The Wrong Complexion
for Protection

# The Wrong Complexion for Protection

*How the Government Response to Disaster*
*Endangers African American Communities*

Robert D. Bullard and Beverly Wright

NEW YORK UNIVERSITY PRESS
*New York and London*

NEW YORK UNIVERSITY PRESS
New York and London
www.nyupress.org

References to Internet websites (URLs) were accurate at the time of writing.
Neither the author nor New York University Press is responsible for URLs that may have
expired or changed since the manuscript was prepared.

Library of Congress Cataloging-in-Publication Data
Bullard, Robert D. (Robert Doyle), 1946-
The wrong complexion for protection : how the government response to disaster endangers
African American communities / Robert D. Bullard and Beverly Wright.
p. cm.
Includes bibliographical references and index.
ISBN 978-0-8147-9993-2 (cl : alk. paper)
ISBN 978-0-8147-7193-8 (ebook)
ISBN 978-0-8147-6384-1 (ebook)
1. Disaster relief--Social aspects—United States. 2. African Americans—Civil rights.
3. African Americans—Social conditions. 4. Racism in public welfare—United States.
5. Racism in social services—United States. 6. Racism—United States. I. Wright, Beverly,
Ph. D. II. Title.
HV555.U6B846 2012
363.34'808996073--dc23
2012004485

New York University Press books are printed on acid-free paper,
and their binding materials are chosen for strength and durability.
We strive to use environmentally responsible suppliers and materials
to the greatest extent possible in publishing our books.

10 9 8 7 6 5 4 3 2 1

*For my mother and father, Nehemiah and Myrtle Bullard—RDB*

*For my father and mother, Morris Bates Sr. and Evelyn Bates Justin; my brother, Morris Bates Jr.; and my uncle, Walter Smith, who survived Hurricane Katrina at age seventy-nine—BW*

# Contents

# Acknowledgments

The research for this book was made possible by support from the Ford Foundation. We would especially like to thank Michelle DePass, who, at the time we began this book project, was program officer at the Ford Foundation, for her support for our work before and after Hurricane Katrina. Many individuals at our host institutions also provided valuable support for our research efforts. We owe a debt of gratitude to staff members from our respective centers, the Environmental Justice Resource Center at Clark Atlanta University (Glenn S. Johnson and Angel O. Torres) and the Deep South Center for Environmental Justice at Dillard University (Celeste Cooper and Myra Lewis) for their assistance in researching and documenting the case studies, retrieving archival materials, fact checking, editing and proofing, and typing the manuscript.

With apologies to anyone we may have left out, we also would like to acknowledge the extraordinary work being performed in New Orleans and along the Gulf Coast. We would also like to give special thanks to William Lucy, president of the Conference of Black Trade Unionists (CBTU), and to representatives from the National Black Environmental Justice Network (NBEJN) and its affiliate organizations for their encouragement, comments, suggestions, and recommendations over the four years that this book project has been under way: Elodia Blanco, Bunyan Bryant, Damu Smith (now deceased), Donele Wilkins, Monique Harden, Leslies Fields, Charlotte Keys, Vernice Miller-Travis, Felicia Eaves, Peggy Shepard, Cecil Corbin-Mark, Lula Odom, Yolanda Sinde, Robin Cannon, Hazel Johnson (now deceased), Henry Clark, and Michael Lythcott. The authors, of course, assume full responsibility for the book's content.

# List of Acronyms and Abbreviations

| | |
|---|---|
| ABC | American Beryllium Company |
| ABPsi | Association of Black Psychologists |
| ACLU | American Civil Liberties Union |
| ACORN | Association of Community Organizations for Reform Now |
| ADEM | Alabama Department of Environmental Management |
| AELOS | Agricultural Economics and Land Ownership Survey |
| AIG | American International Group |
| ARC | Atlanta Regional Commission |
| ATSDR | Agency for Toxic Substances and Disease Registry |
| BFI | Browning Ferris Industries |
| BP | British Petroleum |
| BW | Biological Weapons |
| CAB | Community Advisory Board |
| CAFOs | Confined Animal Feeding Operations |
| CATE | Citizens Against Toxic Exposure |
| CARAT | Community Action and Response Against Toxics |
| C&D | Construction and Demolition |
| CBCF | Congressional Black Caucus Foundation |
| CBTU | Conference of Black Trade Unionists |
| CDBG | Community Development Block Grant |
| CDC | Centers for Disease Control and Prevention |
| CDHS | California Department of Health Services |
| CERCLA | Comprehensive Environmental Response, Compensation, and Liability Act |
| CEQ | Commission of Environmental Quality (Texas) |
| CHDP | Child Health and Disability Prevention |
| CHEERS | Children's Environmental Exposure Research Study |
| CAA | Clean Air Act |
| CIA | Central Intelligence Agency |
| COE | Corps of Engineers |
| CNN | Cable News Network |
| CRA | Community Reinvestment Act |
| CWA | Clean Water Act |
| DDT | *Dichloro-Diphenyl-Trichloroethane* |

| | |
|---|---|
| DENR | Department of Environment and Natural Resources |
| DHS | Department of Homeland Security |
| DME | Dichloromethane |
| DOH | Department of Health |
| DOT | Department of Transportation |
| DSCEJ | Deep South Center for Environmental Justice |
| EJ | Environmental Justice |
| EJRC | Environmental Justice Resource Center |
| EPA | Environmental Protection Agency |
| EPR | Extended Producer Responsibility |
| ERP | Emergency Response Program |
| ESI | Expanded Site Inspection |
| ETC | Escambia Treating Company |
| FEMA | Federal Emergency Management Agency |
| GAO | General Accountability Office |
| GIS | Geographic Information Systems |
| HANO | Housing Authority of New Orleans |
| HBCUs | Historically Black Colleges and Universities |
| HRS | Hazard Ranking System |
| HUD | Housing and Urban Development |
| IDP | Internally Displaced Persons |
| IOM | Institute of Medicine |
| IPCC | Intergovernmental Panel on Climate Change |
| IRB | Institutional Review Board |
| ISTEA | Intermodal Surface Transportation Efficiency Act |
| LAB | Loral American Beryllium |
| LDCs | Least Developed Countries |
| LDEQ | Louisiana Department of Environmental Quality |
| LEED | Leadership in Energy and Environmental Design |
| LULUs | Locally Unwanted Land Uses |
| MARTA | Metropolitan Atlanta Rapid Transit Authority |
| MBTA | Massachusetts Bay Transit Authority |
| MCL | Maximum Contaminant Level |
| MEK | Methyl-Ethyl Ketone |
| MIC | Methyl Isocyanate |
| MPO | Metropolitan Planning Organization |
| MRL | Materials Recovery Landfill |
| MRGO | Mississippi River Gulf Outlet |
| MTBE | Metyl Tertiary Butyl Ether |

| | |
|---|---|
| MTSA | Maritime Transportation Security Act |
| NAACP | National Association for the Advancement of Colored People |
| NBEJN | National Black Environmental Justice Network |
| NRDA | Natural Resources Damage Assessment |
| NCEH | National Center for Environmental Health |
| NECAG | Northeast Community Action Group |
| NEJAC | National Environmental Justice Advisory Council |
| NEPA | National Environmental Policy Act |
| NFHA | National Fair Housing Alliance |
| NGOs | Nongovernmental Organizations |
| NIEHS | National Institute of Environmental Health Sciences |
| NIMBY | Not in My Back Yard |
| NOPS | New Orleans Public Schools |
| NORTA | New Orleans Rapid Transit Authority |
| NOV | Notice of Violations |
| NOx | Nitrogen Oxide |
| NPL | National Priorities List |
| NPR | National Public Radio |
| NRDC | Natural Resources Defense Council |
| NTSB | National Transportation Safety Board |
| NWF | National Wildlife Federation |
| OIG | Office of Inspector General |
| OSHA | Occupational Safety and Health Administration |
| OSWER | Office of Solid Waste and Emergency Response |
| PBS | Public Broadcasting Service |
| PBTs | Persistent, Bioaccumulative, and Toxic pollutants |
| PCBs | Polychlorinated Biphenyls |
| PCP | Pentachlorophenol |
| PGO | Process Gas Oil |
| PHS | Public Health Service |
| PIBBY | Place in Blacks Back Yard |
| ppb | Parts Per Billion |
| PTSD | Posttraumatic Stress Disorder |
| PVC | Polyvinyl Chloride |
| RCRA | Resource Conservation and Recovery Act |
| ROD | Record of Decision |
| RRC | Railroad Commission |
| RSF | Russell Sage Foundation |

| | |
|---|---|
| RTA | Rapid Transit Authority |
| SAFETEA-LU | Safe, Accountable, Flexible, Efficient Transportation Equity Act—A Legacy for Users |
| SARA | Superfund Amendment and Reauthorization Act |
| SARS | Severe Acute Respiratory Syndrome |
| SBA | Small Business Administration |
| SEPs | Supplemental Environmental Projects |
| SI | Site Inspection |
| SJCJE | St. James Citizens for Jobs and the Environment |
| SUNY | State University of New York |
| TCE | Trichloroethylene |
| TCEQ | Texas Commission on Environmental Quality |
| *TDEC* | Tennessee Department of Environment and Conservation |
| TDH | Texas Department of Health |
| TEA-21 | Transportation Equity Act for the Twenty-first Century |
| TRI | Toxics Release Inventory |
| TSU | Texas Southern University |
| TVA | Tennessee Valley Authority |
| UCC | United Church of Christ |
| UCLA | University of California, Los Angeles |
| UNO | University of New Orleans |
| USDA | United States Department of Agriculture |
| USW | United Steel Workers |
| WHO | World Health Organization |
| VMT | Vehicle Miles Traveled |
| VOC | Volatile Organic Compounds |

# Preface

Reflecting upon the process of writing this book, we realized that the journey began in May 2004, when, during the annual convention of the Conference of Black Trade Unionists (CBTU), held that year in Atlanta, we made a commitment to our colleagues at the Community Action and Response Against Toxics (CARAT) Team to write a book on government responses to environmental and health emergencies in African American communities. We attended the CBTU convention to conduct a workshop on the National Black Environmental Justice Network's (NBEJN) multistate Building Just and Healthy Communities Campaign, led by Damu Smith. This was not an easy book to write. Nevertheless, deciding to write it was not a hard decision to make, nor did it take a lot of convincing for us to undertake this project, since there was no such book on the topic at the time. Our goal was to fill this information void with a readable book about government response to disasters using a racial equity lens—one that connected the dots and provided a framework for explaining what many African Americans have seen with their own eyes for decades.

Because of the positive response from the membership, from CBTU president William Lucy and Lula Odom, who coordinates the CARAT Team, invited our panel back the following year. By the time we attended the May 2005 meeting, in Phoenix, much of the basic research on toxic contamination, public health emergencies, industrial accidents, and bioterrorism threat case studies had been completed. On May 28, 2005, some of the preliminary findings of our study were presented in a CBTU workshop webcast. In June 2005, we began retrieving case studies on weather-related disasters, hurricanes, droughts, and floods. After Hurricane Katrina hit New Orleans and the Gulf Coast three months later, in August, our book project was not only delayed but was placed on hold for some time because of personal losses.

Hurricane Katrina inflicted harm on eighty thousand square miles of the Louisiana, Mississippi, and Alabama Gulf Coast. The levee breach flooded 80 percent of New Orleans and destroyed a large block of the research that the

Deep South Center for Environmental Justice had conducted, research that was housed at Xavier University and that was scheduled to be relocated to Dillard University on September 1; the storm delayed our project for nearly two years while the Deep South Center staff put their homes and lives back in order.

The 2005 New Orleans flood destroyed all of the Center's computer files and reports and scattered staff to Baton Rouge, Atlanta, Houston, and Jackson, Mississippi. Nevertheless, we were determined to complete this important book project come hell or high water. The Environmental Justice Resource Center at Clark Atlanta University in Atlanta, Georgia, became the Deep South Center's temporary base of operation; the Center later moved to Baton Rouge and then back to New Orleans, in 2007. Atlanta became home to nearly 100,000 Katrina evacuees shortly after the storm; after five years, nearly fifty thousand New Orleans Katrina evacuees still called Atlanta home.

Our book places the government response to Hurricane Katrina in historical context to compare and contrast how the government has responded to other emergencies, including environmental and public health emergencies, toxic contamination, industrial accidents, bioterrorism threats, and natural and human-induced disasters that disproportionately affect African Americans. Too often, African Americans have experienced slow "Katrina responses" from various local, state, and federal government agencies during a range of emergencies. Slow response or no response has often been the rule—not the exception.

Many African Americans believe that "we have the wrong complexion for protection." Much of this belief emanates from wrong-headed U.S. Supreme Court decisions that have served to buttress "white supremacy," racial apartheid—transportation apartheid, residential apartheid, medical apartheid, food apartheid, parks apartheid, environmental apartheid, and disaster relief apartheid—affecting blacks, from homeowners to public-housing tenants, to transit riders, to hospital patients, to farmers. Race still matters.

Even after more than 150 years, the impact of the 1857 *Scott v. Sanford* (Dred Scott) Supreme Court decision, in which the high court judges ruled, "No black man has any rights that any white man is bound to respect," is still felt by millions of African Americans who are denied basic rights that whites take for granted. Leftovers from the 1896 *Plessy v. Ferguson* Supreme Court ruling, a decision that codified "Jim Crow" segregation, linger, despite the 1954 *Brown v. Board of Education* ruling that made *Plessy* null and void. And the more recent 2001 *Alexander v. Sandoval* Supreme Court decision requiring victims of discrimination to prove "intent" has made discrimination easier to practice and more difficult to prove.

While natural disasters do not discriminate on the basis of race, some government response to disasters place African Americans at elevated health risks. The fact that the people who are most neglected by the government's failure to respond expeditiously and competently are African Americans and the poor places questions of race, institutional racism, and class at the center of this analysis. Therefore, it is extremely important that disaster-response events over the past eight decades be placed within a social and historical context for our analysis.

The United States was built on a system of race-based inequality. Moreover, in every aspect of the existing social structure, certain groups have been denied equal access or opportunity to achieve the inalienable rights to life, liberty and the pursuit of happiness. As the work of two African American sociologists who grew up in the South before the Jim Crow segregation signs came down, this book is more than theory. It reflects not only our keen observations, firsthand experiences, and insights as social scientists but also our understanding of a legacy that the region and the country, for that matter, have yet to overcome.

Writing this book has been a therapeutic venture for us both and has actually helped to channel the negative energy of racism into a positive and constructive analysis of a problem that is systemically embedded in our American culture today. It is an issue that must be placed in the forefront of all that is important to the survival of the principles upon which our nation was founded for the benefit and enjoyment of all citizens. Many African Americans learned a long time ago that "waiting for the government can be hazardous to your health."

The simple but urgent message of this book centers on equity, justice, and fairness. Centuries of black exploitation, experimentation, drug testing, and forced surgeries have engendered mistrust of government, the medical establishment, and biomedical research among African Americans. We believe fairness is essential to building trust and reaching any meaningful solution to natural and human-induced disasters and for achieving sustainability and homeland security. Fairness matters. It matters how we design plans and strategies for addressing public health emergencies, toxic contamination, industrial accidents and spills, earthquakes, extreme weather events such as hurricanes, floods, tornados, droughts, and heat waves, and bioterrorism threats.

The call for climate justice is written largely in the aftermath of Hurricane Katrina. Clearly, those communities that contribute least to global warming and climate change are most vulnerable and feel the negative impacts first, worst, and longest. The catastrophe has left an indelible imprint on our centers, our work, and our collaborations with other organizations. Much of our collaborative research and policy work on disasters took us to faraway places, from Puerto Rico to Alaska, from South Central Los Angles to Soweto, South Africa, and, to the United Nations COP15 climate summit in Copenhagen, Denmark, in 2009 and to COP16, in Cancun, Mexico, in 2010.

Hurricane Katrina brought this work close to home. And we do mean home—with family homesteads, institutions, and community networks destroyed. And, as we write, six years after the partly man-made disaster, many impacted communities along have yet to be made whole—especially African American communities in New Orleans, Mississippi, and Alabama that were vulnerable and marginalized before the storm. Age-old discriminatory practices extended into government dispensation of aid, loans, grants, and recovery dollars—patterns and practices not unlike those that African Americans faced pre-Katrina.

The issues dealt with in this volume will be relevant for decades to come, for the nation is likely to see more public health emergencies, environmental hazards, toxic contaminations, industrial accidents, train wrecks, and toxic spills. We hope we will not have another terrorist attack within our borders. However, whether or not we do, the preparedness and responses to emergencies need to be fair, just, and equitable in order to achieve maximum success.

To some extent, our analysis is a chronicle of lessons not learned, government failures, and inadequate and inequitable government responses to natural and human-induced emergencies. We believe our book will shed new light on issues of health equity, racial and environmental justice, and the government's role in providing equal protection under the law for all Americans, without regard to race, color, national origin, or income.

As the nation moves to strengthen its ability to prepare for and respond to the health consequences of potential bioterrorism, we also cannot forget or ignore the real health and environmental pollution threats posed by chemical plants and railway accidents and explosions that threaten fenceline communities. Much of our contemporary work comes from visiting, working with, and interviewing residents who view their communities as "sacrifice zones." These are ordinary people who are engaged in extraordinary struggles. Finally, we provide the reader with a brief glimpse into the personal circumstances that propelled us on a journey for equity and justice—including health equity and environmental, economic, racial, and climate justice—not just for us but for all.

# Introduction

*Anatomy of Vulnerability*

Much attention has been devoted to natural and man-made disasters since the terrorist attack on the United States in September 2001, the anthrax attack in Washington, D.C., that same year, and the government response to Hurricane Katrina and its aftermath, in 2005. Before these incidents grabbed headlines and shone the national spotlight on government ineptness and incompetence and on severe gaps in disaster preparedness, African Americans for decades had complained about differential treatment, about being left behind, and about outright racial discrimination. Most of these complaints routinely fell on deaf ears long before Hurricane Katrina devastated New Orleans and the Gulf Coast. Katrina raised "a new class of problems that demand rigorous analysis, prudent planning, and courageous political leadership."[1]

This book examines government responses to a range of environmental and health threats to African Americans, including weather-related disasters like hurricanes and droughts, which conventionally have been considered "natural," and disasters that are normally considered human induced, such as industrial accidents, railcar explosions, chemical contamination, and bioterrorist attacks. Our analysis uses an environmental justice and racial equity frame to understand mitigation and adaptation to human-induced threats and to show how best society should both think about, prepare for, and respond to weather-related disasters and prevent public health threats, environmental catastrophes, toxic contamination, industrial accidents, and related human-induced disasters.

We examine the unequal protection and unequal treatment afforded African Americans over eight decades and factors that have made them vulnerable, including their physical location, socioeconomic status, race, and the lingering institutional constraints created and perpetuated by racialized place. We also explore how environmental hazards develop into public health threats and how design factors either mitigate or amplify their effects. The case studies detail special challenges and barriers faced by African Americans in everyday society and how these obstacles are compounded by government's ineptitude, inaction, and slow response to environmental health threats.

Environmental and public health threats from natural and human-made disasters are not randomly distributed. Healthy places and healthy people are highly correlated. It should be no surprise that the poorest of the poor within the United States and around the world have the worst health and live in the most degraded and at-risk environments. While access to insurance and to health care is important, social conditions are also major determinants of health. Social forces acting at a collective level help shape an individual's risk, environmental exposure, and access to resources that promote health.[2]

One of the most important indicators of one's health is one's street address or neighborhood. Where you live affects your health and your chances of leading a flourishing life. It also affects your risk from natural and unnatural disasters. Today, numerous researchers are looking at individual health outcomes through an ecological lens, recognizing that "place matters." They are using geographic information system (GIS) analysis to map relationships between racial and income composition and vulnerability.

The Centers for Disease Control and Prevention (CDC) recognizes this connection in its "Healthy People in Healthy Places" initiative. The initiative operates from the idea that the places where people live, work, learn, and play can protect and promote their health and safety, especially those people at increased risk of health disparities. Among the social determinants of health are factors in the social environment that contribute to or detract from the health of individuals and communities. These factors include the socioeconomic status of community residents, availability of transportation, quality of housing, access to services, existence of discrimination based on social grouping (e.g., race, gender, or class), and social or environmental stressors. Inequitable distribution of these conditions across various populations is a significant contributor to persistent and pervasive health disparities in the United States.

The CDC's 2008 *Promoting Health Equity: A Resource to Help Communities Address Social Determinants of Health* report is a workbook for community-based organizations that seek to affect the social determinants of health through community-based participatory approaches and nontraditional partnerships.[3] The social determinants of health are the circumstances in which individuals are born, grow up, live, work, play, learn, and age and the systems that are created to deal with illness. These circumstances are in turn shaped by a wider set of societal forces such as economics, social policies, and politics, as well as psychosocial factors such as opportunities for employment, access to health care, hopelessness, and freedom from racism, including institutional racism and discrimination.[4]

Race and place in America have always been connected.[5] In the South, during the Jim Crow era and even after "separate but equal" laws were struck down by the courts, there were places where black people could not buy homes, ride public transit, play in parks and beaches, gain access to schools and hospitals, or sit down at a restaurant. These "special places" for whites and blacks were artificially created by racism, with privilege and advantage biased in favor of whites. White elites reserved the best of the best for themselves and, not surprisingly, doled out the worst of the worst for blacks.

Place affects access to jobs, education, public services, culture, shopping, and medical services, as well as level of personal security.[6] Place even affects the air we breathe. Although there is no "white air," "Hispanic air," or "black air," race maps closely with bad air quality. African Americans and other people of color live in the most polluted places and suffer the health consequences. Race does not cause illness; racism does. More than one hundred studies now link racism to worse health.[7]

All communities are not created equal. Some communities are more equal than others. If a community happens to be poor or working class or is in a geographic area made up predominantly of people of color, its residents generally have fewer choices and opportunities—on a range of residential amenities, such as housing, schools, jobs, shopping, parks, green space, hospitals, police, and fire protection—than residents of affluent, middle-class, or white neighborhoods.[8]

Using a racial equity lens, this book builds on more than three decades of environmental justice, health equity, and disaster research and policy work that challenge the dominant environmental protection paradigm and the traditional quantitative-risk model. The dominant environmental protection paradigm manages, regulates, and distributes risks.[9] This paradigm also institutionalizes unequal enforcement; trades human health for profit; places the burden of proof on the "victims" and not on the polluting industry; legitimates human exposure to harmful chemicals, pesticides, and hazardous substances; promotes "risky" technologies; exploits the vulnerability of economically and politically disenfranchised communities; subsidizes ecological destruction; creates an industry around risk assessment and risk management; delays cleanup actions; and fails to develop pollution prevention as the overarching and dominant strategy. The dominant paradigm seldom challenges environmental racism and other forms of environmental injustice.

On the other hand, the environmental justice framework rests on developing tools, strategies, and policies to eliminate unfair, unjust, and inequitable conditions and decisions. The framework rests on prevention, precaution, and avoidance of harm. It also attempts to uncover the underlying assumptions that may contribute to and produce differential exposure and unequal protection. The framework brings to the surface the *ethical* and *political* questions of "who gets what, when, why, and how much."

## A Focus on the Southern United States

We chose the southern United States for our analysis. We recognize that issues addressed in this book are not unique to the South. Additionally, we recognize that many of the circumstances detailed in our analysis are not unique to African Americans. However, the southern region of the United States and its treatment of African Americans present some unique circumstances that deserve isolation. Our analysis shines a special spotlight on "slow-moving" disasters in a region whose legacy includes slavery, Jim Crow segregation, and entrenched white supremacy. It also gives perspective to pre- and postgovernment responses to natural and unnatural disasters that disproportionately impact African Americans.

The South gave birth to the modern civil rights movement and to the environmental justice movement.[10] It is also a region that is vulnerable to weather-related disasters, including hurricanes, floods, and droughts. Today, the South is the favorite destination for black migration and black vacationing.

The 2000 census showed that African Americans ended the twentieth century by returning "home" to the South—the same region they had spent most of the century escaping or being pushed out. The southern United States grew by more than 3.6 million people in the 1990s.[11] Blacks' search for a "New South" began in the mid-1970s; between 1970 and 1980, more than 100,000 more blacks moved to the South than moved out.[12] This pattern continued unabated in the 1990s. The 1970s saw the South become a leader in the creation of nonagricultural jobs, and this increased economic opportunity attracted migrants from the postindustrial economy of the North; the region is attracting large numbers of black middle-class, post–baby boomers.

Millions of African Americans who left the South for other parts of the country decades ago are returning to reclaim the region.[13] Searching for the

"New South" that was prominently displayed in booster campaigns under-taken by southern cities, many have moved back to Alabama and Georgia to retire or to seek new job opportunities in the "New South." They moved to the South for many other reasons, as well, including the region's warm cli-mate, the improved racial climate, the cheaper cost of living, and to be near elderly parents.

In the 620 counties that make up the southern "Black Belt," stretching from Delaware to Texas, African Americans make up about 12 percentage of the total population, a larger percentage than in the country as a whole. In the fifteen southern states (excluding Texas and Florida), blacks make up 22.8 percent of the population, far more than the 3.5 percent of the popula-tion that is Hispanic.[14]

The African American population in cities, suburbs, and rural areas of the South is growing at twice its rate of growth than in any other region in the country. The 1990s saw the black population increase in metropolitan cen-ters in every state of the former Confederacy. Florida and Georgia posted the largest gains, adding 674,000 and 632,000 black residents, respectively. Sev-eral other southern states—Texas, North Carolina, and Maryland—added more than 300,000 African Americans.

At the same time African Americans were moving to the South, the North-east, the Midwest, and the West all saw blacks leaving as African Americans sought better jobs, safer neighborhoods, and warmer weather in cities like Atlanta, Washington, D.C., Memphis, and Dallas. Other top southern desti-nations for black Midwesterners included Norfolk, Virginia; Houston; Nash-ville; and Louisville. Atlanta, however, which calls itself the "Black Mecca," was by far the top urban destination for African Americans.[15] In the 1990s, metropolitan Atlanta continued to serve as the "premier African American magnet."[16]

As the "region of choice," the South attracted both the skilled and the unskilled, the educated and the undereducated, as well as low-income and middle-income African Americans who sought to make their fortune in this "land of new opportunity." If the South "rises again," blacks want to reap some of the benefits of this rebirth.

Many newcomers settle in the suburbs. The two most affluent African American counties in the nation, Prince George's County, Maryland, and DeKalb County, Georgia, are suburban and in the South.[17] Some 76 per-cent of all southern blacks live in metropolitan areas, and 43 percent live in the suburbs. Seven of the ten fastest growing U.S. counties in terms of African American population are located in the suburban part of metropolitan Atlanta.[18] Black suburbanization has often meant re-segregation. Separate translates into unequal, even for the most affluent African American enclaves.[19]

Today, African Americans voters are a key constituency in general elections in at least fifteen states and represent a key voting bloc in Democratic primaries in more than twenty states. There are more than nine thousand African American elected officials in America.[20] Eight of the ten states with the highest number of black elected officials are in the South. African Americans have been elected mayor in most of the nation's big cities, there are roughly six hundred African Americans in state legislatures nationwide, and blacks now hold about 10 percent of the seats in the U.S. Congress. Still, African Americans are underrepresented at most levels of government.

Environmental decision making and local land-use planning operate at the juncture of science, economics, politics, and special interests that place communities of color at special risk. In many instances, the only science involved is "political" science. This is especially true in America's Deep South. By default, the southern United States became a "sacrifice zone," a dump for the rest of the nation's toxic waste.[21] Unfortunately, "sacrifice zones" cheapened the lives and damaged the health of the most vulnerable people and places.[22]

There is a direct correlation between exploitation of land and exploitation of people. It should not be a surprise to anyone to discover that African Americans have to contend with some of the worst pollution in the region. A colonial mentality exists in Dixie, where local government and big business take advantage of people who are both politically and economically powerless. The region is stuck with a unique legacy—the legacy of slavery, Jim Crow, and white resistance to equal justice for all. This legacy has also affected race relations and the region's ecology. It has also affected how local, state, and federal officials respond to public health threats from natural and human-induced disasters.[23]

The South is characterized by "look-the-other-way environmental policies and giveaway tax breaks" and a place where "political bosses encourage outsiders to buy the region's human and natural resources at bargain prices."[24] Lax enforcement of environmental regulations has left the region's air, water, and land the most industry-befouled in the United States.

Toxic-waste discharge and industrial pollution are correlated with poorer economic conditions. An Institute for Southern Studies report, *Gold and Green 2000*, used two separate lists of indicators to evaluate states' economic performance and stresses on the natural environment.[25] The twenty economic indicators include annual pay, job opportunities, number of business startups, and number of workplace injury rates; the twenty environmental measures range from toxic emissions and pesticide use to energy consumption and urban sprawl. Ten states, mostly in the South, are among the worst fifteen on both lists. Louisiana ranks forty-eighth on economic performance and fiftieth on the environment. Others ranking at the bottom are Alabama, Texas, Tennessee, Mississippi, Indiana, Arkansas, West Virginia, Kentucky, and South Carolina.

Having industrial facilities in a community does not automatically translate into jobs for that community's residents. Many industrial plants are located at the fenceline with black communities. Some are so close that local residents could walk to work. More often than not, however, communities of color are stuck with the pollution and poverty, while other people commute in for industrial jobs.

Similarly, tax breaks and corporate welfare programs have produced few new jobs at polluting companies for black residents who live on the fenceline with industry. However, state-sponsored pollution and lax enforcement have allowed many communities of color and poor communities to become dumping grounds for industrial waste. Louisiana is the poster child for corporate welfare. The state is mired in both poverty and pollution. It is no wonder that Louisiana's petrochemical corridor, the eighty-five-mile stretch along the Mississippi River from Baton Rouge to New Orleans, dubbed "Cancer Alley," became a hotbed for environmental justice activity long before Hurricane Katrina struck and the levee breach drowned 80 percent of the city in 2005.[26]

The environmental justice movement has set out clear goals of eliminating unequal enforcement of environmental, civil rights, and public health laws; unmasking differential exposure among populations to harmful chemicals, pesticides, and other toxins in the home, school, neighborhood, and workplace; exposing faulty assumptions used in calculating, assessing, and managing risks; revealing discriminatory zoning and land-use practices and exclusionary policies and practices that limit some individuals and groups from participation in decision making. Many of these problems could be eliminated if existing environmental, health, housing, and civil rights laws were vigorously enforced in a nondiscriminatory way.

The poisoning of African American residents and workers in Louisiana's "Cancer Alley" and in other black communities across the South has its roots in an economic system characterized by economic exploitation, racial oppression, and devaluation of human life and the natural environment.[27]

This same thinking drives waste and risky technologies to the poorest communities in this country and the poorest nations around the world.

The unwritten policy of targeting Third World nations for waste trade received international media attention in 1991. Lawrence Summers, at the time chief economist at the World Bank, shocked the world and touched off an international firestorm when his confidential memorandum on waste trade was leaked. Summers wrote: "'Dirty' Industries: Just between you and me, shouldn't the World Bank be encouraging more migration of the dirty industries to the LDCs (Least Developed Countries)?"[28] Summers's memorandum was newsworthy not so much for the view expressed but because he put this policy in writing for the world to see.

The events that unfolded in New Orleans and the Gulf Coast region before and after Hurricane Katrina provide the sociohistorical backdrop for our examination of social vulnerability and government responses to environmental and health threats to African Americans that date back more than eight decades. Our analysis focuses on government response to weather-related events, such as hurricanes, floods, and droughts, but also includes case studies on toxic contamination, industrial accidents, train derailments and explosions, medical experimentation, and bioterrorism threats.

Over the past three decades, environmental justice and disaster scholars have compiled an impressive record of research detailing unfair, unjust, and disparate treatment by government of African Americans and other people of color in a wide array of policy areas, including siting enforcement, cleanup, mitigation, and emergency response to man-made and natural disasters. While progress has been made in addressing inequities, much work is still needed to ensure that all populations receive environmental justice and equal protection from natural and human-induced hazards.

In the nine chapters that follow, we describe and provide explanations of government response to natural and unnatural disasters that have impacted African Americans in the southern United States. Although we confine ourselves to the South, our approach and findings may have implications well beyond the region and African Americans, given the nature of institutional racism in America, which is a national phenomenon. We have provided lessons learned and lessons not learned and a framework for addressing the legacy of unequal protection.

Finally, we offer policy strategies for preventing disastrous responses by government to various threats to African Americans. Eliminating disparities and providing equal protection will make us a stronger and healthier people and nation as a whole.

# Race, Place, and the Environment in a Small Southern Town

*A Personal Perspective from Robert D. Bullard*

Who we are often defines what we do. Many of our experiences also help define and shape our worldview. This chapter chronicles my early years growing up in the racially segregated South (Alabama and Louisiana) and the influence of those years on my thinking about race, environment, disaster, social equity, and government responsibility. It is written from a first-person perspective and provides unique insights into my journey to becoming an environmental sociologist and one of the founders of the environmental justice movement in the United States.

The analysis places in context three decades of research, policy work, and activism—all directed toward getting various levels of government to respond fairly and equitably to natural and man-made disasters and health emergencies in communities inhabited by African Americans and other people of color.[1] It should be made clear that much of what has transpired in my efforts to move environmental justice into mainstream thinking was largely a result of events and circumstances beyond my control and had a lot to do with being "drafted" into this struggle before the national movement took hold.

Much of the credit for getting me started is owed to Linda McKeever Bullard, my former wife, who for more than six years singlehandedly held back one of the second largest waste disposal companies in the world, Browning Ferris Industries (BFI), with her lawsuit and legal challenges. While I have gained some degree of notoriety for my environmental justice work, her contribution to developing the legal theory behind challenging environmental racism has pretty much gone unnoticed in the field. However, a few legal scholars, such as the late Luke Cole, recognized Linda's work early on and patterned many of his legal theories and much of his analysis on her *Bean v. Southwestern Waste Management Corp.* lawsuit.

Over the past three decades, I have written more than fifteen books and hundreds of articles that address environmental justice, environmental racism, land use and industrial facility siting, housing and residential segregation, transportation, suburban sprawl, smart growth, livable communities, regional equity, sustainable development, disaster response, and climate justice. All of my writings use an environmental justice and racial equity framework. Environmental justice is seen as not only a civil right but a basic human right.[2] Race matters. Also, place matters.

Long before I became a sociologist and an environmental justice scholar, growing up in the segregated South, I witnessed up close and personal how race and place combine to create opportunity for whites and barriers for blacks. For me, it was not theory or something I had to read in a book or discover in the library. Nevertheless, my parents provided me with a wealth of books and other reading materials so that I could expand my mental boundaries beyond my isolated small-town southern roots. This exposure led me to believe early on that clean air, clean water, and safe housing are basic human rights—even though they were denied me and many of my fellow black residents who lived in my segregated hometown in southern Alabama.

### Making the Race-Environment Connection—My Early Years in Elba

Much of my writings over the past years are rooted in my early years growing up in the region that gave rise to the modern civil rights movement in Montgomery, Alabama, in December 1955—which began with Rosa Park's single defiant act of refusing to give up her seat on the bus to a white man.

Elba is a city located in Coffee County, Alabama. In 2000, the population was 4,185. The racial makeup of the Elba is 64 percent white, 34 percent black, and 2 percent other races. Elba is a typical small southern town where blacks and whites live in segregated neighborhoods. Although blacks made up one-third of the city's population, whites governed the town as if its African American citizens were invisible. As late as 1964, a decade after *Brown v. Board of Education*, Elba's blacks attended segregated schools and were still being served at the back door of restaurants or at the "colored" window (though the "colored" signs had come down).

In Elba, Jim Crow translated into white neighborhoods receiving the "best of the best," including libraries, street lighting, paved roads, sewer and water lines, garbage pickup, swimming pools, and flood control measures years before black neighborhoods received these tax-supported services.

For decades, Elba's segregated black neighborhoods flooded, while white neighborhoods remained high and dry. Streets in my all-black Mulberry Heights neighborhood and the school ground were often flooded. We were frequently forced to walk in ankle-deep water on unpaved muddy streets without sidewalks to get to school. On some occasions, floodwaters even made it into our classrooms. Not a hospitable place for a young black student to become an environmentalist—but a perfect laboratory for a black boy to learn about the harsh facts of life, fairness, and justice through a racial equity lens. Even the secondhand textbooks doled out to our school reminded us five days a week that life was not fair.

Because of it precarious location—the town sits at the confluence of Beaver Dam Creek, Whitewater Creek, and the Pea River—Elba has repeatedly flooded over the years. Some hard-hit black neighborhoods have not recovered from the 1990, 1994, and 1998 floods. Many black inhabitants have sunk deeper into poverty after each flood. Seven years after the last major flood, many streets in Elba's black neighborhoods are not maintained, and scores of homes are boarded up. Few opportunities exist in this small southern town for blacks. Each subsequent flood has worsened their chance of economic mobility. Generally, high school graduation has meant a one-way ticket out of town. I left town to attend college in 1964. I was a graduating senior in 1968 at Alabama A&M University, a historically black university located in Huntsville, Alabama, when Dr. Martin Luther King Jr. was assassinated in Memphis, Tennessee.

Every time I get a request for assistance from a black community fighting a landfill, garbage dump, or waste facility, a voice in my head always reminds me that Dr. King was called to Memphis in 1968 to support the environmental and economic justice struggle of 1,300 striking sanitation workers from Local 1733. The strike shut down garbage collection and sewer, water, and street maintenance. Clearly, the Memphis struggle was much more than a garbage strike. The "I AM A MAN" signs that black workers carried reflected the larger struggle for human dignity and human rights. Although Memphis was Dr. King's "last campaign," his legacy lives on even to this day.[3] King's legacy remains an integral part of my environmental, health, transportation, land use, smart growth, and climate justice research and policy work.

## Impact of My Houston Years—the 1970s and Early 1980s

After receiving my Ph.D. degree in sociology from Iowa State University, I moved to Houston in 1976 and accepted a teaching position at Texas Southern University (TSU), one of the largest historically black colleges and universities (HBCUs) in the country.

A decade after Dr. King was killed, I found myself drafted into a garbage struggle in Houston. In 1978, when I was just two years out of graduate school, my attorney wife, Linda McKeever Bullard, asked me to conduct research for a community she was working with that was trying to block the Whispering Pines landfill from being sited in the mostly black suburban Northwood Manor subdivision. The community formed the Northeast Community Action Group (NECAG) and led protests and demonstrations in front of the proposed landfill entrance, located just 1,400 feet from a school.

In 1979, Bullard filed a class-action lawsuit, *Bean v. Southwestern Waste Management Corp.*, on behalf of black residents who were seeking to block Browning Ferris Industries (BFI), the second-largest waste disposal company in the world, from locating a "sanitary landfill" (we all know there is nothing "sanitary" about a place where household garbage is dumped) in the midst of a predominantly black middle-class neighborhood in northeast Houston.

Northwood Manor consists primarily of single-family moderate and middle-income homes. Residents in the neighborhood are served by the suburban 17,800-pupil North Forest Independent School District, a district where, in 1980, blacks made up more than 80 percent of the student body. The North Forest Independent School administration building is located at East Houston Dyersdale Road (Mesa Drive) and East Little York. A total of seven North Forest schools are located in the Northwood Manor area and within a one-mile radius of the landfill.

The 195-acre Whispering Pines landfill, located at 11800 East Houston-Dyersdale Road (Little York Off Mesa), is across East Little York Road from the North Forest Independent School District bus facilities, the Smiley High School Complex, a service center, and the Jones-Cowart Stadium and athletic fields. The landfill is only 1,400 feet from the three-thousand-student Smiley High School Complex, which did not have air conditioning in 1982.

The Whispering Pines landfill mound, as early as 1983, could be seen rising above the surrounding landscape on East Little York. A more graphic and panoramic view of Northwood Manor's "Mount Trashmore" (a name given to the landfill by area residents) can be seen from modern Jones-Cowart Stadium, an outdoor arena where mostly young black high school students practice and play across the road from the sanitary landfill.

Overall, housing in Northwood Manor is well maintained; more than 88 percent of the residents own their homes. (Nationally, about 46 percent of blacks own their homes.) Driving through the neighborhood, one often sees children playing in the yards and on the sidewalks; the neighborhood appears to be composed largely of younger families with children.

My previous research on housing discrimination and residential segregation proved useful in making the transition to examining and mapping the spatial location of landfills, incinerators, and garbage dumps and the racial composition of the neighborhoods in which they are sited. The central theme of my analysis was that all communities are not created equal when it comes to the siting of locally unwanted land uses (LULUs) such as garbage dumps, landfills, and incinerators. Also, race and class dynamics, along with political disenfranchisement, interact to place some communities at special environmental and health risk from waste facility siting.[4] If a community happens to be poor, black, and powerless, it receives less environmental protection in the placement of LULUs than an affluent, white, and politically powerful community.

In my research methods class, I designed a student project in which ten graduate students were able to assist me in tracking the location of solid-waste facility siting in Houston from the 1920s through 1978, when the permit for the Whispering Pine sanitary landfill was granted by the Texas Department of Health. At times, it seemed as though my students and I were more detectives than sociologists when trying to locate and map waste facilities in Houston over more than five decades. We were "connecting the dots" between race and waste facilities at a time when no standard methodology or research protocol was in place.[5]

In order for us to obtain the history of waste disposal facility siting in Houston, government records (city, county, and state documents) had to be manually retrieved because the files were not computerized in 1979. On-site visits, windshield surveys, and informal interviews, done in a sort of "sociologist as detective" role, were conducted as a reliability check. This was not an easy task. I often joke about the work that was done "BC" (Before Computers). It was also initiated pre-GIS (Geographic Information Systems).

Houston is basically flat, with many low-lying sections located below sea level. It is also the only major U.S. city without zoning. In our search for landfills, we discovered a few "mountains." Anytime we found a mountain in Houston, we immediately became suspicious. They usually turned out to be old landfills. Houston also has more than five hundred neighborhoods spread over six hundred square miles. Houston's black population is located in a broad belt that extends from the south-central and southeast portions of the city into northeast and north-central.

Houston's no-zoning policy allowed for an erratic land-use pattern. The NIMBY (Not in My Back Yard) practice was replaced with the PIBBY (Place in Blacks' Back Yard) policy. The all-white, all-male Houston city government and private industry targeted Houston's black neighborhoods to serve as the sites for landfills, incinerators, garbage dumps, and garbage transfer stations. Clearly, white men decided that Houston's garbage dumps were not compatible with the city's white neighborhoods. Having white women on the city council made little difference to where Houston sited landfills. This idea changed somewhat when the first African American, Judson Robinson Jr., was elected to the city council in 1971. Robinson had to quell a near-riot over the opening of a landfill in the predominantly black Trinity Gardens neighborhood.

Five decades of discriminatory land-use practices lowered black residents' property values, accelerated the physical deterioration of black communities, and increased disinvestment in Houston's black neighborhoods. Moreover, the discriminatory siting of solid-waste facilities stigmatized the black neighborhoods as "dumping grounds" for a host of other unwanted facilities, including salvage yards, recycling operations, and automobile "chop shops."

Renewable deed restrictions were the only tool many residents had at their disposal to regulate nonresidential uses. However, residents in low-income areas often allowed deed restrictions to lapse because they were preoccupied with making a living and perhaps did not have the time, energy, or faith in government to get the signatures of neighborhood residents necessary to keep their deed restrictions in force. Moreover, the high occupancy turnover and large renter population in many Houston inner-city neighborhoods further weakened the efficacy of deed restrictions as a protectionist device.

Ineffective land-use regulations have created a nightmare for many of Houston's neighborhoods—especially the ones that are ill equipped to fend off industrial encroachment. From the 1920s through the 1970s, the siting of nonresidential facilities heightened animosities between the black community and the local government. This was especially true in the case of solid-waste disposal siting. It was not until 1979, with *Bean v. Southwestern Waste Management Corp.*, that black Houston mounted a frontal legal assault on environmental racism in waste facility siting. A new environmental justice theme emerged around the idea that "since everybody produces garbage, everybody should have to bear the burden of garbage disposal." This principle made its way into the national environmental justice movement and later thwarted subsequent waste facility siting in Houston.

Public officials learned fast that solid-waste management could become a volatile political issue. Generally, controversy centered on charges that disposal sites were not equitably distributed among the city's quadrants. Finding suitable sites for sanitary landfills had become a critical problem mainly because no one wanted to have a waste facility as a neighbor. The burden of having a municipal landfill, incinerator, transfer station, or some other type of waste disposal facility near one's home was not equally borne by Houston's neighborhoods.

In our research in support of the *Bean* lawsuit, we discovered some alarming trends. From the 1920s to the 1978, a total of seventeen solid-waste facilities were located in black Houston neighborhoods. Thirteen solid-waste disposal facilities were operated by the City of Houston from the late 1920s through the mid-1970s. The city operated eight garbage incinerators (five large units and three mini-units), six of which were located in mostly black neighborhoods, one was in a Hispanic neighborhood, and one was in a mostly white area.

All five of Houston's large garbage incinerators were located in neighborhoods dominated by people of color—four black and one Hispanic; all five of the city-owned landfills were sited in black neighborhoods. One of the oldest city-owned incinerators was located in Houston's Fourth Ward. This site dates back to the 1920s. Other city-owned incinerators included the Patterson Street site, the Kelly Street site, the Holmes Road site, and the Velasco site, located in the mostly Hispanic Second Ward or "Segundo Barrio." The costs of operating these large incinerators and the problems of pollution generated by these systems were major factors in their closing.

Although blacks composed just over one-fourth of the city's population, five out of five city-owned landfills (100 percent) and six of the eight city-owned incinerators (75 percent) were built in black Houston neighborhoods. From the 1920s through the 1970s, eleven of thirteen city-owned landfills and incinerators (84.6 percent) were built in black neighborhoods. Blacks during this same period made up only about 25 percent of Houston's population.

It is clear that *Bean v. Southwestern Waste Management Corp.* exposed the racist waste facility siting practices then prevalent in Houston. The *Bean* lawsuit also changed the city's facility siting and solid-waste management practices after 1979 and forced the city to adopt a more aggressive waste minimization and recycling plan. Since the *Bean* lawsuit, not a single landfill has been sited in Houston.[6]

Bean also signaled a milestone and a turning point in environmentalism as practiced in the United States. Less than a decade after the First Earth Day, in 1970, and the discovery of the Love Canal horror story, in 1978, Houston protests against the Whispering Pines landfill in 1978 and the *Bean* lawsuit in 1979 focused the environmental dialogue on "environmental dumping on black people" as another form of racial discrimination, a framework that was missing from the mainstream, mostly white environmental movement and the mostly black civil rights movement.

Historically, Houston's black neighborhoods were dumped on while receiving less than their fair share of residential services—including garbage collection, water and sewer services, and parks and green space. Black Houstonians had gotten use to living with neglect. While some progress was made over the years, Houston's neglected black neighborhoods were visible signs that race still mattered.

In a 2002 special report on Houston's neglected neighborhoods, the *Houston Chronicle* reporter Mike Snider explained that hasty annexations by the city had left a legacy of blight.[7] Even the best efforts of the Houston Super Neighborhood Program, the cornerstone of the administration of Mayor Lee Brown, Houston's first African American mayor, did little to reverse decades of systematic neglect. Under the program, the city was divided into eighty-eight "super neighborhoods." These neighborhoods could choose to create resident councils and develop "action plans," which were essentially wish lists, to deal with a range of urban problems, including improved routine maintenance such as ditch cleaning and regrading; more rapid construction of sidewalks and street repaving; increased numbers of parks and green spaces, libraries, and multipurpose centers; and other capital improvement projects.[8] This "experiment" was a failure.

Many of Houston's "invisible" black neighborhoods were easily identified by their substandard housing, lack of sewer and water lines, unpaved and narrow streets, open ditches, illegal dumps, and lack of sidewalks, curbs, and storm drains. When it rained, these areas flooded. The *Houston Chronicle* reporter Kristen Mack concluded that a sizable share of the mostly black Acres Homes neighborhood was as impoverished in 2002 as it had been ten years earlier.[9] Homoizelle Savoy, a thirty-year resident of the Acres Homes area, summed up her community's plight: "Thirty years is neglected, isn't it? Ain't no feeling. I know we've been overlooked."

It is ironic that some of the residents who were fighting the construction of the Whispering Pines landfill had moved to Northwood Manor in an effort to escape landfills and garbage dumps in their former Houston neighborhoods. Patricia Reaux relayed her experience with landfills: "About seven years ago, I lived near another dump on Hirsch Road. . . .There were rats so big you would have to use a gun to kill them. The smell was awful, and the water sometimes was not drinkable."

After collecting data for the *Bean v. Southwestern Waste Management* lawsuit and interviewing citizens from other African American neighborhoods, my graduate students and I came to realize that waste facility siting in Houston was not random. Moreover, this was not a chicken-or-egg (which came first?) problem, as some "environmental racism skeptics" wanted us to believe. Black Houstonians did not move in next to the dumps. In all of the cases we observed, the residential and racial character of the neighborhoods had been established long before the waste facilities invaded the neighborhoods.

## My Dumping in Dixie Years—The Early 1990s

My early collaborations with the Reverend Benjamin Chavis—who was with the United Church of Christ (UCC) Commission for Racial Justice—and Warren County, North Carolina, activists helped ground me to the emerging national environmental justice movement. The national environmental justice movement was born in the 1980s in mostly rural, black Warren County—where more than five hundred blacks and whites, young and old, went to jail protesting the placement of a toxic-waste dump in the mostly black and poor county. Protesters were asking legitimate questions: why would the government clean up dangerous toxic chemicals that threatened public health but then truck it to and dispose of the chemicals in the heart of the black community? Did black people's health matter just as much as white people's health? Why were black communities the targets for so many dangerous and risky facilities?[10]

Although the demonstrations in Warren County, North Carolina, and Houston, Texas were not successful in halting the landfill construction, the protests brought into sharper focus the convergence of civil rights and environmental rights and mobilized a nationally broad-based group to protest these inequities. For me, the Warren County case made it clear that the Houston landfill case was not an isolated problem. This fact was later reinforced by the General Accounting Office (1983) report and by UCC's groundbreaking *Toxic Wastes and Race* report.[11]

Not wanting to go it alone, I recruited my friend and colleague Beverly Wright, a young, untenured sociology professor at the University of New Orleans whom I had met at a Mid-South Sociological Association meeting in Monroe, Louisiana, in 1977, to work with me on environmental justice and environmental racism. I now had a sociologist colleague to pursue a line of research in as yet untested waters. We were able to collaborate on a half-dozen articles and scholarly papers in the mid-1980s.

Although my book *Dumping in Dixie* later became widely associated with the national environmental justice movement, at least a dozen book publishers rejected my manuscript in 1989. They failed to see the connection between race and environmental protection. I did not take the rejections personally. In general, the book publishing industry, dominated by whites who live in the suburbs and have little or no contact with blacks—did not have a clue about what we were seeing on the ground or about what we were writing. This is understandable, given the extreme racial segregation in our society and the racism and elitism that permeate the publishing world. Fortunately, Westview Press, based in Boulder, Colorado, published the book, and hundreds of colleges and universities adopted it as a required text.

In 1990, the National Wildlife Federation (NWF) gave me the Conservation Achievement Award in Science for *Dumping in Dixie* and invited me to spend the summer in Washington, D.C., as a visiting scholar. NWF even put my family and me up in a swank apartment near its headquarters. That summer, my wife and kids had a ball doing the Washington, D.C., "tourist thing" while I gave a couple of lectures and schooled NWF staffers on environmental justice and the importance of diversifying its staff, board, message, and agenda.

On the other hand, my colleagues in the American Sociological Association were slow to recognize environmental justice as a movement. However, the Environment and Technology Section did give me an award in 1998 for *Dumping in Dixie*, a full eight years after it was first published. My position was "better late than never." I reluctantly accepted the award—not that I needed the ASA or the NWF to validate my environmental justice work or the existence of the national environmental justice movement.

It has now been nearly two decades since *Dumping in Dixie* was first published. During this period, the terms "environmental justice," "environmental racism," and "environmental equity" have become household words. Out of the small and seemingly isolated environmental struggles emerged a potent grassroots movement. The 1990s saw the environmental justice movement become a unifying theme that crosses race, class, gender, age, and geographic lines.

*Dumping in Dixie,* now in its third edition, examines the widening economic, health, and environmental disparities within the United States as we enter the twenty-first century. Today, many Americans, from constitutional scholars to lay grassroots activists, recognize that environmental discrimination is unfair, unethical, and immoral. The practice is also illegal. I carried out this research under the assumption that all Americans have a basic right to live, work, play, go to school, and worship in a clean and healthy environment.

This framework became the working definition of the environment for many environmental justice activists and analysts alike. I made a deliberate effort to write a readable book that might reach a general audience while at the same time covering uncharted areas of interest to environmentalists, civil rights advocates, community activists, political leaders, and policymakers.

The issues addressed in *Dumping in Dixie* center on equity, fairness, and the struggle for social justice by African American communities. The struggles against environmental injustice are not unlike the civil rights battles waged to dismantle the legacy of Jim Crow in Selma, Montgomery, Birmingham, and some of the "Up South" communities in New York, Boston, Philadelphia, Detroit, Chicago, and Los Angeles. The analysis chronicles the environmental justice movement in an effort to develop common strategies that are supportive of building sustainable communities for African Americans and other people of color.

In the South, African Americans just happen to make up the region's largest racial minority group. This analysis could have easily focused on Latino Americans in the Southwest or Native Americans in the West. People of color in all regions of the country bear a disproportionate share of the nation's environmental problems. Racism knows no geographic bounds.

Limited housing and residential options, combined with discriminatory facility practices, have contributed to the imposition of all types of toxins on African American communities through the siting of garbage dumps, hazardous-waste landfills, incinerators, smelter operations, paper mills, chemical plants, and a host of other polluting industries. These industries have generally followed the path of least resistance, which has been to locate in economically poor and politically powerless African American communities.

I found that poor African American communities were not the only victims of facility siting disparities and environmental discrimination. Middle-income African American communities were also confronted with many of the same land-use disputes and environmental threats as their lower-income counterparts. Increased income has enabled few African Americans to escape the threat of unwanted land uses and potentially harmful environmental pollutants. In the real world, racial segregation is the dominant residential pattern, and racial discrimination is the leading cause of segregated housing in America.

Since affluent, middle-income, and poor African Americans live near to one another, the question of environmental justice can hardly be reduced to a poverty issue. The black middle-class community members in Houston's Northwood Manor neighborhood quickly discovered that their struggle was not unlike that of their working-class and poor counterparts who had learned to live with that city's garbage dumps and incinerators.

For those who make environmental and industrial decisions, African American communities—regardless of their class status—were considered to be throw-away communities; therefore, land could be used for garbage dumps, transfer stations, incinerators, and other waste disposal facilities. A growing number of grassroots activists, from communities of African Americans and other people of color, have challenged public policies and industrial practices that threaten the residential integrity of their neighborhoods. Activists began to demand environmental justice and equal protection. The demands were reminiscent of those voiced during the civil rights era—they sought an end to discrimination in housing, education, employment, and the political arena. Many exhibited a growing militancy against industrial polluters and government regulatory agencies that provided companies with permits and licenses to pollute.

## The EJ Movement in the 1990s and Beyond

The decade of the 1990s was different from the late 1970s and 1980s.Some progress was made in mainstreaming environmental protection as a civil rights and social justice issue. In the early 1990s, I began to get calls from all kinds of groups that wanted me to speak at forums, symposia, and conferences. Many groups covered travel expenses, and some even paid me to speak. I was getting so many calls in 1991 that my colleague Beverly Wright jokingly suggested I get a booking agent. I took her advice and hired Jodi Solomon, of the Speakers Bureau in Boston, to handle my speaking engagements. Jodi sure has made my life easier.

In the 1990s, groups like the NAACP Legal Defense and Education Fund, the Earthjustice Legal Defense Fund, the Lawyers Committee for Civil Rights Under the Law, the Center for Constitutional Rights, the National Lawyers Guild's Sugar Law Center, the American Civil Liberties Union, and the Legal Aid Society teamed up to work on environmental justice and health issues that differentially affect poor people and people of color. Environmental racism and environmental justice panels became hot topics at conferences sponsored by law schools, bar associations, public health groups, scientific societies, social science meetings, and even government workshops.[12]

Environmental justice leaders have also had a profound impact on public policy, industry practices, national conferences, private foundation funding, and academic research. Environmental justice courses and curricula can be found at nearly every university in the country. In the 1990s, a growing number of academics built careers and got tenure, promotions, and merit raises in departments of environmental justice.

Environmental justice trickled up to the federal government and the White House. Environmental justice activists and academicians were key actors in convincing the U.S. Environmental Protection Agency (during the administration of President George H. W. Bush) to create an Office on Environmental Equity. In 1990, the Reverend Benjamin Chavis (who at the time was executive director of the United Church of Christ Commission for Racial Justice) and I were selected to work on President Bill Clinton's Transition Team in the Natural Resources Cluster (the Environmental Protection Agency and the Departments of Energy, the Interior, and Agriculture).

The 1991 First National People of Color Environmental Leadership Summit was probably the most important single event in the movement's history. The Summit, coordinated by the New York-based United Church of Christ Commission for Racial Justice, broadened the environmental justice movement beyond its early antitoxics focus to include issues of public health, worker safety, land use, transportation, housing, resource allocation, and community empowerment. As a member of the National Planning Committee, I flew to New York twice a month for meetings.

Environmental justice leaders quickly got the Clinton administration to establish a National Environmental Justice Advisory Council (NEJAC) to advise the EPA. In response to growing public concern and mounting scientific evidence, President Clinton, on February 11, 1994 (the second day of the national health symposium), issued Executive Order 12898, "Federal Actions to Address Environmental Justice in Minority Populations and Low-Income Populations." I was present in the Oval Office on that cold, snowy day in February 1994 when President Clinton signed the EJ executive order. Clinton gave us all pens and, later, a photograph of the historic signing.

This executive order attempts to address environmental injustice within existing federal laws and regulations. It reinforces the Civil Rights Act of 1964, Title VI, which prohibits discriminatory practices in programs receiving federal funds. The order also focuses the spotlight back on the National

Environmental Policy Act (NEPA), a twenty-five-year old law that set policy goals for the protection, maintenance, and enhancement of the environment. NEPA's goal is to ensure for all Americans a safe, healthful, productive, and aesthetically and culturally pleasing environment. It requires that federal agencies prepare detailed statements on the environmental effects of proposed federal actions that significantly affect the quality of human health.

In October 2002, we convened the Second National People of Color Environmental Leadership Summit (Summit II), in Washington, D.C. Summit II organizers planned the four-day meeting for five hundred participants. More than 1,400 individuals representing grassroots and community-based organizations, faith-based groups, organized labor, civil rights, youth, and academic institutions made their way to the nation's capital to participate in the historic gathering.

When the First National People of Color Environmental Leadership Summit was held, in 1991, no state had passed an environmental justice law or issued an executive order. In 1993, New Hampshire passed its pioneering environmental justice policy. By 2007, at least three dozen states and the District of Columbia had adopted formal environmental justice statutes, executive orders, or policies. In addition, forty-one states had a policy or program in place that paid attention to the issue of environmental justice. By 2009, all fifty states and the District of Columbia had instituted some type of environmental justice law, executive order, or policy. Although permitting and facility siting still dominate state programs, a growing number of states are beginning to use land-use planning techniques, such as buffer zones, to improve environmental conditions, reduce potential health threats, and prevent environmental degradation in at-risk communities of low-income people and people of color. A few states are also incorporating environmental justice principles in their brownfields, Supplemental Environmental Projects (SEPs), and climate policies.

## Action-Oriented Policy Research

I left UCLA and the University of California, Riverside, for Atlanta in 1994 to start the Environmental Justice Resource Center at Clark Atlanta University (EJRC), my alma mater. The Center was founded that year to assist, support, train, and educate students of color, professionals, and grassroots community leaders, with the goal of facilitating their inclusion into the mainstream of environmental decision making. The EJRC staff played an instrumental role in introducing the environmental justice framework onto the national and international scene. Three decades of cutting-edge research, policy, and community outreach initiatives have emphasized application and action.

Our Center works across the various disciplines in building partnerships and collaborations to achieve environmental and economic justice and healthy communities in the United States and abroad. It has developed strong international collaborations with nongovernmental environmental and human rights organizations in the developing world, including Nigeria, South Africa, and Brazil.

It is no accident that the United Church of Christ (UCC) in 2005 (before Hurricane Katrina) asked our Center to assemble a team of national environmental justice scholars to update its landmark 1987 report to help mark the twentieth anniversary of the original report. The 2007 study, *Toxic Wastes and Race at Twenty: 1987–2007*, was released in March at the National Press Club in Washington, D.C. The new UCC study was the first to use 2000 census data, a current national database of commercial hazardous-waste facilities, and Geographic Information Systems to count persons living near these facilities to assess nationally the extent of racial and socioeconomic disparities in facility locations. *Toxic Wastes and Race at Twenty* also examines racial disparities by region and state and in metropolitan areas, where most hazardous-waste facilities are located.

People of color make up the majority (56 percent) of those living in neighborhoods within three kilometers (1.8 miles) of the nation's commercial hazardous-waste facilities, nearly double the percentage living in areas beyond three kilometers (30 percent). People of color make up a much larger (more than two-thirds) majority (69 percent) of people who live in neighborhoods with clustered facilities. Percentages of African Americans, Hispanics/Latinos, and Asians/Pacific Islanders who live in host neighborhoods are 1.7, 2.3, and 1.8 times greater in host neighborhoods than in nonhost areas (20 percent vs. 12 percent, 27 percent vs. 12 percent, and 6.7 percent vs. 3.6 percent), respectively. In nine out of ten EPA regions, there are racial disparities in the location of hazardous-waste sites.

In forty of forty-four states (90 percent) with hazardous-waste facilities, these facilities are located in neighborhoods whose residents are disproportionately people of color—on average about two times more than the percentages in nonhost areas (44 percent vs. 23 percent). Host neighborhoods in an overwhelming majority of the forty-four states with hazardous-waste sites have disproportionately high percentages of Hispanics (thirty-five states), African Americans (thirty-eight states), and Asians/Pacific Islanders (twenty-seven states). Host neighborhoods of 105 of 149 metropolitan areas with hazardous-waste sites (70 percent) have disproportionately high percentages of people of color, and 46 of these metro areas (31 percent) have host neighborhoods where people of color constitute a majority.

Racial and socioeconomic disparities in the location of the nation's hazardous-waste facilities are geographically widespread throughout the country. People of color are concentrated in neighborhoods and communities with the greatest number of facilities, and people of color in 2007 were more concentrated in areas with commercial hazardous sites than in 1987. Race continues to be a significant independent predictor of the location of commercial hazardous-waste facility when socioeconomic and other nonracial factors are taken into account.

Hurricane Katrina opened a window on a world of hurt often ignored by media, policymakers, and the public. Facing enhanced environmental vulnerability and stranded by a lack of public transit, residents of the poorest and blackest neighborhoods of New Orleans quickly educated America to the fact that disasters and rescues are not equal opportunity affairs. For centuries, African Americans learned the hard way that waiting for the government can be hazardous to their health and the health of their communities. And, in some cases, government action or inaction is the problem.

## Conclusion

My work over the past three decades has pointed to a clear connection between race and place. Vulnerable places often map closely with race. This is the case for natural and human-made disasters. Historically, in the South, this meant that black people occupied the most threatened and vulnerable places. This was certainly the case in my hometown of Elba, Alabama. This uneven and racialized system was buttressed by government, industry, housing markets, financial institutions, and the education system. We now know that by not protecting the most vulnerable in our society, we place everyone at risk. Hurricane Katrina and the levee breach in New Orleans is a clear example of this principle.

The environmental justice paradigm is now being integrated into national dialogues on poverty and pollution, transportation equity, suburban sprawl, smart growth, regional equity, sustainable development, livable communities, and climate change. There is growing consensus among disaster experts that the devastation, destruction, and death that occurred in New Orleans after Katrina was not an act of God or a "natural disaster" but a human-induced disaster worsened by government failures, systematic neglect, and political corruption.

Although Jim Crow was legally declared dead by the courts in 1954, the legacy and residuals of this unfair system relegated black neighborhoods and their inhabitants to unequal environmental protection and unjust health and safety standards. Housing discrimination and forced racial segregation compounded the social and environmental vulnerability and marginalization of African Americans. Erasing this shameful and hurtful legacy has not been an easy task. It is to be hoped that, in time, the nation will come to realize that no community—no matter how poor or no matter what color its residents—is expendable.

Today, millions of Americans, ranging from constitutional scholars to lay grassroots activists, recognize that environmental discrimination is unfair, unethical, and immoral. They also recognize that environmental justice is a legitimate area of inquiry inside and outside the academy. Environmental justice is also a civil rights and human right issue. This was not always the case. Three decades or so ago, few academicians, government bureaucrats, environmentalists, or civil rights or human rights leaders knew anything about or understood the racial dynamics involved in environmental decision making.

The environmental justice movement has continued to make its mark in the twenty-first century. From New York to California, and in a host of cities in between, environmental justice activists are challenging environmental racism, international toxics trade, economic blackmail, corporate welfare, and human rights violations. Groups are demanding a clean, safe, just, healthy, and sustainable environment for all. They see this as not only the right thing to do—but as the moral and just path to ensuring our survival.

In October 2011, I returned to Houston and Texas Southern University as Dean of the Barbara Jordan-Mickey Leland School of Public Affairs—to the city and university that launched my environmental justice career some three decades earlier.

# Growing Up in a City That Care Forgot, New Orleans

## *A Personal Perspective from Beverly Wright*

Growing up in New Orleans was a uniquely delightful experience, filled with the warmth of family and friends who felt like family. My early beginnings in the City of New Orleans bring forth nothing but wonderful memories. The air was always filled with the smell of good food and the sounds of music. As I remember it, we all truly celebrated life. These memories serve as an ironic backdrop for that period of harsh segregation where Jim Crow ruled.

However, within the confines of segregation, the black community was able to nurture and maintain its unique cultural traditions, which were taught to the young and practiced by all, even across income and class lines. Even more so than Christmas, probably the most remembered and cherished holiday of my childhood, as well as in the lives of most adults, was Mardi Gras, or "Fat Tuesday," as it is called here. I can still recall the first time I heard, in the distance, the sounds of tambourines and crowds of people chanting in a language I could not understand.

I could see a large group of people coming up the middle of the street singing and dancing and playing tambourines to the booming sounds of different drummers. The crowds were huge, so much so that I could not tell where the street ended and the sidewalk began. My eyes, widened by childhood curiosity, could hardly take in the beauty of the magnificent costumes I saw, with colors so brilliant it almost hurt to look at them through the bright sunshine. I had never seen anything so beautiful in all of my four-year-old life! Ah, yes, these were the Mardi Gras Indians in all their splendidly feathered glory, and they were coming toward me! As fate would have it, they stopped right in front of my door to begin a spectacular display of chanting and dancing.

Even to this day, I still cannot translate their chanting, but it was on that day I learned the beginning steps of the famous "Second Line." And, as I made the steps my little feet could grasp, the "Big Chief" emerged from the crowd to declare, "Aay pockaway!" With that, everyone started singing and dancing with such intensity that I did what any other four-year-old would do—I joined in trying to mimic what I saw most everybody doing.

An older cousin of mine saw me trying my feeble best and was impressed with my efforts. She immediately stopped me from gyrating in a frenzy and told me, "No, no, watch me. You move your feet like this." As she began to give me my first official second line lesson, I watched and followed her steps. And so, I, like everyone in my community, became an authentic second line dancer. It was much later in life that I cultivated an appreciation for this unique form of an African/Haitian and New Orleans-inspired cultural tradition that has helped to shape the character of my city, making it a "place to visit" for most Americans regardless of race, ethnicity, or culture. The Spirit of New Orleans is in its people, and, without black people, New Orleans would lose its "soul."

In our most recent New Orleans vernacular since Katrina, "hurricane" is synonymous with danger, but, in my experience of growing up in New Orleans, the word "hurricane" was synonymous with heavy rain and a party. Why, we even named a very powerful alcoholic drink after this weather event. What I remember most was the rush to the supermarket for bread, milk, hot dogs, hamburger meat, and cold cuts. These were the staples necessary to survive the power outages that accompanied a "storm." With an impending storm, the family would all meet at one house to "ride it out." Inevitably, the storm would arrive during the night when we were tucked safely into our beds, the children huddled together not so much because we feared disaster but because it was fun for us to be with our extended family at this unique time. In the morning, the family would go out to survey the neighborhood. The greatest devastation that occurred, as I recall from those pre-Katrina days, were the garbage cans thrown about and tree branches blown to the ground.

As I grew into adulthood, the hurricanes seemed to increase in intensity, leaving more and more water, more and more often. Several hurricanes over the years left water high enough to wash into houses, damaging carpets and low-lying furniture and appliances. In 1965, Hurricane Betsy hit the City of New Orleans. It devastated the Lower Ninth Ward and New Orleans East.[1] Hundreds of people lost their lives, and many homes were flooded. Black mold was also a problem, even though the water did not sit for weeks as it did in the wake of Katrina and the New Orleans levee failures. As Betsy's waters began to recede, people began to immediately repair their homes with a little help from insurance companies, the Red Cross, and the Federal Emergency Management Agency (FEMA). We survived, and New Orleanians went on with their lives.

However, one thing this 1965 hurricane left behind was an increasing perception that our federal government had no desire to protect the African American population of this city. To this day, black New Orleanians still believe that the levees were broken intentionally to protect very wealthy white homes and business owners Uptown and in the French Quarter. Victor Schiro, who was then mayor, was blamed for the devastation, and the question of race and who will be protected was settled in the minds of African Americans in this city. We knew that we would be the last to receive protection, and Hurricane Katrina has further validated this belief.

After Hurricane Betsy, hurricanes and rumors or warnings of hurricanes were more frequent. But, for the greater part of forty years, New Orleans was not hit by a major hurricane. We continued to feel the effects of hurricanes through their heavy winds and rains. What this meant for most people was the loss of electricity and a bit of water in our houses. These somewhat frequently occurring weather events each year were seen as an annoyance, not a "danger." When we saw the storms as annoyances or an inconveniences that interrupted our lives, we viewed the imminent repairs as an "upgrade." We got new floors, carpets, or appliances, and that was our reality relating to hurricanes.

## My Katrina Experience

My academic life and research agendas have been indelibly shaped by extremely personal experiences and curiosities. Over the past three decades, I have been involved in the struggle for equality and social justice for all people. A large portion of my work has evolved around a framework of environmental justice. This circuitous journey still did not prepare me for the injustices perpetrated, which resulted in the government's utter failures during Katrina, as well as those that occurred in the storm's aftermath.

The year leading up to Katrina had already been particularly hard for me on a personal level. In January of 2004, my only brother, three years younger than I, was diagnosed with cancer. The doctors gave him three months to live. My family and I were devastated and just could not believe or accept this diagnosis. We, just as most families have done in this situation, did everything humanly possible to keep him alive. But we lost the battle, and Morris died on August 6, 2004.

At the same time that we were battling to save my brother's life, my family was dealing with another familiar family illness. My mother was diabetic and had been placed on dialysis nearly two years before Morris was diagnosed. He had been her major caregiver because my work kept me on the road most of the time. This, too, was a very stressful ordeal. After my brother's death, my mother's health seemed to deteriorate. In April 2005, eight months after the death of my brother, my mother died. I was completely devastated, heart-broken, and inconsolable. I felt that surely nothing else could happen to me. Then came Katrina, only four months after my mother's death. That terrible storm washed away everything that I owned, everything that I had inherited, and every tangible bit of memorabilia that captured my life and family experiences. Every picture, every card, every letter and keepsake that I had of my mother and brother all washed away in those horrible floodwaters. Katrina swept away the pictorial history of my life and ancestry. Every picture of children growing up, grandparents hugging, great-grandparents' wisdom-weathered faces smiling, camera-shy aunts and uncles hiding, and genera-tions of laughing and playing cousins captured in time were lost forever, and there was nothing I could do to bring back these treasured possessions.

I was the official keeper of the family pictures. I kept pictures from both my husband's and my own family. I proudly displayed them throughout my house, carefully arranging them as focal points of my souvenir and art collec-tion from my travels around the world. The tribal masks from South Africa, a porcelain faced image of Nelson Mandela in tribal garb, a didgeridoo and a boomerang from Australia, a porcelain faced puppet from Indonesia, and many more treasured art pieces were meticulously placed to accent family portraits. All were lost in the storm.

The Katrina tragedy was worsened by the fact that I too had a missing relative as a result of this storm. My seventy-seven-year-old uncle, who was my Mom's only brother, was missing. The events that led up to his being left in New Orleans had more to do with the loss of my mother and brother than the storm itself. My brother and I were the primary caregivers for our now very small number of elderly family members. When the storm hit, I was out of town, and my uncle was home alone. He and my mother and brother had all lived together. I have one sister who lives in Jackson, Mississippi. The two of us made arrangements for my uncle to evacuate with his cousins. Some-how, the evacuation plans were not carried out, and they all remained in the city, and were all missing after the storm. We received word early on that my cousins were safe, but it was two weeks after the storm before we heard anything about Uncle Walter.

After riding out the storm and flooding on the second floor of our New Orleans East family home, Uncle Walter was eventually rescued by boat, and the Coast Guard airlifted him to Reese Air Force Base in Lubbock, Texas, located more than 870 miles from New Orleans. He survived Katrina and lived the rest of his life in Baton Rouge—which he never saw as home. New Orleans was his birthplace and his home. He died in May 2008, one month before his eightieth birthday. He is buried in New Orleans.

The emotional stress created by this situation for my entire family can only be described as pure agony, anger, and disbelief. Recall the horrific scenes of devastation and the abandonment of people left behind all over the city, viewed by the world as the days slowly crept by. Now imagine not knowing where a loved one is as you watch as this tragedy unfold before your very eyes. I was heartbroken and angry. It was as if I were watching some cataclysmic event in a Third World country, far, far away. This couldn't possibly be happening in the United States! Who would have ever believed that this country would respond to the suffering of its people in such a callous and indifferent manner? When I reflect on my feelings in the first days after Katrina, I can honestly identify my central emotion as fear couched in anger and disbelief at the incompetence of our government. I could not believe the utter failure of our government to grasp the nature of the tragedy and to understand that it required a truly compassionate, immediate, and coordinated response. For the first time in my life, I felt that, as a nation, we were unprepared and vulnerable. Even the tragedy of 9/11 did not evoke such fear and emotional upheaval in me. When and how did this country come to this?

## Loss of Inheritance

When I was a child, every Sunday after church, my father would take us all for a ride in the family car. We always ended up in the same places. We would sightsee in the white neighborhoods lined with white-framed houses with perfectly manicured lawns and large oak trees spreading their branches over the streets. My father's words were always the same: "You see, children. This is what you should work for."

My father believed that every generation should do better than the one before it and that it was the responsibility of each generation to do everything to make the American Dream possible for the next generation. As Dad would say, "It's hard to get ahead when you are starting from scratch. This house is your scratch." In fact, my mother and father bought two houses and three lots in their lifetimes. Katrina destroyed them all.

Like many African American families in New Orleans, my family was just beginning to realize the dreams of our parents and grandparents. The property they had worked so hard to secure for their families was paid for in full, and their children now had an inheritance, or, as Dad would say, their "scratch."

Eighty percent of homes destroyed by Katrina in New Orleans were owned by African Americans. For many families, their first ever inherited property was lost in the storm, and all the dreams and hard work of their parents and grandparents were destroyed along with them. To add insult to injury, African American New Orleanians watched with horror as the first rebuilding plan was presented to the City Council. What became perfectly clear after a first glimpse of the new map, or, as it was called, the smaller footprint, was that the footprints of African Americans in New Orleans were to be erased. The map clearly showed that the areas slated for immediate redevelopment were those that had received the least amount of water—areas where white citizens lived. The areas that were mostly inhabited by African Americans, specifically New Orleans East and the Lower Ninth Ward, were not slated for redevelopment and were instead to be converted into "green space." With one stroke of a pen, our land was being taken away and our inheritance lost, along with our family's legacy. I could think only how arrogant and racist this plan was to take our land.

After the dreadful storm, my first visit to my home could only be described as surreal. As we drove toward the city, there were literally thousands of people traveling both ways with trailers attached to cars that held the family's remaining, salvageable personal belongings. The ride was quiet and solemn, a kind of funeral procession. There were also numerous accidents and breakdowns. The scene reminded me of scenes from World War II movies in which villages were bombed and people were fleeing the devastation. The only difference was that people were driving, rather than walking.

When I arrived at my house, I immediately donned protective clothing and breathing apparatus. Upon entering through my front door, which was swollen and bent shut, I immediately realized that all of the furniture was rearranged. In fact, the refrigerator was toppled over and sitting in the den. The leather sofa was completely white, although the original color was black. I later discovered that it was completely overgrown with mold. Everything was covered with mold. The floor was slippery, and the odor was indescribably foul.

Mold had traveled up the wall to the upstairs bedrooms, and my younger daughter's room was completely destroyed. I cried. The roof had been blown off in one corner, and everything was ruined. It was clear to me that the entire house needed to be gutted and rebuilt. I left my house, however, determined to rebuild. I was coming back come hell or high water. The one question I had centered on was the extent of the contamination left by Katrina.

For the previous ten years at least, I had worked with communities contaminated by toxic emissions and people living with lead-contaminated soil. I had also worked to train young men and women in hazardous-materials abatement and with superfund sites for cleanup. I kept trying to imagine what level of contamination would be so bad that it would keep us from being able to clean it up. I left my home with a determination fueled by the words of my father: "This is your scratch." I needed to understand the contamination left by Katrina and to develop a plan to clean it up.

The Deep South Center for Environmental Justice, where I am founding director and currently work, had previously established a relationship with the Natural Resources Defense Council (NRDC) and was keenly aware of the Council's research, scientific, and legal capabilities. We immediately developed a partnership with them to test the air and soil contamination left by Katrina. The results showed that there was contamination that needed to be cleaned up and contained. Post-Katrina contamination had rendered some communities unsafe.

The NRDC took air and soil samples and reviewed sample data taken by the Environmental Protection Agency (EPA) and found very similar results. There were high levels of lead and arsenic and derivatives of benzopyrene. What I determined was that the cleanup was a doable project to undertake. New Orleans could be cleaned up, and its citizens would be able to return to a safe and clean environment. Not to do what was needed to achieve this end would be criminal.

## A Safe Way Back Home

The Deep South Center for Environmental Justice (DSCEJ) was founded in 1992 in collaboration with community environmental groups and universities within the region to address issues of environmental justice. The Center provides opportunities for communities, scientific researchers, and decision makers to collaborate on programs and projects that promote the rights of all people to be free from environmental harm as it impacts health, jobs, housing, education, and general quality of life.

The DSCEJ's Minority Worker Training Program is funded by the National Institute of Environmental Health Sciences (NIEHS) and provides training for young men and women in an array of hazardous-materials abatement and construction skills. Our program is a part of a consortium of union organizations, universities, nonprofit training organizations, and HBCUs that provides training for workers and supervisors in hazardous-materials mitigation and construction. At our first meeting after the storm, member organizations were encouraged to assist Gulf Coast organizations in their recovery. All of the union organizations offered their support; however, an extensive conversation with Paul Renner of the United Steel Workers was the most productive. While sitting in the airport awaiting return flights to our respective locations, drinking a glass or two of wine, we came up with the idea of a demonstration project that would clean up one solid block in a devastated neighborhood. Our intent was to show the government what could and should be done in order for citizens to return home safely. The "Safe Way Back Home" project emerged out of the frustration of many citizens over the lack of information available on environmental contamination, health, and safety. Even more disconcerting was the actual double-talk that we were receiving from the EPA on contamination levels and risks and how residents should respond.

The Center has been conducting environmental remediation training with a grant from the National Institute of Environmental Health Science (NIEHS) since 1995. The specialized expertise and the trained workforce that it provided were of great benefit to New Orleans after Katrina. They also meant that our University Center could and would play a critical role in providing a vital service in the cleanup of the city. We could supply trainers and workers in areas where they were gravely needed to clean up and rebuild the city. But, there was one more thing that we could provide besides our professional expertise, and that was the actual implementation of a program that would result in the actual cleanup of a site. After Katrina, however, there was mass confusion on the ground. The information that we received from EPA's website showed contamination levels for lead, arsenic, and PCBs to be extremely high, exceeding the recommended safe levels set by both the EPA and the Louisiana Department of Environmental Quality (LDEQ).

We consulted with scientists from the NRDC and consulted the EPA's website, which reported sampling data, to determine the type and extent of remediation needed to reduce the risk of exposure from chemicals found in the soil. In our attempt to be responsive in the midst of what we saw to be slow to no action by government in the cleanup of neighborhoods and at the same time watching residents return to their homes every day without protective gear or information on risk levels for sediment, we decided to implement a demonstration project that the government could model in the cleanup of the city. In the project's development, we spoke with EPA (off the record), FEMA, the United Steelworkers Union (USW), volunteer organizations, and student organizations.

After a short planning period and coordination of partners, the DSCEJ at Dillard University and the USW developed a plan to remediate twenty-five homes or one block in the New Orleans East area. With approximately 180 volunteers over two weekends, we removed six inches of top soil, deposited clean soil, and planted sod on the twenty-five homes whose residents had agreed to the terms of participation.

FEMA committed to pick up the soil, the Red Cross agreed to provide supplies, and the volunteers agreed to assist. The United Steelworkers operated the bobcats to remove the soil. We were well on our way to completion of what we saw as a precedent-setting event when, on the third day, FEMA stopped picking up the soil. All of our efforts to get the agency to honor its commitment were thwarted. We were actually stuck with several large piles of contaminated soil on a block we had just returned to normal, with beautiful green grass on front and back lawns, lawns safe enough for children to play outside. We could not understand why FEMA discontinued picking up the dirt. We were later informed that the soil was contaminated and considered hazardous material and under the Stafford Act could not be removed by FEMA. The EPA and the LDEQ were insisting that the soil was not contaminated. The residents were caught in the middle of an unbelievable dispute. What were we to do with these large mounds of soil now sitting in the street in front of our homes?

The story does have a happy ending, but not because the federal government resolved this issue. Eventually, the City of New Orleans removed the soil from the median where we moved it so as not to recontaminate the entire block.

What has become clear through my interaction with the EPA and this experience is that the agency has lost sight of its true mission to protect the public health and the environment. We experienced a bureaucratic response in a crisis. The agency followed "the letter of the law and not the spirit" of the law. For example, state and federal officials labeled the voluntary cleanup efforts as "scaremongering." EPA and LDEQ officials said that they had tested soil samples from the neighborhood in December 2005 and found there was no immediate cause for concern.

According to Tom Harris, administrator of LDEQ's environmental technology division and state toxicologist, the government originally sampled eight hundred locations in New Orleans and found cause for concern in only forty-six samples. According to Harris, the soil in New Orleans was consistent with "what we saw before Katrina." He called the "Safe Way Back Home" program completely unnecessary. However, all requests for soil sampling data before the storm have gone unanswered. Moreover, initial sampling results of soil collected before Katrina are showing arsenic and lead levels much lower than those reported by LDEQ post-Katrina.

A week after the March 2006 voluntary neighborhood cleanup project began, an LDEQ staffer ate a spoonful of soil scraped from the piles of soil left by FEMA in front of the beautiful new lawns planted by volunteers of the "Safe Way Back Home" project. The soil-eating publicity stunt was clearly an attempt to disparage the proactive neighborhood cleanup initiative. I immediately invited Mr. Harris back to eat a spoonful of soil every day for the next ten years. Only then would I be convinced that his exposure to the chemicals in the soil would be comparable to that of my children or grandchildren if they played outside in the soil every day. I offered to buy him lunch and bury the hatchet if he was still alive and well at the end of the ten years.

While I initially was totally confused by the EPA's response to the contamination threats to my hometown presented on their website, I was truly angry after reading the June 2007 U.S. General Accountability Office (GAO) report. The EPA did not assess and properly mitigate the environmental impacts posed by Katrina. The EPA's December 2005 assessment stated that the "majority" of sediment exposure was safe.[2] It is clear that existing policies are not adequate to protect the public in matters related to disasters, especially catastrophic events like Hurricane Katrina. It seems that the existing policies actually work in a manner that diametrically opposes the agency's mission—monitoring and protecting the environmental health and safety of the public.

The "Safe Way Back Home" project generated excitement and increased hope for the neighborhood's return. All of this happened without any assistance from the local, state, or federal government. It has been the unrelenting resolve of New Orleans East residents to rebuild their homes and their lives that has given us a glimmer of hope for recovery.

In attempting to understand how and why federal agencies (e.g., EPA, FEMA, U.S. Army Corps of Engineers) were unable to assist citizens in their quest to remediate their own properties after the storm, the GAO's *Hurricane Katrina: EPA's Current and Future Environmental Protection Efforts Could Be Enhanced by Addressing Issues and Challenges Faced on the Gulf Coast* report offers much insight on the inner workings of these agencies, which fostered their failure to act. In fact, their actions served as a deterrent to citizens' efforts.[3]

The response to the health implications of this enormous environmental catastrophe fell far below any logical or reasonable response to this disaster. Second only to "rebuilding the levees," environmental health should be the issue of greatest concern in the rebuilding and repopulating plan for the city. Unfortunately, issues related to health and the environment have barely been mentioned in the discussions of rebuilding the city. This piece of the rebuilding process is missing. Its omission has given life to numerous rumors and panic that stalled the rebuilding process. At stake was not only the health of the community but also the loss of property and wealth for a large portion of the New Orleans African American community and a possible dramatic shift in the city's demographics, with negative implications for the black electorate.

## Congressional Hearings

Shortly after Katrina, I was invited to testify at two congressional hearings. Senator Barbara Boxer invited me to testify before the Committee on Environment and Public Works Subcommittee on Superfund and Waste Management, and Senator Hillary Rodham Clinton invited me to testify before the Subcommittee on Superfund and Environmental Health of the Senate Environment and Public Works Committee. The July 2007 Clinton hearing was the first-ever Senate hearing on environmental justice. The goal was to understand exactly what had gone wrong with the government's preparation and response to natural disasters. There was also great interest in obtaining the facts and in getting assistance with plans for Gulf Coast recovery.

In the months immediately following Katrina, Congress rushed pass laws designed to support the cleanup and recovery of the Gulf Coast. Moreover, a number of bills were submitted to allow the waiver of many important environmental regulations and laws, as well as to limit legal responsibility for damages by private businesses involved in the cleanup of the Gulf Coast.

My second testimony took place on June 25, 2007, at a hearing before the Subcommittee on Superfund and Environmental Health of the Senate Environment and Public Works Committee. The intent of the committee was to investigate environmental justice concerns related to health in the aftermath of Katrina, with particular emphasis on Superfund sites.

In my testimony, I was eager to raise the case of the Agriculture Street landfill (discussed in chapter 5) and the irony of effects from both Hurricanes Betsy and Katrina. It was debris from Hurricane Betsy, forty years ago, that led to the reopening of the Agriculture Street landfill, atop which a community was built. Contamination from was later found in the community and for years local residents fought to be bought out and relocated. But it was Hurricane Katrina, not the government, that relocated the community nearly fourteen years after the community began its struggle to relocate. Moreover, the responses of government to many of the new environmental health risks caused by Katrina were almost identical to the way it responded to the plight of the Agriculture Street landfill community.

My testimony included a request that Congress investigate the latest report and flood maps produced by the U.S. Army Corps of Engineers post-Katrina, which provided no increased levee protection for the mostly African American areas of the city. One of my major concerns at the time of this hearing, however, was the health of the children who attended some of New Orleans's public schools; I strongly believed the results of testing done in 2007 indicated the need for additional investigation into the safety of a number of school grounds.

In March 2007, a coalition of community and environmental groups collected more than 130 soil samples in sixty-five sites in residential neighborhoods in Orleans Parish where post-Katrina EPA testing had previously shown elevated concentrations of arsenic in soils. Testing was then performed by the Natural Resources Defense Council. Sampling was also done at fifteen playgrounds and nineteen schools. Results from the independent laboratory testing for the nineteen schools are as follows:

Six results indicate levels of arsenic in excess of the LDEQ's soil screening value for arsenic. The LDEQ soil screening value of 12 milligrams per kilogram (mg/kg) normally requires additional sampling, further investigation, and a site-specific risk assessment. It is clear that the levels of arsenic in the sediment are unacceptably high for residential neighborhoods. We are especially concerned about potential health risks to children playing in areas with arsenic-contaminated sediments. At some of the sites sampled in March, lab results indicate that arsenic levels have increased in the time that has passed since earlier post-Katrina studies.

In June 2007, the coalition sent a letter to LDEQ requesting that it take action and recommending that it take advantage of the window of opportunity provided by the upcoming summer vacation to take several steps: to conduct additional sampling of school playgrounds in previously flooded areas, to conduct a site-specific risk assessment, and to work with the schools and community to examine potential remediation options. Because we felt it would be unethical to withhold these data from potentially affected parties, we also notified school officials in the six schools where the elevated arsenic levels were detected. The response that we received from the EPA was basically that it was reviewing our letter and would respond within thirty days.[4]

The response that we received from LDEQ concerning the high arsenic levels found on the school grounds of New Orleans public schools once again supports criticisms of the EPA's response to Katrina: that the agency did not assess and properly mitigate Katrina's environmental impacts. Specifically, the letter from LDEQ, first of all, addresses the fact that "15 of the 19 schools sampled fell below health-based levels of concern and are consistent with background levels for Louisiana." Our data actually showed that thirteen of the nineteen schools were at safe levels. However, this was not the point. We were and are interested only in those schools with problems.

Second, the letter from LDEQ immediately speaks to its process for collecting samples and the fact that LDEQ and the EPA together collected more than two thousand sediment and soil samples in the impacted area, whereas NRDC "collected only one sample." This implied that, because we had taken only one sample, our results, while high, did not warrant further testing or concern. Consequently, we were told that we should inform the schools in question. The letter also stated that, although LDEQ was under no legal obligation because the public schools were strapped for funds, it would provide further testing if the principal of a school made the request. My reply to that was, "Well, thanks for the favor," but isn't it the job of citizens to assess and mitigate the impacts of Katrina?

In the letter from LDEQ, there was an attempt to educate the coalition on a few facts of which we were not aware. These involved the possibility that the arsenic contamination existed on these school grounds before Katrina. I found this to be an absolutely incredible statement. Did this mean that LDEQ was actually aware of the elevated arsenic on the playgrounds of these schools? If not, then why were we discussing pre-Katrina arsenic levels?

The point is that LDEQ and EPA seemed much more interested in justifying their existing position—that they were not obligated and were even forbidden by law to clean up pre-Katrina contamination—than they were in protecting the public. Nonetheless, it was our hope that LDEQ and EPA would rise to the challenge of its mission to ensure that Louisiana's citizens "have a clean and healthy environment to live and work in for present and future generations" by responding to these data in a time-sensitive manner.

Although contamination levels discovered at New Orleans schools exceeded state and federal clean-up standards and posed a risk of cancer and chronic illness to children who play in the dirt and put their hands in their mouths, federal and state clean-up funds were earmarked for contamination that was from the storm, not from preexisting contamination, regardless of the public health significance. Contamination on the school grounds was not cleaned up. Once again, the health of the most vulnerable population in New Orleans, African American school children, is placed at risk because of a government rule that gives clean-up priority to time of contamination rather than health impacts.

## Conclusion

In September 1965, I left my beloved city of New Orleans to attend Grambling College. I was seventeen years old and leaving home for the first time. My first week at Grambling was the exciting experience of freshmen orientation. I remember returning from a student assembly and watching the 6:00 news, which was airing a special report. I was paying minimal attention to the broadcast while laughing, joking, and becoming acquainted with my new roommates and friends. I did, however, notice a street sign that seemed to be leaning over and was partially covered by water. The street sign read "Rampart!" My attention was then turned to the television, not only because Rampart is a famous street in New Orleans but also because it was the street where my former high school was located.

My high school, McDonogh #35, was more than a hundred years old and was the only high school for African American youth during the era of segregation. I guess it would today be described as a school for the gifted, but, for us, it was a "college prep" school for students with the highest grade point averages in their classes. This school trained the best of the best public school students in the African American community. It served a very important function and was also an historic landmark for the community. Needless to say, when I saw a mound of bricks near the street sign, I was flabbergasted. Could this pile of bricks actually be my alma mater? To my chagrin, the news reporter validated my suspicion. It was my school! Even worse, I discovered that my city had been hit by a powerful and dangerous hurricane named

Betsy. The news of the storm only worsened. I later found out that my neighborhood was flooded, that, indeed, all of New Orleans East and the Lower Ninth Ward were flooded by waters from Lake Ponchartrain.

The week of freshmen orientation at Grambling College is forever etched in my mind because of Betsy. The excitement of going away to school was inevitably replaced by the urgent need to contact family and to return home to make sure that everyone was safe. I could not act on either of these urges, however; phone lines were down, and transportation into the city was not available. I had to sit nervously and patiently, waiting for someone to contact me. The only phones we had in the dormitories back then were located at the end of the hall on each floor. We didn't have the convenience of cell phones. The lines of students trying to call home were continuously long, and most of us encountered the same nerve-wracking problem—we could not connect with any of our family members.

Finally, after nearly four days, a call came through to me from my parents. Overjoyed at the sound of their voices, I was grateful to hear that they were fine. But I was devastated upon hearing that the first floor of our new split-level home (which was only three years old) was completely flooded. My mother described the damage created by the five or six feet of water that had inundated the ground floor of our home. The first-floor bedroom, bathroom, utility room, and den (or, as we considered it, playroom) had been destroyed in the storm. I was also told that ten of our neighbors, whose houses were single-story homes, were staying with my family in the upper floor of our home.

My father told me how he had walked miles from work "Uptown," where there was no water, into the East, where the water rose above his shoulders after he crossed the Industrial Canal. He walked all those miles so that he could reach his family. And, as he walked through the floodwaters in our neighborhood, he was joined by other neighbors. Remembering an elderly couple who lived alone, they decided to force open their front door, only to discover that this couple, both of whom were past eighty, had resigned themselves to die in the floodwaters. My father, being the man he was, helped our neighbors out of their house and up the stairs into our home. The triumph of the New Orleans spirit rose above the floodwaters that day and in many days to come.

When I was able to return home for Thanksgiving break in November, I discovered that a vile, fishy odor still lingered in our neighborhood. It would prove to be many months before the odor dissipated. However, I don't ever remember feeling that recovery was not possible after Betsy. There was never any discussion about the possibility that the many African American neighborhoods affected by the storm were no longer safe for residents. I remember President Lyndon Johnson visiting New Orleans and the Lower Ninth Ward within twenty-four hours of the hurricane and his assurances that our government would assist us in recovering from the storm. I also vividly remember my parents telling me that they were going to get a FEMA grant to renovate the ground floor of the house. It would include money for a new refrigerator and a new roof. In less than one year, my entire neighborhood was cleaned up and back to normal, all shining and new.

Many African Americans, to this day, however, still believe that Mayor Schiro had holes blown in the levees to save Uptown and the French Quarter at the expense of African American neighborhoods. There is no evidence of record to support this theory, but some even say that Mayor Schiro admitted that he had given the order. What we do know as fact is that the floodwaters grew to almost six feet in only three minutes. Many people drowned, and many New Orleans residents still don't trust local government to protect them from disasters, whether natural or man-made. At that time, in a pre-Katrina New Orleans, residents did, however, have some faith in the federal government and in FEMA in particular.

Hurricane Betsy was a powerful storm. In 1965, Betsy was deemed the costliest hurricane in the history of the United States. It was nicknamed "Billion Dollar Betsy." Levees for the Mississippi River Gulf Outlet (MRGO) along Florida Avenue in the Lower Ninth Ward and on both sides of the Industrial Canal failed during the storm. Floodwaters reached the tops of houses in some places and covered the roofs of single-story homes in the Lower Ninth Ward and in New Orleans East. Many residents drowned in their attics trying to escape the rising floodwaters. Breaches in the levee system flooded parts of Gentilly, the Upper and Lower Ninth Ward, and Eastern New Orleans. Arabi and Chalmette, in St. Bernard Parish, were also flooded. It took nearly ten days for most of the water to recede and for most of the residents living in flood-ravaged single-story homes to return in order to clean up. Those who did not have family members or friends to take them in lived in trailers until they were able to return home. A total of 164,000 homes were flooded. Just as with Katrina, the evidence suggests that substandard construction and poor maintenance of the levee system led to its failure.

A look at both hurricanes Betsy and Katrina reveals some interesting similarities but also some glaring differences. Hurricane Katrina and its impacts should not have been a surprise to anyone in government, which was not the case with Betsy. While citizens were not privy to important scientific information concerning weather patterns and trends or to assessments of the storm-worthiness of the levees or the viability of the pumping system, government had this information. Several computer models and accompanying predictions of the impact on the city of a Category 3 or a Category 5 hurricane were made available to government officials on the local, state, and federal levels. These models and predictions should have better guided the decisions made by government at all levels in its response both pre- and post-Katrina.

The government's response in the aftermath of Hurricane Betsy was quick and efficient. Within a very short period of time, the city, along with its citizens, was back up and running. Hurricane Betsy, which hit the city more than forty years ago, was followed by another dangerous storm, Hurricane Camille, in 1969. Although this storm was deadly, it did not bring with it the devastating floodwaters that Betsy had. However, since that time, the citizens of New Orleans and the Gulf Coast have experienced increases in both the number and the intensity of hurricanes. We have also seen an increase in citizen awareness and evidence that government takes seriously the need to prepare for these storms, as evidenced by improved advance planning for evacuation. In fact, approximately eight months prior to Hurricane Katrina, the City of New Orleans was evacuated in preparation for the coming of Hurricane Ivan.

Fortunately for us, New Orleans was not hit by Ivan, although Florida did take a direct hit from it. However, what was evident at the time of this storm were the increasing tensions and stress brought on as hurricane season approached, lingered, and waned. In fact, I can honestly say that, in my life-time of living in the City of New Orleans, I had never experienced a degree of anxiousness and cautiousness as the hurricane season approached as I had in the three years before Hurricane Katrina. Even before Katrina, our attitude about hurricanes was reflected in the naming of an alcoholic drink with a powerful kick that became popular in the French Quarter as a "hurricane." The time spent preparing for a storm, formerly dubbed a "hurricane party," had also taken on a new seriousness. Since Katrina, as citizens of New Orleans, our fear of the storms has been heightened, and, even worse, our trust in our government and the belief that it will respond to our plight both efficiently and fairly has deteriorated into mistrust and unbelief.

Government's response to the impacts of Katrina on New Orleans and the Gulf Coast has challenged the beliefs of most Americans, black and white alike, that our government is competent to meet the challenges posed by most major disasters and, for African Americans particularly, that it will respond equally to the needs of all of its citizens, regardless of race or ethnicity. Many of my white friends expressed outrage toward the government for its slow response to a mostly African American city but also confessed to me their fears concerning our government's ability to protect even them against any threat, foreign or domestic. It is clear that the lethargic and inept emergency response after Hurricane Katrina was a disaster that overshadowed the deadly storm itself. Nearly a decade after the storm and the beginning of the cleanup, it just may be a policy "surge," not the storm surge, that completes the job. If policies are not developed to protect vulnerable populations, there will be a permanent and systematic depopulation and displacement of the African American communities of New Orleans.

In 2010, just as I was thinking, "Things certainly couldn't get any worse," I heard something about an oil spill in the Gulf. Explosions at chemical plants and oil leaks in the Gulf are pretty commonplace where I live, but this "rumor" seemed to be lingering. After pretty much ignoring the incident, despite the eleven men who died in the explosion, news reporting on the oil spill seemed to increase, although we were told that the oil leak was under control. Then, suddenly, the very quiet rumbling about the spill burst into a panicked outcry related to the future the Gulf of Mexico and the impact of the spill on the people and industries that rely on it for a living.

Information from the media exposed me to the complexities of the process of oil drilling. Most of us knew that oil drilling played a major role in the destruction of the coastline as it led to erosion of the wetlands and marshes so precious to the wildlife and marine life in our area. Most of us who live along the coast understood that wetlands and marshes serve as natural barriers against flooding and that they had protected us well before Hurricane Katrina. But I am certain that we never knew that there was a drilling accident just waiting to occur, with the potential to completely destroy the Gulf of Mexico, or at least our way of life, for a very long time.

The reality is that the fisher community of Louisiana and other Gulf states was devastated. Beaches and the related tourism industry and community have also lost their economic base. For most, all income for 2010 was lost and showed signs of struggling in 2011. Small and minority businesses have been slowest to recover from the Gulf Coast disasters.

Who should be blamed for this disaster? After Katrina, it became obvious that much of the human suffering that followed the flood could be blamed on the government's slow response. We later learned of the problems with levees, pump stations, and coastal erosion. In the end, a failure of government at all levels—federal, state and local—was responsible for the magnitude of the devastation from the storm and the enormous amount of human suffering.

Let's compare the results of this analysis to our effort to decipher the cause of the BP oil rig disaster and to determine the responsible parties. Initially, one might very easily have believed that this was "just" an accident, the outcome of a risk that must be taken in our efforts to supply our country with oil. Let's say that, in this instance, the good outweighed the bad and that, moreover, the greater good was served. Americans are not unaccustomed to accepting high risk for the greater good. For example, during war, we know that there will be a loss of life; we also accepted the risks posed by manned space travel as we attempted to reach the moon despite the loss of life to astronauts.

The oil spill and the attempts by BP to cap the well created an emotional roller-coaster for Gulf Coast residents. Every day was one of wonder and worry over the well's closure, with all good news receiving only cautious acceptance. After months of hoping for the best, we learned to expect the worst.

After nearly eighty-five days of oil spilling into the Gulf, on July 15, 2010, we finally received good news. The well had been capped. The caution, however, was that it would be forty-eight hours before we could be certain that the cap would hold. Well, the forty-eight hours passed, the cap held, but there were concerns about leakage from the bottom of the well. As it turned out, the cap was only a temporary fix, and engineers, as in the past, disagreed on what would be the best next steps.

Capping the well was only part of the headache that gripped my community and me. We constantly worried about the lasting economic and psychological impact of the spill. Some estimates have valued the lost ecosystem services from the BP Deepwater Horizon spill at between $1.2 and $23.5 billion per year into the indefinite future (until ecological recovery), or between $34 and $670 billion in present value. We later learned that our psychological fears were not wild paranoia but fears documented by health scientists. The researchers concluded that "Current estimates of human health impacts associated with the oil spill may underestimate the psychological impact in Gulf Coast communities that did not experience direct exposure to oil. Income loss after the spill may have a greater psychological health impact than the presence of oil on the immediately adjacent shoreline."[5]

Intertwined in this ongoing dilemma was the relationship between the federal government and BP. At what point could the federal government force BP to comply with its directives for sealing the well? What I found most disturbing is that neither the government nor BP had a scientifically conclusive remedy to expeditiously seal the well or to clean up the coast. To quote an old TV show, "What a revolting development this is!"

This takes us to the more perplexing and complicated parts of this saga, the offshore deepwater drilling moratorium imposed by the Obama administration, which suspended new drilling projects so that the government could study the risks revealed by the disastrous BP oil spill. While I was completely baffled by the response of our state and some of our local governments to the moratorium, in some ways it came as no surprise. Not long after the burial and memorial services for the eleven men burned alive in the BP oil explosion and the announcement by the president of a moratorium on deep-well drilling, our state governor and many small parishes whose family members were not killed in this accident were yelling for a lifting of the moratorium.

Sadly, many of my fellow New Orleanians did not return home after Katrina. And those of us who did return and who were continuing to rebuild their homes and communities found themselves threatened by the BP oil spill—a man-made disaster that spilled more than 210 million U. S. gallons of oil into the Gulf—equivalent to one Exxon Valdez disaster every ten days. The 2010 environmental disaster in the Gulf complicated the fragile recovery from Hurricane Katrina—especially among communities of low-income people and people of color that were marginalized before the storm.

Residents in New Orleans and the Gulf Coast are a resilient people. We have lived through numerous disasters and have come back. However, one has to wonder how many additional natural and man-made disasters and inept responses we can shoulder. No community should be asked to live with health-threatening pollution, whether from a hurricane, a flood, or an oil spill. The 2010 BP oil spill was a disaster waiting to happen. It turned out to be Gulf Coast residents' worst nightmare economically and environmentally.

In July 2010, winds from Hurricane Alex blew tar balls and an oily sheen into Lake Pontchartrain, the 630-square-mile brackish lake that drowned much of New Orleans after the levee breach during Hurricane Katrina. The lake is located just a few blocks from my East New Orleans home and is a bountiful fishing ground and a popular spot for boating and swimming. Gulf Coast residents, including me, are worried about the future of our region. The BP disaster heightened stress levels and added mental strains on a population that had yet to fully recover from Hurricane Katrina.

In September 2011, federal investigators from the Bureau of Ocean Energy Resource Management and Enforcement (BOERME) issued their long-delayed report on the causes of the 2010 Deepwater Horizon blowout and oil spill. The joint investigation conducted by the Bureau of Ocean Energy Management and the Coast Guard concluded that BP and its contractors Transocean and Halliburton violated at least a half-dozen federal regulations. It also found that the disaster resulted from "a culture of complacency."[6] The BOERME report includes dozens of recommendations for new ways to improve safety in offshore drilling, including measures that would strengthen blowout prevents and would require operators to more frequently report well-control problems. Gulf Coast residents need a break from disasters and they need it now.

# The Legacy of Bias

*Hurricanes, Droughts, and Floods*

Much of the death and destruction attributed to "natural" disasters is unnatural and human-induced. Many unnatural disasters result from "human error or malicious intent," negligence, or the failure of a system.[1] Human activity is affecting our environment so much that the so-called natural disasters framework is being reassessed.[2] Quite often, preventable human error figures heavily in much of the death, damage, and destruction left behind by natural disasters. Such is the case for industrial accidents, toxic chemical contamination, and even climate-related disasters that are exacerbated by human activity that meddles with already fragile environments.

Some scholars argue that "there is no such thing as a 'natural' disaster."[3] What we often term "natural" disasters are in fact acts of social injustice perpetuated by government and business on the poor, minorities, and the elderly—groups least able to withstand such disasters. In his book *Acts of God: The Unnatural History of Natural Disasters in America*, Case Western University history professor Ted Steinberg says humans prefer to make "Mother Nature" or "God" the villain in catastrophic losses from tsunamis, earthquakes, droughts, floods, and hurricanes, rather than place responsibility squarely on social and political forces.[4]

More than two billion people worldwide were affected by disasters between 2000 and 2010. In the 1990s, disasters such as hurricanes, floods, and fires caused more than $608 billion in economic losses worldwide, losses greater than those incurred during the previous four decades. Global insured economic losses from climate-related disasters was $27 billion in 2010 alone. Climate change was a big share of the $109 billion in economic damage in 2010.

The catastrophic "effects of a disaster are magnified by ecologically destructive practices, like degrading forests, engineering rivers, filling in wetlands, and destabilizing the climate."[5]

When extreme weather events hit, we often hear about the property loss and insurance loss. However, the healthcare costs are seldom reported. A 2011 NRDC study estimated deaths and health problems from six floods, drought, and other U.S. disasters related to climate change cost an estimated $14 billion between 2000 and 2009. The six events resulted in 1,689 premature deaths, 8,992 hospitalizations, 21,113 emergency room visits, and 734,398 outpatient visits.[6]

The number of people forced to flee their homes because of extreme weather events is increasing globally. More than 90 percent of all disaster displacement around the world in 2010 was caused by climate-related disasters. More than 38.3 million women, men, and children were forced to move, mainly by floods and storms in 2010. Today, there are more "environmental refugees" (twenty-five million) than "political refugees" (twenty-two million). By 2050, the number of "environmental refugees" is expected to top 150 million, mainly because of the effects of global warming.[7]

Weather-related disasters, including hurricanes, floods, droughts, and windstorm, are growing in frequency and intensity. Globally, the number of reported weather-related natural disasters has more than tripled since the 1960s. Every year, these disasters result in more than sixty thousand deaths, mainly in developing countries, and have forced millions to flee their homes.

Generally, "rich people tend to take the higher land leaving to the poor and working class more vulnerable flooding and environmental pestilence."[8] Assigning nature or God as the primary culprit has helped to hide the fact that some Americans are better protected from the violence of nature than their counterparts lower down the socioeconomic ladder. As more Americans move to coastal regions, future losses from "unnatural" disasters will continue to be formidable because of increased development in these high-hazard areas.[9] Blaming nature has become a political tool.

Quite often, the scale of a disaster's impact, as in the case of Hurricane Katrina, has more to do with the political economy of a country or region than with the hurricane category strength.[10] Measures to prevent or contain the effects of disaster vulnerability are not equally provided to all. What is vulnerability, and how does it operate? Vulnerability is "the characteristics of a person or group and their situation that influence their capacity to anticipate, cope with, resist and recover from the impact of a natural hazard."[11]

Clearly, some populations are more prone to damage, loss, and suffering in the context of different hazards. Vulnerability also denotes "capacity," or the ability of a group or population to resist a hazard's harmful effects and to rebound easily. Disasters compound vulnerability, and vulnerable groups "find it hardest to reconstruct their livelihood following disaster, and this in turn makes them more vulnerable to the effects of subsequent hazards events."[12]

## Vulnerability and Risk

The law professors Lani Guinier and Gerald Torres in their book, *The Miner's Canary: Enlisting Race, Resisting Power, Transforming Democracy*, view race in America like the "miner's canary."[13] Guinier and Torres write:

> Miners often carried a canary in the mine alongside them. The canary's more fragile respiratory system would cause it to collapse from noxious gases long before humans were affected, thus alerting the miners of danger. The canary's distress signaled that it was time to get out of the mine because the air was becoming too poisonous to breathe.
>
> Those who are marginalized are like miner's canary: their distress is the first sign of a danger that threatens us all. It is easy enough to think that when we sacrifice this canary, the only harm is to communities of color. Yet others ignore problems that converge around racial minorities at their own peril, for these problems are symptoms warning us that we are all at risk.[14]

Typically, disaster mitigation and investments provide location-specific benefits that are available only to populations that live or own assets in the protected areas. Thus, "by virtue of where we live, work, or own property, some members of society are excluded from the benefits of these investments."[15] While Mother Nature may not discriminate, the individuals who hold power and the purse strings and make decisions often do. In his article "Let Them Eat Risk: Wealth, Rights, and Vulnerability," University of Massachusetts economist James K. Boyce wrote:

> The idea that every person is endowed with equal rights to life, liberty, the pursuit of happiness, and to a safe and healthy environment, is a universalistic ethical precept. To be sure, it is not universally accepted, let alone universally honored. But this principle has won increasingly widespread acceptance throughout the world, and is today formally incorporated in the constitutions of governments that span the globe.[16]

Human vulnerability in disasters is caused not only by the natural environment but even more by the social, political, and economic environment.[17] Socially created vulnerabilities are largely ignored in the hazards and disaster literature.[18] Moreover, science is not sufficiently developed to allow us to adequately model or predict future risk exposures or social vulnerabilities.[19] University of South Carolina geography professor Susan L. Cutter summed up this problem:

> Social vulnerability is partially a product of social inequalities—those social factors and forces that create the susceptibility of various groups to harm, and in turn affect their ability to respond, and bounce back (resilience) after the disaster. But it is much more than that. Social vulnerability involves the basic provision of health care, the livability of places, overall indicators of quality of life, and accessibility of lifelines (goods, services, emergency response personnel), capital, and political representation.[20]

Race and class factors explain a large part of social and environmental vulnerability to disasters. Generally, people with resources and means evacuate before a disaster hits, whereas individuals and families who have limited resources and means are often forced to "ride it out." Generally, the most vulnerable get left behind.[21] Policymakers face a complex set of challenges as they strive to "fix" social vulnerability (by improving the overall quality of life for low-income African Americans), environmental vulnerability (by shoring up levees, constructing disaster-resistant buildings, changing land use, and restoring wetlands and floodways), and economic vulnerability (by dismantling income and wealth gaps). It is far easier for the U.S. Army Corps of Engineers to retrofit and rebuild levees than it is for other government agencies to root out racial injustice, dismantle centuries of mistrust, and rebuild "community."

## Legacy of Unfairness

The "legacy of unequal protection" too often places residents in mostly black communities on the frontline of environmental assault and subjects them to elevated health risks. In the real world, all communities are not created equal; some are more equal than others. If a community happens to be poor or black or is located on the "wrong side of the tracks," it receives less protection than communities inhabited largely by affluent whites in the suburbs. Generally, this holds true both for government responses to human-induced environmental catastrophes and for weather-related disasters, including climate change.

While the science on global climate change is clear, the answers to questions about mitigation (actions taken to minimize the effects of global warming) and adaptation (physical and behavioral changes that would allow us to survive) are less clear. What do we do about the harmful effects of global warming? How will the mitigation plans impact different people and the environment? How is fairness addressed? How will different populations adapt? Clearly, these climate justice questions remain unanswered.[22]

Climate change poses special health and environmental threats, especially to vulnerable populations.[23] Will the U.S. government's response to climate change be fair? Does fairness matter? The jury is still out, given the way government has handled health and environmental threats in the past and its gross mismanagement of both its emergency preparation and its response to Hurricane Katrina and its aftermath.[24]

Climate change looms as *the* global environmental justice issue of the twenty-first century. It poses special environmental justice challenges for communities that are already overburdened with air pollution, poverty, and environmentally related illnesses.[25] This is especially the case for African American communities that are already overburdened with pollution and health-threatening environmental hazards.

A 2005 study from the Associated Press reported that African Americans are 79 percent more likely than whites to live in neighborhoods where industrial pollution is suspected of posing the greatest health danger.[26] Using EPA's own data and government scientists, the AP study revealed that in nineteen states, blacks were more than twice as likely as whites to live in neighborhoods where air pollution seems to pose the greatest health danger. The AP analyzed the health risk posed by industrial air pollution using toxic chemical air releases reported by factories to calculate a health risk score for each square kilometer of the United States. The scores can be used to compare risks from long-term exposure to factory pollution in different areas.

A 2004 Congressional Black Caucus Foundation report, *Climate Change and African Americans: Unequal Burden*, concluded that there is a stark disparity in the United States between those who benefit from the causes of change and those who bear the costs of climate. The report concluded:

African Americans are already *disproportionately burdened* by the health effects of climate change, including deaths during heat waves and from worsened air pollution. Similarly, unemployment and economic hardship associated with climate change will fall most heavily on the African-American community. African Americans are *less responsible* for climate change than other Americans. Both historically and at present, African Americans emit less greenhouse gas. Policies intended to mitigate climate change can generate large health and economic benefits or costs for African Americans, depending on how they are structured. Unless appropriate actions are taken to mitigate its effects or adapt to them, climate change will worsen existing equity issues within the United States.[27]

Global warming will increase temperatures on hot summer days, potentially leading to more unhealthy "red alert" air pollution days in the coming years.[28] In a study of fifty U.S. cities, Bell et al.[29] report that future ozone concentrations and climate change could detrimentally affect air quality and thereby harm human health. The most vulnerable populations will suffer the earliest and most damaging setbacks, even though they have contributed the least to the problem of global warming.

The most recent report of the Intergovernmental Panel on Climate Change (IPCC), *Climate Change 2007: Impacts, Adaptation and Vulnerability*, identified key vulnerabilities associated with climate-sensitive systems, including food supply, infrastructure, health, water resources, coastal systems, ecosystems, global biogeochemical cycles, ice sheets, and modes of oceanic and atmospheric circulation. The IPCC predicts that the impacts of future changes in climate will fall disproportionately on the poor and on communities in low-lying coastal and arid areas, with many who are highly dependent on farming, fishing, or forestry seeing their livelihoods severely curtailed or destroyed.

More social research is needed to better inform and provide data-based support for the response to climate change, including research on the association between climate change and public health (including mental health), models to forecast health impacts and vulnerabilities, and development and testing of strategies to reduce risk. The issue of "who gets left behind before and after disasters strikes and why" is a core climate justice research and policy question. In Hurricane Katrina, which hit the Gulf Coast in 2005, the effects of climate change fell heaviest on the poor and people of color.[30]

The deadly pattern of climate change in the United States is also likely to fall disproportionately on the poor and on people of color, who are concentrated in urban centers, coastal regions, and areas with substandard air quality—including high levels of ground-level ozone. Nonetheless, in October 2007, the Bush administration made deep cuts in written testimony given to a U.S. Senate committee by Dr. Julie L. Gerberding, director of the Centers for Disease Control and Prevention, on the health risks posed by global warming.[31] Entire sections of her original written testimony on health-related effects of extreme weather, air pollution-related health effects, allergic diseases, water- and food-borne infectious diseases, food and water scarcity, and the long-term impacts of chronic diseases and other health effects were edited out of the of the testimony. The following passages on vulnerable populations were deleted entirely:

> In certain Southern coastal communities with little economic reserve, declining industry, difficulty accessing health care, and a greater underlying burden of disease, these stressors could be overwhelming. Similarly, in an urban area with increasingly frequent and severe heat waves, certain groups are expected to be more affected: the home-bound, elderly, poor, athletes, and minority and migrant populations, and populations that live in areas with less green space and with fewer centrally air-conditioned buildings are all more vulnerable to heat stress. Some populations of Americans are more vulnerable to the health effects of climate change than others.
>
> Children are at greater risk of worsening asthma, allergies, and certain infectious diseases, and the elderly are at higher risk for health effects due to heat waves, extreme weather events, and exacerbations of chronic disease.
>
> In addition, people of lower socioeconomic status are particularly vulnerable to extreme weather events. Members of racial and ethnic minority groups suffer particularly from air pollution as well as inadequate health care access, while athletes and those who work outdoors are more at risk from air pollution, heat, and certain infectious diseases.
>
> Given the differential burden of climate change's health effects on certain populations, public health preparedness for climate change must include vulnerability assessments that identify the most vulnerable populations with the most significant health disparities and anticipate their risks for particular exposures. At the same time, health communication targeting these vulnerable populations must be devised and tested, and early warning systems focused on vulnerable communities should be developed. With adequate notice and a vigorous response, the ill health effects of many exposures from climate change can be dampened.[32]

A 2011 Union of Concerned Scientists report, *Climate Change and Your Health: Rising Temperatures, Worsening Ozone Pollution*, found that unchecked global warming could increase ground-level ozone, threatening U.S. public health, and could cost the economy approximately $5.4 billion in 2020.[33] Climate-change-induced ozone increases could result in 2.8 million additional serious respiratory illnesses, 5,100 additional hospitalizations of infants and seniors for serious breathing problems, and 944,000 additional missed school days in the United States in 2020. A 2011 Natural Resources Defense Council report puts the health cost of six U.S. climate events at $14 billion.

Climate-related disasters in the South have outnumbered those in other regions of the U.S. annually in both scale and magnitude by a ratio of almost 4:1 during the past 10 years.[34] Climate change poses special health risks to vulnerable populations who are already marginalized because of their limited means and their concentration in areas that already face environmental problems, whether coastal areas and low-lying areas that are prone to flooding and nonattainment areas or areas that fail to meet EPA ambient air-quality standards. African Americans and Latinos are concentrated in the nation's dirtiest cities. For example, air pollution exacerbates asthma and other respiratory illnesses, and inner-city children have the highest rates for asthma prevalence, hospitalization, and mortality.

African Americans and Latinos are almost three times more likely than whites to die from asthma.[35] More than 72 percent of African Americans live in counties that violate federal air pollution standards, whereas only 58 percent of the white population does. One of every four American children lives in areas that regularly exceed the EPA's ozone standards, and half the pediatric asthma population, two million children, lives in these areas. More than twenty-seven million children under age thirteen live in areas with ozone levels above the EPA standard. More than 61.3 percent of African American children, 69.2 percent of Hispanic children, and 67.7 percent of Asian American children live in areas that exceed the 0.080 ppm ozone standard, while 50.8 percent of white children live in such areas.

## When Disasters Hit Home

Each year, communities along the Atlantic and Gulf Coasts are hit with tropical storms and hurricanes, forcing millions to flee to higher ground. Hurricanes Dennis, Katrina, and Rita displaced hundreds of thousands of people, destroyed tens of thousands of homes, and disrupted oil rigs and refineries. Historically, the Atlantic hurricane season produces ten storms, of which about six become hurricanes and two or three become major hurricanes.[36]

The 2005 hurricane season produced a record twenty eight storms with twenty-seven of them named, of which a record fifteen became hurricanes, topping the previous record of twenty-one storms set in 1933 and outpacing the twelve hurricanes that occurred in 1969.[37] Three of the hurricanes in the 2005 season reached Category 5 status, meaning they had wind speeds greater than 155 miles per hour at some point during the storm. Katrina's death toll (1,325) made it the third most deadly hurricane in U.S. history—surpassed only by the 1928 hurricane in Florida that killed 1,836 and the 1900 Galveston hurricane that killed 8,000.[38]

Emergency responses to major storms reflects the preexisting social and political stratification structure, with black communities receiving less priority than white communities. Equity issues arise around which communities' needs are addressed first and which communities are forced to wait. Race and class dynamics also play out in disaster survivors' ability to rebuild, replace infrastructure, obtain loans, and locate temporary and permanent housing. Race even impacts how disasters are covered in the mainstream and ethnic media.[39] Generally, people of color sustain higher levels of loss due to physical damage but lower dollar losses than whites; they live largely in segregated housing and occupy older, poorly built homes.[40]

Weeks of rain and snowmelt in May 2011 caused the Mississippi River to swell to an all-time high, breaking high-water records set in the 1920s and 1930s and surpassing the Great Mississippi Flood of 1927. The flooding in the Mississippi Delta hit a fourteen-county area where more than one in five residents lives in poverty, the highest level in the nation. The vast majority of the Mississippi Delta residents are blacks only a generation or two removed from the days of sharecropping. Most have no insurance or savings to cushion a disaster's blow. The floodwaters ravaged many of the majority-black towns along the Mississippi River made famous by Civil War buffs, blues artists, and civil rights struggles, including The Mississippi towns of Clarksdale (68.9 percent black), Greenwood (65.7 percent black), Greenville (69.6 percent black), Yazoo City (70.2 percent black), and Vicksburg (60.4 percent black). Many of the poverty-stricken Delta residents are left with no homes, no jobs and no money.

*Mississippi River Flood (1927)*

In his 1997 book, *Rising Tides: The Great Flood of 1927 and How It Changed America*, John M. Barry details one of the most destructive natural disasters in American history.[41] The 1927 flood along the Mississippi was the worst to strike the country until the Hurricane Katrina flood of 2005. In the spring of 1927, incessant rains pushed the Mississippi River to more than thirty feet in height and began eroding the levees from Cairo, Illinois, to Greenville, Mississippi. More than twenty-seven thousand square miles were inundated; thousands of farms and hundreds of towns were wiped away by floodwater. Estimates of the damage ranged from $246 million to $1 billion (roughly $2 billion to $7.8 billion in today's dollars). The official death toll reached 246, with perhaps thousands more African American deaths uncounted. Nearly a million people in the Mississippi Delta were left homeless.

White racism and Jim Crow added to the disaster. Government response to the flood was a classic case of environmental injustice. More than thirteen thousand flood victims near Greenville, Mississippi, were taken from area farms, evacuated to the crest of an unbroken levee, and stranded there for days without food or clean water, while boats arrived to evacuate white women and children.[42]

While whites were evacuated, thousands of black work gangs and their families were held as virtual prisoners in 154 dreadfully squalid "concentration camps" set up along miles of the Greenville levee.[43] Local landowners kept the government from relocating blacks because to do so would deprive them of their primary source of cheap labor. The economic system of sharecropping and peonage, an illegal state of partial slavery used to hold blacks to the land, prevailed in the rural South before the catastrophe, and the black refugee camps were a convenient means of keeping sharecroppers in one place. "The whole question seems to have been whether guards were stationed there to keep the refugees in or to keep the public out."[44]

Some sources estimate that, of the 608,000 people who lost their homes in the flood, 555,000 were black. Black flood victims were "double sufferers," attempting to save themselves, their families, and their belongings at the same time that they were trying to keep from being enslaved by white people.[45] Blacks were forced to load and unload supplies without pay. Those who refused to work were cut off from Red Cross relief rations. When the levee first broke at Mounds Landing, the National Guard commander in charge forced black levee workers to continue filling sandbags at gunpoint. As many as two hundred of these workers drowned when the levee finally gave way. Thousands of displaced residents, black and white, left the land and never returned, accelerating black migration to the North and thus changing the political landscape of the country.

## Florida Okeechobee Hurricane (1928)

In September 1928, the Okeechobee hurricane struck Florida with devastating force. It was the first Category 5 hurricane officially recorded in the Atlantic. The eye of the storm passed ashore in Palm Beach County with 140-mile-per-hour winds, then struck a populated area on the southern edge of Lake Okeechobee.[46] The only thing between the low-lying communities and the massive lake was a five-foot mud dike constructed to hold back Lake Okeechobee during the summer rains. In his 2003 book, *Black Cloud: The Deadly Hurricane of 1928*, Eliot Kleinberg provides a graphic account of Florida's deadliest storm.[47] When the hurricane had passed, the dike broke, and somewhere between 1,800 and 3,000 people drowned, making it the second deadliest hurricane in U.S. history, behind the Galveston, Texas, hurricane of 1900, which killed 8,000 people.[48]

Nobody really knows how many people died in the storm. For years, the Red Cross set the death toll at 1,836. In the summer of 2003, the National Hurricane Center increased the death toll from 1,836 to 2,500, with an asterisk suggesting that the total could be as high as 3,000. Some accounts put the death toll closer to 3,500.[49] Half of the 6,000 people living in the farming communities between Clewiston and Canal Point perished. More than 75 percent of the recorded victims were black migrant workers, segregated in life and abandoned in death.

Palm Beach County in the 1920s, as today, was home to one of the world's great wealth enclaves, with its glittering ocean drawing tourists from around the world. But just a thirty-minute drive to the west takes you into a world of dirt roads, farm fields, poverty, and shantytowns, inhabited largely by black migrant workers from the Deep South and the impoverished islands of the Caribbean. The 1928 Okeechobee hurricane "killed more people than the 1906 San Francisco earthquake (about 700), more than sinking of the *Titanic* (1,505), and probably more than the estimated 3,000 who died on September 11, 2001."[50] Author Eliot Kleinberg questions why so little attention has been given to this American catastrophe. He writes:

> The hurricane may have also accounted for the most deaths of black people in a single day in U.S. history. One has to wonder: Had the storm drowned 3,000 white businessmen in downtown West Palm Beach, or smashed a black-tie affair on ritzy Palm Beach, instead of killing mostly black migrant workers from the Caribbean in vegetables fields of Florida's interior, might it have received more attention?[51]

The disaster occurred in an isolated area within a few miles of a large city. However, it was not until three days later that the state's own governor learned of the storm's enormity.

Dead bodies were scattered everywhere. Some who survived the storm are believed to have perished later as they wandered the vast Everglades.[52] The devastation was complete. Although the storm destroyed everything in its path with impartiality, it hit the poor, low-lying black areas around the lake hardest.

Belle Glade, Pahokee, and South Bay were virtually wiped off the map.[53] Bodies, livestock, and lumber floated everywhere. Some survivors used bloated cows as rafts and splintered lumber as paddles. The dead bodies overwhelmed officials. The few caskets available were used to bury the bodies of whites. Other bodies were either burned or buried in mass graves. Burials were segregated, and the only mass gravesite to receive a memorial contained only white bodies. A *St. Petersburg Times* reporter, Nicole Sterghos Brochu, described the differential treatment of the remains of black and white storm victims:

> The burned remains, along with those of many others, 600 in all, were trucked to Port Mayaca on the lake's eastern shore. Makeshift graveyards in roadside ditches from Pahokee to Sebring contain the remains of scores of others. Sixty-nine white people were buried in pine boxes at Woodlawn Cemetery in West Palm Beach. Another 674 black people were dumped, unceremoniously and without a sign to mark the spot, in a 20-foot hole in the city's pauper cemetery, forgotten for more than 70 years. The number of known graves approaches 2,500, but more bodies were never found, swallowed whole by the Everglades muck or left to the elements after the government called off the search for lack of money.[54]

The Florida Hurricane of 1928 is referred to as Florida's forgotten storm. Local politicians did not want the horror of the storm to impact tourism in the area, so the deaths and devastation were undercounted. The savage storm was immortalized in the African American writer Zora Neale Hurston's classic novel *Their Eyes Were Watching God.*[55] No amount of public relations and government coverup could hide the horror left by the floodwaters—especially the damage the storm inflicted on the black population and the racism by whites that followed.

The 1928 hurricane changed the way the Florida Everglades was managed.[56] In the three decades after the storm, the U.S. Army Corps of Engineers constructed a 150-mile dike around the lake. In some places, the Hoover dike, named after President Herbert Hoover, is 45 feet high and 150 feet wide. Built out of mud, sand, grass, rock, and concrete, the dike has withstood several major hurricanes.

### Hurricane Betsy, New Orleans, Louisiana (1965)

Hurricane Betsy struck the state of Louisiana and the City of New Orleans in 1965.[57] At the time, Betsy was the most destructive hurricane on record ever to strike the Louisiana coast.[58] The damage and flooding throughout the state covered 4,800 square miles, killed 81 persons, caused about 250,000 persons to be evacuated, and disrupted transportation, communication, and utilities service throughout the eastern coastal area of Louisiana for weeks.

Betsy hit the mostly black and poor New Orleans Lower Ninth Ward, the same neighborhood that was inundated by floodwaters from Katrina in 2005, especially hard. More than 98 percent of the Lower Ninth Ward residents are black, and a third live below the poverty level. Betsy accelerated the decline of the neighborhood and the outmigration of many of its longtime residents.

A disproportionate share of Lower Ninth Ward residents did not receive sufficient postdisaster financial assistance in the form of loans and other support to revitalize the area. As a consequence, a growing number of black New Orleanians lost faith that the EPA, FEMA, the Centers for Disease Control and Prevention (CDC), the U.S. Housing and Urban Development (HUD), the state of Louisiana, and the city government would do the right thing for the city's poor and African American citizens.

A group of New Orleans residents sued the Louisiana Road Home program over the way it handed out recovery dollars. The suit alleged that the formula used to allocate grants to homeowners through the Road Home program—the single largest housing recovery program in U.S. history—had a discriminatory impact on thousands of African American homeowners. In July 2011, HUD, Louisiana, the Greater New Orleans Fair Housing Action Center, National Fair Housing Alliance, NAACP Legal Defense and Education Fund and others agreed to end the legal challenge. The settlement agreement caused HUD and the State of Louisiana to change the Road Home program grant formula to provide full relief to more than thirteen thousand homeowners. All eligible low- and moderate-income homeowners received supplemental grant awards totaling $473 million based upon the estimated cost of damage to their homes, rather than the original grants based merely upon the much lower prestorm market value of their homes.[59]

Many older blacks are still bitter about being trapped in attics as they tried to avoid the rising floodwaters from Hurricane Betsy in 1965. Blacks from diverse socioeconomic backgrounds believe that the flooding of the Lower Ninth Ward and other black areas after Betsy was a deliberate act stemming from orders given by Mayor Victor Schiro, who was not known for his progressive views on race, to breach the levees and have the floodwaters pumped out of his well-to-do white subdivision, Lake Vista, and into the Lower Ninth Ward.[60]

Whether a conspiracy rumor, urban legend, or fact, the "Betsy experience" is the number one reason why many Lower Ninth Ward residents keep hatchets and axes in their attics to cut holes through the rooftops. This mistrust of government probably saved thousands of lives after the levee breach four decades later when Hurricane Katrina struck in 2005 in this neighborhood where mistrust lingers.

## Hurricane Alicia, Houston-Galveston, Texas (1983)

In 1983, Hurricane Alicia devastated the Houston Gulf Coast.[61] Debris from the hurricane was scattered all across the Houston-Galveston area. Disaster cleanup in Houston's black neighborhoods, such as the Third and Fifth Wards, Sunnyside, South Park, and the South Main area, lagged behind the cleanup of the city's affluent white neighborhoods. An even more pressing problem was what to do with the estimated four million tons of hurricane debris. Houston's majority-white city leaders selected an all-black neighborhood in northeast Houston community, Bordersville, as a site for the "emergency burning" of debris from Alicia. This angered local residents, who saw their neighborhood being used as a dumping ground for hurricane debris.[62] The Bordersville's "emergency" landfill case study, chronicled in the 1987 book *Invisible Houston: The Black Experience in Boom and Bust*, is a textbook example of how environmental racism changed the life of local residents.[63] The burning left ash on rooftops, cars, and trees. Trucks filled with decaying branches and trunks barreled in and out of the dump day and night, turning once-quiet dirt roads into dusty thoroughfares. "I think poor people have enough to worry about without something like this. . . . Our people here can't afford washers and dryers and a lot of them don't have the means to go to the Laundromat. Now, they can't wash their clothes outside. It's a real problem. The smoke is terrible, it's just disgusting,"[64] observed A.W. Jones, president of the Three-H Community Center of Bordersville.

The all-black suburban Bordersville, located nearly thirty miles north of downtown Houston, is an old sawmill settlement that was annexed by Houston in the mid-1960s as part of a corridor to the new Houston Intercontinental Airport, now named for President George H. W. Bush. Bordersville is a black "poverty pocket" in the midst of white suburban affluence. The rapid development of the area surrounding the airport overshadowed the conditions that existed for nearby Bordersville residents. Ginger Hester described the conditions in the Bordersville community:

> This black community on the fringes of FM 1960 and suburbia is catching up with the 20th century. Jessie Doyle heads a household teaming with children; four are her daughter's, one is her brother's, one youngster is her own. Almost 10 people share the three-room shack, built in the late 1920s, like similar shanties along the dirt and gravel road, to house workers at Edgar Borders' now-defunct sawmill. Like the rest of the "sawmill quarters," it barely hangs together with scraps of tarpaper and rotting wood. The front door is broken, without pane, allowing cold air to blow in next to a small wood-burning stove. She pays $10 a month rent and subtracts from that any repair costs, and repairs are not high on the priority list.[65]

The Bordersville neighborhood lacked running water, sewer lines, paved streets, regular street repairs, and other neighborhood amenities that many Houstonians took for granted. Some of the two hundred houses in the neighborhoods had indoor plumbing; mostly these were houses that were built later than the others. Most of the residents in the neighborhood had to get their water from a "yellow city tank truck that made door-to-door deliveries three times a week. Residents were charged $2.98 per month for all the water delivered."[66]

In 1981, Bordersville became part of Houston's Community Development Block Grant (CDBG) program, a federally funded program designed to assist lower-income neighborhoods in making capital improvements, upgrading housing, and promoting economic development to create jobs. As a neighborhood target area, Bordersville was earmarked to receive funds to improve services in the area, and City Hall spent more than $500,000 on new water lines for the area. But many of the residents could not benefit from the new water lines because of the poor condition of their houses. The city required that homes meet the housing code before they could receive a hookup, but most residents could not afford the repairs needed to meet the minimum standard, and City Council policy limited the amount of federal funds that could be spent on individual residences. In a situation that sings of Catch-22, some Bordersville residents continued to go without.

This was not the first time a black Houston neighborhood had been chosen for a waste dump, and black resistance to the siting and operation of landfills, garbage dumps, and incinerators in black Houston neighborhoods was not new. As early as 1967, black Houstonians picketed the Holmes Road dump in the southeast Sunnyside neighborhood, where an young child had drowned in a pond formed at the dump. These Holmes Road dump protesters joined forces with another protest group that was marching for equal education, fueling the conditions for the 1967 Texas Southern University "riot," the only major civil disturbance that occurred in the city during the turbulent 1960s.[67]

In 1971, the first major controversy surrounding the newly elected city council member Judson Robinson Jr., Houston's first black city councilman, had to deal with involved a city-owned dump. Councilman Robinson had to quell a near-riot at the Kirkpatrick landfill in the mostly black Trinity Gardens neighborhood. Black protesters were demanding that the city-owned landfill be closed. The facility was in fact later closed after six months of intense protest demonstrations.

Houston, the nation's fourth largest city, has more than five hundred neighborhoods. It is also the only major American city that does not have zoning restrictions. This no-zoning policy has allowed for a somewhat erratic land-use pattern in the city. Houston's black neighborhoods were unofficially "zoned" for garbage. In Houston, NIMBY (Not in My Back Yard) was replaced by the policy of PIBBY (Place in Blacks' Back Yard).[68] The all-white, all-male city government and private industry targeted Houston's black neighborhoods to receive landfills, incinerators, garbage dumps, and garbage transfer stations. The burden of having a municipal landfill, incinerator, transfer station, or some other type of waste disposal facility near one's home has not been borne equally by Houston's neighborhoods. Black Houston has become the dumping grounds for the city's household garbage.[69]

The city has used two basic methods of disposing of its solid waste: incineration and landfill. From the 1920s to the 1978, a total of seventeen solid-waste facilities were located in black Houston neighborhoods. Thirteen solid-waste disposal facilities were operated by the City of Houston from the late 1920s to the mid-1970s, including eight garbage incinerators (five large units and three mini-units), six of which were located in mostly black neighborhoods, one in a Hispanic neighborhood, and one in a mostly white area. All five of Houston's large garbage incinerators were located in minority neighborhoods—four black and one Hispanic. All five of the city-owned landfills were sited in black neighborhoods. One of the oldest city-owned incinerators was located in Houston's Fourth Ward. This site dates back to the 1920s. Other city-owned incinerators included the Patterson Street site, the Kelly Street site, the Holmes Road site, and the Velasco site, located in the mostly Hispanic Second Ward or "Segundo Barrio." The costs of operating these large incinerators and the problems of pollution generated by these systems were major factors in their closing.

Although blacks composed just over one-fourth of the city's population, five out of five city-owned landfills (100 percent) and six of the eight city-owned incinerators (75 percent) were built in black Houston neighborhoods. From the 1920s through the 1970s, eleven of thirteen city-owned landfills and incinerators (84.6 percent) were built in black neighborhoods. Blacks during this same period made up only about 25 percent of Houston's population.

Five decades of these discriminatory practices lowered the property values in Houston's black neighborhoods, accelerated their physical deterioration, and increased disinvestment in them. Moreover, the discriminatory siting of solid-waste facilities stigmatized the black neighborhoods as "dumping grounds" for a host of other unwanted facilities, including salvage yards, recycling operations, and automobile "chop shops."[70] Many of Houston's residential areas and their inhabitants experienced greater health and environmental risks than residents of other neighborhoods because of the unregulated growth, the ineffective regulation of industrial toxins, and public policy decisions authorizing industrial facilities that favored those with political and economic clout.

Renewable deed restrictions were the only tool many residents had at their disposal to regulate nonresidential uses. However, residents in low-income areas often allowed deed restrictions to lapse because they were preoccupied with making a living and lacked the time, energy, or faith in government to get the signatures of neighborhood residents necessary to keep their deed restrictions in force. The high occupancy turnover and large renter population in many Houston inner-city neighborhoods further weakened the efficacy of deed restrictions as a protectionist device.

Ineffective land-use regulations have created a nightmare for many of Houston's neighborhoods—especially the ones that are ill equipped to fend off industrial encroachment. Black Houston, for example, has had to contend with a disproportionately large share of garbage dumps, landfills, salvage yards, automobile chop shops, and a host of other locally unwanted land uses. The siting of nonresidential facilities has heightened the animosity between the black community and the local government. This is especially true in the case of waste disposal facility siting.

The *Bean v. Southwestern Waste Management Corp.* lawsuit finally went to trial in 1984. Earlier, in 1979, the residents and their attorney had sought a temporary injunction to block the opening of the 195-acre landfill. That effort was argued in front of U.S. District Judge Gabrielle McDonald, the only African American female judge in Texas. In December 1979, Judge McDonald denied the temporary injunction.

In her written order denying the temporary injunction, Judge McDonald said she "might very well have denied this permit" by the Texas Department of Health (TDH) licensing the landfill site. "It simply does not make sense to put a solid waste site so close to a high school, particularly one with no air conditioning. . . . Nor does it make sense to put the landfill so close to a residential neighborhood. But I am not TDH. For all I know, TDH may regularly approve of solid waste sites located near schools and residential areas, as illogical as that may seem." Judge McDonald also described the landfill siting as both "unfortunate and insensitive," but she felt the plaintiffs had failed to prove that the permit was motivated by "purposeful racial discrimination."[71]

The case was transferred to U.S. Federal District Judge John Singleton's court in 1984. During my expert-witness testimony, in which I described the location of Houston's black neighborhoods and their proximity to solid-waste sites, Judge Singleton repeatedly referred to the black plaintiffs as "nigras" and their neighborhoods as "nigra areas." Most people from the South know that the word "nigra" is code for "nigger." The judge's clerk softly reminded the judge that blacks in his court were offended by his referring to them as "nigras."[72] The judge later ruled against the residents, and the landfill was built.

### Hurricane Hugo, South Carolina (1989)

In September 1989, Hurricane Hugo made its way to shore in South Carolina. The toll of this hurricane was forty-nine deaths, widespread damage and losses estimated to exceed $9 billion, temporary displacement of hundreds of thousands of people, and disrupted lives for about two million people. Twenty-six of South Carolina's forty-six counties, covering two-thirds of the state, were declared federal disaster areas.[73] Following Hugo, African Americans and less educated victims received less help than similarly affected victims who were white or more educated.[74] Bureaucratic blindness and biased relief assistance in South Carolina following Hugo left behind many African Americans who lacked insurance and other support systems.[75]

### Hurricane Andrew, Miami-Dade and South Florida (1992)

Hurricane Andrew struck south Florida in 1992 and forced an estimated 700,000 residents from their homes.[76] More than 250,000 people were left homeless, 15 people were killed, 75,000 homes were destroyed, 1.5 million individuals were left without water, electricity, and telephones, 108 schools were damaged, and 3 were destroyed. Andrew caused an estimate $25 billion in losses, a record until Katrina, in 2005. An estimated 100,000 South Dade residents moved away from the area after the storm, and this migration changed the area's racial makeup. In studying race and social vulnerability in Hurricane Andrew, disaster researchers at Florida International University wrote:

> Some neighborhoods are located on the *wrong* side of the tracks, the *bad* side of town, or in slums and urban war zones. Others are on the *right* side of the *tracks*, uptown, upscale, or on the good side of down. Minorities, particularly Black households, are disproportionately located in poor quality housing segregated into low-valued neighborhoods. This segregation creates *communities of fate* that can take on added salience in a disaster context. Race and ethnicity linked to housing quality—not because of ethnically based cultural variations in housing preferences as is true in some societies—but because race and ethnicity are still important determinants of the economic resources, such as income and credit, critical for obtaining housing.[77]

Blacks were more vulnerable to hurricane damage because of residential segregation, the location of their neighborhoods, and the condition of their housing. Andrew marginalized the already marginalized. Recovery was also problematic for black Miami neighborhoods where poorer-quality building construction and insufficient insurance left residents more vulnerable.[78]

Posthurricane relocation was impeded for blacks, not only because of possible economic constraints but because of housing barriers created by residential segregation.[79]

### Tropical Storm Alberto (1994)

In July 1994, Tropical Storm Alberto dumped at least seventeen inches of rain on parts of Georgia, flooding the Flint and Ocmulgee River Basins. The floods were responsible for thirty deaths. Albany, whose nearly eighty thousand residents make up most of the population of Dougherty County, got the worst of Alberto; African Americans make up 65 percent of Albany's population. On average, the education level of Albany residents is lower than the state average, and poverty is greater than the national average. More than 27 percent of the city's population is below the poverty level. Medical facilities and transportation are lacking.

Alberto generated a flood that crested on July 7, 1994, at 44.3 feet. Albany and areas adjoining the Flint River system experienced the worst flooding in recorded in the city's history. The flood killed people, displaced more than twenty-two thousand residents in Albany, and damaged 6,500 buildings. A Georgia State University economist estimated that the flood would have a $1 billion impact on the state overall, including $500 million in damage to uninsured property and $200 million in agricultural losses.[80]

As in earlier floods, those hit hardest lived in south Albany, the Radium Springs-Putney area, and along the larger creeks. The devastation in south-central Albany was so widespread that local leaders feared that many residents would not resettle there, thereby weakening black voting strength in a city where blacks make up a majority of the population but have only since 1994 won a majority of the seats on the city commission.

Floodwaters from the Flint River consumed nearly two-thirds of the 204-acre campus of historically black Albany State University. Founded in 1903, Albany State University has 4,463 students as of the fall of 2011. About 40 percent of the students live in campus housing; 40 percent are older adults. Sixty percent are women. Located on the banks of the Flint River, the campus required $112 million in reconstruction and renovation as the result of the devastating flood in 1994. The aftermath of this natural disaster created a new spirit of determination on campus—along with the motto "Unsinkable Albany State." The construction created a new campus for Albany State students and the Albany community. More than $59.6 million was spent on the rehabilitation and relocation of Albany State University structures damaged by the flood.[81]

From 1994 through 2004, the institution grew from an enrollment of approximately 3,100 students to nearly 3,700 students.   Post-Alberto construction projects completed at the university include the federally funded $1 million Early Learning Center, and a $33 million public-private dormitory. The institution's $25 to $30 million Ray Charles Fine Arts Building is in the planning stages. In addition, the university recently completed the construction of a $7 million athletic stadium.[82]

Seven weeks after floods ravaged southwest Georgia and parts of Alabama and Florida, the hardest-hit sections of the mostly black Albany community had barely begun to recover from the storm.[83] The legacy of racial separation and distrust tore people apart and kept help from getting to the most needy storm victims quickly. Many African Americans believe that city and county officials deliberately diverted water to their neighborhoods in order to save the northern areas where affluent white people live. White officials strongly deny this. Racial tension, which is generally high, was heightened by the way disaster relief and rebuilding efforts were handled.

## Black Farmers and USDA Disaster Relief (1997)

Land ownership has long been a key asset in wealth accumulation. Although more a promise than policy, the "forty acres and a mule" idea was one of the first notion of reparations for slavery and was premised on allowing newly freed slaves to build, accumulate, and pass on wealth derived from such a government land grant. In 1865, as General William Tecumseh Sherman and his Union soldiers advanced through the South, tens of thousands of freed slaves left their plantations and marched with the Union army to the sea. Sherman issued Special Field Order No. 15, granting each freed family forty acres of tillable land on offshore islands and along the coast of Georgia. The Army also granted a number of unneeded mules to settlers.

Because of the backlash from white landowners, this temporary plan never became the policy of the federal Bureau of Refugees, Freedmen and Abandoned Lands, popularly known as the Freedmen's Bureau. By the summer of 1865, forty thousand former slaves had received 400,000 acres of abandoned Confederate land. However, in 1866, Congress defeated the portion of the Freedmen's Bureau Act that gave it the authority to assign land to former slaves, and President Andrew Johnson ordered all land titles rescinded, forcing the freedmen off their land, and returned to the former white plantation owners.

Nevertheless, by 1910, just forty-five years after the end of slavery, African Americans had acquired more than fifteen million acres of farmland on their own without the help of government land grants. According to the U.S. Department of Agriculture, they owned less than a sixth of that by 1997. A 1999 Agricultural Economics and Land Ownership Survey (AELOS) found that sixty-eight thousand African American rural landowners owned 7.7 million acres of land valued at $14 billion—less than 1 percent of all privately owned rural land in the United States. Sixty percent of the rural land owned by blacks is owned by nonfarmers.

Today, land ownership continues to be a key ingredient for blacks in building wealth in rural, urban, and suburban America. Nevertheless, black land loss continues unabated. The Federation of Southern Cooperatives attributes this land loss a number of factors: the preponderance of property ownership by heirs, a lack of estate planning, tax sales, court-ordered partition sales, voluntary sales to individuals outside the African American community, blacks' lack of access to legal counsel, and violence, exploitation, and injustice.

Black farmers have suffered severe damage from natural disasters such as floods, droughts, tornados, and hurricanes. They, like other farmers, suffer in the aftermath of such natural disasters through loss of crops, livestock, supplies, equipment, barns, and storage areas. These losses result in reduced family income, delayed production, stunted business growth, and, for some, a total loss of livelihood.

For decades, black farmers were subjected to institutional racism when applying for disaster relief. Unlike black farmers, white farmers get results from the U.S. Department of Agriculture (USDA) when they apply for disaster relief, emergency loans, and operating loans. Black farmers get the runaround. Testifying at the Eatonton, Georgia, stop of the Economic Human Rights Bus Tour, along with several other black farmers, Melvin Bishop summarized the problem: "Even more devastating than the tornado was being denied USDA funds appropriated for emergency disaster and relief purposes. The process involved waiting and standing in long lines to shuffle paper, completing forms and applications and was physically, mentally, and emotionally draining."[84]

Bishop is among hundreds of black farmers who filed administrative complaints or lawsuits charging that, for decades, USDA loan officials have discouraged, delayed, or rejected loan applications because of the applicant's race. Federal officials have upheld these charges. The farmers say that such discrimination is a major reason that the nation's already tiny corps of black farmers is dwindling at three times the rate for farmers overall.

In 1997, African American farmers brought a lawsuit against the USDA, charging it with discrimination in denying them access to loans and subsidies mandated by law. The lawsuit was filed in August 1997 on behalf of four thousand of the nation's seventeen thousand black farmers and former farmers. A consent decree was signed in January 1999. The estimated cost of the settlement was set at $2.5 billion.[85]

In June 2008, more than eight hundred black farmers, mostly from Alabama and Mississippi, filed a new lawsuit against the USDA just two weeks after Congress reopened a 1999 settlement over past discrimination. The new lawsuit was made possible under a provision in a recently enacted farm bill that allows applicants who were denied reviews after missing earlier deadlines to reapply. An estimated seventy-five thousand individuals could fall into that group. If their suits are successful, the case could cost the government several billion dollars on top of the $980 million in damages already paid under the original settlement. Roughly two-thirds of the nearly 22,500 farmers who filed suit were awarded damages.[86] The government had paid just more than $1 billion to settle nearly sixteen thousand claims. About ninety-four thousand black farmers applied for compensation under this second round, but most of those applications, eighty-one thousand, were rejected.

In 2008, Congress appropriated $100 million to address the claims that were shut out of the process. In February 2010, Congress and President Barack Obama announced a second government payout of $1.25 billion to settle the decade-old discrimination class-action lawsuit with black farmers who were left out of the federal farm loan and assistance program because of their race. In October 2011, federal judge Paul L. Friedman in Washington, D.C., signed off on the $1.25 billion settlement for black farmers. Only time will tell whether or not this latest settlement is implemented in a just and fair way.

### Hurricane Floyd, Eastern North Carolina (1999)

Hurricane Floyd pounded more than thirty North Carolina counties on September 15–16, 1999 and dropped an estimated fifteen to twenty inches of rain.[87] It left seventeen thousand homes uninhabitable, fifty-six thousand homes damaged, and forty-seven thousand people living in temporary shelters in eastern North Carolina, a poor rural area with a large concentration of African Americans.[88]

In North Carolina, the top fifteen hog-producing counties have large African American and poor communities. Of these fifteen counties, twelve have African American populations of at least 30 percent; thirteen have a poverty rate of 25 percent or higher among their African American residents; and fourteen rank in the bottom 50 percent of North Carolina's family income distribution. African Americans were more likely than whites to live in the areas with confined animal feeding operations (CAFOs) that are high-poverty areas and areas with a high dependence on wells for drinking water.[89]

Hurricane Floyd's floodwater exposed residents to contaminants from a variety of sources, including municipal solid-waste facilities, sewage treatment facilities, hazardous-waste facilities, underground storage tanks containing petroleum products, and thousands of dead hogs.[90] More than six years after Hurricane Floyd, many black families suffered from respiratory infections, skin irritations, moldy homes, and unmet home repair needs that left them vulnerable to future storms.[91]

### Flooding of Princeville, North Carolina (1999)

In September 1999, Hurricane Floyd flooded the banks of the Tar River in Eastern North Carolina, drowning Princeville, the nation's first chartered town by blacks in the United States.[92] Princeville is located in Edgecombe County, which was 57.5 percent black, according to the 2000 census. Much of the all-black town was lost when flooding from back-to-back hurricanes hit it. Before the flood struck, Princeville was a town of 2,100 residents, 850 homes, thirty businesses, and three churches. The town covered forty streets spread over 1.3 square miles. Having survived slavery, Jim Crow, and previous floods, many Princeville residents were concerned about the town's ability to recover from Hurricane Floyd.

Founded in 1865 by former slaves on low, swampy land across the Tar River from the white town of Tarboro, Princeville was originally called Freedom Hill in honor of the grassy knoll that was under the protection of Union soldiers. After the Civil War, blacks were allowed to settle on the land whites didn't want. On February 20, 1885, two decades after the Civil War ended, Freedom Hill residents voted to incorporate and legally govern themselves. They named the town Princeville after Turner Prince, a former slave and carpenter who was one of Freedom Hill's earliest residents.[93]

Hurricane Floyd dumped between fifteen and twenty inches of rain on the area, pushing the Tar River to record level. Most residents lost everything. The Tar River crested twenty-three feet above its nineteen-foot flood stage, breaching a dike built in 1965 by the U.S. Army Corps of Engineers to protect Princeville, which had flooded seven times between 1800 and 1958. The Princeville Dike, which formed a three-and-a-half-mile semicircle around the town, rose forty-nine feet above sea level. The dike was designed to protect Princeville against the type of flood estimated to happen once every three hundred years, enough protection to officially remove the town from the flood plain.[94]

The handling of the Princeville flood is "one of government neglect and even malfeasance."[95] It seems that Mother Nature may not have caused all of the devastation. City officials from Rocky Mount, a town on the Tar River upstream from Princeville, opened the floodgates of the Tar River Reservoir Dam just twenty miles away. It is unclear how much water was dumped from the spillway and how much it contributed to the downstream flooding of Princeville.

After Floyd, federal, state, and local government officials pressured Princeville residents to consider abandoning their town. This pressure came at the same time whites in the flooded region were receiving flood assistance. Government aid to Princeville residents was slow in coming. Six months after Floyd flooded the town, only 100 of the 875 Princeville families had moved back into their homes, with more than 300 families housed at the sprawling temporary camper park nicknamed "FEMAville." A year later, many residents were still waiting for assistance.[96]

The federal government gave Princeville townspeople two choices—rebuild or accept a buyout. A buyout meant that the historic town would be lost forever. Much talk about "not rebuilding the historically black town" was heard around the state among non-Princeville residents. Rebuilding would be costly and would require the Army Corps of Engineers to reconstruct the levee, theoretically providing another one hundred years of protection, as well as payments to Princeville property owners equal to the preflood market value of their homes, businesses, and churches. Renters would also be given money to relocate. Only 50 of Princeville's 2,100 residents voted for the buyout. And, by a three-to-two vote, the Board of Commissioners voted to reject the buyout and return home. Clearly, Princeville residents were not going anywhere but home.

On February 29, 2000, President Bill Clinton issued an executive order forming the President's Council on the Future of Princeville, North Carolina. The Council brought together representatives from fifteen federal agencies, including FEMA, the Department of Labor, and the Department of Housing and Urban Development, along with several key members of Clinton's cabinet. A month after President Clinton established the Council on the Future of Princeville, FEMA released a 145-page Princeville Recovery Plan. Five years after Floyd nearly wiped Princeville off the map, the historic town celebrated its 120th birthday, in February 2005.The town's population is nearly back to its preflood size of 2,029 residents. Jonathan Tilove summed up Princeville's miraculous rise from the floodwaters: "as the waters receded, it became plain that even as the flood had nearly wiped Princeville off the map, it also had served to put it back on the map."[97]

## Conclusion

In examining selected floods, droughts, and hurricanes over the past eight decades, we have found that race and class dynamics are potent factors that impact vulnerability and adaptation. Race maps closely with geographic vulnerability. Generally, whites take the high ground, leaving the poor, the working class, and African Americans to inhabit the more vulnerable low-lying land.

Weather-related disasters expose marginalized and vulnerable communities to economic and political exploitation. They also expose the survivors to price gouging, home repair scams, banking and insurance redlining, and predatory lending practices. African Americans have also experienced heightened poststorm stressors (emotional, health, environmental, and economic), a type of "second disaster" that is compounded by institutional and structural discrimination in the distribution and allocation of postdisaster resources. Much of this differential treatment mirrors the discrimination that predates the disaster—an extension of the social, economic, and political conditions society creates for different population groups.

Disasters create scarcities—in housing, health care, schools and access to banks and lending institutions, among others. Scarcities intensify competition and discrimination and place a special burden on black renters and black homebuyers seeking replacement housing, exposing them to housing discrimination and locking them in for longer stays in temporary housing.

# Recovery and Reconstruction in Post-Katrina New Orleans

## A Time for Healing and Renewal

On August 29, 2005, Hurricane Katrina laid waste to New Orleans, an American city built below sea level in 1718 on the banks of the Mississippi.[1] Katrina was complete in its destruction of houses, neighborhoods, institutions, and communities.

New Orleans was a vulnerable city before Katrina's floodwaters devastated it.[2] It sits in a bowl—bounded by the Mississippi River, Lake Pontchartrain, and the Gulf of Mexico. In this case, the city's coastal wetlands, which normally serve as a natural buffer against storm surge, had been destroyed by offshore drilling, Mississippi River levees, and canals for navigation, pipelines, highway projects, and agricultural and urban development.

Over the past century, more than two thousand of the original seven thousand square miles of coastal marsh and swamp forests that formed the coastal delta of the Mississippi River have vanished. An average of thirty-four square miles of South Louisiana land, mostly marsh, has disappeared each year for the past five decades. More than 80 percent of the nation's coastal wetland loss in this time occurred in Louisiana. From 1932 to 2000, the state lost 1,900 square miles of land to the Gulf of Mexico.[3] Hurricane Katrina pushed New Orleans even closer to the coast because of extensive erosion at the coastal edge. This is a national problem. A range of groups, including researchers, policymakers, and environmentalists, are calling for restoration of wetlands and barrier islands to help protect New Orleans the next time a hurricane strikes.

The disaster that unfolded in New Orleans after Katrina was unnatural and caused by humans. Flooding in the New Orleans metropolitan area largely resulted from breached levees and flood walls.[4] A May 2006 report from the Russell Sage Foundation, *In the Wake of the Storm: Environment,*

*Disaster, and Race After Katrina*, observed that people of color and the poor often experience a "second disaster" after the initial storm.[5] Prestorm vulnerabilities limited the participation of thousands of low-income communities of color along the Gulf Coast in the poststorm reconstruction, rebuilding, and recovery. In these communities, days of hurt and loss are likely to become years of grief, dislocation, and displacement.[6]

## A Twenty-Point Plan to Destroy Black New Orleans

Hurricane Katrina exposed the limitation of local, state, and federal government operations to implement an effective emergency preparedness and response plan. As reconstruction and rebuilding move forward in New Orleans and the Louisiana, Mississippi, and Alabama Gulf Coast region, it was clear that the lethargic and inept emergency response after Hurricane Katrina was a disaster that overshadowed the deadly storm itself. Yet, there was a "second disaster" in the making, driven by racism, classism, elitism, paternalism, and old-fashioned greed. The "Twenty-Point Plan to Destroy Black New Orleans" presented here is based on trends and observations Beverly Wright and I made four months after the devastating storm. Other trend data and observations were added that further illustrate how the "plan" was implemented.[7]

1. *Selectively hand out FEMA grants.* The Federal Emergency Management Agency (FEMA) was consistent in its slow response in getting aid to Katrina survivors. FEMA's grant assistance program favors middle-income households, making it difficult for low-income and black Katrina survivors to access government assistance and directing the bulk of the grant assistance to middle-income white storm victims. The Lawyers Committee for Civil Rights and several other legal groups sued FEMA over its response and its handling of aid to storm victims. FEMA referred more than two million people, many of them with low incomes, to the Small Business Administration (SBA) to get the loans.

2. *Systematically deny the poor and blacks SBA loans.* The SBA screened out poor applicants and denied black households disaster loans. A December 21, 2005, *New York Times* editorial summed up this problem: "The Poor Need Not Apply." As of that date, the SBA had processed only a third of the home loan applications it had received. However, the SBA rejected 82 percent of the applications it received, a higher percentage than in most previous disasters. In well-off neighborhoods like Lakeview, 47 percent of the loans were approved, whereas in poverty-stricken neighborhoods, only 7 percent were.

Middle-class black neighborhoods in the eastern part of the city had lower than average loan rates.[8]

3. *Award insurance claims using the "wind or water" trap.* Because of the enormity of the damage in the wake of Katrina, insurance companies categorized a lot of legitimate wind claims as flood- or water-related. The "wind or water" problem hit black storm victims the hardest because they were likely to have their insurance through small companies, since the major companies had "redlined" many black neighborhoods. Most rebuilding funds after disasters came from private insurance, not the government.

4. *Redline black insurance policyholders.* Numerous studies show that African Americans are more likely than whites to receive insufficient insurance settlement amounts. Insurance companies target black policyholders in majority-black zip codes and offer them low and inadequate insurance settlements as a way to subsidize fair settlements made to white policyholders. If black homeowners and business owners were to recover from Katrina, then they had to receive full and just insurance settlements. FEMA and the SBA could not be counted on to rebuild black communities.

5. *Use "greenbuilding" and flood-proofing codes to restrict redevelopment.* Requiring that rebuilding plans conform to "green building" materials and new floodproofing codes priced many low- and moderate-income homeowners and small-business owners out of the market. This hit black homeowners and black business owners especially hard, since they generally had lower incomes and less wealth.

6. *Apply discriminatory environmental cleanup standards.* Failure to apply uniform cleanup standards can kill off black neighborhoods. A full-scale cleanup of white neighborhoods was undertaken to meet residential standards, while no or partial cleanup (industrial standards) took place in black residential neighborhoods. Failure to clean up black residential areas can act as a disincentive for redevelopment. It can also make people sick. Some people used the argument that black neighborhoods were already highly polluted with background contamination "hot spots" that exceeded EPA safe levels pre-Katrina and thus did not need to be cleaned to more rigorous residential standards.

7. *Sacrifice "low-lying" black neighborhoods in the name of saving the wetlands and environmental restoration.* Some people advocated allowing black neighborhoods like the Lower Ninth Ward and New Orleans East to be "yielded back to the swamp," while allowing similar low-lying white areas to be rebuilt and redeveloped. This is a form of "ethnic cleansing" that was not possible before Katrina. Instead of emphasizing equitable rebuilding,

uniform cleanup standards, equal protection, and environmental justice for African American communities, public officials sent mixed signals for rebuilding vulnerable "low-lying" black neighborhoods.

8. *Promote a smaller, more upscale, and "whiter" New Orleans.* Concentrating on getting less-damaged neighborhoods up and running could translate into a smaller, more upscale, and whiter New Orleans and a dramatically down-sized black community. Clearly, shrinking New Orleans neighborhoods disproportionately shrinks black votes, black political power, and black wealth. A February 2011 *Bloomberg News* headlines read "Census Finds Hurricane Katrina Left New Orleans Richer, Whiter, Emptier." The city lost 140,845 residents, a decrease of 29 percent from 2000. Whites were far more likely to make it back to New Orleans than blacks. The percentage of the population that was black fell to 60.2 percent from 67.3 percent.[9] This drop in population will translate into one fewer congressional seat for Louisiana—now six instead of seven.

9. *Revise land-use and zoning ordinances to exclude.* Katrina could be used to change land use and zoning codes to "zone against" undesirable land uses that were not politically possible before the storm. Also, "expulsive" zoning could be used to push out certain land uses and certain people.

10. *Employ phased rebuilding and restoration scheme that concentrates on the "high ground." New* Orleans officials were advised to concentrate rebuilding on the areas that remained high and dry after Katrina. These areas are disproportionately white and affluent. This scenario builds on preexisting inequities and "white privilege" and ensures future inequities and continued "white privilege." By the time rebuilding got around to black "low-lying" areas, there were not likely to be any rebuilding funds left. This is the "oops, we are out of funds" scenario.

11. *Apply eminent domain as a black land grab.* Another proposal was to give Katrina evacuees one year to return before the city was allowed to legally "take" their property through eminent domain. Clearly, it would take much longer than a year for most New Orleanians to return home. This proposal could turn into a giant land grab of black property and a loss of the wealth that blacks have invested in their homes and businesses.

12. *Offer no financial assistance for evacuees to return.* Thousands of Katrina evacuees were shipped to more than three dozen states with no provisions for return, the equivalent of being given a "one-way" ticket. Many Katrina evacuees ran short of funds. No money translates into no return to their homes and neighborhoods. Promoting the "right to return" without committing adequate resources to assist evacuees to return doesn't help.

13. *Keep evacuees away from New Orleans jobs.* The nation's unemployment rate was 5 percent in November 2005. That month, the jobless rate for Katrina returnees was 12.5 percent, while 27.8 percent of evacuees living elsewhere were unemployed. The jobless rate among blacks who had not returned was 47 percent in November 2005, whereas the rate was only 13 percent for whites who had not gone back. Katrina evacuees who made it back to their home region thus had much lower levels of joblessness. This is especially important for African Americans, whose joblessness rate was more than 30 percentage points lower for returnees. The problem was that the vast majority of black Katrina evacuees had not returned to their home region. Only 21 percent of black evacuees—but 48 percent of white evacuees—had returned by November.

14. *Fail to enforce fair housing laws.* In the aftermath of the storm, housing discrimination against blacks was allowed to run rampant. Katrina created a housing shortage and opened a floodgate of discriminatory acts against black homeowners and renters. In December 2005, the National Fair Housing Alliance (NFHA) found high rates of housing discrimination against African Americans displaced by Hurricane Katrina. In 66 percent of the test runs conducted by the NFHA, forty-three of sixty-five instances, whites were favored over African Americans.[10]

15. *Provide no commitment to rebuild and replace low-income public housing.* Shortly after Katrina struck, even the Secretary of the U.S. Department of Housing and Urban Development (HUD) spoke of not rebuilding all of the public housing lost during the storm. The HUD secretary's statement was a powerful signal to New Orleans poor that public housing might not be around for them to return to.

16. *Downplay the black cultural heritage of New Orleans.* Some officials tried to promote rebuilding and the vision of a "new" New Orleans as if the city's rich black culture did not matter or as if it could be replaced or replicated in a "theme park"-type redevelopment scenario. Developers tried to capture and market the "black essence" of New Orleans without including black people.

17. *Treat mixed-income "integrated" housing as superior to all-black neighborhoods.* First, there is nothing inherently inferior about an "all-black" neighborhood or all-black anything, for that matter. Black New Orleanians who chose to live in neighborhoods that happened to be all black (whites have always had the right to move in or move out of these neighborhoods) should not have been forced to have their neighborhoods rebuilt as "integrated" or "multicultural" neighborhoods. Also, for many blacks, "mixed-income" housing conjures up the idea that 10 percent of the fair-market

housing units will be set aside for them. Many blacks are battle-weary of being some generic 10 percent. New Orleans was 68 percent black before Katrina, and most black folks were comfortable with that.

18. *Allow "oversight" (overseer) board to manage Katrina funds that flow to New Orleans.* Some officials tried to take away "home rule," since the billions of Katrina redevelopment dollars that were to flow to New Orleans would be too much money for a majority-black city council and a black mayor to oversee or manage. More important, the oversight board needed to represent "big-money" interests (real estate, developers, banking, insurance, hotels, law firms, the tourist industry), well beyond the oversight of a democratically elected city government, to ensure that the vision of the "new" New Orleans, "smaller and more upscale," was implemented.

19. *Delay rebuilding and construction of New Orleans schools.* The longer New Orleans schools stayed closed, the longer families with children stayed away. Schools are a major predictor of racial polarization. Before Katrina, more than 125,000 New Orleans children were attending schools in the city. Blacks made up 93 percent of the students in the New Orleans schools. Evacuated children were enrolled in school districts from Arizona to Pennsylvania; three months after the storm, only one of the New Orleans 116 schools was open.[11]

20. *Hold elections without appropriate Voting Rights Act safeguards.* Almost 300,000 registered voters left New Orleans after Katrina. The powerful storm damaged or destroyed 300 of the 442 polling places. Holding city elections posed major challenges in terms of registration, absentee ballots, availability of city workers to staff the polls, polling places, and identification for displaced New Orleanians. Identification is required at the polls, and returning residents might well have lost traditional identification papers (e.g., birth certificates, driver's licenses) in the hurricane. More than three months after Katrina struck, 80 percent of New Orleans voters had not made their way back to the city, including most African Americans, who made up two-thirds of the city's population before the storm.

Holding elections while a substantial portion of African American New Orleans voters were displaced outside of their home district and even their home state is unprecedented in the history of the United States, but also raises racial justice and human rights questions.

## Cleaning Up after Katrina

Katrina has been described as one of the worst environmental disasters in U.S. history. A September 2005 *Business Week* commentary described the handling of the untold tons of "lethal goop" as the "mother of all toxic clean-ups."[12] However, the billion-dollar question facing New Orleans was which neighborhoods would get cleaned up, which ones would be left contaminated, and which ones would be targeted as new sites where storm debris and waste from flooded homes could be dumped.

Hurricane Katrina left debris across a ninety-thousand-square disaster area in Alabama, Mississippi, and Louisiana, far more extensive than the sixteen-acre tract in New York that was destroyed on September 11, 2001.[13] According to the Congressional Research Service, debris from Katrina could well top 100 million cubic yards, far more than the 8.8 million cubic yards of disaster debris generated after the 9/11 terrorist attacks on New York City.

Ten months after the storm, FEMA had spent $3.6 billion to remove 98.6 million cubic yards of debris from Katrina.[14] This is enough trash to pile two miles high across five football fields. An estimated 20 million cubic yards of debris still littered New Orleans and Mississippi waterways—with about 96 percent, or 17.8 million cubic yards, of the remaining wreckage in Orleans, St. Bernard, St. Tammany, Washington, and Plaquemine Parishes.

Louisiana parishes hauled away twenty-five times more debris than was collected after the 9/11 terrorist attack in 2001.[15] The Army Corps of Engineers originally estimated it would complete its debris mission, including demolitions, by the end of September 2006.[16] However, the mission did not conclude until August 31, 2007.

In addition to wood debris, EPA and LDEQ officials estimated that 140,000 to 160,000 homes in Louisiana might need to be demolished and disposed.[17] More than 110,000 of the 180,000 homes in New Orleans were flooded, and half sat for days or weeks in more than six feet of water.[18] Government officials estimated that as many as thirty thousand to fifty thousand homes citywide might have to be demolished, while many others could be saved with extensive repairs. As many as fifteen thousand buildings were set for demolition once local authorities got permission from property owners. Getting this permission was a drawn-out process because people were coming back slowly to damaged areas. Demolishing damaged homes in the hard hit Lower Ninth Ward proved to be a hot political issue.[19]

More than 350,000 automobiles in the Gulf Coast had to be drained of oil and gasoline and then recycled; 60,000 boats were destroyed; and 300,000 underground fuel tanks and 42,000 tons of hazardous waste required cleanup and proper disposal at licensed facilities.[20] Government officials pegged the numbers of cars lost in New Orleans alone at 145,000.[21]

What was been cleaned up, what got left behind, and where the waste was disposed of appear to have been affected more by political science and sociology than by toxicology, epidemiology, and hydrology. Weeks after Katrina struck, LDEQ allowed New Orleans to open the two-hundred-acre Old Gentilly landfill to dump construction and demolition waste from the storm.[22] Federal regulators had ordered the unlined landfill closed in the 1980s.The dump was being readied for reopening just before Katrina hit. By December, after it reopened, more than two thousand truckloads of hurricane debris were entering the landfill in east New Orleans every day.[23]

Just four months after the storm, the Old Gentilly landfill had grown about one hundred feet high.[24] LDEQ officials insisted that the old landfill, which is still operating, met all standards. But residents and environmentalists disagreed. Even some high-ranking elected officials expressed fear that the reopening of the Old Gentilly landfill could create an ecological nightmare.[25] In November 2005, four days after environmentalists filed a lawsuit to block the dumping, the landfill caught fire.

In April 2006, the U.S. Army Corps of Engineers and the Louisiana Department of Environmental Quality issued permits that would allow Waste Management, Inc., to open and operate a landfill in New Orleans East to contain construction- and demolition-related material (C&D). The new landfill was located on Chef Menteur Highway, which runs through much of New Orleans East, where the majority of the population is African American. Waste Management pledged to give the city 22 percent of all revenue derived from the site. Every week, Waste Management picked up an average of forty-five pounds of trash from each home, twenty pounds more per home than pre-Katrina. But, after Katrina, the state LDEQ expanded its definition of what it considered "construction debris" to include potentially contaminated material.[26] Yet, regulators acknowledged the potential toxic contamination threat from storm-related wastes. Much of the disaster debris from flooded neighborhoods in New Orleans was mixed to the point that separation was either very difficult or essentially impossible.[27] David Romero of the EPA said that it would be "lucky" if even 30 percent of the hazardous waste was removed from the waste stream. In an October 2005 interview on CNN, LDEQ Assistant Secretary Chuck Carr Brown said hazardous material was hidden "like toxic needles in a haystack" in the hurricane debris.[28]

Nevertheless, government officials asserted that the risk that hazardous materials were being dumped at the Chef Menteur site was insignificant and that existing sorting practices were adequate to keep hazardous waste out of the landfill. They also insisted that protective liners were not needed for

C&D landfills because demolition debris was cleaner than other rubbish.[29] C&D landfills are not required under federal law to have protective liners as is required for municipal landfills, which are expected to receive a certain amount of hazardous household waste. However, an LDEQ official, Chuck Carr Brown, told the *New York Times* in May that "there's nothing toxic, nothing hazardous" going to the landfill.[30]

Landfill opponents thought otherwise. Many feared that the government's willingness to waive regulations would mean that motor oil, batteries, electronics, ink toner, chlorine bleach, drain cleaners, and other noxious material would almost certainly wind up at the unlined landfills.[31] Historically, government has done a poor job policing what goes into landfills—especially after hurricanes, when contents from gutted homes get mixed together. Community leaders beat back two other efforts, in 1990 and 1997, to locate landfills along U.S. 90 near their homes in New Orleans East. The Chef Menteur Highway landfill was about four miles west of the Old Gentilly landfill in a mostly African American and Vietnamese community.[32] More than a thousand Vietnamese American families lived less than two miles from the edge of the new landfill. African American and Vietnamese homeowners saw the landfill as a direct assault on their health, their homes' property values, and their efforts to rebuild their lives, which had been shattered by the storm.

## Impact of the Demolition of Public Housing

All eyes were watching the rebuilding efforts in New Orleans, especially how the city addressed the repopulation of its historically African American neighborhoods and its strategically sited public housing. The Housing Authority of New Orleans, or HANO, as it is popularly called, had been dismantling traditional public housing for nearly a decade before Hurricane Katrina struck through Hope VI, a Clinton-era program that favors vouchers and mixed-income developments. Dramatic population shifts occurred in New Orleans as a result of the Hope VI project, which displaced thousands of public-housing residents. Gentrification of historically black areas of the City was becoming a problem for many citizens.

The St. Thomas redevelopment in New Orleans in the late 1990s became the prototype for elite visions of the city's future. Strategically sited public housing projects like the St. Thomas homes were demolished to make way for neotraditionalist townhouses and stores (in the St. Thomas case, a Wal-Mart) in the New Urbanist spirit. These "mixed-use, mixed-income" developments were typically advertised as little utopias of diversity, but—just as in the Olympic Village (formerly Techwood Homes) in Atlanta and in similar cases around the country—the real dynamic operating was exclusionary rather than inclusionary, with only a few project residents being rehoused at the development site.

HUD announced that it would invest $154 million in rebuilding public housing in New Orleans and that it would assist the city in bringing displaced residents home. But critics feared that government officials and business leaders were quietly planning to demolish the old projects and privatize public housing. Four years after Katrina, at least 80 percent of public housing in New Orleans remained closed. Six of ten of the largest public housing developments in the city were boarded up, with the other four in various states of repair. As of the beginning of 2011, the Housing Authority of New Orleans lists nine public housing developments with the majority of them being mix-income developments.

More than forty-nine thousand people lived in public housing before Katrina, twenty thousand in older, large-scale developments such as St. Bernard, and twenty-nine thousand in Section 8 rental housing, which was also devastated by the storm. The number of public housing units in New Orleans has been on a steady decline since the mid-1990s. In 1996, the city had 13,694 units of conventional public housing; in 2005, right before Katrina, it had 7,379 such units.

The homeless population of New Orleans skyrocketed after Hurricane Katrina, reaching an unprecedented level of one resident in twenty-five in 2008. The city's estimated homeless population of twelve thousand that year was nearly double the pre-Katrina homeless count. New Orleans's homeless rate is more than four times that of most U.S. cities, whose homeless populations are less than 1 percent of their total populations. The cities with homeless rates closest to that of New Orleans are Atlanta (1.4 percent) and Washington, DC (0.95 percent), both majority-black cities.[33]

Although the city faced a severe housing crunch and a growing homeless problem, plans to rebuild the seventy-seven thousand rental units lost to Katrina largely failed.[34] In June 2006, federal housing officials announced that more than five thousand public housing apartments for the poor would be razed and replaced by developments for residents from a wider range of incomes. The demolition plan would eliminate 4,500 public housing units in the city while building only about 800 units of traditional public housing.[35] This move heightened the anxiety of many low-income black Katrina survivors, who feared they would be pushed out in favor of higher-income families.[36]

Powerful forces have been trying to demolish public housing in New Orleans for decades. When Katrina emptied New Orleans of its public-housing residents, the *Wall Street Journal* reported that U.S. Congressman Richard Baker, a ten-term Republican from Baton Rouge, told lobbyists: "We finally cleaned up public housing in New Orleans. We couldn't do it, but God did."[37] The demolition of four sprawling public housing projects—the St. Bernard, C. J. Peete, B. W. Cooper, and Lafitte housing developments—eliminated more than half of all of the conventional public housing in the city, where only 1,097 units were occupied ten months after the storm.

HUD raised 35 percent the value of disaster vouchers for displaced residents because the city's housing shortage caused rents to skyrocket. However, Hurricane Katrina drove up housing prices as individuals competed for the limited supply that survived the storm and for newly constructed units; the average two-bedroom apartment that would have cost $676 a month in 2005 in 2011 rented for $847 to $1,371 per month.[38] Housing discrimination becomes rampant when the supply is scarce, hitting African American renters and homebuyers especially hard.[39] A Greater New Orleans Fair Housing Action Center study of the New Orleans metro area after Hurricane Katrina found discrimination in nearly six out of ten transactions, with African Americans receiving less favorable treatment because of their race.[40] Housing providers often simply didn't return phone calls from African Americans, didn't provide applications to African Americans, or didn't show available rental units to African Americans. With obstacles like these, it is no wonder that African American Katrina survivors had difficulty recovering from the storm. Many African American households began their road to recovery not by returning to work and home but by looking for jobs and housing.

Although Hurricane Katrina did not discriminate, a May 2008 progress report from the Louisiana Family Recovery Corps found a wide disparity between African American and white storm victims in both adaptation and recovery:

> There is great disparity in the progress towards recovery, disruption from the storms and levels of progress between black and white households, even for those with similar incomes. On nearly every indicator, the storm impact and recovery experience for black households is significantly different than for whites, even after examining these issues by income levels.[41]

A June 6, 2008, CNN *Money Magazine* report indicated that the price of the average single-family home in the New Orleans metropolitan area had risen in the first three months of 2006 to $215,179, up from an average of $195,377 just before the storm. Rents in the Mid-City and Lakefronts sections of New Orleans, both of which were flooded, had risen to a poststorm average of $1,584 a month in 2008 from $986 before the storm. As of July 2008, nearly four thousand displaced New Orleans residents lived in trailers. Some one-fourth of the trailer residents were renters, and 16 percent had special needs. Most of the people still living in trailers three years after the storm were families who faced the greatest challenges in a tight housing market.[42] In May 2008, African American storm victims were more than twice as likely as white storm victims to be still living in trailers.[43]

### Seeking a "Safe" Road Home

Estimates vary on how many people actually made it back to New Orleans within three years after the storm. Some demographers place the number between 315,000 to 320,000 residents, basing their figures on utility and water hookups, mail delivery, and other public service accounts. In May 2008, the Brookings Institution estimated that New Orleans had reached 72 percent of its pre-Katrina population of 453,726.[44] The storm cut deeper for the city's African American households than for its white households; in 2006, nearly half (47 percent) of African Americans households lived someplace other than New Orleans, whereas only one-fifth (19 percent) of white households did so.[45]

By March 2008, FEMA had paid Louisiana 93 percent of the $6.6 billion infrastructure allocation, but only 47 percent had actually reached localities. Overall, Katrina relief and rebuilding funds only trickled down to local governments and residents alike. Given the enormity and the urgency of the need, one would think much more would have been done after three years.

FEMA even withheld disaster relief supplies from Katrina victims. In June 2008, nearly three years after the storm, the first truckload of $85 million in federal relief supplies, lost in a bureaucratic hole, arrived in Louisiana and was distributed to those still displaced by both Katrina and Rita. The supplies had been stored in Fort Worth, Texas, for two years and were deemed surplus goods in 2008 after the building's owner decided to demolish the structure.

The road home for many Katrina survivors has been a bumpy one, largely because the government was slow to distribute the $116 billion in federal aid to residents to enable them to rebuild. At the end of 2007, two years after the storm, only about $35 billion had been appropriated for long-term rebuilding. Most of the Katrina money coming from Washington hasn't gotten to those most in need—and the funding squeeze is stopping much of the Gulf Coast from coming back.[46]

Eighteen months after the storm, only 630 homeowners had received checks from the Louisiana Road Home program, a program designed to provide compensation to Louisiana homeowners affected by Hurricanes Katrina or Rita for the damage to their homes. The program provided eligible homeowners up to $150,000 in compensation for their losses to get back into their homes. In August 2007, only 22 percent of the applicants to Louisiana's Road Home program had gone to closing. In July 2008, the Road Home program had made 114,679 awards totaling $6.7 billion, making it the largest home rebuilding program in American history. The average Road Home award was $58,688 in Louisiana but $73,090 in Mississippi.

Although government officials insisted that the dirt in residents' yards was safe, Church Hill Downs, Inc., the owners of New Orleans's Fair Grounds, felt it was not safe for its million-dollar thoroughbred horses to race on. The Fair Grounds is the nation's third-oldest track; only Saratoga and Pimlico have been racing longer. The owners hauled off soil tainted by Hurricane Katrina's floodwaters and rebuilt a grandstand roof that had been ripped off by the storm's wind.[47] The Fair Grounds then opened on Thanksgiving Day 2006. Certainly, if tainted soil is not safe for horses, surely it is not safe for people—especially children who play and dig in the dirt.

Families that choose to return to rebuild their communities shouldn't have to worry about their children playing in yards, parks, and schoolyards contaminated with cancer-causing chemicals left by Katrina's floodwaters. In March 2006, seven months after the storm slammed ashore, organizers of the Safe Way Back Home initiative, the Deep South Center for Environmental Justice at Dillard University (DSCEJ), and the United Steel Workers (USW) undertook a proactive pilot neighborhood cleanup project—the first of its kind in New Orleans.[48] The cleanup project, located in the 8100 block of Aberdeen Road in New Orleans East, removed several inches of tainted soil from the front and back yards, replacing the soil with new sod, and disposed of the contaminated dirt in a safe manner.

Residents who chose to remove the top soil from their yards—which contained sediments left by flooding—found themselves in a "Catch-22" situation, with the LDEQ and EPA insisting the soil in their yards was not contaminated and local landfill operators refusing to dispose of the soil because they believed that it was contaminated. This dilemma over what to do with the topsoil remained unresolved a year and a half after the devastating flood.

The Safe Way Back Home demonstration project served as a catalyst for a series of activities that attempted to reclaim the New Orleans East community following the devastation caused by Hurricane Katrina. It is the government's responsibility to provide the resources required to address areas of environmental concern and to assure that the workforce is protected. However, residents did not wait for the government to ride in on a white horse to rescue them and clean up their neighborhoods.

The DSCEJ/USW coalition received dozens of requests and inquiries from New Orleans East homeowners associations to help clean up their neighborhoods block by block. State and federal officials labeled the voluntary cleanup efforts as "scaremongering."[49] EPA and LDEQ officials said that they had tested soil samples from the neighborhood in December 2006 and that there was no immediate cause for concern.

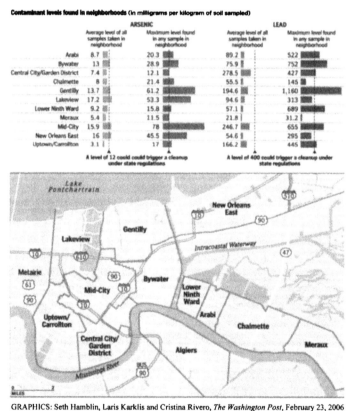

GRAPHICS: Seth Hamblin, Laris Karklis and Cristina Rivero, *The Washington Post*, February 23, 2006

Figure 4.1: Contamination levels left behind by Hurricane Katrina

According to Tom Harris, administrator of LDEQ's environmental technology division, state toxicologist, the government originally sampled 800 locations in New Orleans and found cause for concern in only 46 samples. Generally, the soil in New Orleans is consistent with "what we saw before Katrina," says Harris. He called the "A Safe Way Back Home" program "completely unnecessary."[50]

A week after the voluntary cleanup project began, an LDEQ staffer ate a spoonful of dirt scraped from the Aberdeen Road pilot project. The dirt-eating publicity stunt was clearly an attempt to disparage the proactive neighborhood cleanup initiative. LDEQ officials later apologized.

Despite the barriers and red tape they encountered, Katrina evacuees moved back into their damaged homes or set up travel trailers in their yards. Homeowners gutted their houses, treated the mold, fixed roofs and siding, and slowly got their lives back in order. One of the main questions returning residents had was: is this place safe? They got mixed signals from government agencies. In December 2005, LDEQ announced that "there is no unacceptable long-term health risk directly attributable to environmental contamination resulting from the storm." Yet, contamination was found all across the city's flooded neighborhoods.

Two months later, in February 2006, the Natural Resources Defense Council (NRDC) published test results with different findings.[51] NRDC's analyses of soil and air quality after Hurricane Katrina revealed dangerously high levels of diesel fuel, lead, and other contaminants in Gentilly, Bywater, and Orleans Parish and in other New Orleans neighborhoods.

Although many government scientists insisted the soil was safe, an April 2006 multiagency task force press release distributed by the EPA raised some questions.[52] Though it claimed that the levels of lead and other contaminants in New Orleans soil were "similar" to soil-contaminant levels in other cities, it also cautioned residents to "keep children from playing in bare dirt. Cover bare dirt with grass, bushes, or 4-6 inches of lead-free wood chips, mulch, soil, or sand."

Surely, if the federal government can pay for debris removal, blue tarp roofs, and temporary trailer housing (which have already cost an estimated $4.5 billion), it can make funds available to address the "silent killer" of childhood lead poisoning. Making government grants of from $2,000 to $3,000 available to homeowners to test and clean up contamination in their yards would be a bargain, given the millions of hurricane relief dollars wasted on profiteering, no-bid contracts, and material markups.[53] The "band-aid" approach, for example, covering bare dirt with grass and wood chips, stops short of addressing the root problem—environmental hazards found inside and outside homes in older neighborhoods.

Instead of cleaning up the mess that existed before the storm, government officials allowed dirty neighborhoods to stay dirty forever. Just because lead and other heavy metals existed in some New Orleans neighborhoods before Katrina doesn't mean that they are safe or that there wasn't a moral or legal obligation to remediate any and all contamination uncovered. Government scientists have assured New Orleanians, including gardeners, that they did not need to worry about soil salinity and heavy-metal content. They also said that residents need not worry about digging or planting in the soil. But, given the uncertainties built into quantitative-risk assessments, how certain were these government officials that all of New Orleans neighborhoods were safe?

In August 2006, nearly a year after Katrina struck, the federal EPA gave New Orleans and surrounding communities a clean bill of health, while pledging to monitor a handful of toxic hot spots.[54] EPA and LDEQ officials concluded that Katrina did not cause any appreciable contamination and that existing contamination had preceded the storm. Although EPA tests confirmed the widespread presence of lead in the soil—a prestorm problem in 40 percent of New Orleans —EPA dismissed residents' calls to address this problem as outside the agency's mission.

And, in June 2007, the U.S. General Accountability Office (GAO) issued a report, *Hurricane Katrina: EPA's Current and Future Environmental Protection Efforts Could Be Enhanced by Addressing Issues and Challenges Faced on the Gulf Coast,* that criticized the EPA's handling of contamination in post-Katrina New Orleans and elsewhere along the Gulf Coast.[55] The GAO found inadequate monitoring for asbestos around demolition and renovation sites. Additionally, the GAO investigation revealed that "key" information released to the public about environmental contamination was neither timely nor adequate and that, in some cases, it was "easily misinterpreted to the public's detriment."

The GAO also found that the EPA did not state until August 2006 that its 2005 report, which said that the great majority of the data showed that adverse health effects would not be expected from exposure to sediments from previously flooded areas, applied only to short-term visits, such as to view damage to homes.[56]

In March 2007, a coalition of community and environmental groups collected more than 130 soil samples in Orleans Parish. Testing was conducted by the Natural Resources Defense Council.[57] Sampling was done at 65 sites in residential neighborhoods where post-Katrina EPA testing had previously shown elevated concentrations of arsenic in soils. Sampling was also done at 15 playgrounds and 19 schools. Six school sites had arsenic levels in excess of the LDEQ's soil screening value for arsenic. The LDEQ soil screening value of 12 milligrams per kilogram (mg/kg) normally requires additional sampling, further investigation, and a site-specific risk assessment. It is clear that the levels of arsenic in the sediment are unacceptably high for residential neighborhoods.

## *"Home": The Toxic FEMA Trailers*

Right after Katrina, FEMA purchased about 102,000 travel trailers for $2.6 billion, or roughly $15,000 each, to house homeless Katrina victims.[58] Surprisingly, there were reports that residents became ill in these trailers from the release of potentially dangerous levels of formaldehyde.[59] In fact, formaldehyde is the industrial chemical (used in glues, plastics, building materials, composite wood, plywood panels, and particle board) that was used to manufacture the travel trailers.

In Mississippi, FEMA received forty-six complaints from individuals who indicated that they had symptoms of formaldehyde exposure, which include eye, nose, and throat irritation, nausea, skin rashes, sinus infections, depression, irritated mucus membranes, asthma attacks, headaches, insomnia, intestinal problems, memory impairment, and breathing difficulties.[60] The Sierra Club conducted tests on thirty-one trailers and found that twenty-nine of them had unsafe levels of formaldehyde.[61] According to the Sierra Club, 83 percent of the trailers tested in Alabama, Louisiana, and Mississippi had formaldehyde levels above the EPA limit of 0.10 parts per million.[62]

Even though FEMA received numerous complaints about the toxic trailers, the agency tested only one occupied trailer to determine the levels of formaldehyde in it.[63] The test confirmed that the level of formaldehyde was extraordinarily high and presented an immediate health risk to the trailer's occupants.[64] Unfortunately, FEMA did not test any more occupied trailers and released a public statement discounting any risk associated with formaldehyde exposure.

According to findings from a congressional committee hearing, FEMA deliberately neglected to investigate any reports of high levels of formaldehyde in trailers so as to bolster FEMA's litigation position just in case individuals affected by the agency's negligence decided to sue.[65] More than five hundred hurricane survivors and evacuees in Louisiana did in fact pursue legal action against the trailer manufacturers for exposure to the toxic chemical. Two years after Katrina hit, more than sixty-five thousand Gulf Coast families, an estimated 195,000 people, were still living in FEMA trailers. The vast majority of the trailers, about forty-five thousand, were located in Louisiana.[66]

In July 2007, FEMA stopped buying and selling disaster relief trailers because of the formaldehyde contamination.[67] FEMA administrator R. David Paulison admitted that the trailers were toxic and concluded that the agency should have moved faster in addressing the health concerns of residents.[68] In August 2007, FEMA began moving families out of the toxic trailers and finding them new rental housing.[69] Testing of FEMA travel trailers for formaldehyde and other hazards began in September 2007.[70] The Centers for Disease Control and Prevention was named the lead agency in developing parameters for testing the travel trailers.

In February 2008, more than two years after residents of FEMA trailers deployed in the Gulf Coast after Katrina began complaining of breathing difficulties, nosebleeds, and persistent headaches, officials of the Centers for Disease Control and Prevention (CDC) announced that the long-awaited government tests had found potentially hazardous levels of toxic formaldehyde gas in both travel trailers and mobile homes provided by FEMA. The CDC tests found levels of formaldehyde gas in 519 trailer and mobile homes tested in Louisiana and Mississippi that were, on average, about five times the level that people are exposed to in most modern homes.[71] In some trailers, the levels were nearly forty times the customary exposure levels, raising fears that residents could suffer long-term respiratory problems and perhaps other health effects. CDC tests showed an average formaldehyde level of 77 parts per billion (ppb), with a low of 3 ppb and a high of 590 ppb. The average level in new homes, in contrast, is 10 to 20 ppb. Formaldehyde is a known carcinogen, and long-term exposure to levels of 77 ppb can have serious health effects, and exposure to the higher levels can cause eye irritation, coughing, and other respiratory problems. These health findings came twenty-three months after FEMA first received reports of health problems and test results showing formaldehyde levels at seventy-five times the U.S.-recommended workplace safety threshold.

In 2007, the federal government approved $400 million to build "Katrina Cottages," or alternative affordable housing designed to survive a storm.[72] However, this did not happen because of internal political fights between the state government and private contractors that sought to build homes for Katrina evacuees.

## A Food Desert Among Plenty

Before Katrina, predominantly African American communities in the City of New Orleans were struggling with the mass closings of shopping centers and grocery stores in their communities. Many watched with horror at the explosion of unhealthy fast-food chains, liquor stores, dollar stores, pawnshops and check-cashing establishments being erected in their neighborhoods in rapid succession. Life was becoming more difficult as residents were forced to travel great distances because they could not obtain the ordinary amenities of life close to home. Ironically, income did not seem to matter. Residents of middle- and upper-middle class black neighborhoods all fell victim

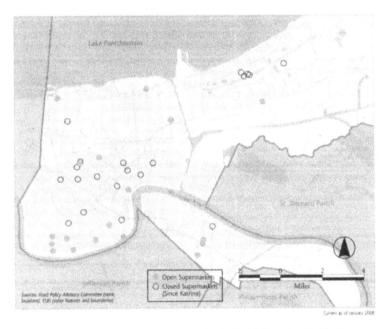

Map created by the Louisiana Public Health Institute for the New Orleans Food Policy Advisory Committee. (January 2008). Originally Published in: The Prevention Research Center at Tulane University and the Food Trust. (2008, March). *Building healthy communities: Expanding access to fresh food retail. A report by the New Orleans Food Policy Advisory Committee.* New Orleans, LA: Authors.

Figure 4.2: Supermarkets in New Orleans before and after Hurricane Katrina

to the same fate; all had to drive long distances to white neighborhoods to find supermarkets, shopping centers, and quality restaurants.

A 2007 survey of low-income Orleans Parish residents showed that nearly 60 percent of low-income residents had to drive more than three miles to get to a supermarket, while only 50 percent of those surveyed owned cars. Additionally, of those surveyed, 70 percent reported that they "would buy" or "might buy" most fresh produce items if they were available in their neighborhoods. Moreover, the study shows that low-income people "like" to eat fruit and vegetables as much as or more than unhealthy foods.[73]

Access to fresh, nutritious food was inadequate in New Orleans even before Katrina. At that time, there were about 12,000 residents per supermarket in New Orleans while the nation's average was 8,800 residents per supermarket.[74] Five years after Katrina, the availability of these types of foods had only declined. There were nearly eighteen thousand residents per supermarket, an increase of six thousand residents per supermarket compared to pre-Katrina data. There were only twenty-three supermarkets open in New Orleans after the storm. Adding to this woeful lack of stores was the fact that the smaller stores that have reopened did not meet the demand for fresh produce.

In 2006, in the predominately black New Orleans East area, populated by sixty thousand people, there was only one supermarket. News of the reopening of this Winn Dixie created such excitement in the area that opening day felt like the local jazz festival. People gathered and greeted friends they had not seen since before the storm and catching up on stories of loved ones and tales of surviving Katrina. The checkout lines extended into the grocery aisles. There was joy and merriment all over the store, but especially in the fruit and vegetable section. People were "ooohing" and "ahhhing" over the fresh tomatoes, strawberries, and melons like kids in a candy store. Cabbages and fresh stringbeans were in every basket.

Who would have thought that one supermarket could bring such joy? Yet this level of excitement is not uncommon in African Americans urban neighborhoods that have become "food deserts," neighborhoods devoid of full-service supermarkets, grocery stores, and farmers markets. New Orleans East residents are forced to accept extremely long checkout lines in exchange for access to a full-service supermarket.

Healthy foods like fruits and vegetables are high in nutrients and low in salt, fat, and calories. Therefore, access to fresh healthy foods is vital to good health. Research conducted in the city's Central City neighborhood revealed that greater access to fresh vegetables led to increased consumption of these foods by residents of the neighborhood. Improving access to healthy foods would lead to better dietary practices and better health for individuals and families in underserved communities. In the rebuilding of New Orleans, we must reverse this trend of poor access to healthy foods leading to poor dietary health.

## Improving Levee Protection in New Orleans Post-Katrina

The U.S. Army Corps of Engineers worked to fix and or replace 220 miles of levees and floodwalls, build new flood gates and pump stations at the mouths of three outfall canals, and strengthen existing walls and levees at important points. By May 2008, the Corps had spent $4 billion of the $14 billion set aside by Congress to repair and upgrade the metropolitan area's hundreds of miles of levees by 2011. As early as 2008, some outside experts said the new

| *Neighborhoods* | *Average Depth of Flood Water Decrease* | *Fatalities Decreased* | *Property Loss Decreased* |
|---|---|---|---|
| *Table 4.1: Inter-agency Performance Evaluation Task Force Risk and Rehabilitation Report Army Corps of Engineers June 20, 2007* | | | |
| | 5.5 ft | 70% | 32% |
| Upper Ninth | .5 | 31% | 11% |
| Lower Ninth | 2 ft | 29% | 4% |
| Gentilly | .5 ft | 19% | 5% |
| N.O. East (West Lake Forest) | NC | NC | NC |
| Michoud | NC | NC | NC |
| New Orleans East | 1 ft | 83% | 24% |

Source: Army Crops of Engineers Interagency Performance Evaluations Task Force (IPET), Risk & Reliability Report (June 20, 2007) found at http://nolarisk.usace.army.mil/.

levees were already leaking, meaning that billions more will be needed and that some of the work already completed may need to be redone.[75]

A 2007 report that included flood maps produced by the Army Corps of Engineers showed that levee protection to New Orleans East residents had not improved since Katrina.[76] A disproportionately large swath of black New Orleans was once again left vulnerable to future flooding. After nearly two years and billions spent on levee repairs, the Army Corps of Engineers estimated that there was a one in one hundred annual chance that about one-third of the city would be flooded with as much as six feet of water.[77]

Mostly African American parts of New Orleans are still likely to be flooded in a major storm. Increased levee protection maps closely with neighborhoods' racial composition, with predominantly black neighborhoods such as the Ninth Ward, Gentilly, and New Orleans East receiving little, if any, increased flood protection. These disparities could lead insurers and investors to redline and think twice about supporting the rebuilding efforts in vulnerable black areas.

Lakeview area residents can expect 5.5 feet of increased levee protection. This translates into 5.5 feet less water than they received from Katrina. Lakeview is mostly white and affluent. New Orleans East, in contrast, is mostly black and middle class. This same scenario holds true for the mostly black Lower Ninth Ward, Upper Ninth Ward, and the Gentilly neighborhood. There is a racial component to the post-Katrina levee protection. Whether you are rich, poor, or middle class, if you are a black resident of New Orleans, you are less protected and you have received less increased flood protection from the federal government than if you live in the more white and affluent community of Lakeview.

Race has taken an unmeasured toll on the lives of minorities and the poor because institutionalized racism has influenced policy that discriminates in ways that serve the needs of the white and more affluent populations and communities. Katrina and its impacts, in a very powerful and revealing way, showed the world how race and class are intrinsically tied to policy. Moreover, it pointedly displayed how government policy can actually be harmful to the health and well-being of vulnerable populations (i.e., racial minorities, the poor, the sick, the elderly, and children).

The scenes of stranded New Orleanians trapped on the roof of the crumbling Superdome and images of children, the sick, and the elderly dying on the street outside the Superdome and the New Orleans Convention Center are visions tragically etched in our memory. What was painfully obvious to all watching was that policies for responding to disasters were woefully inadequate and needed to change.

What the New Orleans recovery process has showed is that policies intended to be race neutral can further devastate the most vulnerable populations, rather than alleviate the destruction caused by a disaster, if our policies are not race sensitive. This is especially true when race has been a determining factor in the disparate response to a disaster, as it was in New Orleans.

The city's new post-Katrina levee system will not provide the same level of protection for all of the city's residents. One need not be a rocket scientist to predict who is most likely to receive the least amount of protection or which communities are likely to be left behind and left vulnerable after the flood-proofing is completed—the same groups that were deserted environmentally and economically before the devastating storm.

In March of 2007, African Americans citizens of New Orleans have uncovered another initiative that completely excludes them. FEMA has created a Hazardous Mitigation Fund that provides millions of dollars to mitigate flooding in communities. Site selections are based partly on participation in the National Flood Protection Program. Most homeowners in the City of New Orleans in fact have flood insurance through that program. In fact, the City of New Orleans has a participation rate higher than the national average.

A second basis for receiving funds to mitigate hazards relies on policy decisions that result in the exclusion of neighborhoods by race and that are discriminatory. The number of claims submitted by neighborhoods for flooding is taken into consideration in allocating the funds. In New Orleans, Uptown neighborhoods where there were large concentrations of white homeowners before Katrina tended to flood every time there was a very hard rain. New Orleans East and the Lower Ninth Ward are much more vulnerable to hurricanes but rarely flooded when it rained before Katrina.

Consequently, FEMA Hazardous Mitigation Funds that were intended to help the populations most vulnerable to hurricanes will not go to the black neighborhoods of New Orleans. Once again, the program benefits the more affluent and white populations. What is being experienced in New Orleans is a "policy surge" more powerful than the storm surge, which could facilitate a permanent and systematic depopulation and displacement of New Orleans's African American communities.

## Policy Recommendations

After considering what happened in New Orleans in the wake of Katrina, we have several policy recommendations that could prevent the occurrence of similar delays and unfairness should a similar disaster strike New Orleans in the future. They include these:

- *Implement environmental justice.* Ensure equal funding, equal cleanup standards, and equal protection in implementing public health and environmental responses in minority and low-income communities. The EPA, FEMA, and the U.S. Army Corps of Engineers need to enforce Executive Order 12898, "Federal Actions to Address Environmental Justice in Minority Populations and Low-Income Populations" ensuring environmental justice in the cleanup and rebuilding of the hurricane-affected Gulf Coast region.
- *Enforce existing environmental and health standards.* Cleanup standards should not be weakened or compromised in low-income and minority neighborhoods. Allowing waivers of environmental standards can compound the harms already caused by Katrina and undermine the health protections afforded the most vulnerable members of our society.
- *Provide environmental guidance on comprehensive waste management.* Provide detailed guidance to state and local entities to help them develop a comprehensive waste management plan before and after disasters to better ensure that the public health and the environment are protected and to avoid the need for future Superfund sites. This guidance should address the selection of landfill sites for disaster debris, including advance selection of potential landfill sites, and practices to consider when making special accommodations for debris disposal in emergencies. Guidance should be put in place so that public health risks are minimized during the demolition and renovation of buildings containing asbestos, which can release asbestos fibers into the air. Currently, homes being demolished and renovated by or for individual homeowners are generally not subject to the EPA's asbestos emissions standards aimed at limiting releases of fibers into the air.
- *Conduct an environmental assessment.* Federal and state government agencies include additional sampling, assessment, and cleanup of toxic sites, establishing an effective process for debris and waste management, fully informing the public of health risks, and providing access to protective equipment and treatment, if necessary. The city should ensure that state and federal agencies continue to fully assess health risks for residents returning to contaminated areas before making any official declarations that it is safe for them to do so.
- *Conduct independent environmental testing and monitoring.* Because of the loss of trust in government, independent testing and monitoring of the water, soil, sediment, and air in the affected areas are needed and should use the

best testing technology and methods available. This testing must provide an assessment of current contamination levels, as well as continuous monitoring.

- *Remove contaminated sediments.* The city should immediately request that FEMA and the EPA remove contaminated sediment from New Orleans's communities and conduct further investigation and remediation of toxic hot spots.

- *Monitor the air and water.* There is a need for ongoing monitoring of the air and water quality in New Orleans. In many cases, data have not been updated since 2006, yet we know that there were documented problems with mold, endotoxin, heavy metals, particulate matter, and drinking water contamination. These findings need to be followed up to ensure that they have been resolved. The EPA should develop a plan for additional air monitoring and evaluate the number and location of the air monitors to ensure sufficient coverage of areas with substantial demolition and renovation activities, both regulated and unregulated. If air monitors are not appropriately located in neighborhoods undergoing demolition and renovation, the monitoring network will not be adequate to ensure that public health is being protected. While the EPA took steps to monitor asbestos after the hurricane—for example, more than doubling the number of ambient (outdoor) air monitors and monitoring emissions at debris reduction sites—monitors were not placed in areas undergoing substantial demolition and renovation, such as the Ninth Ward.

- *Provide residents access to treatment for exposure to toxins.* The city should demand that the federal Public Health Service and Agency for Toxic Substances Disease Registry provide ongoing medical care and testing to residents exposed to toxins, as required by the Comprehensive Environmental Response, Compensation and Liability Act (section 104(i)(1)).

- *Ensure safe and healthy schools for returning children.* Flood-damaged schools should be rebuilt in a manner that fully protects children's health. It is imperative that schools and the land on which they sit be safe, clean, and free from health-threatening contamination. Rebuilt schools should be LEED-certified and incorporate guidelines developed by the Collaborative for High Performance Schools for the design of energy-efficient, healthy, comfortable, well-lit schools. Care should be taken to make design, engineering, and materials choices that prevent mold from growing indoors. The city also should guarantee that soil on school grounds is clean and safe by making sure it is tested and cleaned to at least the level of the most protective cleanup guidelines in the country.

- *Balance green building and social justice.* Rebuilding efforts in the Gulf Coast region should adopt smart growth and green building principles to ensure that past environmental inequities are repaired along with the physical infra-structure. However, greenness and justice need to go together. Green building in New Orleans and elsewhere on the Gulf Coast could involve exorbitant fees for architects, materials, and construction—and greening that fails to address issues of affordability, access, and equity may open the floodgates for perma-nent displacement of low-income and minority homeowners and business owners.

- *Implement an environmental training and "green jobs" initiative.* Implement a comprehensive environmental cleanup, restoration, and "green jobs" training program for local residents who live in environmental "hot spot" areas.


## Conclusion

As the waters began to recede and the light of day was cast on the enormous, even unbelievable, extent of the damage to New Orleans and the rest of the Gulf Coast, speculation about whether the city would recover or die began to echo across the media. How extensive was the environmental contamina-tion? Had New Orleans become a Superfund site? Was it safe for residents to return? The inability of both federal and state agencies (the EPA, LDEQ, CDC, the Agency for Toxic Substances and Disease Registry) to effectively and accurately answer these questions created a quandary that both slowed the recovery and paralyzed the ability of citizens to make a decision about returning.

To date, the information made available on the environmental safety of residents in New Orleans has been nothing short of double talk. The EPA tells citizens that the city is safe, although its own test sampling says other-wise and is refuted by credible environmental scientists. Furthermore, after giving the city a clean bill of health, the EPA then provides instructions for parents to follow in order to keep their children safe when they play outside. LDEQ attempts to discredit citizen action groups when they organize their communities to work with labor unions, nonprofit organizations, and volun-teers to clean up their own neighborhoods. This schizophrenic response by government to what has been described as the largest environmental disaster this country has ever seen and as the "mother of all toxic cleanups" bears some of the responsibility for the slow recovery of the City of New Orleans.

We can only speculate on what progress could have been made toward rebuilding New Orleans and the return of most of its citizens if the environ-mental cleanup that was deserved had been done. What if the same attention to cleanup and safety paid to the French Quarter, the Central Business District, and the racetrack for horses had been paid to the Lower Ninth Ward, New Orleans East, and other hard-hit sections of the city?

Just after the storm, a story appeared in the *Dallas Morning News* that quoted the Army Corps of Engineers as saying that it would take the Corps three months to scrape the city clean of all contaminated soil and sediment. This, of course, did not happen. What did occur was politics as usual, and the losers were the citizens of New Orleans, with African Americans taking the biggest hit.

Residents of devastated New Orleans neighborhoods did not need government agencies debating the "chicken or egg" contamination argument ("which came first, the contamination or Katrina?"). They needed the government to clean up the mess. All levels of government had a golden opportunity to get it right this time. Cleanup and reconstruction efforts in New Orleans were shamefully sluggish and patchy, and the environmental injustice may be compounded by forcing residents to rebuild on poisoned ground.

The opportunities faded as Katrina slowly slipped off the political radar. It is no accident that not one word about Katrina and the Gulf Coast reconstruction was mentioned in President Bush's State of the Union address in January 2007—some seventeen months after the devastating storm. Displaced residents needed a "road home" program that was not only fair but also safe. It is immoral—and should be illegal—to unnecessarily subject Katrina survivors to contamination—whether the pollution was there before or after the storm.

Clearly, prevention and precaution should have been the driving force behind the environmental cleanup in post-Katrina New Orleans. Either we all pay now or we pay later. Delaying the cleanup will cost more in terms of dollars and ill health down the road. The nation cannot allow another immoral, unethical, and illegal "human experiment" to occur in New Orleans and the Gulf Coast. The solution is prevention.

# The Wrong Complexion
# for Protection

*Response to Toxic Contamination*

The federal Superfund program was created in 1980 when Congress enacted the Comprehensive Environmental Response, Compensation, and Liability Act (CERCLA). This law imposed a tax on the chemical and petroleum industries that went into a trust fund to be used for cleaning up abandoned or uncontrolled hazardous-waste sites and allowed the federal government to respond to releases or potential releases of hazardous wastes that might harm people or the environment. CERCLA was amended by the Superfund Amendments and Reauthorization Act (SARA) on October 17, 1986.

The Superfund program was designed to clean up the nation's uncontrolled hazardous-waste sites. Under the Superfund program, abandoned, accidentally spilled, or illegally dumped hazardous waste that poses a current or future threat to human health or the environment is cleaned up. This chapter examines how government responds to toxic contamination in African American communities and the health consequences for the residents of those communities.

## Legacy of Unequal Protection

In 1992, the *National Law Journal* uncovered glaring inequities in the way the U.S. Environmental Protection Agency enforces its Superfund laws. The authors wrote: "There is a racial divide in the way the U.S. government cleans up toxic-waste sites and punishes polluters. White communities see faster action, better results and stiffer penalties than communities where blacks, Hispanics and other minorities live. This unequal protection often occurs whether the community is wealthy or poor."[1]

These findings suggest that unequal protection is placing African Americans and other communities of color at a special risk. The *National Law Journal* study supplements the findings of earlier studies and reinforces what many grassroots leaders have known for generations: not only are black people differentially impacted by industrial pollution, but also they can expect different treatment from the government.[2]

In October 2009, environmental justice leaders representing more than a dozen environmentally impacted communities from six southern states (Alabama, Florida, Georgia, Mississippi, South Carolina, and Tennessee) met in Atlanta with EPA Region IV acting administrator A. Stanley Meiburg and senior staff. The meeting, convened by the Environmental Justice Resource Center, allowed leaders of impacted communities and their representatives to present documentation of environmental injustice, unequal protection, and failures on the part of EPA Region IV and state environmental agencies to protect the health and environment of communities that were home to African Americans and other people of color.[3] This was the first meeting of this type at Region IV in more than a decade.

The meeting between EPA officials and EJ leaders was held at the same time as and just a few blocks from the Centers for Disease Control and Prevention (CDC) National Environmental Public Health Conference—where thousands of federal, state, tribal, and local public and environmental health professionals, academic researchers, physicians, nurses, other health-care professionals, representatives from communities and organizations, and policy and decision makers were "exploring new research and innovative practice in ecosystems and public health, healthy places and communities, sustainability, public health and chemical exposures."

The CDC's National Center for Environmental Health (NCEH) and the Agency for Toxic Substances and Disease Registry (ATSDR), headed by Dr. Howard Frumkin, was the next target to which these environmentally impacted communities turned their attention. Many environmental justice leaders view ATSR and EPA Region IV as "evil twins" that have historically provided unequal protection and a "Katrina response" in response to toxic health threats to communities of low-income people and people of color long before that deadly storm ravaged the Gulf Coast. Ironically, it was NCEH/ATSDR's lethargic and inept response to the formaldehyde-laden FEMA trailers provided to homeless people after Hurricane Katrina that figured largely in getting Frumkin reassigned in 2010 to a position with less authority, a smaller staff, and a smaller budget. Frumkin, who inherited many of the problems noted in the report from previous ATSDR directors, had led the embattled agency since 2005.

A 2008 congressional report concluded that the failure of ATSDR's leadership "kept Hurricane Katrina and Rita families living in trailers with elevated levels of formaldehyde . . . for at least one year longer than necessary." In the wake of a congressional inquiry, the majority staff of the Subcommittee on Investigations and Oversight of the Committee on Science, Space, and Technology released a report in 2009 that revealed other cases in which the ATSDR had relied on scientifically flawed data, causing other federal agencies to mislead communities about the dangers they faced from exposure to hazardous substances.

African Americans and other people of color have long been suspicious of ATSDR. For the most part, they did not trust the agency. Now it's clear that these groups and others have good reason to be suspect of the agency's findings. People of color are not only disproportionately exposed to current chemicals from industrial polluters, and chemical plants in their neighborhoods, but also these same communities are the ones most frequently afflicted by legacy chemicals from many previous uses, for example in abandoned brownfield sites in their neighborhoods, and from multiple sources of lead that poisons their children. Numerous bad decisions have turned communities of far too many low-income people and people of color into "sacrifice zones" and toxic dumping grounds, lowering nearby residents' property values (thereby stealing their wealth) and exposing them to unnecessary environmental health risks.

Leaders from contaminated communities in October 2009 were hoping to communicate to the Obama administration the deadly impact of environmental racism and to make the elimination of environmental hazards in communities of low-income people and people of color a top priority for the EPA's new administrator, Lisa P. Jackson, the first African American to hold the post. The community leaders presented the Region IV acting administration with their own written reports and conveyed personal "horror stories" that highlighted the devastating impact of toxic contamination and of the EPA's flawed protection model that appears to value good relations with state environmental regulators over enforcing the laws, in many cases allowing polluters to walk away unpunished. All of the written reports were e-mailed to EPA headquarters in Washington.

The environmental justice leaders who came to Atlanta were part of the thirty-six environmental justice, civil rights, faith, academic, and legal groups from all eight Region IV states that signed a letter sent to Congressman John

Lewis, longtime civil rights and environmental justice advocate, requesting him to call for an Inspector General (OIG) or a U.S. General Accountability Office (GAO) investigation of EPA Region IV's treatment of African Americans and its poor track record on environmental justice. In November 2009, the EPA Office of the Inspector General began a preliminary investigation into the environmental justice complaints filed in Region IV. An OIG investigative review of the allegations found no evidence that EPA contracts, assistance agreements, or programs were involved or that an EPA employee had committed any actionable offenses.[4]

The EPA was created in December 1970 under President Richard M. Nixon. From the very beginning, EPA's ten regions were set up as nearly autonomous subagencies. Fundamental change is needed in the way EPA regions operate, especially those that cover states that have a legacy of slavery, Jim Crow segregation, and resistance to civil rights and equal environmental protection. It is not an accident that the modern civil rights movement and the environmental justice movement were both born in the South.

Historically, EPA regional administrators have served as a bridge between EPA headquarters and state and local governments. While on the surface this traditional role may be appealing to state and local government officials, who thus move the center of power and authority away from Washington, D.C., and to the regional offices, it has been a disaster for African Americans in the Deep South.

The nation got into this mess by allowing EPA's ten regions to operate as nearly autonomous subagencies and by letting "look-the-other-way" collusion with state environmental agencies rule the day. Many of the bad facility siting and permitting decisions have resulted directly from deals and compromises made between Region IV and state and local governments—often at the expense of and over the opposition of African American residents.

In 1974, for example, EPA Region IV nominated Sumter County, Alabama as a possible hazardous-waste landfill site. The county, located in the heart of Alabama's Black Belt, is 71.8 percent black. More than 35.9 percent of the county's population are below the poverty line. In 1977, Resource Industries, Inc., purchased a three-hundred-acre tract of land just outside Emelle, Alabama, more than 90 percent of whose residents are black. The permit for the facility was approved by the Alabama Department of Environmental Management (ADEM) and EPA Region IV over the opposition of local residents, who thought they were getting a brick factory. In 1978, Chemical Waste Management, a subsidiary of Waste Management, Inc., bought the permit from Resource Industries, Inc., and opened the nation's largest hazardous-waste landfill, often tagged the "Cadillac of dumps."[5]

Sumter County has a legacy of farming and cotton production dating back to the plantation system of slavery and the sharecropper tenant farming system that succeeded it. The hazardous-waste facility was lured to the predominately black county during a period when the residuals of Jim Crow segregation still ruled the day. Blacks did not hold public office or sit on bodies that govern the predominantly black county, including the state legislature, county commissions, and the industrial development board.

A 2009 *New York Times* headline, "Toxic Waters—Clean Water Laws Are Neglected, at a Cost in Suffering," is clear evidence that the traditional role of EPA's ten regions is a dismal failure.[6] Between 2004 and 2009, polluters violated federal clean water laws more than 500,000 times, with many violators escaping fines and punishment. About 60 percent of the polluters were deemed in "significant noncompliance," which translates into the most serious violations, like dumping cancer-causing chemicals. The *New York Times* research team discovered that 10 percent of Americans have been exposed to drinking water that contains dangerous chemicals or that fails to meet a federal health benchmark and that 40 percent of the nation's public water systems have violated the Safe Water Drinking Act at least once.

The lapse in enforcement is caused by EPA regional administrators averse to "risking their relationship" with the states. Many regional administrators are not that keen on ruffling the feathers of the industry they regulate—which are often big political campaign contributors. These relationships appear more important than the enforcement of environmental laws and the protection of public health.

Making families wait for clean water while the EPA, state, and local governments meet and debate the families' water contamination problem does little to foster residents' trust. Allowing polluters and violators of clean-water laws to escape punishment and to endanger the public should be a crime. The nation's clean-water laws should be enforced equally across the board—not selectively enforced on the basis of residents' income or a community's capacity to hire lawyers, experts, and scientists.

This slow response to environmental justice and civil rights complaints continued at EPA under the Obama administration. In September 2009, a three-judge panel on the Ninth U.S. Circuit Court of Appeals in San Francisco found widespread failure by EPA to investigate Title VI civil rights complaints.[7] A March 2011 report by Deloitte also criticized EPA's slow response in processing Title VI complaints.[8] And a December 2011 Center for Public Integrity report found the EPA neglected discrimination claims from polluted communities.

The following case studies offer a sampling of African American communities that have suffered from government collusion with state and industry officials in preventing the application of equal environmental and health protection. They are offered to illustrate the widespread occurrence of environmental racism and slow government response in the face of threats to the health and welfare of African Americans in the Deep South.

## Triana, Alabama

In 1980, Barbara Reynolds, in *National Wildlife*, described Triana, a small, all-black town in northern Alabama, as the "unhealthiest town in America."[9] Residents of this rural town of about one thousand people were tested by the Centers for Disease Control and were found to be contaminated with the pesticide DDT and the highly toxic industrial chemical PCB (polychlorinated biphenyl). Some of the residents were contaminated with the highest levels of DDT ever recorded in humans. The source of the PCBs was not determined.

The DDT was produced by Olin Chemical Company from 1947 to 1971 for the Redstone Arsenal Army missile base. DDT was banned in the United States in 1971. The manufacturing plant was torn down, and more than four thousand tons of DDT residues remained buried in the area and eventually worked their way into Indian Creek, a popular fishing place for Triana residents. Indian Creek is a tributary of the Tennessee River and is under the jurisdiction of the Tennessee Valley Authority (TVA).

While the elevated level of contamination of these black residents was documented as early as 1978, actions on the part of the U.S. Army Corps of Engineers or the federal government did not materialize until five years later. Triana residents wanted to know why the government kept this information from them. Clyde Foster, then mayor of Triana, spoke to this lack of concern and inaction on the part of government:

> I did not want a confrontation. I just wanted the scientific investigation to speak for itself. Why did the TVA suggest Triana be studied if DDT was not at all dangerous? How can it kill insects, fish, and birds and not be potentially harmful to people? I knew the stuff was real stable, that it stays in a body for years. Who knows what effects massive doses could have over a long period of time? The TVA has known about the presence of DDT in

the fish of Indian Creek for years, and I found later that the Army checked in 1977 and found a fish with one hundred times the safe DDT level. We received the TVA analysis of the fish from our freezers. Our fish had even higher DDT levels than those they had first tested. . . . Many of us eat its [Indian Creek's] fish every day. Already there is a hardship among the very poor people who customarily derive sustenance from the river. Our whole community is upset. We needed some help.[10]

It was not until Mayor Foster filed a class-action lawsuit in 1980 against Olin Chemical Company that the problems of these citizens were taken seriously.[11] After many delays and attempts to coopt the local citizens, the lawsuit was settled out of court in 1983 for $25 million. The settlement agreement had three main points. Olin Chemical Company agreed (1) to clean up residual chemicals, (2) to set aside $5 million to pay for the long-term medical surveillance and health care of Triana residents, and (3) to pay "cash-in-pocket" settlements to each resident. The legal claim against the federal government was withdrawn in order to make the settlement with Olin.

The tragedy at Triana is not an isolated incident. There are numerous other cases of poor, black, and powerless communities being victimized and ignored when it comes to the equitable enforcement of environmental quality standards. These disparities form the basis for the environmental justice movement.

### West Dallas, Texas

A lead smelter operated by the RSR Corporation poisoned the mostly African American and Latino West Dallas, Texas, neighborhood for more than five decades. The smelter was located next to an elementary school, a day care center, and a 3,500-unit public housing development. The housing project, which was built in the mid-1950s, was located just fifty feet from the sprawling West Dallas RSR lead smelter's property line and was in the direct path of the prevailing southerly winds.

During peak operation in the mid-1960s, the plant employed more than four hundred persons. The smelter pumped more than 269 tons of lead particles each year into the West Dallas air. Lead particles were blown by the prevailing winds through the doors and windows of nearby homes and onto the West Dallas streets, sidewalks, ballparks, and children's playgrounds. Few West Dallas residents can afford the luxury of air conditioners to contend with the long and hot Texas summers. People usually leave their windows open, sit underneath shade trees, or socialize outside on their porches to keep cool.[12]

In 1968, the City of Dallas enacted one of the strongest lead ordinances in the country. The ordinance prohibited the emission of lead compounds in excess of 5 ug/m3 (micrograms per cubic meter) over any thirty-day period and prohibited any particulate concentration greater than 100ug/m3. The ordinance, however, proved to be a worthless piece of legislation because city officials systematically refused to enforce its lead emission standards.

Dallas officials were informed as early as 1972 that lead was finding its way into the bloodstreams of the children who lived in the two minority neighborhoods (West Dallas and East Oak Cliff, near a smelter operated by Dixie Metals) near lead smelters.[13] The Dallas Health Department study found that living near the smelters was associated with a 36 percent increase in blood lead level. Children who lived near the smelters were exposed to elevated levels of lead in the soil and air and in their homes. The city was urged to restrict the emissions of lead to the atmosphere and to undertake a large screening program to determine the extent of the public health problem. The city failed to take immediate action on this matter.

After repeated violations of the lead ordinance, the city in 1974 sued the local smelters to force compliance. The suits were settled a year later after the companies agreed to pay fines of $35,000 and install pollution equipment. The city amended its lead ordinance in 1976, but the amended ordinance was much weaker than its 1968 predecessor. The new ordinance—like the old version—was not enforced consistently, while lead companies in Dallas chronically and repeatedly violated the law. The Dallas Alliance Environmental Task Force, a citizen group appointed by the Dallas City Council in 1983 to address the health concerns of West Dallas, highlighted this point in its study:

> We believe that the City has missed many opportunities to serve and protect the community-at-large and two neighborhoods in particular in relation to the lead problem we now address. It is clear that the state and Federal governments have also failed in their opportunities to regulate an industry of this type with regard to the general welfare of citizens.[14]

The EPA in 1978 established the National Ambient Air Quality Standard, setting a limit for airborne lead of an average of 1.5 micrograms per cubic meter of air in samples taken over a ninety-day period. Two years later, the EPA, concerned about health risks associated with the Dallas lead smelters, commissioned another lead screening program. A 1981 study confirmed what had basically been found a decade earlier. Children living near the lead smelters were likely to have greater lead concentrations in their blood than children who did not live near smelters. Soil-lead concentrations near the RSR smelter in West Dallas, for example, averaged nine times those in the control area, while the average near the Dixie Metals smelter in East Oak Cliff was thirteen times the norm.

Federal officials received the report in February 1981. The city and the two companies had the report three months later. West Dallas and East Oak Cliff residents, however, did not receive formal notification of the health risks associated with living so close to the lead smelters. It was not until June 1981 that the *Dallas Morning News* broke the headline-grabbing story of the "potentially dangerous" lead levels discovered by EPA researchers. The series of articles presented in the local newspaper on the lead contamination triggered widespread concern, public outrage, several class-action lawsuits, and legal action by the City of Dallas and the State of Texas against the smelter operators.

Soil levels found near the West Dallas Boys Club, located just a short distance from the three-hundred-foot smokestack of the RSR smelter, forced the directors to suspend outdoor activities. The first city-sponsored tests of soil at the Boys Club showed one sample that contained sixty times the level considered potentially dangerous to children. RSR voluntarily removed and replaced the soil at the Boys Club and at the nearby school. The West Dallas Boys Club, a program that enrolled more than 1,200 youths between the ages of six and twenty-eight, and the Maro Booth Day Care Center, a facility that served children from seventy-five low-income families, were later forced to close in 1983 because of the lead problem.

After publicity exposed the health threat, no immediate action was forthcoming from the EPA or the city to alleviate the lead contamination problem in West Dallas. Local opposition mounted against the company. At one meeting in the spring of 1983, more than 150 angry citizens packed a room in the George Loving Place public housing project to voice their opposition to a plan to move them out rather than close the lead smelter. Residents felt that their plight was being ignored because they were poor, black, and politically powerless. In an April 27, 1983, *Dallas Morning News* article, Patricia Spears, a homeowner, community leader, and operator of a West Dallas funeral home, summed up her community's dilemma: "If we lived in Highland Park or Northeast Dallas [affluent white areas], the lead plant would have been closed in 1981. Instead of them moving us, why don't they pull together and shut the lead plant down?"

It was later revealed in the March 1983 hearings conducted by U.S. Representative Elliot H. Levitas (D-Ga.) that former EPA Deputy Administrator John Hernandez had needlessly scrapped a voluntary plan by RSR to clean up the lead-contaminated "hot spots" in West Dallas. Hernandez blocked the cleanup and called for yet another round of tests to be designed and conducted by the Centers for Disease Control (CDC) with the EPA and the Dallas Health Department. The results of this study were available in February 1983. Although the new study showed a lower percentage of children affected than the earlier study had shown, it established the smelter as the dominant source of elevated lead in the children's blood.[15] The smelter ceased operation in 1984.

Nearly a decade passed before the neighborhood was declared a Superfund site in 1993. Covering some 13.6 square miles and with a population of approximately seventeen thousand persons, the RSR Superfund Study Area was one of the nation's largest Superfund sites. Although three government studies, dating back to 1972, documented the lead smelter as presenting a health risk to children in West Dallas, it was not until September 2004 that EPA completed cleanup activities in West Dallas and eliminated the sources of RSR smelter contamination from the community.[16]

Government officials allowed West Dallas residents, and especially children, to be harmed by lead for more than two decades after the source of the problem was pinpointed. Again, one must ask why it took so long for the government to act. Would the government have responded quicker if children in mostly white affluent North Dallas were being poisoned?

## Warren County, North Carolina

In December 2003, after waiting more than two decades, an environmental justice victory finally came to the residents of predominately black Warren County, North Carolina. Since 1982, county residents had lived with the legacy of a 142-acre toxic-waste dump. Detoxification work began on the dump in June 2001, and the last cleanup work ended late in December 2003. In the process, state and federal sources spent $18 million to detoxify or neutralize contaminated soil stored at the Warren County PCB (polychlorinated biphenyl) landfill, owned by the North Carolina Department of Environment and Natural Resources (DENR) and located about sixty miles northeast of Raleigh off North Carolina SR 1604 and U.S. Highway 401.[17] A private contractor hired by the state dug up and burned 81,500 tons of oil-laced soil in a kiln that reached more than eight hundred degrees Fahrenheit to remove the PCBs. The soil was then put back in a football-field size pit, re-covered to form a mound, graded, and seeded with grass.

Local Warren County environmental justice leaders and their allies across the state deserve a gold medal for not giving up the long fight and for pressuring government officials to keep their promise and clean up the mess they had created. This was no small win, given state deficits, budget cuts, and past broken promises. Residents and officials were left to grapple with what to do with the site.

The sign at the entrance to the fenced in Warren County PCB landfill in 2003 read, "PCB Landfill—No Trespassing." Clearly, a sign reading "Justice Delayed Is Justice Denied" might be more appropriate to post at the entrance to the site. The toxic-waste dump was forced on the tiny Afton community—more than 84 percent of which was black in 1982—helping trigger the national environmental justice movement. While the "midnight dumpers" were fined and jailed, the innocent Afton community was handed a twenty-year sentence of living in a toxic-waste prison.

The PCB landfill later became the most recognized symbol in the county. Despite the stigma, Warren County also became a symbol of the environmental justice movement. Warren County residents pleaded for a permanent solution, rather than a cheap "quick fix" that would eventually end up with the PCBs leaking into the groundwater and wells. Their voices fell on deaf ears. State and federal officials chose to build a landfill, the cheap way out. By 1993, the landfill was failing, and for a decade community leaders pressed the state to decontaminate the site.

Residents of Warren County were searching for guarantees that the government was not creating a future Superfund site that would threaten nearby residents. North Carolina state officials and federal EPA officials could give no guarantees, since there is no such thing as a 100-percent-safe hazardous-waste landfill, one that will not eventually leak. It all boiled down to trust. Can communities really trust government (state and federal) to do the right thing? Recent history and hundreds of books are filled with case studies of government deception and "whitewashing" real threats to public health.

Even after the landfill was detoxified, some Warren County residents still questioned the completeness of the cleanup, especially contamination that may have migrated beyond the three-acre landfill site into the 137-acre buffer zone that surrounds the landfill and the nearby creek and outlet basin. PCBs are persistent, bioaccumulative, and toxic pollutants (PBTs). That is, they are highly toxic, long-lasting substances that can build up in the food chain to levels that are harmful to human and ecosystem health. PCBs are not something most Americans would want to have next door. They are probable human carcinogens, cause developmental effects such as low birth weight, and disrupt hormone function.

Warren County is located in Eastern North Carolina, and it is vulnerable to a "quadruple whammy" of being mostly black, poor, rural, and politically powerless. The county had a population of 16,232 in 1980. Blacks made up 63.7 percent of the county population and 24.2 percent of the state population in 1980.The county continues to be economically worse off than the state as a whole on all major social indicators. Per capita income for Warren County residents was $6,984 in 1982, whereas the state per capita income was $9,283. Warren County residents thus earned about 75 percent of the state per capita income.

The county ranked ninety-second out of one hundred counties in median family income in 1980.The economic gap between Warren County and the rest of the state actually widened during the 1990s. Warren County per capita income ranked ninety-eighth in 1990 and ninety-ninth in 2001. According to U.S. Census Bureau statistics, one fourth of Warren County residents and more than a third of children (those under eighteen years of age) live in poverty, although the state's poverty rate for children is 20.8 percent.

It is important that the state finally detoxified the Warren County PCB landfill—a problem it had created for local residents. This was a major victory for local residents and for the environmental justice movement. However, it was also important that the surrounding land area and local community be made environmentally whole. Detoxifying the landfill did not bring the community back to its pre-1982 PCB-free environmental condition. Soil that contains low levels of PCBs remained buried at least fifteen feet below the surface in the dump.

Government officials claimed the site was safe and suitable for reuse. However, none of them lived next door to the dump. While there remained some questions about suitable reuse of the site, there was no evidence that the land had been brought back to its pre-1982 condition—where homes with deep basements could have been built and occupied and backyard vegetables gardens grown with little worry about toxic contamination or safety.

The placement of the PCB landfill in Afton is a textbook case of environmental racism. Around the world, environmental racism is defined as a human rights violation. Strong and persuasive arguments have been made for reparations as a remedy for serious human rights abuse. Under traditional human rights law and policy, we expect governments that practice or tolerate racial discrimination to acknowledge and end this practice and to compensate the victims. Environmental remediation is *not* reparations. No reparations have been paid for the two decades of economic loss, psychological damage, and mental anguish suffered by the Warren County residents.

Justice will not be complete until the twenty thousand Warren County residents receive a public apology and some form of financial reparations from the perpetrators of environmental racism against the local citizens. How much reparations should be paid is problematic, since it is difficult for anyone to put a price tag on peace of mind. At a minimum, Warren County residents should be paid reparations equal to the cost of detoxifying the landfill site, or $18 million. Another reparations formula might include a payment of a minimum of $1 million a year for every year the mostly black Afton community hosted the PCB-landfill, or $21 million. Some people may think the idea of paying reparations or monetary damages a bit farfetched. However, until the impacted community is made whole, the PCB landfill detoxification victory won by the tenacity and perseverance of Warren County residents will remain incomplete.

When it comes to enforcing the rights of poor people and people of color in the United States, government officials often look the other way. Too often, they must be prodded to enforce environmental and civil rights laws and regulations without regard to race, color, national origin, or socioeconomic (class) background. Laws, regulations, and executive orders are only as good as their enforcement. Unequal enforcement has left a gaping hole in the environmental protection afforded many communities of poor people and people of color. Waiting for government to act is a recipe for disaster.

### Agriculture Street Landfill, New Orleans

Dozens of toxic time bombs along Louisiana's Mississippi River Industrial Corridor, the eighty-five-mile stretch from Baton Rouge to New Orleans, made the region a major environmental justice battleground in the 1990s and early 2000s. The corridor is commonly referred to as "Cancer Alley." For decades, black communities all along the petrochemical corridor have been fighting against environmental racism and demanding relocation from polluting facilities.[18]

Two mostly black New Orleans subdivisions, Gordon Plaza and Press Park, have special significance for those interested in environmental justice and emergency response. Both subdivisions were built on land that was part of a municipal landfill for more than fifty years. The Agriculture Street landfill, covering approximately 190 acres, was used as a city dump as early as

1910. After 1950, the landfill was mostly used to discard large solid objects, including trees and lumber. The landfill was a major source for dumping debris from the very destructive Hurricane Betsy, which struck New Orleans in 1965. It is important to note that the landfill was classified as a solid-waste site and not as a hazardous-waste site.

In 1969, the federal government created a home ownership program to encourage lower-income families to purchase their first home. Press Park was the first subsidized housing project to be built in New Orleans under this program. The federal program allowed tenants to apply 30 percent of their monthly rental payments toward the purchase of a family home. In 1987, seventeen years later, the first sale was completed. In 1977, construction began on a second subdivision, Gordon Plaza. This development was planned, controlled, and constructed by the U.S. Department of Housing and Urban Development (HUD) and the Housing Authority of New Orleans (HANO). Gordon Plaza consists of approximately sixty-seven single-family homes.

In 1983, the Orleans Parish School Board purchased a portion of the Agriculture Street landfill site for a school. The fact that this site had previously been used as a municipal dump prompted concerns about the suitability of the site for a school. The board contracted with engineering companies to survey the site and assess it for contamination of hazardous materials, and the companies detected heavy metals and organics at the site.

In May 1986, the EPA performed a site inspection (SI) in the Agriculture Street landfill community. Although lead, zinc, mercury, cadmium, and arsenic were found at the site, according to the Hazard Ranking System (HRS) model used at that time, the score of three was not high enough to place the site on the National Priority list. Despite the warnings, Moton Elementary School, an $8 million state-of-the-art public school, opened with 421 students in 1989.

On December 14, 1990, the EPA published a revised HRS model in response to the Superfund Amendment and Reauthorization Act (SARA) of 1986. Upon the request of community leaders, in September 1993, an Expanded Site Inspection (ESI) was conducted. On December 16, 1994, the Agriculture Street landfill community was placed on the National Priorities List (NPL) with a new score of fifty.

The Agriculture Street landfill community is home to approximately nine hundred African American residents. The average family income is $25,000, and the educational level is high school graduate and above. The community pushed for a buyout of their property and asked to be relocated. However, this was not the resolution chosen by the EPA. A cleanup was ordered at a cost of $20 million, although the community buyout would have cost only $14 million. The actual cleanup began in 1998 and was completed in 2001.[19]

Disagreeing with the EPA's cleanup plans, the Concerned Citizens of Agriculture Street Landfill filed a class-action suit against the City of New Orleans for damages and the cost of relocation. In 2002, the EPA sued the city and several companies that owned or operated portions of the landfill where hazardous material was found to recoup the $20 million it had spent on cleanup. The case was settled in federal court in a May 2008 consent decree that called for the city to maintain a synthetic liner and a soil cap over the site. The city was not required to pay any cleanup costs or civil penalties after the court determined that New Orleans could not afford to pay any part of the settlement because of the "extraordinary financial difficulties" it faced after Hurricane Katrina.[20] As far back as 2005, CFI, Inc., and its parent company, IPC, Inc., had already agreed to pay $1.75 million plus interest as part of the settlement, and BFI Waste Systems of North America, Inc., had agreed to pay $335,000 plus interest. The U.S. Department of Justice reached tentative settlement agreements with Delta By-Products, Inc., and Edward Levy Metal, Inc.[21]

The settlement between the EPA and the city had no impact on the Agricultural Street landfill class action lawsuit judgment issued by Civil District Court Judge Nadine Ramsey. In 2006, Judge Ramsey ruled in favor of the residents, declaring the neighborhood "unreasonably dangerous" and "uninhabitable." The judge order HANO, the city, and the insurers to pay fair market value, plus $4,000 to $50,000 for emotional distress, to each community resident, depending on how long the resident had lived in the neighborhood before contamination was found in 1993.The ruling was appealed, and, in January 2008, Louisiana's Fourth Circuit Court of Appeals largely upheld Judge Ramsey's ruling. However, it cut the emotional stress awards in half.[22] The case has been beset by a number of legal maneuverings by the defendants that have resulted in delays on final settlement payments. There also has been a series of judges who have recused themselves from the case or have been removed from the case due to conflicts of interest noted by the court. As 2011 ended, none of the plaintiffs had been paid by the City of New Orleans, HANO, and the New Orleans Public School Board.

Nearly one year after Hurricane Katrina and the levee breach flooded 80 percent of New Orleans, the EPA gave the city a clean bill of health. There was one glaring exception—the Ninth Ward Agricultural Street landfill neighborhood. EPA scientists discovered cancer-causing benzo(a)pyrene in residents' yards at levels fifty times the normal level. No new cleanup was in the works. Yet, FEMA trailers were supplied to residents in the contaminated area. These same residents later learned that the FEMA trailers themselves posed a health hazard from deadly formaldehyde fumes.[23]

When Agriculture Street homeowners applied under Louisiana's $10.3 billion Road Home program to rebuild their homes, they were flatly refused funds. Residents were told that their applications were put on hold indefinitely because they lived on a Superfund cleanup site. HUD, the federal agency that financed and guaranteed loans in the neighborhood, also took the position that none of its money could be used to purchase contaminated land.[24] Road Home officials later placed former residents of the landfill neighborhood back in the Road Home pipeline for consideration pending the drafting policies for Superfund neighborhoods. Homeowners would have the option of having their Road Home grants calculated on the basis of a regular rebuilding grant, but they would also be allowed to use the money to relocate.

In July 2008, after nearly fifteen years of struggle, the Louisiana Supreme Court handed a legal victory to some eight thousand Agriculture Street residents who had sued the City of New Orleans, its public housing authority, and its school board for putting their homes and school on a toxic-waste dump without warning them. As noted earlier, in a five-to-two vote, the Louisiana Supreme Court upheld the 2006 ruling by Judge Ramsey.[25]

## Texarkana, Texas

Texarkana is a twin city that straddles the Texas-Arkansas state line. In 1990, the population of the Texas side of the city was 31,656, of which about a third were African Americans. Jim Crow shaped residential patterns. Carver Terrace was one of the few neighborhoods where upwardly mobile middle-income African Americans could own homes in racially segregated Texarkana. The all-black Carver Terrace neighborhood was built on a one-hundred-year flood plain and on an old wood treating site with the full knowledge of city officials.

Koppers Company, a wood-treating company, operated on the site until 1961. Carver Terrace was built in the 1960s and served as "strivers row" (a residential enclave for upwardly mobile middle-class families) for the seventy-nine African American homeowners, who included teachers, ministers, mail carriers, and factory workers. Over the years, residents' homes had been flooded repeatedly. In 1980, the State of Texas discovered that the soil and groundwater were contaminated with chemicals commonly used in wood preserving: pentachlorophenol (PCP), arsenic, and creosote. The neighborhood became a Superfund site in 1984,[26] and a health assessment was conducted at the site that same year.

The EPA concluded that the Koppers Superfund site posed a "potential risk to humans resulting from possible exposure to hazardous substances concentrations that may result in adverse health effects."[27] Clean soil and sod were placed in some of the yards. The EPA made a Record of Decision (ROD) in 1988 that called for a cleanup of the community. Residents were instructed not to let their children play outside and not to dig in their yards or eat food from their gardens. Some of the residents were not satisfied with the EPA's handling of the contamination problem and turned to their local congresspersons. In fact, it took a congressional act for Carver Terrace residents to be heard. The EPA was mandated by Congress to amend its 1988 ROD on the site and to buy out and relocate the affected residents.

The EPA contracted with the U.S. Army Corps of Engineers (COE) to handle the $5 million federal buyout. On April 23, 1991, COE official Richard O. Murray, chief of the Real Estate Division, mailed letters to Carver Terrace residents informing them of the buyout. Some residents were confused, and many were intimidated by the content and tone of the letters and by subsequent visits from COE officials who explained the property appraisals. In an April 23, 1991, letter to homeowner Nathaniel and Patsy Oliver, Richard O. Murray, Department of Army, Fort Worth District, Corps of Engineers, wrote these troubling words:

> Your property is being acquired on behalf of the EPA. If we are unable to negotiate a direct purchase from you, it will be necessary to acquire the property through condemnation proceedings. This information is not to be considered a threat, but in our opinion, it is necessary that we provide it to you so that you are fully informed of the laws and procedure applicable to this acquisition program. Please be assured that we will make every effort to negotiate a fair settlement with you. Should it be necessary to acquire your property through condemnation proceedings, the property will be reappraised. The Department of Justice, who will represent the United States, has directed that the reappraisal be based on the value of the property in its actual condition, which would necessitate consideration of the fact that the property is located within an environmentally unsafe area. This, in all probability, would lower the appraised value of your property.

In June 25, 1992, a "citizen accountability hearing" was held at which EPA and COE officials were queried about the language and origin of the controversial statements in the letter. The hearing panel was made up of representatives from the Southwest Organizing Project, the National Association for the Advancement of Colored People's Legal Defense Fund, the Panos Institute, and the Texas Network. A COE representative informed the panel that "an official from the Justice Department" had insisted that the paragraph be included. The government representatives have been unable to determine which Justice Department official authorized the statement.

In addition to being threatening, insensitive, and racist, the COE letter failed to grasp the sociohistorical significance of a community like Carver Terrace. Because of institutional racism, housing and residential options were more restrictive for Texarkana's African American residents than for their white counterparts.

These problems were compounded by the fact that many of the Carver Terrace residents were elderly, retired, disabled, or living on fixed incomes. After enjoying nearly three decades of home ownership, which is still an integral part of the American dream, many Carver Terrace residents were being involuntarily uprooted from their homes, social institutions, and community and dispersed throughout the greater Texarkana area.

Some of the residents asked to be relocated as a community. This proposal was rejected by the COE. The $5 million government buyout had no provisions for compensating the residents for the "loss of community." The federal buyout turned some of the owners into renters, push some of the residents back into Texarkana's ghetto, and otherwise worsened the economic conditions and overall quality of life (mental health and psychological well-being) for some individuals who thought they had planned for their retirement in a safe, quiet neighborhood near family and friends.

The last residents in Carver Terrace signed an agreement to sell their homes on August 6, 1992. Once the residents were relocated from the contaminated community, the COE and the EPA had no further contact with them. However, the trauma of the move may well have manifested itself six months, a year, or even longer after COE and EPA officials closed the files on the Koppers Superfund sites.

The federal government is mandated to provide a resident with "comparable" housing under the Uniform Relocation Act. Since Carver Terrace was the premier African American neighborhood in the city, which neighborhoods were the residents able to secure comparable housing? How did they cope with the move and with their new physical surroundings?

A community is more than merely houses and yards; it is made up of homes, families, neighbors, friends, churches, civic clubs, and other social institutions. What government body will protect residents of unincorporated communities, many of whom are often members of the most vulnerable groups in society—the elderly, the disabled, and persons living on fixed incomes? Will these individuals and families become environmental refugees? It is fairly safe to assume that neither government nor industry buyouts should worsen residents' situations after their move. The results (and mistakes) from these buyouts will likely have broad implications for future grassroots organizing and environmental education campaigns in the South and in other regions of the country.

Clearly, the time is long overdue for the United States to provide equal protection for all Americans—in their homes, workplaces, and playgrounds—and places (whether rural, urban, suburban, reservations, or other).Environmental justice and pollution prevention must become overarching principles of environmental protection if existing inequities are to be eliminated.

## "Mount Dioxin," Pensacola, Florida

The Escambia Treating Company (ETC) Superfund site is located in a mixed industrial and residential area in north central Pensacola, Florida. The company operated from 1943 to 1982, using creosote and pentachlorophenol (PCP) to treat wood for use as utility poles and foundation pilings. Few environmental precautions were taken. Wastes were placed in an unlined landfill, in an unlined containment pond, and in unlabeled drums.

The EPA data confirm that dangerous levels of dioxins migrated from the landfill into some residents' yards. The elevation of the site, which is more than sixty feet above much of downtown Pensacola, and conditions during the plant's operation suggest that storm water runoff often carried contaminants well beyond the closest residential neighborhoods.

Ceasing operations in 1982, the plant was abandoned and left in disarray. The plant had leaking drums, a lab full of broken equipment and open containers, an overturned electrical transformer, and crumbling asbestos insulation around a boiler. It also left soil, sludge, and groundwater contamination from forty years of wood-preserving activities. By the mid-1980s, the extent of the contamination had become obvious, and the site was abandoned through bankruptcy in 1991.

In October 1991, the EPA excavated 225,000 cubic yards of soil contaminated with dioxins, one of the most dangerous compounds ever made, and stockpiled it under a plastic cover on-site in the neighborhood. The Escambia Wood Treating site was dubbed "Mount Dioxin" because of the sixty-foot high mound of contaminated soil dug up from the neighborhood. Some fifty people in the community of only 358 families died of cancer between 1991 and 1997.[28] Margaret Williams, at the time a seventy-three-year-old retired Pensacola schoolteacher, led a five-year campaign to have her community relocated to a site away from the environmental and health hazards posed by the nation's third largest Superfund site. She led Citizens Against Toxic Exposure (CATE), a neighborhood organization formed to win relocation, into battle with EPA officials, who first proposed to move only the sixty households most affected by the site. After prodding from CATE, EPA then added thirty-five more households to the list, for a total cost of $7.54 million. The original government plan called for 257 households, including an apartment complex, to be left out. CATE refused to accept any relocation plan unless everyone was moved. The partial relocation was tantamount to partial justice.

CATE took its campaign on the road to EPA's National Environmental Justice Advisory Council (NEJAC). The group was successful in getting EPA's NEJAC Waste Subcommittee to hold a Superfund Relocation Roundtable in Pensacola. At this meeting, CATE's total neighborhood relocation plan won the backing of more than one hundred grassroots organizations. EPA nominated the Escambia Wood Treating Superfund site as the country's first pilot program to help the agency develop a nationally consistent relocation policy that would consider not only toxic levels but also welfare issues, such as property values, quality of life, health, and safety.

On October 3, 1996, EPA officials agreed to move all 358 households from the site at an estimated cost of $18 million. EPA officials deemed the mass relocation "cost efficient" after city planners decided to redevelop the area for light industry, rather than clean the site to residential standards.[29] This decision marked the first time that an African American community had been relocated under EPA's Superfund program, and it was hailed as a landmark victory for environmental justice.

The Escambia relocation was the third largest Superfund relocation in U.S. history. The relocation was completed in 2001.The abandoned homes were finally demolished in November 2003. The demolition project was funded by the Escambia County Commission and the City of Pensacola, with assistance from the Army Corps of Engineers, the U.S. Environmental Protection Agency, and the Florida Department of Environmental Protection.[30]

## DeBerry, Texas

A July 2006 *New York Times* article detailed what many environmental justice advocates have known for decades.[31] It described a clear racial divide in the way government responds to toxic contamination in blacks and whites communities. This sad state of unequal environmental protection was typified by what happened in DeBerry, a small black community in East Texas. The case involves Frank and Earnestene Roberson and their relatives who lived on County Road 329 in a historically black enclave in the East Texas oilfields. The Roberson family is descended from a black settler, George Adams, who bought forty acres and a mule for $289 there in 1911. In the 1920s, oil was discovered in the area, and DeBerry enjoyed a brief boom.

The families suspect that their wells were poisoned by a deep injection well for saltwater wastes from drilling operations that began around 1980. Years before the saltwater injection wells were constructed, cool water flowed from wells drilled into the ground and through the pipes inside the families' homes. By 2005, the seven families along County Road 329 in Panola County could not drink their well water because various levels of methyl tertiary butyl ether (MTBE), benzene, petroleum hydrocarbons, arsenic, lead, barium, cadmium, mercury, fecal coliform, and E. coli were detected in multiple samples. Their water was unsafe for domestic use.[32]

Because of the contamination, some families were forced to drive twenty-three miles to a Wal-Mart near Shreveport for clean water. Other family members depended upon visits from the Music Mountain truck for water delivery, which cost about $40 a month. The closest public water systems within reach of the County Road 329 are about just five hundred yards to the east and serve Spring Ridge and Keithville. The Panola-Bethany Water System is about 1.5 miles to the west and serves lines on both sides of the Texas-Louisiana state line.

In August 2005, free drinking water was delivered weekly in five-gallon containers to residents' homes, compliments of the Environmental Protection Agency Region VI Emergency Response, located in Dallas, and the Texas Commission of Environmental Quality.[33]

The Roberson family first complained about spillover from the Basic Energy Services' injection well to the Texas Railroad Commission back in 1987. Nearly a decade later, in 1996, the railroad commission took samples and found "no contamination in the Robersons' household supply water that can be attributed to oilfield sources." Basic Energy Services, a Midland, Texas-based oil- and gas-producing company, is the nation's third largest well-servicing contractor.

In 2003, the railroad commission tests found benzene, barium, arsenic, cadmium, lead, and mercury in the wells at concentrations exceeding primary drinking water standards. In October 2003, after a second round of well testing showed high levels of hazardous chemicals, the Railroad Commission sent letters to affected residents advising them that their water contained material "that may pose adverse health effects. We do not recommend that it be used for any domestic purposes."

Still, no government cleanup actions were taken to protect the Robersons and other black families in the community. In June 2006, the Roberson family filed suit in federal court, accusing the Texas Railroad Commission, which regulates the state's oil and gas industry, of failing to enforce safety regulations and of "intentionally giving citizens false information based on their race and economic status."

The Robersons pointed to the slow government response to the toxic contamination in their mostly black community and to the rapid cleanup response in 2004 by the railroad commission in Manvel, a largely white suburb of Houston. One need not be a NASA scientist to see the racial disparity.

The site was closed only after the Panola County District Attorney discovered that a pipe for waste runoff had been illegally drilled under the country road. Because the site sits on an incline, it seems logical that runoff would go downhill and into the Reverend David Hudson's and his neighbors' homes. Because of this, the Reverend Hudson, the Robersons' nephew and a retired California radio and television station manager, waged a one-man crusade to get justice for his community.

Tests performed in April 2004 on wells on the disposal site and at Hudson's home detected levels of dichloromethane (DME), which is a colorless organic liquid often used as a paint remover, industry solvent, and cleaning agent. Residents' wells and a nearby spring had an oil sheen and odor. Ron Kitchens, executive director of the Texas Railroad Commission, agreed that the families' wells were contaminated, but he stopped short of saying the contamination was from oil and gas operations. While there was a general consensus that the residents' wells were fouled, no one was willing to finger the culprit.[34] Basic Energy's monitoring wells at the disposal site and the neighborhood spring registered nearly identical concentrations of barium and chloride. Someone wrote in the margin, "interesting coincidence," on a CEQ document reviewing Basic Energy's test results.

According to a 2004 report by the Texas Groundwater Protection Com-mittee, of which the RRC is a member, since 1989, of the 230 closed cases of groundwater contamination related to oilfield operations in Texas, 222 were linked to commercial saltwater-disposal wells. *Shreveport Times* reporter Lisa Sorg[35] contrasted distinctions on how Louisiana and Texas handle salt-water disposal:

> In Louisiana, commercial saltwater-disposal wells are considered hazard-ous enough that state regulations prohibit their property boundaries to be within 500 feet of a residence, church, or school. But in Texas, there are no such regulations, although local governments can pass ordinances to restrict their use. Panola County has passed no such law, and the property boundary of the Basic well is within 300 feet of the church and two homes. All the houses on CR 329 are within 700 feet of the disposal-well property.

It is cheaper for energy companies to haul their waste to East Texas where, thanks to laxer rules, the wells are abundant. Hudson and his neighbors sought relief from the Railroad Commission, the Texas Commission of Envi-ronmental Quality, and the Environmental Protection Agency. In January 2005, the Railroad Commission canceled the company's permit. In April, Basic Energy plugged the wells, removed the tanks, and plugged lines with cement. A July 6, 2006, memorandum from the EPA Office of the Inspector General presented its preliminary findings on the Basic Energy site.[36] The EPA's OIG found that "neither EPA nor the State has a plan to permanently provide safe drinking water for the affected community, to fully assess the contamination and implement remedial measures to ensure the protection of human health, or to remediate the effect on the environment" and noted that, "As overseer, EPA has not ensured that the State's efforts were sufficient. EPA has not carried out its enforcement responsibilities as outlined in the Safe Drinking Water Act and applicable Code of Federal Regulation to pro-tect human health and the environment."

Hudson and his neighbors' civil lawsuit against Basic Energy Services was settled out of court in June 2006. A federal judge dismissed part of the resi-dents' lawsuit. In September 2007, the OIG completed its final report, *Com-plete Assessment Needed to Ensure Rural Texas Community Has Safe Drinking Water*, which confirmed that the groundwater in the community was con-taminated and should not be used for domestic purposes (U.S. Environmen-tal Protection Agency 2007). However, it did not determine the source of the groundwater contamination. The OIG report cost taxpayers $375,251. The cost for the RRC to drill a monitoring well in 2008 was $45,000 (they have drilled a total of twelve at the time). In comparison, the original cost to connect residents who lived on County Road 329 to a public water supply system only a mile and half away was only $60,000.

In February 2007, the EPA did not link the contamination to the abandoned injection well. It determined that the private water wells of Hudson and his neighbors who brought the lawsuit tested positive only for fecal coliform and placed the blame for that contamination on surface water carrying contaminates from septic systems and possible oilfield spills, not from the Basic Energy Services operations. However, the natural springs and monitoring wells were found to be contaminated with metals and radionuclides at levels that exceed those considered safe for drinking water. The radionuclides include materials such as barium, cadmium, and beryllium, which are by-products of oil and gas production.

In June 2008, EPA Region VI announced that fresh water finally would be coming to DeBerry residents.[37] After the water lines were installed, families were responsible for installing service lines to their homes and water meters. Residents viewed the decision as a partial victory, since toxic contamination remained in their community. The families continued to bathe in the contaminated water because they had no other options, given their limited means. The families were hooked up to the public water system in 2009.

## Athens, Georgia

In 1990, the City of Athens and the *County* of Clarke merged to form the *unified government* of Athens-Clarke County. The Athens-Clark County Municipal Solid Waste Landfill was sited in 1976 on Highway 78 in the middle of Athens's historically black Dunlap Road community and next door to the homestead of the African American Nash family, whose family landholdings in the community date back more than one hundred years. For decades, Dunlap Road residents grew their gardens and enjoyed a peaceful life in their rural Athens neighborhood. For the most part, they were left alone. Although the Dunlap Road community received few city and County services, such as paved streets, street lights, bus service, sewer and water lines under Jim Crow segregation, the resident had little fear that their wells would be contaminated or their water poisoned with dangerous chemicals.

This all changed once the landfill was forced on the community. Residents' property values were lowered by their unwanted landfill neighbor.They could no longer have outdoor BBQ events and family reunion picnics because of the odor and dust from the landfill and from truck traffic. Their once quiet, close-knit community was trashed by their own government—the same government to which they paid property taxes.

In 1988, contamination was detected at the unlined landfill, and a $7 million cleanup was performed to bring it up to the new state environmental protection standards. The landfill contaminated the groundwater with deadly chemicals, including vinyl chloride (at levels that exceeded the reportable quantity of one pound of release, volatile organic compounds, pesticides, and heavy metals—all linked to adverse health effects.[38]

Some Dunlap Road residents were provided access to the county water system to prevent their having to drink and bathe in contaminated well water.[39] In March 2001, more than four acres of a twenty-five-acre tract owned by the Nash family—land that had been in the Nash family for more than a century—were condemned and seized by the Athens-Clark County government under eminent domain to buffer them from the contaminated groundwater plumes. As late as May 2008, when the community held its "Walk for Awareness" event, some Dunlap Road residents were still on well water—even though groundwater contamination had been found in the area. For many, the delay was a result of their limited incomes and their inability to afford the water hookup costs required to run lines from the main to their homes.

In December 2007, county commissioners proposed expanding the landfill, despite the language of a 1992 agreement, signed by Gwen O'Looney, then Athens-Clarke CEO, and W. A. Bryant, at the time the Oglethorpe County Commission chairman, as well as by three representatives of an ad hoc citizens committee. A sentence in the "Long Range Use of Landfill," reads, "There shall be no expansion onto adjacent or contiguous properties for the purposes of landfill operations." The landfill, which straddles the Clarke-Oglethorpe county line, had three to five years of space left, and the expansion would add about twenty-five to thirty years to its life.[40]

The 1992 agreement was unenforceable since, under Georgia law, commissions are prohibited from binding other, future commissions made up of different members. The agreement was based on the assumption that a regional landfill would be built, but that effort failed in 1998 after a NIMBY (Not in My Back Yard) outcry from white residents living near twenty-five proposed landfill sites.[41] The compromise was to burden the Dunlap Road community with an expanded landfill facility for another three decades.

The expansion would add seventy-nine acres in Oglethorpe County at the current site of the now four-hundred-acre landfill.[42] However, there was no discussion with the Dunlap Road community about what a landfill expansion would look like, how it would proceed, or what would be done to protect the surrounding communities.[43] Residents felt they had borne the burden of Athens and of Clark and Oglethorpe counties long enough. They did not want to be saddled with the landfill for another three decades. In December 2011, the expansion permit application was still pending at the Georgia Environmental Division.

## Conclusion

All communities are not created equal. Millions of African Americans have learned the hard way that waiting for government to respond to environmental crises can be hazardous to their health. And, in some cases, it is not the polluting industry that is the culprit. Too often, it is government that is to blame for poisoning black people and their communities. It becomes problematic for victims of poisoned communities to ask that government for protection, equal treatment, and justice when government is the perpetrator.

There continues to be a racial divide in the way government at its various levels (local, state, and federal) protects African Americans from toxic contamination. Since toxic chemicals do not discriminate in their harmful effect, one would expect the government to treat all communities, regardless of race, ethnicity, or class, the same. Arsenic kills blacks just as quick as it kills whites. Thus, government's response to toxic contamination should aim to protect public health and the environment.

Sadly, we have not reached a race- and class-neutral or colorblind society where everyone is equally protected under the law. The United States has some of the best environmental laws in the world. The problem rests in the fact that they are not uniformly applied or enforced in all communities. This fact of life is not unique to environmental protection. The environmental justice movement has attempted to level the playing field by making it clear that poor people and people of color have a right to be protected from toxic chemicals just like rich people and white people. It is the responsibility of the government to protect all Americans—not just Americans who can afford lawyers, scientists, and experts or Americans who can "vote with their feet" and exit polluted or contaminated communities.

# Nightmare on Eno Road

*Poisoned Water and Toxic Racism
in Dickson, Tennessee*

Access to clean water is something most Americans take for granted. When we turn on the faucet in our kitchens, we expect the colorless liquid flowing into our sink to be clean and safe. Never in our wildest dreams would we expect that the baths and showers that we take could make us sick or even kill us. However, for some Americans whose wells and springs have been poisoned with chemicals, clean water is a dream, and toxic contamination and slow government response have turned their lives into a nightmare.

This chapter provides a real-life example of the deadly mix of toxic waste, water, and race in the early years of the twenty-first century—the Dickson County, Tennessee, landfill and the contamination of an African American family's wells on their homestead. The goal of our analysis is to illustrate how sluggish and inept government response to an environmental emergency is endangering the health and safety of African Americans more than two decades after the United Church of Christ published *Toxic Wastes and Race* and six years after Hurricane Katrina and the levee breach that flooded New Orleans. Our analysis also illustrates that the combination of institutional racism and poisoned water creates a deadly mix for African Americans.

## The "Dumping Grounds" in a Tennessee Town

What would you call an individual who climbs the water tower in tiny Dickson, Tennessee, and dumps deadly chemicals into the town's drinking water supply that ultimately make local residents sick? Most of us would label that person a toxic terrorist. We would mostly likely see the Department of Homeland Security, the FBI, the EPA, state and local officials, and a host of other government agencies deployed to the tiny town in warp speed. The emergency response would be swift and thorough. If such an unthinkable event ever happened, the culprit would be hunted down and, if found, tried and mostly likely convicted and sent straight to jail.

Dickson's water was poisoned not by an individual but by a corporate polluter. And the government response was not swift—especially when the contamination involved black families. Dickson is a textbook case—the poster child for environmental racism.[1] Dickson is a town of 12,244 located about thirty-five miles west of Nashville. Dickson County was about 4.5 percent black in 2000.[2] For more than four decades, Dickson's mostly African American Eno Road community has been used as the dumping ground for garbage and toxic wastes.

For decades, Jim Crow segregation created and maintained the racially segregated Eno Road community and kept it from receiving the same benefits enjoyed by white homeowners and property owners, such as paved streets, sewer and water service, and fire protection. Although black property owners paid taxes to Dickson County, they had little to show for their contribution. Black tax dollars were used to subsidize whites—who were generally more financially secure than black residents. This "reverse Robin Hood" scenario—"take money and taxes from the poor and give it to the rich"—was commonplace in the southern United States and formed the economic foundation for white privilege.

The Eno Road community was used first as the site of the Dickson "city dump" and later for city and county Class I sanitary landfills and for Class III and IV construction and demolition (C&D) landfills, balefills, and solid-waste processing centers. In 2007, the site was being used as a C&D landfill, garbage transfer station, and recycling center (see Table 6.1). The Town of Dickson purchased the land for a city dump in 1946. Sometime between 1946 and 1956, the newly acquired land, which was bounded on one side by the old "Negro Coaling School," a one-room county school with grades first through ninth that dates back to 1895, became the Dickson city dump, an open unlined dump. This point is made clear in Johnnie Hall's property deed dated September 22, 1956. The deed described the location of the Hall property as follows:

Located in the First Civil District of Dickson County, State of Tennessee, bounded and described as follows: Beginning at an iron pin in the east boundary line of the Town of Dickson's "City Dump" tract at the northwest corner of Roy Holt's 7.4 acre tract; runs south 87½ deg. East 44 poles to a stake, the northeast corner of the aforesaid 7.4 acre tract; thence North 1 deg. East 16 poles to an iron pin; thence North 87½ deg. West 43.6 poles to a pile of stones in the aforesaid Town of Dickson's east boundary line; thence South 2 deg. West 16 poles to the beginning, containing 4.4 acres, more or less.

Being a part of the same property conveyed to Johnnie Hall by a deed from Tobe Hall of record in Deed Book No. 67, page 430 in the Register's office of Dickson County Tennessee.[3]

The Dickson County landfill consists of seventy-four acres off Eno Road, 1.5 miles southwest of Dickson. The landfill contains four parts: the City of Dickson landfill, the County landfill expansion, and the balefill, which are all now closed, and a fourth part that consists of approximately five acres located on the eastern portion of the landfill. The balefill disposed of solid waste that was compressed or bound.

The Scovill-Schrader automotive company opened in Dickson, Tennessee, in 1964—the same year the U.S. Congress passed the sweeping Civil Rights Act that outlawed racial discrimination. The plant manufactured automotive tire valves and gauges, using processes that included metal plating, etching, rubber molding and application, polishing, and degreasing and painting, according to documents prepared by the Tennessee Department of Environment and Conservation (TDEC) Division of Water Supply. An industrial operation like this generates lots of hazardous wastes that must be disposed of.

According to government records, in 1968, the same year Dr. Martin Luther King Jr. was assassinated, in Memphis, Scovill-Schrader and several other local industries buried drums of industrial waste solvents at an "open dump" landfill site.[4] In 1972, the unlined landfill was granted a permit by the Tennessee Department of Health and Environment. The town of Dickson operated the landfill until 1977, when it was taken over and operated by Dickson County.[5] Both Dickson City and County government joined forces in making Eno Road the "preferred dumpsite" community for household garbage and toxic waste—and set in motion a pattern of dumping on black residents that went unchecked for decades.

More than 1,400 people obtain their drinking water from private wells or springs within a four-mile radius of the Dickson County landfill.[6] However, it was Dickson's Eno Road black residents who lived closest to the landfill and who bore the brunt of its negative environmental impacts. A 1991 Halliburton report acknowledged the fact that the well used by the Holt family was the closest to the landfill. It states, "The closest private well [the Harry Holt well] is located approximately five hundred feet east of the landfill."[7]

The county landfill initially started as a 41.6-acre expansion of the original City of Dickson landfill, of which 28.6 acres were used for waste disposal. The expansion occurred after the county purchased the original City of Dickson landfill, as well as forty-five additional acres, in 1977. The balefill was established as part of the 1987 expansion (see Table 6.1). For years, drums of toxic industrial waste solvents were dumped at the landfill, and these solvents later contaminated the groundwater.

Contaminated waste material was cleaned up from other areas in this mostly white county and trucked to the landfill in the mostly black Eno Road community. For example, the Ebbtide Corporation (Winner Boats) removed material from an on-site dump and transferred it to the Dickson County landfill for disposal.[8] The company disposed of drummed wastes every week for three to four years. The Scovill-Schrader manufacturing plant buried drums of industrial waste solvents that are known to have contained acetone and paint thinner at the landfill.[9] In addition, a 1991 EPA Site Inspection Report notes that soil containing benzene, toluene, ethylbenzene, xylenes, and petroleum hydrocarbons from underground storage tank cleanups had been brought to the landfill. In 1988, for example, the Dickson County landfill had accepted 275 to 300 cubic yards of solid waste from the CSX White Bluff derailment cleanup.[10]

The Dickson County landfill received citations for unsatisfactory operational conditions. The landfill received five notices of violations (NOV) from July 18, 1988, to April 12, 1999, that cited inadequate daily cover, violation of groundwater protection standards, the presence of cadmium in groundwater and springs at concentrations exceeding the maximum contaminant level (MCL), and inadequate depth cover and pooling of water on the landfill cover.[11] The landfill noncompliance is summarized in the 2004 *Dickson County Landfill Reassessment Report* (Region IV):

> The County has a long history of noncompliance related to groundwater and leachate violations since at least 1983. These violations have resulted in fines, Commissioner's Orders, and NOV (Notice of Violation). These violations were related to such issues as major and minor leachate seeps and flows, failure to provide immediate cover, failure to provide erosion control, excedance of groundwater standards for cadmium and TCE [trichloroethylene], discharge of leachate from the property without a permit,

failure to maintain a stormwater pollution prevention plan, and implementation of required corrective actions.[12]

Despite repeated violations at the Dickson County landfill, TDEC continued to grant permits for the site on Eno Road. TDEC permitted at least four landfills at the Eno Road site beginning in 1988. In February 2007, Dickson County operated a recycling center, a garbage transfer station, and a C&D landfill at the Eno Road site, where twenty to twenty-five heavy-duty diesel trucks entered the sites each day, leaving behind noxious fumes, dangerous particulates, household garbage, recyclables, and demolition debris from around Middle Tennessee. The garbage transfer station alone handled approximately thirty-five thousand tons of waste annually.

Dickson County covers more than 490 square miles—the equivalent of 313,600 acres.[13] However, the only cluster of solid-waste facilities in the county is located fifty-four feet from a 150-acre farm owned by an African American family in the small mostly black Eno Road community. It is no accident or fluke that all the permitted landfills in Dickson County are concentrated in this black community. Yet, blacks make up less than 5 percent of the county's population and occupy less than 1 percent of the county's land mass.

When the former *New York Times* columnist Bob Herbert, for an October 2006 article, "Poisoned on Eno Road," queried Dickson County attorney Eric Thornton about why it was that the Eno Road community had been chosen to absorb so much of the county's garbage and hazardous waste over the years, his reply was, "It has to be at some location."[14] While this statement may be true, the million-dollar question remains unanswered—why must the "somewhere" end up being in Dickson's black Eno Road community?

The "put it in the black community" thinking is not limited to Dickson County but can be found all across the South, where African American neighborhoods are unofficially zoned for garbage and hazardous waste. Historically, all-white city councils and county commissions made a conscious effort to locate locally unwanted land uses (LULUs) in black neighborhoods and away from their white constituents. It is this kind of thinking that gave rise to the national environmental justice movement in Warren County, North Carolina, where the term "environmental racism" was coined in 1982. This kind of thinking robs black residents of their health, their dignity, and their basic civil and human rights.

Dickson city and county officials engaged in environmental racism, destroying black health and diminishing black wealth. Black farmers like the Holt family in Dickson are threatened by toxic contamination from the polluting industry on the one hand and by racism practiced by the government on the other. Much of black family farmers' wealth is vested in their land holdings. Threats to black land are not new but can be traced to the post-Reconstruction era, when a range of hostile actions by government and white citizens groups, including the Ku Klux Klan, colluded to push former slaves off their newly acquired land and to steal their wealth.

A major component in the growing black-white wealth gap can be traced to inheritance. Black families are more likely than white families to have to start from "scratch," with no inheritance. This wealth gap has actually widened over the past generation. Researchers from Brandeis University have found that the "wealth gap between white and African-American families has more than quadrupled over the course of a generation."[15] From 1984 through 2007, the racial gap increased by $75,000, from $20,000 to $95,000. This black-white wealth gap "results from historical and contemporary factors but the disturbing four-fold increase in such a short time reflects public policies, such as tax cuts on investment income and inheritances which benefit the wealthiest, and redistribute wealth and opportunities."[16]

Five generations of Holts have lived on the family's Eno Road homestead. Now, toxic racism threatens to end the transformative wealth the family has accrued over the years—wealth that has been passed on from one generation to the next so that future generations of family members need not start off with nothing. Toxic racism, in effect, has stolen the Holts' inheritance. Contaminated, devalued property is not what most Americans would consider a valuable inheritance.

## Treatment of Black Families in Dickson

After slavery, dozens of black families acquired hundreds of acres of land— not part of the empty "forty acres and a mule" government promise—and lived a quiet and peaceful existence in Dickson's Eno Road community—that is, until their wells were poisoned by the landfill.[17] One African American family in particular, the Harry Holt family, has been especially harmed by the toxic assaults of the city and county landfills and by government inaction. These are some of the medical problems that can be traced to the family's exposure to toxic chemicals:

- Harry Holt—Prostate cancer, bone cancer, Type 1 diabetes, hypertension, kidney disease (died on January 9, 2007)

- Beatrice Holt—Rheumatoid arthritis, diabetes, cervical polyps
- Sheila Holt-Orsted—Breast cancer, diabetes, arthritis, gastrointestinal disorder
- Bonita Holt—Arthritis, colon polyps, hypertension, gastrointestinal disorder
- Demetrius Holt—Diabetes, gastrointestinal disorder
- Patrick Holt—Immune disorder, arthritis

The Holt family's American Dream of land ownership has become a toxic nightmare. For more than a decade, this black family experienced the terror of not knowing what health problems might lay ahead for their children and their children's children. The family still does not know the full health effects of drinking contaminated water, a "TCE cocktail," for the twelve years after the contamination was first discovered by government tests.

Government records show that trichloroethylene (TCE), a suspected carcinogen, was found in the wells used by Harry and Lavenia Holt as early as 1988, the same year the Tennessee Department of Health and Environment (TDHE) issued a permit to Dickson County for operation of the facility as a sanitary landfill. TDHE approved the Dickson County landfill permit on December 2, 1988, even though government test results on the Holts' wells

Table 6.1: History of Landfill Permitting in Dickson, Tennessee,
Eno Road Community

| Site Name | Year Permitted | Type Permit[1] |
| --- | --- | --- |
| Dickson City Dump | N/A (1956)[2] | No Permit |
| Dickson City Dump | N/A (1968) | No Permit |
| Dickson City Landfill | 1972 | Class I |
| Dickson County Landfill | 1977 | Class I |
| Dickson County Landfill | 1988 | Class I |
| Dickson County Balefill | 1988 | Processing |
| Dickson County Balefill | 1990 | Processing |
| Dickson County Demolition | 1992 | Class III/Class IV |

[1] The solid waste facility permits were granted for 100 Virgil Bellar Road, Dickson, Tennessee, located in the heart of the Eno Road community.

[2] The City of Dickson purchased the land for the Eno Road site in 1946. Government records indicate that the land was associated with the Dickson city dump tract as early as 1956. The site was an open dump in 1968 and in 1972 was first permitted by the State of Tennessee for use as a sanitary landfill.

Source: Tennessee Department of Environment and Conservation, Division of Solid and Hazardous Waste Management, Solid Waste Facility Database (2002).

completed on November 18, 1988, had showed TCE contamination. TDHE sent letters to Harry and Lavenia Holt on December 8, 1988, informing the family of the test results. The letter states: "Your water is of good quality for the parameters tested. It is felt that the low levels of methylene or trichloroethene may be due to either lab or sampling error."[18]

TDEC is responsible for water quality in the state and is also in charge of permitting waste facilities. It seems a bit odd that the State of Tennessee would continue permitting landfills in the mostly black Eno Road community even after government tests repeatedly turned up TCE contamination on site and off site in both monitoring wells and in private wells—such as the Holt family wells—that are just a stone's throw from the facility. (Currently, there are fewer than one hundred chemicals for which a maximum allowable concentration in public drinking water systems has been established. However, these represent chemicals that are thought to pose the most serious risk.)

Some of the health effects associated with ingestion of TCE include liver disease, hypertension, speech impediments, hearing impairment, stroke, anemia and other blood disorders, diabetes, kidney disease, urinary tract disorders, and skin rashes.[19] For children whose mothers ingested water contaminated with TCE during pregnancy, reported health effects include leukemia, low birth weight, fetal death, and a range of birth defects, including heart defects, cleft lip and other oral cleft defects, neural tube defects, eye defects, and choanal atresia, a blockage by bone or tissue of the nasal passages (choana) leading from the back of the nose to the throat.

TCE is not something you would want added in your morning cup of coffee. It is not regulated as a toxic substance. Yet, the level of TCE contamination at the Dickson plant caused the EPA to classify it as a Superfund site. This designation was later changed after the company undertook a "voluntary cleanup." The toxic waste from the cleanup was trucked to the Dickson County landfill and the Chemical Waste Management landfill in Emelle, Alabama. More than 95 percent of Emelle's residents are African American.

After twenty-two years of study, the EPA in September 2011 declared TCE a "very hazardous" mutagenic cancer-causing chemical. The new EPA study found that TCE is even more dangerous to people's health than previously thought, causing kidney and liver cancer, lymphoma, and other health problems. This new information also lays the groundwork for reevaluating the federal drinking-water standard for TCE: 5 parts per billion in water, and 1 microgram per cubic meter in air.[20]

On January 28, 1990, government tests found 26 ppb (parts per billion) TCE in the Holt family's well—five times the established MCL of 5ppb set by the federal EPA. On August 17, 1990, government tests found 3.9 ppb of TCE in the same well. On August 23, 1991, government tests showed 3.7 ppb of TCE in that same well.

On January 28, 1991, the EPA performed an inspection of the landfill, looking for potential hazardous wastes. The *Chronology of Events—Dickson County Landfill Appendix B* (*Dickson County Landfill Reassessment Report*) stated:

> Elevated levels of several pesticides were detected within the landfill. Questionable material was placed in the city dump prior to 1973. The private well was contaminated with TCE, and two municipal wells are within 4,000 feet. Soils within the landfill were contaminated with high levels of pesticides, metals and unidentified organics. Mr. Holt owns a home approximately 500 feet east of the landfill; however, the old dump is not used. The area is not fenced, and pedestrian traffic is possible. A landfill directly adjacent to the old city dump to the west is presently being used. Most waste was in drums and the old city dump is not lined.[21]

The Harry Holt homestead property line is actually fifty-four feet (not five hundred feet) from the landfill property line. And, on December 3, 1991, the EPA sent Harry Holt a letter informing him of the three tests performed on his well and telling him that his water was safe. The letter stated: "Use of your well water should not result in any adverse health effects."[22] It went on:

> It should be mentioned that trichloroethylene (TCE) was detected at 26 ug/1 in the first sample. Because this detection exceeded EPA's Maximum Contaminant Level (MCL) of 5 ug/1, the well water was re-sampled. TCE was detected at 3.7 ug/1 in the second sample; however, it was noted this sample contained air bubbles. EPA then took a third sample with results nearly identical to the second (3.9 ug/1). Trichloroethylene (TCE) originates from the disposal of dry cleaning material and the manufacture of items such as pesticides, paints and paint thinners, waxes and varnishes, and metal degreasers.[23]

A December 17, 1991, letter from the TDEC expressed some concern about the level of TCE contamination found in the Holts' well. TDEC officials agreed that Mr. Holt's well should continue to be sampled. However, this was not done. The TDEC letter stated: "Our program is concerned that the sampling twice with one considerably above MCL and one slightly below MCL in a karst area such as Dickson is in no way an assurance that Mr. Holt's well water will stay below MCL's. There is a considerably seasonal variation for contaminants in karst environments and 3.9 ppb TCE is only slightly under the MCL of 5 ppb."[24]

Although Tennessee state officials expressed concern about the tests, they stood by and allowed the Holt family to continue to drink contaminated well water. A January 6, 1992, letter from the Tennessee Department of Health and Environment continued to express concern about the level of contamination found in the Holt well. The letter stated:

> Mr. Holt's well was sampled as a result of the Preremedial Site Investigation and Ranking package on the Dickson County landfill for NPL consideration. Mr. Carr told me the field investigation was complete and that he was not in a position to sample Mr. Holt's well again even though it had sporadically shown TCE contamination above MCL's. He agreed that Mr. Holt's well should continue to be sampled. There may be some chance of the site going NPL, but that will be at least 1–2 years away. Mr. Carr suggested I contact Nathan Sykes at (404) 347-2913 to determine why it was not felt that further monitoring or an alternate water supply was necessary.[25]

A month later, in a letter written on February 12, 1992, Tennessee state officials continued to discuss the Holt family well and allegations that the Dickson County landfill was the source of the TCE contamination. The letter stated:

> A search of our Division's files has been made concerning the allegation that a domestic well, located on the Harry and Lavenia Holt property, may have been adversely impacted by the Dickson County Landfill. No substantial evidence was found in our files to support this allegation.
>
> Attached is a 1988 memo from our Division showing that groundwater samples from the Holt well were obtained and analyzed at that time. Those sample results showed that trichloroethylene (TCE) and methylene chloride were found to be at the upper regulatory limit of the acceptable drinking water standards set by EPA. It was concluded by this Division that these detection levels may have been due to either laboratory or sample error. There is no record that any additional samples were obtained at a later date by either our Division or by the EPA.[26]

A March 13, 1992, internal memorandum from TDEC sided with the EPA and maintained that the Holt family's well water was "safe." The letter stated:

> Since EPA has already completed a site investigation, has identified the pollutants involved, and has, in part, determined the extent of the leaching, I would suggest that they, EPA, continue with their chosen course of action, rather than create the added confusion of various agencies making their own agendas. I would suggest that if Mr. Holt is concerned about possible health risks in using his well water between now and June (when EPA's priority decision is made), that he should rely on bottled or city water for cooking and drinking purposes until he is convinced that his well water is safe.[27]

TDEC and EPA officials traded internal memoranda back and forth about the Holts' contaminated wells but never informed the family of these deliberations. From these internal memoranda, it is clear that the Dickson County landfill was suspect and that the Holt family was thought to be at risk. However, in the final analysis, the state handed the ball off to the federal government and, in doing so, handed the Holt family a death sentence. Government regulators had more than sufficient information and documentation to respond proactively to toxic threat. They chose to not to respond.

Even after the results from a series of tests were in hand, the Harry Holt well was *not* retested or monitored as recommended by Tennessee state officials. Generally, such retesting is standard operating procedure when contamination is found. According to the 2004 EPA *Dickson County Landfill Reassessment Report*, no government tests were performed on the Harry Holt family well between August 24, 1991, and October 8, 2000—a full nine years.[28] No explanation has been given for this gap, even though TDHE and the EPA were periodically performing tests on private wells that were within a one-mile radius of the leaky Dickson County landfill. One has to question why the private well that was closest to the landfill—the Harry Holt family well—was omitted from the government tests.

The Harry Holt well, one of the earliest private wells to show TCE contamination, was routinely left out of government testing and monitoring protocols for wells tested within a one-mile radius of the Dickson County landfill. In February 1997, TCE was detected at 1.3 parts per billion in water from a production well (DK-21) operated by the City of Dickson and located northeast of the landfill. The MCL is 5 parts per billion. The Harry Holt homestead is a mere fifty-four feet from the landfill property line and lies between the landfill and the DK-21 public water supply—yet it was not retested.

An April 7, 1997, TDEC confirmation sample at DK-21 showed TCE at 14 parts per billion and Cis-1, 2 dichloroethene at 1.3 parts per billion. And, on April 18, 1997, the City of Dickson stopped using the DK-21 well as a supplement to the municipal water source after the State of Tennessee informed them that the city would be required to install an aeration or water filtration system, according to the TDEC Division of Water Supply. The city began using the Piney River exclusively (after having closed DK-21) as the municipal water source, according to the TDEC Division of Water Supply.[29]

A dye-tracer study, *Summary and Results of Dye-Tracer Tests Conducted at the Dickson County Landfill, Tennessee, 1997 and 1998*, was conducted to help evaluate whether the landfill was a possible source of the contamination.[30] The study used twenty-four dye-injection and detection sites. The test sites included wetlands, springs, ponds, and wells owned by the City of Dickson, as well as domestic wells. The twenty-four sites were located on all sides of the landfill. One of the dye-tracer test sites was the Humane Society of Dickson County, a facility, located at 410 Eno Road, that housed more than three hundred animals per month. The Harry Holt homestead is located at 390 Eno Road—a few hundred feet from the animal shelter. However, the Harry Holt, Roy Holt, and Lavenia Holt family wells were not part of the 1997–1998 government study, even though they are all within several hundred feet of the landfill.

It appears that Dickson County and EPA officials were more concerned about ducks in a pond and dogs waiting to be euthanized than about protecting the Holt family from TCE released from the county landfill. The Holts' well was not retested until October 9, 2000, when it registered a whopping 120 ppb TCE. A second test, on October 25, 2000, registered 145 ppb— twenty-four times and twenty-nine times, respectively, the MCL of 5ppb set by the EPA.[31] It was only after the extremely high TCE levels found in 2000 that a Dickson County landfill official visited the Holt home to inform the family that their wells were unsafe. No written reports or letters were sent to the Holt family explaining the October 9, 2000, test results.

The Holt family was placed on Dickson City water on October 20, 2000— twelve years after the first government tests found TCE in their well in 1988. Any length of time is too long to drink poisoned water. However, waiting twelve years for clean water is a bit extreme.

At a September 23, 2003, community meeting, TDEC officials discussed the TCE contamination in the Holt family wells.[32] State officials also discussed the one municipal water well (DK-21) that had shown detectable levels of TCE contamination and that had been taken out of service and permanently closed in 1998. The Harry Holt homestead is located between the Dickson County landfill property and the DK-21 site. It stands to reason that if the landfill site was contaminated and the DK-21 water supply site was contaminated, the Harry Holt well was probably also contaminated. And, it turns out, the Holts' well was in fact contaminated.

On December 2, 2003, the Harry Holt family filed a lawsuit against the City of Dickson, the County of Dickson, and Scovill, Inc., the company that owned the former Scovill-Schrader automotive manufacturing plant in Dickson. The Harry Holt family lawsuit was one of the first lawsuits filed against the county landfill. It was also the longest-running citizen lawsuit involving the TCE contamination at the landfill. (In 2009, after nearly a decade of litigation, the Holt family won a victory against Scovill-Schrader in a New York bankruptcy court. The bankruptcy judge awarded the Holts $2.5 million. However, because of the company's bankruptcy, the Holt family received just 10 percent, or $250,000 of the valued amount.

Before the county landfill was sited, the Holt family's wells were clean, the water was safe to drink, and it was free. Not only did the Dickson County Landfill contaminate the Holt family's wells and endanger the family's health; the Holt family was forced incur the added expense of paying the county for clean water. The county began paying the Holts' water bills in 2000 because the well water on the property tested positive for TCE, but, after the Holts filed their lawsuit, the Dickson County Commission stopped paying the family's water bill in 2004.[33]

While a number of white families filed lawsuits against Dickson County and the company that dumped chemicals at the county landfill, the Holt family was the only plaintiff that alleged racial discrimination. In November 2004, Dickson County Circuit Court Judge George Sexton ruled that a racial discrimination amendment could be added to the Holt family's complaint involving the alleged toxic poisoning of their well water near the Dickson County landfill.

In December 2004, twenty-one parents in Dickson County filed a lawsuit against Saltire Industrial, Inc. (a successor company to Scovill-Schrader) on behalf of their twelve minor children. The suit alleged that their children's birth defects were caused by contaminated water. The lawsuit came after a 2001 Centers for Disease Control and Prevention (CDC) study confirmed the existence of a "cleft lip/palate cluster" in Dickson County. The rate of cleft palate birth defects among children born in Dickson County was almost nine times the national average.[34] The lawsuit was settled in 2006.[35] Shortly after, the company filed for bankruptcy.

Earning some $3 million a year from the Eno Road waste operation, Dickson County profited from the suffering inflicted on the Holt family, which lived next door. The Dickson County Landfill was not a "good neighbor." Generally, landfills do not make good neighbors—a reason why they are usually zoned away from residential areas. More important, county officials refused to right the environmental injustice its landfill had created against the Holt family and the other residents of the Eno Road community, an injustice that dated back four decades.[36]

Discrimination against the Holt family did not end with the lawsuit filed in 2003. The Holts continued to receive differential treatment from Dickson County officials as late as November 6, 2006, when, in a special called meeting, Dickson County commissioners voted unanimously to settle lawsuits with several white families that had alleged groundwater contamination from the leaky Dickson County landfill.[37] The city and county settled with all of the white families but refused to deal fairly with the Holt family. The case dragged on for more than seven years. Some Holt family members believe that city and county officials dragged the case out intentionally, waiting for them to die off one at a time. A "war of attrition" of this type is generally biased against the sick victims harmed by toxic racism.

In November 2007, Dickson County accepted a $400,000 settlement from Scovill-Schrader. The county had originally filed a lawsuit for $4 million against the company for allowing TCE to contaminate the county's groundwater, possibly causing county residents to suffer from a number of diseases, including cancer. The county accepted the low offer rather than drag the case out and incur untold costs in legal bills. The county used the contamination found in the Holts' well to justify its claim against the company. Yet, these same Dickson County officials chose to challenge and drag out the Holts' lawsuit. Ironically, there is nothing to preclude county officials from using the $400,000 the country received from the Schrader company to fight the Holts.

## Treatment of White Families

Government testing and monitoring of the black Holt family's wells differed markedly from the treatment accorded the contaminated springs and wells of white families.[38] Treatment differed in terms of testing, notification, remediation, and provision of an alternative water supply, both temporary (providing bottled water) and permanent (connecting to city water system). The racial disparity in government testing is clearly presented in Table 6.2, Summary of TCE and DCE Results, Springs and Private Water Supplies, Dickson County, Tennessee, of the *Dickson County Landfill Reassessment Report.*[39]

On March 5, 1994, TCE was detected in Sullivan Spring, a water supply located one-third mile from the landfill that was used by two white families. On September 1, 1994, tests were conducted on the spring to determine whether it was indeed contaminated. On September 8, 1994, TDEC sent one of the white families a "Notification of Contaminants in Drinking Water" letter. The letter stated:

> As I discussed with you on September 6, 1994, the spring used to supply drinking water to your residence has shown levels of Trichloroethylene-cis-1,2-dichloroethene, and dichloroethene above the allowable levels. It is recommended that you discontinue use of this water as your drinking water supply. As I have been informed, Mr. Lunn of the Dickson County Solid Waste Program contacted you on September 2, 1994, to notify you of the impact to your spring.[40]

Dickson County officials even dug the white family a well to be used as an alternate water supply. The family was placed on the city tap water system after the new well was also found to be contaminated.[41] A total of nine tests were performed on the white family's spring between June 25, 1994, and September 20, 2000.[42] Three tests were performed in 1994, after the initial March 5, 1994, test turned up contamination in the spring. The spring was again tested in 1995, 1996 (two separate tests), 1997, 1999, and 2000.

Government tests were continued for years on the white family's spring even after family members were placed on the city water system. Government records clearly show that nothing of this sort was done for the black Holt family. One has to question why such great lengths were taken to protect the white family but not the black family from the TCE water contamination. No rational explanation has been forthcoming from city, county, state, or federal government agencies charged with environmental and health protection. These same government entities are also charged with providing equal protection under the law, protections guaranteed under the U.S. Constitution.

According to a letter dated August 31, 1993, "Landowner Notification of TCE Contaminated Wells, Scovill-Schrader Site, Dickson, Tennessee," from the state, twenty-nine residential water wells within a one-mile radius of the

Scovill-Schrader Automotive Division Site in Dickson were sampled for volatile organic compounds (VOCs) between May 11, 1993, and May 14, 1993, in accordance with Task 5 of the Phase II RCRA Facility Investigation. TCE was detected in the wells of nine white residents. The Scovill-Schrader site is located near a white neighborhood.

An August 31, 1993, letter contains a detailed table that summarizes the steps taken to immediately notify the affected white residents and the activities undertaken to provide both temporary water supplies and permanent city utilities. The letter stated:

All of the residents with TCE detected in their wells were immediately contacted and all were provided bottled water for drinking and cooking within 48 hours. All other residents sampled within the one-mile radius were contacted and informed that the water samples taken indicated no problems with their water. In addition, all wells within the one-mile radius

Figure 6.1: Map of Dickson City Officials and Proximity to Dickson County Landfill

were re-sampled to verify the original water well sampling results. Residential wells within a one- to two-mile radius of the site were sampled during the month of July. Residents within the one- to two-mile radius will be contacted within the next week to inform them of the results of the last sampling event. It should be noted that all wells within the one- to two-mile radius were non-detectable for VOCs. A listing of the wells sampled within the one- to two-mile radius and date contacted to inform residents of the results will be under separate cover. As a precautionary measure, a water well sampling event is scheduled for the week of August 16, 1993 to re-sample selected wells near the wells found to contain TCE.[43]

Clearly, the care taken and the precautions used by government officials to protect the health of the white families were not extended to the black Holt family. White families near the Scovill-Schrader site benefited from a swift response to the toxic contamination emergencies, while the black family near the leaky landfill was made to wait. White families near the site were notified within forty-eight hours, provided with bottled water, and placed on the city water system. On the other hand, the black family whose property line was just fifty-four feet from the landfill was allowed to drink TCE-contaminated well water for twelve years after the contamination was first discovered by the government in 1988.

### Proximity of Dickson County Landfill to Elected Officials' Homes

There are several interesting observations to be made about the siting of the landfill in Dickson. and officials' handling of the problems growing out of that siting. First, Dickson city and county officials have the power to right a terrible injustice. However, the elected officials have chosen instead to use tax dollars to fight the family whose well was poisoned by a city landfill. It appears that NIMBY (Not in My Backyard) is being practiced by these officials. Harry Holt's property line, as noted, is just 54 feet from the landfill property line; his well is 313 feet from the landfill property line.

How far is the landfill from city and county officials' homes? Only one Dickson city council member's home is within one mile of the landfill. Five of the eight city council members' homes are more than two miles from the landfill. Dickson's mayor lives 3.85 miles from the landfill (see Figure 6.1 and Table 6.3).

Dickson County elected officials live even farther away from the leaky landfill than their Dickson city council counterparts. Two county commis-

Table 6.2. Summary of TCE and DCE Results, Springs
and Private Water Supplies
Dickson County, Tennessee

| Residence/Water Supply | Date | TCE (*g/L) | DCE (*g/L) |
| --- | --- | --- | --- |
| L. Gorley/ private well | October 25, 2000 | 0.6 | BDL |
| L. Gorley/ private well | October 31, 2000 | 0.5J | BDL |
| H. Holt/private well | October 12, 2000 | 3.5 | BDL |
| H. Holt/private well | January 28, 1990 | 26.0 | BDL |
| H. Holt/private well | August 17, 1990 | 3.9 | BDL |
| H. Holt/private well | August 23, 1991 | 3.7 | BDL |
| H. Holt/private well | October 9, 2000 | 120.0 | 6.6 |
| H. Holt/private well | October 25, 2000 | 145.0 | 8.6 |
| H. Holt/private well | January 2001 | 64.0 | 2.9 |
| H. Holt/private well | October 2001 | 160.0 | 2.0 |
| H. Holt/private well | May 2002 | 34.0 | 1.0 |
| H. Holt/private well | April 2003 | 16.0 | 1.1 |
| L. Holt/private well | October 25, 2000 | 1.2J | BDL |
| L. Holt/private well | October 2001 | BDL | BDL |
| L. Holt/private well | May 2002 | BDL | BDL |
| L. Holt/private well | October 2002 | BDL | BDL |
| L. Holt/private well | April 2003 | BDL | BDL |
| R. Holt/private well | November 2000 | 5.0 | BDL |
| R. Holt/private well | January 2001 | 8.0 | BDL |
| R. Holt/private well | October 2001 | 3.0 | 2.2 |
| R. Holt/private well | May 2002 | 2.0 | BDL |
| R. Holt/private well | October 2002 | 2.0 | BDL |
| R. Holt/private well | April 2003 | 9.0 | 134 |
| Sullivan Spring | March 5, 1994 | 18.0 | 5.0 |
| Sullivan Spring | June 25, 1994 | 83.0 | 19.0 |
| Sullivan Spring | September 1, 1994 | 59.0 | 9.8 |
| Sullivan Spring | September 28, 1994 | 84.0 | 17.0 |
| Sullivan Spring | May 22, 1995 | 31.0 | 6.8 |
| Sullivan Spring | August 19, 1996 | <5 | <5 |
| Sullivan Spring | December 3, 1996 | <5 | <5 |
| Sullivan Spring | May 14, 1997 | 230.0 | 31.0 |
| Sullivan Spring | August 26, 1999 | 160.0 | 39.0 |
| Sullivan Spring | September 20, 2000 | 16.0 | 25.0 |
| Sullivan Spring | May 2002 | 23.0 | 1.0 |
| Sullivan Spring | November 2002 | 110.0 | 26.0 |
| Sullivan Spring | April 2003 | 130.0 | 34.0 |

Source: Tetra Tech EM, Inc., Dickson County Landfill Reassessment Report.
A Report Prepared for the U.S. EPA, Region IV. Atlanta: March 4, 2004, Table 2, p. 16.

## Table 6.3: Distance from Dickson City Officials' Homes to the Dickson County Landfill

| City Official | Home Address | Ward Number | Distance to Land-fill (Miles) |
|---|---|---|---|
| 1. R. Arnold | 119 Edgewood Pl. Dickson, TN | 2 | 0.33 |
| 2. J.R. Monsue | 702 West 3rd St. Dickson, TN | 3 | 1.85 |
| 3. M. Corlew | 105 Marley Dr. Dickson, TN | 3 | 1.95 |
| 4. R. Blue | 115 Miller St. Dickson, TN | 4 | 2.22 |
| 5. R.S. England | 711 Henslee Dr. Dickson, TN | 2 | 2.30 |
| 6. B. Rial | 106 Forest Hills Circle Dickson, TN | 1 | 3.65 |
| 7. M. Legg | 105 Steven Nicks Dr. Dickson, TN | 1 | 4.04 |
| 8. J. Jennings | 122 Shady Brook Circle Dickson, TN | 4 | 4.10 |
| 9. D. Weiss, Jr. | 100 Belford Dickson, TN | Mayor | 3.85 |

Source: City of Dickson, Tennessee, "City Council," http://cityofdickson.com/Council. aspx (accessed March 15, 2006).

sioners' homes are within two miles of the landfill; three commissioners live three to four miles from the landfill; and seven of the twelve county commissioners' homes are six or more miles from the landfill. Two of the commissioners live more than fifteen miles from the landfill. The county mayor lives three miles from the landfill (see Figure 6.2 and Table 6.4).

## Conclusion

A major part of the UCC report *Toxic Wastes and Race at Twenty* involved plotting the location of hazardous-waste sites and the sociodemographic composition of the host communities. The Dickson County landfill and the Harry Holt family case study were used to put a human face on the report.

*Table 6.4. Distance from Dickson County Officials' Homes to the Dickson County Landfill*

| City Official | Home Address | District Number | Distance to Land-fill (Miles) |
|---|---|---|---|
| 1. D. Corlew | 1006 West 1st Street Dickson, TN | 8 | 1.79 |
| 2. D. England | 615 W. College St. Dickson, TN | 9 | 1.95 |
| 3. B. Reed | 108 Lone Oak Dr. Dickson, TN | 10 | 3.55 |
| 4. V. Gray | 665 Murrell Rd. Dickson, TN | 7 | 3.70 |
| 5. D. Tidwell | 209 Robinson Dr. Dickson, TN | 11 | 4.00 |
| 6. J. Loggins | 345 Loggins Rd. Burns, TN | 12 | 6.00 |
| 7. R. Wetterau | 325 McElhiney Rd. Dickson, TN | 2 | 6.17 |
| 8. S. Batey | 1128 Old Stage Rd. Dickson, TN | 1 | 6.42 |
| 9. B. Spencer | 885 Tidwell Rd. Burns, TN | 6 | 11.50 |
| 10. G. Larkin | 315 School Rd. White Bluff, TN | 5 | 11.88 |
| 11. G. Suggs | 2645 Wood Valley Rd. Cumberland Furnace, TN | 3 | 15.40 |
| 12. J.B. Smith | 1765 Maple Valley Rd. Charlotte, TN | 4 | 16.50 |
| 13. L. Frazier | 825 North Mount Sinai Rd. Dickson, TN | Mayor | 3.00 |

Source: Dickson County Chamber of Commerce, "County Offices, Elected Officials and County Offices," http://www.dicksoncountychamber.com/community/offices.html (accessed February 26, 2006).

Clearly, Dickson, Tennessee, is the poster child for environmental racism and toxic dumping. The members of the Holt family are paying the ultimate price with their health. Is the health of white families given higher value than the health of black families in Dickson County? Are health and environmental laws applied differently to white and black families in Dickson County? These two questions form the heart of the Holt family's claim of environmental racism. It is clear from reams of government records that all levels of government failed the Holt family.

Even having the facts was not sufficient to get government to respond in a timely manner to protect black families threatened by contamination in their drinking water. White and black families were treated differently. This differential treatment resulted in the African American Holt family's experiencing prolonged exposure to contaminated drinking water and being subjected to unnecessary health risks.

Various levels of government acted promptly to protect the rights (and the health) of white families but failed to protect the rights of black families. Nearly 150 years after the infamous U.S. Supreme Court decision *Scott v. Painter* in 1857, Harry Holt understood how Dred Scott must have felt when the high court judges ruled that "No black man has any rights that any white

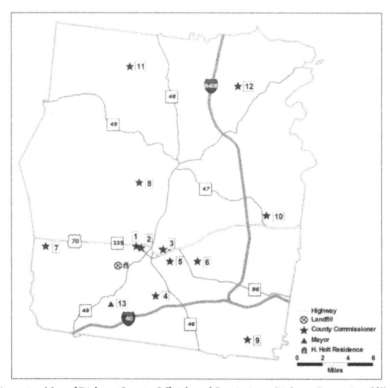

Figure 6.2: Map of Dickson County Officials and Proximity to Dickson County Landfill

man is bound to respect" and when the High Court judges forty years later, in 1896, told Homer Plessy, in the infamous *Plessy v. Ferguson* case, which codified "separate but equal" and fed Jim Crow segregation, to pay his full fare but get on the "back of the train." Harry Holt's 2003 lawsuit was still pending in court when he died, on January 9, 2007. Mr. Holt was sixty-six years old and had lived in the Eno Road community all his life.

In March 2008, the Natural Resources Defense Council, on behalf of two members of the Holt family, filed a federal lawsuit claiming that local governments hadn't done enough to control toxic waste around the contaminated county landfill. The plaintiffs, Sheila Holt-Orsted and her mother, Beatrice Holt, wanted the county and the City of Dickson to clean up toxic-waste barrels they said had been buried at the landfill for decades. Holt-Orsted had undergone six surgeries and chemotherapy for breast cancer. The complaint asked the court to require the defendants to investigate the present extent and the future spread of TCE contamination from the landfill in the soil, surface water, and groundwater of Dickson County. It also asked the defendants to remediate and abate the TCE contamination. Attorneys for the county and the state had denied the claims in the earlier lawsuits.[44]

In January 2009, one of the private defendants, which had filed for bankruptcy after the case was first filed, agreed to settle with the Holts for $2.6 million. According to the NAACP Legal Defense and Education Fund (LDF), in March 2009, the trial court ruled against the remaining government defendants' motions to dismiss the Holts' personal injury, property, and discrimination claims.

After an eight-year legal battle, on December 7, 2011, a $5.6 million settlement agreement was finally worked out with the Dickson City and County governments on the NRDC and the Holts' RCRA lawsuit; $1.75 million was to be paid to eleven Holt family members on the Holts' NAACP civil rights lawsuit from monies from an October settlement reached with three companies that were defendants in the Holts' NRDC case.[45] Ironically, the county spent more than $4 million and the city almost $1.9 million fighting the Holts. The family's quest for environmental justice was not quite complete since the state of Tennessee, a defendant in the Holts' civil rights lawsuit, was not part of the 2011 settlement. The family's civil rights case against the state is scheduled to go to trial in 2012.

In response to the Holts' demand for a personal apology from the City and County of Dickson, the settlement agreement includes the following statement: "The county and city regret the Harry Holt family well was contaminated with TCE and the issues experienced by the Holt family." This is not exactly an apology given the amount of harm, pain, and suffering inflicted on the Holt family from the nearby city and county-owned landfill. The $5 million settlement offers a free permanent connection to the municipal water supply to protect residents from the risk of TCE contamination. Ironically, the Holts still have to pay the county for their water. Finally, the settlement will create a monitoring program to ensure that TCE contamination does not spread beyond its current boundaries.

## Policy Recommendations

Because of the urgency of the environmental health disaster created by the Dickson County Landfill and government inaction, we are making the following recommendations to government and nongovernmental organizations:

*Government*

1. The Dickson County Commissioners should immediately close all solid-waste operations (recycling center, garbage transfer station and Class VI Construction and Demolition landfill) at the facility on Eno Road.
2. The State of Tennessee should institute a moratorium on the siting and permitting of waste facilities and other polluting facilities in the Dickson Eno Road community.
3. The U.S. Congress should hold hearings on the EPA's handling of the Dickson County landfill and the treatment of black and white families whose private wells and springs were contaminated by the leaky landfill.
4. The U.S. Department of Justice, Office of Civil Rights, should conduct an investigation of the City of Dickson, the County of Dickson, and the State of Tennessee regarding their handling of the contamination of the Holt family wells and the protection of the family's civil rights.

*Nongovernmental Organizations*

1. The national environmental and environmental justice groups should "adopt" the Holt family and the Eno Road community as the poster child for environmental racism and use their political and economic clout to pressure the state of Tennessee to repair the harm done to the Holts and to the Eno Road community.
2. The environmental justice, legal, health and medical, scientific, education, civil rights, and religious communities should converge on Dickson, Tennes-

see, to hold a series of national demonstrations to dramatize environmental racism with the goal of making Dickson County the "Warren County" of the 2000s.

Because of overt and intentional discrimination by the City of Dickson, the County of Dickson, the State of Tennessee, and the EPA against the Holt family, the family's health has been adversely affected, its property and land devalued, and its wealth diminished. Generations of Holts survived the horrors of postslavery racism and Jim Crow segregation, but the family may not survive the deadly chemical assault and contamination from the Dickson County landfill and the toxic racism practiced by local, state, and federal government officials.

# APPENDIX A

*Sheila Holt-Orsted Statement to EPA Region IV*

*Atlanta, Georgia*

Good morning. My name is Sheila Holt-Orsted. I'm a member of the Holt family from Dickson, Tenn. Dickson is about 40 miles west from the outskirts of Nashville. I'm here today to say that a change has got to come. EPA, we need you to provide better oversight of environmental problems in our communities. We no longer want to see our communities to be the dumping grounds for hazardous wastes and toxic chemicals. I travel here today to say that I don't appreciate being a statistic. The people you are hearing from today each have their own story about how they've suffered when toxic waste is improperly disposed of in their community. Dr. Robert Bullard has told my story in the report "Toxic Waste and Race at Twenty" (Chapter 7). He called it a toxic terror in a Tennessee town. I call it my horror story. It comes with an "R" rating for waste and race.

In 2002, while in Dickson for the Christmas holiday, I found my community riddled with cancer, including my father. I was so disturbed that I got a full physical when I returned home. A biopsy report revealed that I had Stage 2 breast cancer. I was a former Miss Tennessee Heavyweight and Mixed Pairs Bodybuilding Champion. At the time of my breast cancer diagnosis, I was teaching aerobics and weightlifting classes, working as a personal trainer, and playing in two adult women basketball leagues. That was all replaced by chemotherapy, radiation, numerous surgeries, and a mastectomy.

During my quest to find out why this had happened to me, I learned so many family members were sick so I didn't have to look far. My family's farm—the farm where I grew up—is directly adjacent to the Dickson County Landfill. The Landfill's owners had accepted waste at the Landfill for years with toxic chemicals. Among the chemicals dumped was trichloroethylene or TCE, a cancer-causing chemical that was used as a metal degreaser.

I learned that TCE was seeping from the landfill into groundwater at levels that far exceeded EPA's safety standards. I started going through State documents I found. Horrified, I could not believe what I discovered. Among the State documents were two sets of letters. One group of letters was written to white families. These families were warned that tests indicated their well water was contaminated with high levels of TCE. They were immediately placed on clean drinking water from the municipal supply.

The other letters went out to black families, including my family. The letter my family received said that no levels exceeded EPA standards and that the use of our well water should not result in adverse health effects. Both of these reassurances were untrue. While white families were warned of the dangers and provided with safe drinking water, my family was being poisoned. This is where it turned twisted.

I learned that a State employee went to his supervisor and told him that EPA had misinformed my family about the safety of our water. The supervisor suggested that EPA be contacted and questioned about the letters we had received. EPA said they were not in a position to deal with it at that time. The State of Tennessee decided not to do anything. One letter I discovered said TDEC decided not to warn us of the TCE contamination to avoid the confusion of having various agencies sending different messages. The State of Tennessee was more concerned with not contradicting EPA than it was in protecting my family from a known cancer-causing chemical in our water.

My father lost his battle with cancer and I continued my battle with cancer, while my other family members now live in fear that they might get sick next.

The one bright spot is the team of lawyers, churches, and environmental groups that have joined my family's fight for justice. The Natural Resources Defense Council is representing me in a lawsuit seeking to clean up the toxic contamination at the landfill. The NAACP Legal Defense Fund is representing me in a lawsuit to address the racial discrimination my family faced.

My family is embroiled in what will be one of the biggest environmental justice battles in recent history. EPA, I traveled here today to say, "Do your job!" Support legislation that codifies the Executive Order on Environmental Justice. Support legislation that reinstates the Superfund tax. Protect families and communities like mine around the country. Thank you.

## APPENDIX B

*Chronology of Events Surrounding Dickson
County Landfill*

1964  Scovill-Schrader automotive company opened in Dickson in 1964—the same year the U.S. Congress passed the sweeping Civil Rights Act that outlawed racial discrimination.

1968  According to government records, Scovill-Schrader and several other local industries buried drums of industrial waste solvents at the Dickson "open dump" landfill site in 1968—the same year Dr. Martin Luther King Jr. was assassinated in Memphis.

1972  The unlined landfill was granted a permit by the Tennessee Department of Health and Environment (TDEH).

1977  City of Dickson landfill was taken over by Dickson County, and a forty-five-acre expansion was approved by the state.

7/18/1988  The Dickson County landfill received numerous unsatisfactory operational notices from July 18, 1988, to April 12, 1999

1988  The Dickson County landfill accepted 275 to 300 cubic yards of solid waste from the CSX White Bluff derailment cleanup.

11/18/1988  Government test results completed on the Harry Holt and Lavenia Holt wells showed TCE contamination. The Harry Holt homestead is just fifty-four feet from the landfill property line.

12/2/1988  The TDHE approved the Dickson County landfill permit.

12/18/1988  The Tennessee Department of Health and Environment sent letters to Harry Holt and Lavenia Holt informing the family of the test results and the finding of trichloroethylene in their wells. The letter states: "Your water is of good quality for the parameters tested. It is felt that the low levels of methylene or trichloroethene may be due to either lab or sampling error."

1/28/1990  Government tests found 26 ppb (parts per billion) TCE in the Harry Holt well—five times above the established Maximum Contaminant Level (MCL) of 5 ppb set by the EPA .The MCL is the maximum concentration of a chemical that is allowed in public drinking water systems.

8/17/1990  Government tests found 3.9 ppb TCE in the Harry Holt well.

8/23/1991  Government test showed 3.7 ppb TCE in the Harry Holt well.

12/3/1991 The EPA sent the Harry Holt family a letter informing him of the three tests performed on his well and deeming the water safe. The letter states: "Use of your well water should not result in any adverse health effects." The letter further states: "It should be mentioned that trichloroethylene (TCE) was detected at 26 micrograms per ug/1 in the first sample. Because this detection exceeded EPA's maximum contaminant level (MCL) of 5 ug/1, the well water was resampled. TCE was detected at 3.7 ug/1 in the second sample, however, it was noted this sample contained air bubbles. EPA took then took a third sample with results nearly identical to the second (3.9 ug/1)."

12/17/1991 A letter from the Tennessee Department of Conservation expressed some concern about the level of TCE contamination found in the Holts' well. Tennessee Department of Health and Environment officials agreed that Mr. Holt's well should continue to be sampled. However, this was not done. The letter states: "Our program is concerned that the sampling twice with one considerably above the MCL and one slightly below the MCL in a karst area such as Dickson is in no way an assurance that Mr. Holt's well water will stay below MCL's. There is a considerably seasonal variation for contaminants in karst environments and 3.9 ppb TCE in only slightly under the MCL of 5 ppb." The Holt family was allowed to continue drinking contaminated well water.

1/6/1992 A letter from the Tennessee Department of Health and Environment continued to express concern about the level of contamination found in the Holt well. The letter states: "Mr. Holt's well was sampled as a result of the Preremedial Site Investigation and Ranking package on the Dickson County landfill for NPL consideration. Mr. Carr told me the field investigation was complete and that he was not in a position to sample Mr. Holt's well again even though it had sporadically shown TCE contamination above the MCL's. He agreed that Mr. Holt's well should continue to be sampled. There may be some chance of the site going NPL, but that will be at least 1–2 years away. Mr. Carr suggested I contact Nathan Sykes at (404) 347-2913 to determine why it was not felt that further monitoring or an alternate water supply was necessary."

3/13/1992 A letter from the TDEC sided with the EPA on whether the Holt family well water was "safe." The letter states: "Since EPA has already completed a site investigation, has identified the pollutants involved, and has, in part, determined the extent of the leaching, I would suggest that they, EPA, continue with their chosen course of action, rather than create the added confusion of various agencies making their own agendas. I would suggest that, if Mr. Holt is concerned about possible health risks in using his well water between now and June (when EPA's priority decision is made), that he should rely on bottled or city water for cooking and drinking purposes until he is convinced that his well water is safe."

1997  TCE was detected in water from a production well (DK-21) operated by the City of Dickson and located northeast of the landfill. The Harry Holt property lies between the leaky landfill and DK-21.

2/24/1997 The TDEC Division of Water Supply reported that the city of Dickson had tested the city lake and DK-21 and that trichloroethylene or TCE was detected at 1.3 ppb. The MCL is 5 ppb.

4/7/1997 TDEC Division of Water Supply completed a confirmation sample, testing City Lake, and TCE was not detected. The division's separate test of untreated water at DK-21's well source showed TCE at 14 ppb and Cis-1, 2 dichloromethane at 1.3 ppb.

4/18/97 The City of Dickson stopped using the DK-21 well as a supplement to the municipal water source after a call from the state requiring that an aeration or water filtration system be installed, according to the TDEC Division of Water Supply.

10/9/2000 Harry Holt well tested and registered a whopping 120 ppb TCE, twenty-four times the MCL of 5 ppb set by the EPA.

10/20/2000  The Holt family was placed on Dickson City water—twelve years after the first government tests found TCE in the family's well in 1988.

10/25/2000  A second test performed on the Holt family's well registered 145 ppb—twenty-four the MCL.

12/3/2003 The Harry Holt family filed a lawsuit against the City of Dickson, the County of Dickson, and Scovill, Inc.

11/23/2004 Judge George Sexton of the Dickson County Circuit Court ruled that a racial discrimination amendment could be added to the Holt family's complaint involving the alleged toxic poisoning of the family's well water near the Dickson County landfill.

11/6/2006  In a special called meeting, Dickson County Commissioners voted unanimously to settle lawsuits with several white families that had alleged groundwater contamination from the leaky landfill. The city and county agreed to give the families 75 percent of whatever money they received in New York bankruptcy court in claims that both had filed against Saltire Industrial, Inc., which the lawsuits allege dumped toxic waste at the landfill on Eno Road. Both the City of Dickson and Dickson

County had claims lodged against Saltire Industrial, Inc., in New York, for amounts in excess of $4 million.

1/09/2007 Sixty-six-ear old Harry Holt passed away in Dickson, Tennessee.

3/04/2008 Holt family and the Natural Resources Defense Council filed suit seeking cleanup of alleged water contamination in Dickson County, Tennessee.

12/31/2009 The Holt family wins a $250,000 judgment in New York bankruptcy court against Saltire (formerly Scovill, Inc.).

12/07/2011 Both of the Holt family's lawsuits against the City of Dickson and the County of Dickson were settled. The family's civil rights lawsuit against the state of Tennessee remains pending and awaits trial in federal court in Tennessee.

# Living and Dying on the Fenceline

*Response to Industrial Accidents*

Industrial accidents tend to impact poor communities, communities whose residents are people of color, and environmentally overburdened communities over time. Industrial accidents change the lives of fenceline communities because the residents are always speculating about or waiting for the next chemical spill or toxic contamination that they fear will be the one that destroys the entire community. Many fenceline communities face daily threats from industrial explosions, spills, leaks, and possible terrorist attacks. Accidents and explosions at chemical and industrial facilities are common. Enforcement of safety laws is desperately needed to reduce the frequency, severity, and effects of industrial accidents.

This chapter presents case studies of government response to industrial accidents and other incidents that have affected African Americans dating back to the early 1930s.The cases include the Gauley Bridge, West Virginia, mine disaster in 1930; the Gaylord Chemical tank car accident in Bogalusa, Louisiana, in 1995; the Norfolk Southern Railway train wreck that released toxic chlorine gas in Graniteville, South Carolina, in 2005; the ExxonMobil Baytown, Texas, refinery gas spill in 2006; the 2008 Tennessee Valley Authority (TVA) coal ash spill cleanup in mostly white East Tennessee and the disposal of the waste from that cleanup in 2009 in heavily poor and majority-black Perry County, Alabama. We also discuss the Deepwater Horizon oil rig explosion in the Gulf of Mexico in 2010.

The analysis spans eight decades—with case studies presented from the time before and after the passage of the Civil Rights Act of 1964 and the signing of Environmental Justice Executive Order 12898 in 1994.The analysis examines the role of race and race-based decision making and industrial practices in addressing threats from locally unwanted land uses (LULUs) and risky facilities in African American communities.

## The Risk of Toxic Chemicals

Approximately eighty thousand different chemicals are now in commercial use in the United States, and nearly six trillion pounds of such chemicals are produced annually in the United States. And nearly two thousand new chemicals are introduced annually; more than 80 percent of these have never been screened to learn whether they cause cancer, much less tested to see if they harm the human nervous system, immune system, endocrine system, or reproductive system. Many of the nation's chemical facilities present an unnecessary risk to their surrounding communities. All across the United States, petroleum refineries, chemical plants, and other industrial plants use and store massive amounts of hazardous chemicals that, if subject to an accident, would release dangerous toxins.[1]

The nation is still grappling with securing chemical plants, refineries, water treatment plants, and other vital facilities. Some progress has been made, but more needs to be done to improve safety and security inside and outside the plants. The public is also vulnerable to accidents involving the railways that run in and out of densely population areas. Our railways transport more than 1.7 million shipments of hazardous materials every year, and one hundred thousand tank cars filled with toxic gases like chlorine and anhydrous ammonia travel along rail lines.[2] Many of the trains are rolling time bombs waiting to explode. The explosion of a single car carrying chlorine near a densely populated area could kill as many as one hundred thousand people.

### Gauley Bridge, West Virginia (1930)

Gauley Bridge is a town in Fayette County, West Virginia. In 1930, Union Carbide and Carbon Corporation awarded the Rinehart and Dennis Corporation of Charlottesville, Virginia, $4.23 million to complete a tunnel, dam, and powerhouse for a hydroelectric plant on the New River to help boost West Virginia's economy.[3] The company was given two years to complete the project, which was designed to harness the powers of Gauley River, directing the waters through a tunnel and converting the water into electricity. The tunnel was of singular importance to Union Carbide and Carbon Corporation, making possible what would later be known as the "Chemical Valley of the World."[4] The total tunnel investment was $9 million.

During the early 1930s, more than three thousand men were involved in the project to dig a tunnel through Hawk's Nest in West Virginia. They worked six days a week in ten-hour shifts, while living in a life-threatening environment.[5] Blacks were assigned the dirtiest and most dangerous jobs, paid less, and charged higher rents for housing than white workers.[6]

Black workers, who made up more than 75 percent of the new workers, were assigned to do drilling and mucking, the most dangerous tasks. In *The Hawk's Nest Incident: America's Worst Industrial Disaster*, Martin Cherniack recounts how, over the months, many African Americans died of silicosis, but only with the death of white immigrants did the deaths gain recognition.

In his book, Cherniack chronicles in menacing detail this forgotten event by presenting his findings from an extensive examination of local historical materials, interviews from survivors, and county death records.[7] Cherniack, a physician with expertise in occupational disease, underscored how race and politics informed local residents' memories of this historical incident, even generations after the events took place.

Although a plaque at the tunnel describes its construction as a "marvel of modern engineering," the Hawk's Nest Tunnel did not come without a high price in human suffering and death.[8] Completed in 1936, the tunnel is 16,240 feet (a little over three miles) in length and drops in elevation a total of 163 feet (equivalent to a sixteen-story building). Nobody really knows how many people died working on the tunnel during its five-year construction period.

For nearly a decade, it was dangerous to even talk about the tragedy in West Virginia. In 1939, the governor of West Virginia refused to sanction a Federal Writer's Guide for the State until the writers softened their lengthy and graphic depiction of Hawk's Nest.[9] The Hawk's Nest scandal came to public light only because of militant labor, Franklin Delano Roosevelt's New Deal, and congressional hearings called in 1935, at which one senator described the West Virginia catastrophe as "American industry's black Calcutta." During a congressional hearing, a Union Carbide contractor testified that "I knew I was going to kill those niggers, but I didn't know it was going to be this soon."[10]

In 1936, prompted by findings from the hearings, industry executives gathered at the Mellon Institute and formed the Air Hygiene Foundation (also known as the Industrial Hygiene Foundation and, later, the Industrial Health Foundation) to wage a public relations campaign on behalf of the industry and to allay public concern about silicosis, an often-fatal lung disease caused by the inhalation of silica dust. Writing in *Trust Us, We're Experts*, Sheldon Rampton and John Staubner pointed out how industry manipulated their doctors and gabled with their workers' health at Hawk's Nest:

The exposures that cause disease were only symptoms of a deeper problem—corporate denial regarding the deadly risks associated with growing industrialization. The company doctors who lied to dying workers at Hawk's Nest were following a new version of the Hippocratic Oath: "First, do no harm to the boss." This willingness to subordinate health to profits was common and notorious among physicians who worked for industry. . . . Company doctors were known as the least competent and least ethical of their profession.[11]

Life was cheap during the Great Depression. And black lives were the cheapest. Black deaths were underreported, thus skewing the number of deaths even further. Fifty years after the accident, Cherniack placed the death toll from silicosis at the Hawk's Nest Tunnel at 764 workers, making it the "worst industrial accident" in U.S. history.[12] More lives were lost at Gauley Bridge than were lost in the 1947 ammonium nitrate explosion in Texas City, Texas, where six hundred workers perished.[13]

Silicosis claimed the lives of mostly poor and black Hawk's Nest Tunnel workers, sometimes as quickly as within a single year. The disease infects the lungs and gradually causes the cells to digest themselves. The disaster is a landmark case of environmental racism, a conflict between the powerful and the powerless, between African Americans and the white power structure that devalued human life when measured against profits. The supervisors and the company doctors downplayed the health risks associated with breathing the silica dust created by digging and dynamiting the tunnel shaft, with the result that the lungs of the workers were permanently damaged.

Racism was a determining factor in the actions taken by the corporation. Wet drilling, a process that would have held down the quantity of dust, was not seen as a viable alternative because it would have slowed down the excavation. The white foremen were provided with masks, while the mostly black workers were forced to work in the tunnel unprotected. More than 538 lawsuits were filed against Union Carbide, of which 34 were settled for a total of $200,000.[14] Money was allocated among the plaintiffs on the basis of race and marital status, just as wages and housing had been earlier.[15] A single black man received $400, while a married white man received $1,000. Families of dead workers received an extra $600.[16]

Some of the black disaster victims were hastily buried in mass graves, thrown in the river, or covered in pits to try to hide the deaths. Bodies were transported to Nicholas County and buried unceremoniously on a private farm. "Workers were dying on the job causing the company to hire a local undertaker to dispose of bodies in fields nearby."[17] These workers were disproportionately poor and black and miles away from their family, which encouraged the managers to "believe that they could cover up the deaths."[18] "There were no headstones for the graves that have been found."[19]

After the Hawk's Nest incident, all but two states amended their worker compensation laws to include silica as a hazard that can justify compensation.[20] Rinehart and Dennis never competed for a major project after paying compensation for the deadly accident. On the other hand, Union Carbide, though claiming no responsibility for the silicosis, went on to become a giant multinational chemical company, dominating West Virginia's "Chemical Valley" and employing more than 11,500 employees worldwide. In addition to having enormous economic power from Belgium to Ecuador, the company has come to be known for environmental injustice related to its activities at Hawk's Nest (West Virginia), Bhopal (India), and Institute (West Virginia). In 2007, Dow Chemical acquired Union Carbide for $7.4 billion, creating the world's second largest chemical company, topped only by DuPont.

## Railcar Gas Explosion, Bogalusa, Louisiana (1995)

Bogalusa is a city in Washington Parish, Louisiana. The population was 13,365 at the time of the 2000 census, and it is the only community in Washington Parish incorporated as a city. The population density was 1,407.6 per square mile. The racial makeup of the city was 57.18 percent white, 41.2 percent African American, 0.32 percent Native American, 0.39 percent Asian, 0.16 percent of other races, and 0.73 percent from two or more races. Hispanics of any race made up 0.75 percent of the population.

According to the National Transportation Safety Board (NTSB), on October 23, 1995, at 3:55 p.m., yellow-brown vapors began leaking from the dome of a railroad tank car at the Gaylord Chemical Corporation plant in Bogalusa. The tank car contained a mixture of nitrogen tetroxide, which is a liquefied poisonous gas and oxidizer. The tank car was owned by the Vicksburg Chemical Company.

Vapors from the explosion formed a plume between ten and fifteen feet in diameter. Plant personnel notified emergency response agencies and used two plant fire hoses to spray water into the plume to suppress the vapors. At about 4:30 p.m., Bogalusa fire personnel arrived at the plant and set up fire hoses to help suppress the vapors.

The tank car failed about 4:45 p.m., when an explosion tore away one end of the tank car jacket and threw it about 350 feet. The tank car was then propelled thirty-five feet down the track and later derailed in a populated area. A large reddish-brown vapor cloud was released from the tank car for another thirty-six hours, until the chemical reaction that had occurred within the tank was brought under control through neutralization and dilution.[21]

The NTSB described the probable cause of the accident as "lack of adequate procedures on the part of the Gaylord Chemical Corporation and the Vicksburg Chemical Company to prevent or detect the contamination on [sic] nitrogen tetroxide with water, resulting in the formation of an extremely corrosive product and the subsequent failure of the tank car. Contributing to the severity of the accident were the Gaylord Chemical Corporation's inadequate procedures for emergency transfer of contaminated cargo from the tank car."[22]

Gaylord, it was alleged, had ignored warnings and safety recommendations that could have prevented the accident.[23] The company had failed in "providing safety systems, adequately training their employees, enforcing safe operating and maintenance procedures, and conducting inspections to detect abnormal conditions."[24] The company did not have an emergency response program (ERP) to handle major leaks in the facility. The U.S. Occupational Safety and Health Administration (OSHA) fined Gaylord $15,000 for seven work safety violation rules during the leak.

The "911" records show that the police were kept in the dark after the tanker blast. Police and firefighters, who had no chemical safety equipment, responding to the emergency call knew nothing about how to handle this type of accident or the type of chemical involved.[25] Nitrogen tetroxide has a wide variety of uses; it was used to create a "controlled explosion" to lift Apollo spacecraft off the moon in the 1960s and 1970s. Gaylord uses it to make pharmaceuticals and agricultural chemicals.

More than three thousand of Bogalusa's thirteen thousand residents were evacuated from the area as a result of the vapor cloud. Of a total of 4,710 people who were treated in emergency rooms at local hospitals for burning eyes, skin, and lungs, 81 were admitted. On Monday afternoon, the pinkish cloud of potentially deadly chemical forced the initial evacuation of 1,400 people living within a one-mile radius of the spill. On Tuesday evening, another 1,500 residents were ordered out of their homes as the hazardous-materials experts tried to contain the chemical leak.[26]

Bogalusa's population was 57.2 percent white and 41.2 percent black. Many African Americans viewed the response to the gas leak as racist.[27] Several Bogalusa black leaders say that race was a factor in the evacuation of citizens after the Monday's gas leak. In a letter to Louisiana governor Edwin Edwards,

Citizens Concerned About the Gaylord Gas Poisoning charged that the city's black neighborhoods were evacuated one and a half days after the predominately white neighborhoods were evacuated. The letter reads:

> Immediately following the explosion this week, a forced evacuation took place in the area that first included mostly white families near the plant. Then, after all the shelters were filled, a day and a half later, a much larger area that included most of the African American communities around the plant were evacuated. By that time, many of us had no transportation. The shelters were already full with the people first evacuated. Our phone service was disconnected. We couldn't telephone to get help. This was hell. We had to travel out of town the best way we could to find shelter.[28]

In November 1995, the charge of environmental racism got a shot in the arm from attorney Johnnie Cochran, who promised to create a legal "dream team" to fight this injustice.[29] A cheering crowd of four hundred black residents packed the gymnasium of Bethlehem Baptist Church in Bogalusa to hear Cochran. The lawyer told the crowd he had grown up in Shreveport and that he had long been concerned about environmental racism. He ended up representing between two thousand and three thousand black Bogalusa residents.[30] More than two dozen lawsuits were filed in the state and federal court because of the accident.

Most of the litigation was consolidated in state court into a class action suit with sixteen thousand plaintiffs bringing suit against three defendants: the Vicksburg Chemical Company, which had manufactured the nitrogen tetroxide; the Kansas City Southern and Illinois Central Railroad; and the Westchester Insurance Company. In May 2005, after a decade, the lawsuit was finally settled for $50 million.[31] The settlement also covered an additional 4,500 Louisiana residents who had filed suits in Mississippi. The amount received by the nearly 20,500 victims ranged "from $41.50 up to and in excess of $150,000."

The sixteen thousand plaintiffs in the class-action suit were awarded an additional payout from a $30 million settlement with the Gaylord Chemical Company; the Gaylord Container Corporation, its parent company; and some of the companies' insurers. Also pending in the court system was an award of $92 million in punitive damages awarded to the plaintiffs by a Washington Parish jury in late 2003.[32] In 2008, final settlement was reached in the lawsuit, which had dragged on for more than a decade. The settlements required Gaylord, Vicksburg Chemical, and other companies to pay the plaintiffs more than $120 million, which included $70.9 million distributed in May 2005 and an additional $51 million dispersed by a court order.[33]

## Deadly Train Wreck, Graniteville, South Carolina (2005)

Graniteville is an unincorporated community in Aiken County, South Carolina. It lies along U.S. Route 1, which runs five miles west of Aiken. In 2000, Graniteville reported a population of 7,009, up from around 1,000 in 1990; the area is 34.72 square miles, of which 0.6 percent is water. The population is 2.1 percent Hispanic/Latino, 69 percent white, 26.8 percent black, 1 percent Native American, and 0.3 percent Asian.[34] It is home to Avondale Mills, a company that was at one time the largest denim manufacturer in the United States.

On the early morning of January 6, 2005, two Norfolk Southern Railway Company trains crashed into each other, releasing deadly chlorine gas in Graniteville, killing 9 people, injuring 240, and forcing the evacuation of nearly 5,500 residents.[35] The residents who lived within a mile of the crash site were ordered to evacuate the area for about two weeks while hazardous material (HAZMAT) teams and cleanup crews decontaminated the area.

The derailment occurred when a Norfolk Southern freight train with forty-two cars struck a train with one locomotive and two cars at an Avondale Mills textile facility at about 2:40 a.m.[36] Three of the Norfolk Southern Railway Company tank cars each carried ninety tons of the deadly chlorine gas. Days after the wreck, the railway company was still unable to control the leaking chlorine gas. Eight of the nine victims of the crash died within the first hours after impact. The ninth victim, the train's engineer, died the next day in the hospital.

The Graniteville disaster highlights the risks to communities through which railroads passes. In 2002, three million tons of chlorine, about thirty-seven thousand tank car loads, were moved by rail in North America.[37] It is possible for another Graniteville disaster to occur if the railroad industry does not upgrade its tank cars and lines. In October 2004, government safety officials warned that more than half of the nation's sixty thousand pressurized rail tank cars did not meet industry standards and raised questions about the safety of the rest of the fleet, as well. The tragedy also points to the issue of fairness in emergency response.[38] Some residents in Graniteville's all-black New Hope community complained that the Aiken County government emergency responders left the black community behind while evacuating whites.[39] "The New Hope community on the east side of town roughly between Gregg Highway and A. P. Nievens Street has an estimated population of more than 1,000 residents."[40] African Americans claim that white residents were evacuated shortly after the 2:39 a.m. wreck but that many black New Hope community residents were not evacuated until 3:30 p.m. that afternoon, almost thirteen hours later. Residents say they were ignored because they were poor, black, and politically powerless.

New Hope resident Pamela Hall reported that she could not get the county or Norfolk Southern officials to inspect her school, the Hall Gaffney Learning Center, a private school that serves prekindergarten through second-grade children, for safety before the students were allowed to re-enter it after the disaster, although the EPA eventually sent a worker to inspect the school.[41] Some of the residents strongly believe that the New Hope section of Graniteville is always the last to get any attention, services, or aid from the government even during an incident like the train wreck disaster. Pamela Hall has firsthand experience with her community being slighted over the years. In an interview conducted a few months after the accident, she said:

> It's always been a display of racism in this area for us. When I was a small child growing up in this segregated community, there were two Church Streets, one in the New Hope area and another Church Street on the other side of town in the white area. I can remember when we would have to call the volunteer fire department; they would always go to the Church Street in the white community before they would come to the Church Street in the New Hope community. By the time they would get to the fire in the black community nine times out of ten the house would have burned down.[42]

The financial cost of the train disaster was estimated at between $30 million and $40 million. On May 25, 2005, Norfolk Southern reached a preliminary agreement on settlements for impacted residents. The agreement covered all residents who had been evacuated and who had not sought medical attention within seventy-two hours of the accident. According to the agreement, each plaintiff received $2,000 for the evacuation plus $200 for each day of the evacuation.[43] This settlement did not cover property damage, injuries, or death.

Avondale Mills filed suit against Norfolk Southern, claiming that the company was negligent in its operations through Graniteville and that the alleged negligence was the root cause of the accident. Avondale Mills was closed; in the suit, it claimed that it had laid off thousands of employees and paid more than $140 million in cleanup and repair expenses.

In 2008, Avondale Mills and Norfolk Southern settled for an undisclosed amount in lieu of the $420 million that Avondale Mills was seeking. A federal judge approved a class action lawsuit to compensate those badly injured in the accident by Norfolk Southern and estimated that it would cost $16.2 million to pay those claims. As of 2008, at least fifteen injury cases were still pending against Norfolk Southern.[44]

In March 2010, Norfolk Southern Railway Company agreed to pay the U.S. Justice Department a $4 million penalty to resolve alleged violations of the Clean Water Act (CWA) and hazardous materials laws for a 2005 chlorine spill. The money is to be deposited in the federal Oil Spill Liability Trust Fund.[45]

## ExxonMobil Refinery Oil Spill, Baytown, Texas (2006)

Baytown is a city in Chambers and Harris counties in the Gulf Coast region of the state of Texas. It is located within the Houston Sugar Land-Baytown metropolitan area along both state Highway 146 and Interstate 10. According to the 2000 census, Baytown's population was 66,430, making it the fourth largest city within the metropolitan area.[46] The population density was 2,034.4 people per square mile. The racial makeup of the city was 67.87 percent white, 13.38 percent African American, 0.5 percent Native American, 0.98 percent Asian, 0.08 percent Pacific Islander; 14.42 percent identified themselves as being of other races, and 2.77 percent said they were of two or more races. Hispanics of any race made up 34.24 percent of the population.

On Sunday, January 25, 2006, a 150,000-barrel storage tank at the ExxonMobil refinery in Baytown spilled its contents, a heated substance called process gas oil, or PGO, releasing 1,400 barrels of oil droplets into the nearby neighborhood. Steam from the plant spread an oily film over homes, cars, and playground equipment.[47] Process gas oil contains benzene, a known carcinogen. ExxonMobil safety information reveals that process gas oil, a close relative to crude oil, can irritate the skin after prolonged exposure.[48] Nonetheless, "Investigations by the company and the Harris County Public Health and Environmental Services Office determined that the incident was caused because the tank overfilled and operators failed to notice because of a malfunctioning gauge."[49]

Residents of Archia Court, a fifty-eight-unit federally subsidized public housing complex located across the street from the refinery, described hearing two instances of what sounded like thunder, fifteen minutes apart, around 11:00 p.m. on Sunday. The noise was so loud that it shook the windows in their homes. The housing complex residents woke up on Monday morning to find their homes and cars covered in an oily film. Residents complained that this was the worst spill from ExxonMobil that they had seen in the time they had lived in the area. The residents were suspicious about how the company went about cleaning up the spill, as described by one resident:

> The trucks, emblazoned with the names of environmental cleanup companies arrived first, clogging the entrance of the Archia Courts [sic] public housing complex Tuesday morning. By the time Judy Mixon's husband roused her from bed, 30 men, some carrying buckets and brooms, others wearing backpacks full of cleaning liquid, were spraying down the playground equipment, scrubbing aluminum siding and washing the caramel-colored splatter that coated residents' cars. You come out of your house and they are cleaning, and you say "Something ain't right."[50]

Residents for years have complained to officials about noise, odors, and the glow of flares burning off gases at the refinery.[51] After the spill, some residents described a "chemical smell" and said the air was "like a fog." ExxonMobil officials insisted that the release was not harmful. Monday afternoon, hours after residents bombarded the company with complaints, ExxonMobil sent a team of thirty workers wearing jumpsuits and plastic gloves. On Tuesday, the company distributed a letter, signed by the manager, describing and apologizing for the incident to the residents and the Baytown Housing Authority.

Local residents and state and county environmental officials questioned why ExxonMobil took so long to report the accident.[52] The Texas Commission on Environmental Quality (TCEQ), the state agency in charge of protecting the public from pollution, launched an investigation into the delayed notification. Current Texas law calls for reporting spills within twenty-four hours.

ExxonMobil first reported the spill to the TCEQ more than twelve hours after the spill. And it was not until Tuesday that the company informed TCEQ officials of the cleanup and reported that the spill extended beyond the plant's grounds and was affecting the nearby community. Harris County's Pollution Control and Environmental Health Division officials learned of the off-site release from media accounts on Wednesday, more than two days after the incident.

Penalties for late reporting and creating a nuisance are set between $2,500 and $10,000—hardly a deterrent for ExxonMobil, the largest energy company in the world. The company does business in nearly two hundred countries and on six continents. It has thirty-seven refineries located in twenty-one countries. The ExxonMobil petroleum refinery/petrochemical complex, located in Baytown, is the largest of its kind in the world.

Harris County filed a civil lawsuit against ExxonMobil over violations resulting from the release of process oil from the company's Baytown refinery.[53] The lawsuit cites many violations of state regulations that were found, including these: (1) the spill created a nuisance condition for Archia Court residents such that it interfered with their enjoyment of the property and adversely affected their human health; (2) the company violated the refinery's flexible permit because the spill could have been avoided with good design and better operation and maintenance practices; (3) the company violated the Texas Health and Safety Code by emitting air contaminants that contributed to air pollution; and (4) the company violated the Texas Administrative Code by failing to notify the Texas Commission on Environmental Quality as soon as it discovered that the process gas oil spill had gone off site and affected the nearby neighborhood.[54]

The lawsuit stated that violators of the Texas Water Code could face penalties of $50 to $250,000 per day. In fact, after the spill, ExxonMobil officials renewed the company's efforts to purchase the Archia Court neighborhood from the Baytown Housing Authority, which owns the 1940s-era complex. In 2003, the company offered the Authority $2.1 million for the property as part of its "'greenbelt' program."[55]

Environmental advocates pressured ExxonMobil to buy Archia Court and to relocate the residents.[56] The company had already expressed interest in buying the housing complex but the purchase cannot take place until they find an alternate location for the housing complex and its residents. "It is time for these folks to be relocated and be in a safer area than ExxonMobil's fenceline."[57] In April 2009, HUD approved a proposal from the the the Baytown Housing Authority to relocate the residents from the Archia Housing development.

### TVA Toxic Coal Ash Disposal, Perry County, Alabama (2009)

On December 22, 2008, a wall holding back eighty acres of sludge at the Kingston Fossil Plant, operated by the Tennessee Valley Authority (TVA), the nation's largest public utility, broke, spilling more than five cubic yards of toxic coal ash over a dozen homes and across up to three hundred acres of the surrounding landscape, endangering aquatic life and the water supply for more than twenty-five thousand residents.[58] The cost of the TVA spill pre-vention and cleanup was estimated to perhaps top $3 billion, with about $1.2 billion for just the cleanup.

Six months after the gigantic spill, on July 2, 2009, EPA Region IV approved TVA's decision to ship 5.4 million cubic yards of toxic coal ash by railcar from the mostly white Roane County in eastern Tennessee to the Arrowhead landfill, located in predominately black Perry County, Ala-bama.[59] More than 3.9 million tons of the TVA coal ash were destined for Perry County, which is 69 percent African American and where more than 32 percent of the residents live in poverty; the county is located in the heart of the Alabama "Black Belt."[60] A proposal also called for shipping some of the toxic coal ash to rural Taylor County, Georgia, where 41 percent of the population is African American and more than 24 percent of residents live in poverty.

TVA also considered shipping the coal ash to two communities in eastern Tennessee: Athens, in McMinn County, which is more than 93 percent white, with 18 percent of its residents living in poverty, and Oneida, in Scott County, which is more than 98 percent white, with 21 percent of its residents living in poverty. However, TVA officials sought state regulators' approval only for the Alabama and Georgia sites.[61] The bulk of the toxic goop was shipped by rail to Uniontown, Alabama, more than three hundred miles from the spill. Uniontown has about 1,600 residents, 88 percent of whom are black.[62] TVA's toxic-waste disposal decision is consistent with the racially biased "Dumping in Dixie" disposal pattern documented more than two decades ago—con-firming that all communities in the South are still not created equal.[63]

TVA's Off-Site Ash Disposal Option Analysis Work Plan described the Arrowhead landfill as located in "an isolated area, surrounded by large tracts of property, farms and ranches."[64] However, "isolated" is not defined. More than three hundred residents, homeowners, and cattle farmers lived within a half-mile of the landfill. Ruby Holmes, an eighty-year-old great grand-mother, lived less than one hundred feet from the landfill property lines. She had lived in the community all of her life.

The TVA plan of June 30, 2009, also stated that "TVA officials met with six local elected officials, including county commissioners, a Mayor, and a City Council member to discuss the potential use of the Arrowhead facil-ity as a disposal site for the KIF material." However, no public hearing was held in Perry County prior to EPA's decision, on July 2, 2009, to approve the disposal plan. Only after charges of environmental racism were raised did EPA Region IV conduct a cursory environmental justice analysis as required under Executive Order 12898. The normal procedure is to have such an analysis performed before a decision is made. EPA's seventeen-page "draft," "Perry County Environmental Justice Analysis: Perry County, Alabama," dated September 23, 2009, came nearly three months after the agency had approved the TVA plan to dispose of the toxic coal ash at the Arrowhead landfill.[65]

Since July 2009, the Arrowhead landfill has disposed between eight thousand and eleven thousand tons of waste every day, most of it coal ash from East Tennessee. The coal ash arrives on railcars sealed in thick plastic that TVA officials call "burrito wraps."[66] The decision by the TVA to ship the toxic coal ash to the 976.5 acres Subtitle D Municipal Solid Waste Arrowhead landfill (a facility that is licensed to accept household garbage) in Perry County raised a cry of "environmental racism." Uniontown residents were not given the opportunity to comment before the agreement was finalized. On July 20, 2009, more than two weeks after the plan was approved by EPA Region IV, the Alabama Department of Environmental Management (ADEM) modified the Arrowhead landfill permit "service area, disposal volume, and minor operational changes" to allow it accept the TVA coal ash. ADEM had issued the permit for the landfill in 2006, allowing it to receive a maximum of fifteen thousand tons of waste a day from seventeen states.

The controversial disposal decision, hammered out by top EPA Region IV holdovers from the Bush administration and TVA officials, caught EPA officials in Washington off guard and placed EPA administrator Lisa P. Jackson and Mathy Stanislaus, her newly confirmed assistant for the Office of Solid Waste and Emergency Response (OSWER), on the defensive. Grassroots and national groups pressed the Obama administration to make environmental justice and equal protection top priorities and to address the Perry County injustice, which had happened on his watch.

Environmental justice groups also reminded the EPA not to forget that, in 1982, it had been the shipment and disposal of dirt contaminated with polychlorinated biphenyls (PCBs) in a 142-acre landfill in rural, poor, and mostly black Warren County, North Carolina, that had set off citizen protests, demonstrations, and arrests, sparking the national environmental justice movement. They emphasized that EPA Region IV had assured Warren County residents that the PCB-contaminated landfill was safe and would not leak. Yet, the landfill was shown to be leaking as early as 1993—a decade after the toxic waste was deposited.[67]

EPA and ADEM officials assured Perry County residents that they would receive the same level of protection as that given to residents of Roane

County, Tennessee. All of these assurances were made at the time the Arrowhead landfill operator faced threats of legal challenges related to the Perry County ash disposal. In January 2010, the Arrowhead landfill owners filed for protection under Chapter 11 of the federal bankruptcy code. The action halted any new legal actions against the operators of the landfill.[68]

Since July 2009, nearly a million tons of coal ash, which contains toxins and heavy metals such as arsenic, mercury, and other toxins, have been disposed of at the Arrowhead landfill. Coal ash is the second-largest industrial waste stream in the United States. When coal ash comes in contact with water, hazardous chemicals leach out of the waste and can contaminate groundwater and surface water. A 2007 EPA risk assessment found extremely high risks to human health and the environment from the disposal of coal ash in waste ponds and landfills.[69] These disturbing findings were reaffirmed in 2009 by a coalition of environmental groups, indicating that some coal ash poses significant threats to public health and the environment.[70]

In April 2010, environmental leaders from 239 national, state, and local public interest groups from all fifty states, in a letter, appealed directly to President Obama to issue federal coal ash safeguards that protect public health and the environment. In May 2010, ten months after the first railcars loaded with TVA coal ash rolled into Uniontown, Alabama, the EPA announced the first-ever national rules to ensure the safe disposal and management of coal ash from coal-fired power plants. The EPA's assessment and damage cases indicate that, unless proper protective measures are taken, coal ash can pose significant public health concerns.[71] The spill in Kingston, Tennessee, and the coal ash disposal problem in Perry County, Alabama, raised awareness of the dangers of coal ash and made clear the need for strict EPA oversight, since unregulated dumping of coal ash had already contaminated groundwater and surface water at more than one hundred sites across the country with arsenic and other heavy metals.

Perry County is not the only Alabama "Black Belt" county targeted for waste dumping. In 2000, national civil rights and environmental justice groups successfully blocked the construction of landfills in Macon County (86.4 percent black) near Tuskegee University and in Lowndes County (75.7 percent black), off U.S. Highway 80, which in 1996 was designated the "Selma to Montgomery National Historic Trail." Some waste companies and government agencies see nothing wrong with "trashing" black history or black communities.[72] Six years after the successes in Macon and Lowndes Counties, in 2006, Perry County's Uniontown residents fought the Arrowhead landfill.

However, without national support, they were unsuccessful in stopping the landfill from being built.

Because of lax environmental regulations and "look-the-other-way" practices, Alabama has become the dumping grounds for all types of waste, including household garbage.[73] A growing number of Alabama landfills have become magnets for out-of-state waste. Because Alabama charges the lowest dumping fees per ton of any state in the country, Alabama landfills have been permitted to receive nineteen million tons of garbage per year—almost five times more trash than is generated in the state annually.

Simply put, Alabama has become one of the best places in the nation to dump garbage and other wastes, including toxic coal ash. African Americans and other people of color make up 66.3 percent of the residents who live within two miles of commercial hazardous-waste facilities in Alabama.[74] Generally, landfill fees are lower in the southern United States than anywhere else in the country. It is no wonder that so much waste from other parts of the country make its way south. And, when the waste gets sorted out and disposed of in the region, it is no surprise that black and poor communities get more than their fair share of the waste. This pattern has continued unabated for decades—despite contamination, health threats, protests, and lawsuits.

### The Deepwater Horizon Oil Spill, Gulf of Mexico (2010)

Tens of thousands of industrial accidents, leaks, and spills occur each year in the United States. Many of the spills go unnoticed. Few accidents grab the headlines and the attention of the nation and the world as happened after the April 20, 2010, explosion of an oil rig owned by British Petroleum (BP) in the Gulf of Mexico off the coast of Louisiana. The oil spill started when the Deepwater Horizon rig, leased by BP from Transocean Ltd., exploded and burned, killing eleven workers.

The BP oil accident was a disaster waiting to happen. Environmental groups for decades have called on the government to pay closer attention to abandoned oil and gas wells in the Gulf of Mexico, as federal regulators do not typically inspect or monitor the plugging of leaky offshore wells.[75]

The BP accident created the largest oil disaster in U.S. history—even larger than the 1989 Exxon Valdez spill in Alaska. Efforts to tracking the amount of oil spewing into the Gulf were mired in secrecy and controversy. BP kept changing the numbers, adding to the mounting public mistrust of the oil giant. BP first estimated the spill to be releasing a paltry five thousand barrels (210,000 gallons) of oil per day. Government and independent scientists later confirmed that the well was in fact pouring as much as sixty thousand barrels, or 2.5 million gallons, of oil into the Gulf every day. Documenting the amount of oil released is crucial since the London-based BP PLC is likely to be fined per gallon spilled.

BP also used more than 1.8 million gallons of dispersants on the Gulf's surface and at depths up to five thousand feet deep at the source of the leak —the largest amount ever used on a U.S. oil spill. Dispersants are supposed to neutralize the oil spill's toxic effects by breaking the oil down and spreading it around. The government and BP lack scientific information on the long-term effects of dispersants. Some Gulf Coast residents, fishermen, environmentalists, and marine biologists fear that dispersants may kill more sea life than the oil. In defiance of an EPA order, BP pumped more than a million gallons of the Corexit dispersant, a neurotoxin pesticide, into the Gulf of Mexico. Corexit was banned as a dispersant in the United Kingdom in 1998.

The oil spill created an environmental nightmare on the Gulf Coast from Florida to Texas, and BP's oil cleanup and containment plan received widespread criticism. According to the National Oceanic and Atmospheric Administration (NOAA), the government closed more than 81,181 square miles of the Gulf, or approximately 33.5 percent of the Gulf's federal waters, to fishing. The spill fouled 120 miles of U.S. coastline, imperiled multi-billion-dollar fishing and tourism industries and killed birds, sea turtles, and dolphins. The full health, environmental, and economic impacts of this catastrophe may not become clear for decades.

While the media spotlight has focused attention on efforts to stop the massive oil leak and clean up the spill, the same level of attention was not given to where the oil-spill cleanup waste would eventually be dumped— even after an Associated Press spot check showed mishandling of waste and shoddy disposal work.[76] Before one drop of oil was cleaned up, black people were asking, "Where will the oil- spill waste go after it has been collected from the beaches and skimmed off the water?" The answer: solid-waste landfills. Concern mounted about which communities would be selected as the final resting place for BP's garbage. Because of the size of the massive oil spill, even white communities in the Gulf Coast began asking this same question: "Where is the waste going?"[77]

Given the sad history of waste disposal in the southern United States, it should be no surprise to anyone that the BP waste disposal plan mirrored past "Dumping in Dixie" patterns and became a core environmental justice concern, especially among low-income communities and communities of people of color along the Gulf Coast—communities whose residents have historically borne more than their fair share of solid-waste landfills and hazardous-waste facilities before and after natural and man-made disasters.[78]

A large segment of the African American community was skeptical of BP, the oil and gas industry, and the government long before the disastrous Gulf oil spill, since black communities too often have been on the receiving end of polluting industries without receiving the benefit of jobs and have been used as a repository for other people's rubbish. It is more than ironic that black and other communities of color get BP's garbage, while mostly white companies rake in millions in BP contracts. It does not take a rocket scientist to figure out that this flow of benefits is inequitable.

Black communities were getting more than their fair share of BP oil-spill waste, yet they were locked out of cleanup contracts and other opportunities related to addressing this disaster. Using the latest Federal Procurement Data System (FPDS) information (July 9, 2010), the environmental writer Brentin Mock found that "minorities see little green in BP oil spill jobs."[79] He discovered that only $2.2 million of $53 million in federal contracts, a paltry 4.8 percent, had actually gone to small, disadvantaged businesses. Women-owned businesses had received 4.2 percent of contracts, and, of the 212 vendors with contracts, just 2 were African American, 18 were minority owned, and none were historically black colleges or universities (HBCUs), even though there are three just in New Orleans: Xavier University, Dillard University, and Southern University at New Orleans.

In mid-June 2010, environmental justice and equity concerns were aired at the EPA National Environmental Justice Advisory Council (NEJAC) in New Orleans and on an EPA conference call meeting "attended" by more than 370 callers.[80] EPA administrator Lisa P. Jackson, who was on the call for thirty minutes, emphasized that environmental justice was a priority and indicated that her agency had added staffers to the Joint Information Center to work specifically on environmental justice concerns in the agency's day-to-day operations.

In August 2009, Mathy Stanislaus, EPA assistant administrator for the Office of Solid Waste and Emergency Response (OSWER), posited some key questions and challenges for his office. One question seems especially relevant for the BP spill. Stanislaus asks, "How can we develop better strategies for handling waste or cleaning up contaminated sites?" The answer is simple: make the strategies fair, just, and equitable without regard to race, color, or national origin, or income status.

This has not happened. African American communities along the Gulf Coast still see the PIBBY (Place in Blacks' Back Yard) principle operating: a mindset that allows a disproportionate share of black communities to be targeted for BP oil-spill waste disposal. Gulf Coast residents who live on the fenceline with landfills are determined not to see a repetition of past mistakes that allowed waste from major industrial accidents or disasters to be dumped on poor and politically powerless African American communities.

Because of the haphazard handling and disposal of the wastes from the destroyed well, the U.S Coast Guard and the EPA leaned on BP and increased their oversight of the company's waste management plan approved on June 13, 2010.[81] BP hired private contractors, including Waste Management, Inc., the nation's largest trash hauler, to cart away and dispose of thousands of tons of polluted sand, crude-coated boom and refuse that washed ashore.

In a January 12, 2010, letter, EPA administrator Lisa P. Jackson declared environmental justice as one of "seven priorities" for EPA's future.[82] However, no environmental justice or equity analysis was conducted with regard to where the BP oil-spill cleanup waste actually ended up. Some community leaders insist that such an analysis should have accompanied the waste management plan before any landfill facilities were approved by the EPA and the U.S. Coast Guard. The approved Gulf Coast solid-waste landfills (Subtitle D landfills) and the percentage of minority residents among the population living within a one-mile radius of the facilities are presented in Table 7.1.

Although people of color make up about 26 percent of the coastal counties in Alabama, Florida, Mississippi, and Louisiana, government officials approved a plan that would allow most of the BP oil waste to be trucked to communities often shortchanged in terms of environmental justice. For example, on July 15, 2010—the earliest reporting period—39,399 tons of BP waste went to nine landfills; of this, 21,867 tons (55.4 percent) were disposed of in communities of color. More than 30,338 tons (77.0 percent) of oil waste went to communities where the percentage of people of color was greater than the percentage of people of color in the host county.

As of April 10, 2011—the latest reporting period—106,409 tons of BP waste had gone to eleven landfills. Of this amount, 45,032 tons (42.3 percent) went to landfills in communities where a majority of the residents are people of color, and 90,554 tons (85.1 percent) went to landfills located in communities whose percentage of people of color population exceeded the county's percentage. Clearly, one year after the BP oil disaster, communities with high percentages of minority residents still bear the brunt of the oil-waste disposal. Residents who live in fenceline communities abutting land-

*Table 7.1. Solid Waste Landfills Approved to Receive BP Oil-Spill Waste (July 2010)*

| Approved Landfills (Subtitle D Facilities) | One-Mile Population | One-Mile Percent Minority | One-Mile Percent below Poverty | County | Percent Minority (County) | Percent Poor (County) |
|---|---|---|---|---|---|---|
| Chastang Landfill (Waste Management) Mount Vernon, AL | 156 | 56.2 | 16.7 | Mobile, AL | 36.9 | 19.7 |
| Magnolia Landfill (Waste Management) Summerdale, AL | 295 | 11.5 | 13.2 | Baldwin, AL | 12.9 | 10.0 |
| Timberland Landfill (Allied Services) Brewton, AL | 111 | 15.4 | 17.4 | Escambia, AL | 35.6 | 19.7 |
| Springhill Regional Landfill (Waste Management) Campbellton, FL | 55 | 76.0 | 23.3 | Jackson, FL | 29.8 | 15.0 |
| Colonial Landfill (Allied Waste) Sorrento, LA | 316 | 34.7 | 14.4 | Ascension, LA | 22.6 | 12.8 |
| Jefferson Parish Sanitary Landfill (Waste Management) Avondale, LA | 1,433 | 51.7 | 20.4 | Jefferson, LA | 30.2 | 13.6 |
| Jefferson Davis Parish (Allied Waste) Welsh, LA | 187 | 19.2 | 18.0 | Jefferson Davis, LA | 19.4 | 20.6 |
| River Birch Landfill (Waste Management) Avondale, LA | 2,205 | 53.2 | 16.5 | Jefferson, LA | 30.2 | 13.6 |
| Tide Water Landfill (Environmental Operators LLC) Venice, LA | 48 | 37.6 | 18.0 | Plaquemines, LA | 30.2 | 17.5 |
| Central Landfill (Millard) (Waste Management) Poplarville, MS | 356 | 5.0 | 12.1 | Pearl River, MS | 14.4 | 18.1 |
| Pecan Grove Landfill (Waste Management) Pass Christian, MS | 336 | 12.5 | 12.4 | Harrison, MS | 26.9 | 14.0 |
| Average | 500 | 33.9 | 16.6 | | 26.3 | 15.9 |

*Source*: U.S. Census Bureau, Summary File 1 (2010).

fills are invisible and forgotten Americans—another injustice that needs to be corrected.

Even as the Obama administration oversaw BP's waste management plan, the oil giant was allowed to dump oil-spill waste on a disproportionately large share of African Americans and communities of other people of color in the Gulf Coast states. This targeting of people of color for BP oil-spill waste is consistent with past practices in the region.

The two government-approved landfills in Mississippi are located in mostly white communities. The disposal of BP waste in the Pecan Grove landfill in Harrison County and in the Central landfill in Pearl River County generated an inordinate amount of media and government attention, unlike that generated when similar waste was dumped in mostly black communities.[83] Oil-spill waste was dumped in the Harrison County Pecan Grove landfill over the objections of county supervisors.[84] However, because of a "contingency plan," as of mid-July 2010, no BP oil waste had made its way to the Central landfill in Pearl River County. Dan Bell, the market area engineer for Waste Management, Inc., informed Pearl County supervisors that there was no "economic value" in dumping any of the oil-spill waste at its Central landfill. Ball added, "It is just more feasible right now and closer to the site at this time to use Pecan Grove. Right now we have no plans to use Central Landfill, but that could change tomorrow."

Clearly, Environmental Justice Executive Order 12898, "Federal Actions to Address Environmental Justice in Minority Populations and Low-Income Populations," signed by President Bill Clinton in 1994, requires the EPA and the U.S. Coast Guard to do a better job of monitoring where waste from spills like the BP oil spill ends up to ensure that minority and low-income populations do not bear an adverse and disproportionate share of the burdens and negative impacts associated with such spills. Allowing BP, the Gulf Coast states, and the private disposal industry to select where the oil-spill waste is dumped only adds to the legacy of unequal protection.

## Conclusion

Residents who live on the fenceline with industrial facilities face elevated risks from accidents, explosions, and routine exposure to toxic emissions. Many of these same residents face danger from trains hauling deadly cargo through the heart of their community. It is only a matter of time before leaks, accidents, and tank car derailments chase unsuspecting residents from their homes.

The government must continue to oversee and severely penalize those companies that have inadequate or faulty safety equipment and warning devices for residents in fenceline communities, especially during a chemical spill or an accident. The oversight agencies should share emergency evacuation plans with residents, conduct evacuation drills, and develop a system to identify and evacuate special-needs populations, such as the elderly, the disabled, individuals in hospitals and nursing homes, nondrivers, and persons without cars.

In recent years, "shelter-in-place" (the process of staying where you are and taking shelter, rather than trying to evacuate) has received quite a bit of attention regarding its effectiveness as an emergency response measure. While proponents feel that it is an effective measure, opponents are equally confident that shelter-in-place could represent a threat and serve as the cause of injuries, fatalities, and general loss of comfort. Shelter-in-place should not be the only alternative considered by emergency-response planners, but, at the minimum, it should be considered as a high-level element in the hierarchy of response options available to emergency response planners, emergency responders, and incident commanders.

Thousands of industrial and military facilities and agricultural operations place millions of Americans at risk of serious injury or death due to accidental chemical releases, explosions, fires, and grossly inadequate occupational exposure standards. Some companies are moving toward "greener" production, while others are doing just the minimum to meet EPA requirements. Facility workers and residents in the surrounding areas are forming alliances to reduce their exposure to chemicals and to build a healthy and sustainable environment inside the plant and in the host community.

Many of the environmental problems facing African Americans and other people of color are systemic and will require institutional change, including new legislation and a paradigm shift that emphasizes precaution and prevention. Government alone cannot solve these problems but needs the support and assistance of concerned individuals, groups, and organizations from various walks of life. Private industry must also change. The 2007 *Toxic Wastes and Race at Twenty* report outlined some strategies to move the nation toward a more just and healthier industrial policy.[84]

Residents who are on the frontline of toxic assault, like those in Tennessee, Alabama, and Georgia, have requested that EPA administrator Lisa P. Jackson and her assistant administrator for the Office of Solid Waste and Emergency Response (OSWER), Mathy V. Stanislaus, conduct site visits and take "toxic tours" of impacted communities in their states so they can see, hear, and learn firsthand. Residents who live near "ground zero"—places where hazardous wastes are treated, stored, and disposed of—want to see aggressive steps taken to address the legacy of unequal protection and encourage government decisions that increase health and environmental vulnerability of low-income people and people of color.

Environmental justice leaders from New York to California want the Obama administration to put *protection* back in the EPA. Community leaders want to see this administration fully implement the 1994 Executive Order 12898, Federal Actions to Address Environmental Justice in Minority Populations and Low-Income Populations, which seeks "to ensure that no segment of the population, regardless of race, color, national origin, income, or net worth bear disproportionately high and adverse human health and environmental impacts as a result of EPA's policies, programs and activities." Under this order, each federal agency (all eleven of them covered under the order) must make achieving environmental justice part of its mission by identifying and addressing, as appropriate, disproportionately high and adverse human health and environmental effects of its programs, policies, and activities on minorities and low-income populations.

Finally, environmental justice advocates want to see a "new" EPA reverse the legacy of unequal protection and stop environmental injustice in its tracks. They suggest the following measures:

*Adopt clean production principles and methods.* Clean production is rooted in the Precautionary Principle and requires manufacturing processes that produce clean and safe products. As a healthy business strategy to transform the toxic chemical economy, industry is urged to reduce its use of toxic products, reduce waste, aim for zero waste, and employ closed-loop production systems that promote use of renewable energy, nontoxic materials, safer chemical practices, and sustainable product design. Industry must invest in research on and development of sustainable chemicals, products, materials, and processes. It can begin by adopting the Louisville Charter for safe chemicals developed in 2004 by a broad array of environmental justice and health organizations and professionals.

*Phase out persistent, bioaccumulative, or highly toxic chemicals.* Companies must prioritize the elimination of chemicals that are slow to degrade, that accumulate in our bodies or in other living organisms, or that are highly hazardous to humans or the environment, including those that disrupt hormones and the immune system and are particularly dangerous to children and other vulnerable populations. They must also ensure that chemicals eliminated in the United States are not exported to other countries.

*Adopt extended producer responsibility.* Extended Producer Responsibility (EPR) requires that producers take responsibility for the entire product life cycle, including the postconsumer phase, thereby promoting closed-loop systems. EPR makes producers responsible for the environmental and public health impacts of their products, for example by prohibiting the export of end-of-life product waste to other countries as a commodity. Industry must establish minimum recovery, reuse, and material recycling targets. Incineration or combustion should not be considered "recycling." Industry also must widely adopt end-of-life product buybacks and phase out plans to send all product wastes to landfills, incinerators, cement kilns, or combustion facilities.

*Support community and worker right-to-know.* The public, workers, and communities must be well informed and have access to information about industries' use and release of toxic chemical and product chains. Companies must disclose the chemicals and materials they use, list quantities of chemicals produced, used, released and exported, and provide access to information. The public and workers must be made sufficiently aware of chemical hazards, uses, and exposures to make informed decisions. Access to information must include inspections by citizens and community residents. Corporations also must provide adequate information such as life-cycle assessments and product labeling so that consumers and governments can use their spending power to support clean production. Industry must also provide meaningful involvement for the public and workers when making decisions on use and disposal of chemicals.

*Adopt and uphold legally binding Good Neighborhood Agreements.* Companies must uphold performance standards negotiated with fenceline communities that may include community access to information, environmental and health monitoring, communities' right to inspect the facility, accident preparedness, pollution prevention, support of good local jobs and union jobs, attention to local economic needs, and means for dispute resolution.

*Enact legislation promoting clean production and waste reduction.* Legislation must require that industry use clean production technologies and support necessary R&D leading to a reduction in the use of toxic products and closed-loop production systems. Industry should create incentives and buyback programs to achieve full recovery and reuse of products, recycling of waste, and product design that enhances waste-material recovery and reduction. Policies must include restrictions on the use of highly toxic and carcinogenic materials.

*Require comprehensive safety data for all chemicals.* Chemical manufacturing companies must be required to provide publicly available safety information about a chemical if it is to remain on or be added to the market. The information must allow for reasonable evaluation of the safety of the chemical for human health and the environment and must include hazard, use, and exposure information. This is referred to as the "No Data, No Market" principle.

*Require cumulative risk assessments in facility permitting.* The EPA should require assessments of multiple, cumulative, and synergistic exposures, unique exposure pathways, and impacts on sensitive populations in issuing environmental permits and promulgating regulations under the Resource Conservation and Recovery Act (RCRA), the Clean Air Act (CAA), the Clean Water Act (CWA), and other federal laws. Similar considerations should be taken into account in establishing site-specific cleanup standards under Superfund and Brownfields programs.

*Require that companies establish safety buffers before they can receive a permit and provide fenceline community performance bonds for variances.* The EPA and states should adopt site location standards requiring that there be a safe distance between a residential population and an industrial facility so that the population is not located within the area where deaths or serious injury to health or property are likely to result in the event that a toxic or flammable substance stored or processed at or generated by the facility is released into the environment through explosion, fire, or spill. If safety buffer exemptions are granted, the company should be required to post a locally administered fenceline community performance bond to provide recovery resources for residents impacted by chemical accidents.

# Separate and Unequal Treatment

*Response to Health Emergencies, Human Experi-
ments, and Bioterrorism Threats*

When societal resources are distributed unequally by class and by
race, it should be no surprise population health will be distributed unequally
along those lines, as well. African Americans have long struggled with structural inequities that impact their physical and social health. More than one
hundred studies now link racism to poor health. A 2008 Public Broadcasting
Service (PBS) documentary, *Unnatural Causes: Is Inequality Making Us Sick*,
made clear that "there's more to our health than bad habits, health care, or
unlucky genes."[1] The social environment in which we are born, live, work,
and play profoundly affects our well-being, health, and longevity.

This chapter explores factors that create and exacerbate health disparities, government response to public health threats to African Americans,
and sociohistorical factors that impact variations in perceived fairness of the
public health system. We also examine the legacy of racial discrimination
and bias treatment in medical research, the health-care establishment, and
government responses to epidemics and bioterrorism threats.

## *The Quest for Health Equity*

Disparities exist across the entire health-care establishment, from clinics
to hospitals to nursing homes. They exist in public and private health-care
settings—even within publicly funded programs where the population is
insured and has equal access to services. For example, African Americans
Medicare recipients receive lower levels of care, including fewer office visits,
mammograms, and colonoscopies, than whites.[2]

Addressing these and related health disparities is not an easy task. It
requires new thinking, new paradigms, and new initiatives.[3] While African

Americans, Hispanics, and Native Americans make up more than 25 percent of the U.S. population, they account for only 9 percent of nurses, 6 percent of physicians, and 5 percent of dentists. The Sullivan Commission, chaired by Louis W. Sullivan, M.D., a former secretary of the U.S. Department of Health and Human Services, cited the shortage of minority health workers as a key factor in explaining the discrepancies that citizens of color experience in health care:

> The ghosts of segregation continue to haunt the health professions. . . . The nation's projected upcoming medical school graduating classes for 2007 include only 2,197 Black, Hispanic, and Native Americans out of a total of more than 16,000 students. The picture in nursing and dentistry is similar.[4]

Tackling health disparities requires broadening our lens to bring into view the ways in which the environment (natural, built, social, and cultural), working conditions, education, housing, social inclusion, and even political power influence individual and community health. The concept of *health equity* expands the questions beyond the conventional paradigm and seeks to understand, explain, and address "unnatural" causes of ill health.[5] How can we target dangerous conditions and reorganize land use and transportation policies to ensure healthy spaces and places? How can we eliminate inequities in the distribution of resources and power that shape health outcomes? What kinds of community organizing and alliance building are necessary to protect communities? Here, we refer to the World Health Organization's (WHO) definition of health: "Health is a complete state of physical, mental and social well being, and not merely the absence of disease or infirmity."

Many studies have documented that African Americans receive lower-quality health care than white patients at the same medical facility. Researchers at UCLA reported that race-based discrimination may help explain why African Americans, despite gains in civil rights and targeted health programs, continue to have the highest rates of diabetes, cardiovascular heart disease, hypertension, and stroke among all other racial or ethnic groups in the United States. The experience of racial discrimination may be a key factor in explaining why African Americans have higher rates of obesity and suffer higher rates of diseases such as diabetes and cardiovascular disorders.[6]

In 2002, the Institute of Medicine (IOM) study *Unequal Treatment: Confronting Racial and Ethnic Disparities in Health Care* suggested that the sources of racial disparities are "rooted in historic and contemporary inequities, and involve many participants at several levels, including health systems, their administrative and bureaucratic processes, utilization managers, health care professionals, and patients."[7] In general, IOM research showed that:

> African Americans and Hispanics tend to receive a lower quality of health-care across a range of disease areas (including cancer, cardiovascular disease, HIV/AIDS, diabetes, mental health, and other chronic and infectious diseases) and clinical services; African Americans are more likely than whites to receive less desirable services, such as amputation of all or part of a limb; Disparities are found even when clinical factors, such as stage of disease presentation, co-morbidities, age, and severity of disease are taken into account; disparities are found across a range of clinical settings, including public and private hospitals, teaching and non-teaching hospitals, etc.; and disparities in care are associated with higher mortality among minorities who do not receive the same services as whites (e.g., surgical treatment for small-cell lung cancer).

The IOM report discovered significant variation in the rates of medical procedures by race, even when insurance status, income, age, and severity of conditions are comparable. It also found that U.S. racial and ethnic minorities are less likely to receive even routine medical procedures and experience a lower quality of health services.

A large body of research underscores the existence of racial disparities and show that African Americans adults receive worse medical care than whites across a range of health quality measures.[8] A 2007 study from researchers at Massachusetts General Hospital and other institutions affiliated with Harvard University showed evidence of deeply internalized unconscious racial bias in physicians that may contribute to racial/ethnic disparities in the use of medical procedures. Physicians who were racially biased were less likely to prescribe aggressive heart attack treatment for black patients than for whites.[9]

African Americans are less likely to be given appropriate cardiac medications or to undergo bypass surgery and are less likely to receive kidney dialysis or transplants. By contrast, they are more likely to receive certain less desirable procedures, such as lower-limb amputations for diabetes and other conditions. African Americans are less likely than whites to receive breast cancer screening, eye examinations for patients with diabetes, beta blocker medication after myocardial infarction, and follow-up after hospitalization for mental illness. Overall, African Americans receive a poorer quality of health care than whites.[10]

## Why Trust Matters—Abuse Disguised as Research

The history of black people in the United States is replete with examples that justify blacks' general mistrust of the government and of the health-care system.[11] The public's level of trust in public health officials—and for good reasons—differs widely across racial and ethnic groups.[12] A legacy of slavery, Jim Crow segregation, institutionalized discrimination, human experimentation, and unequal treatment and unequal protection has left Africans Americans with greater distrust of physicians, medical research, and the health-care system than is found among whites.[13] The distrust that many African Americans feel toward the public health establishment and government in general is an issue of social justice, and the government has an obligation to eliminate or mitigate it.[14]

Many people of color in the United States view the world and their health-care situations differently from and, often, more negatively than do whites. A substantial proportion of minorities perceive discrimination in receiving health care, and many feel that they would not receive the best care if they were sick.[15] Researchers at the University of Pennsylvania found that African Americans were significantly more likely than whites to report low trust in health-care providers. They found that 44 percent of African Americans but only 33 percent of whites reported having low levels of trust in health-care providers.[16]

Researchers at Johns Hopkins University found that people of color are 200 percent more likely to perceive harm coming from participating in research.[17] More than twice as many African Americans as whites believe physicians secretly experiment on patients. The study shows that distrust of researchers lingers some thirty-five years after the infamous Tuskegee syphilis experiment and provides direct evidence that distrust of researchers explains the lower participation of blacks in cardiovascular disease prevention trials research. Only 27 percent of African American respondents but 39 percent of whites were willing to participate in a mock trial of a cardiovascular drug.

Other findings indicate that 24 percent of African Americans but 13 percent of whites reported that their doctors would not fully explain research participation to them; 72 percent of African Americans but 49 percent of whites said doctors would use them as guinea pigs without their consent; 35 percent of African Americans but only 16 percent of whites said doctors would ask them to participate in research even if it could harm them; 8 percent of African Americans but 2 percent of whites believed that they could not freely ask questions of doctors; 58 percent of African Americans but only 25 percent of whites said that doctors had previously experimented on them without consent.

The researchers found that the "impact of race was attenuated and nonsignificant after adjustment for potential mediating factors of racial differences in medical researcher distrust and perceived risk of harm."[18] The trust factor appears to explain much of the higher resistance among African Americans than among whites to participation in clinical trials.

Mistrust runs deep. It is rooted in experiences extending back to slavery and the antebellum period and continuing to the present day.[19] Long before the Tuskegee experiment, a form of "medical apartheid" allowed slaves and free blacks to be used as subjects for dissection and medical experimentation. Medical exploitation was rampant on southern plantations. The South was a particularly unhealthy region of the country and was home to 90 percent of American blacks, the majority of whom were enslaved until 1865.

In her groundbreaking book *Medical Apartheid: The Dark History of Medical Experimentation on Black Americans from Colonial Times to the Present*, the journalist and ethics scholar Harriett A. Washington summed up the ugly legacy in our nation's history: "Dangerous, involuntary, and nontherapeutic experimentation upon African Americans has been practiced widely and documented extensively at least since the eighteenth century."[20]

The United States was the first country to overtly undertake compulsory sterilization programs for the purpose of eugenics. More than sixty-five thousand individuals were sterilized in thirty-three states under state compulsory sterilization programs in the United States.[21] Many black women were sterilized against their will, often without their knowledge, while they were in hospitals for other reasons, such as childbirth.[22] The 1914 Model Eugenical Sterilization Law inspired the eugenics program in Nazi Germany in the 1930s and 1940s. The practice of "rendering black women infertile without their knowledge during other surgery was so common that the procedure was called a 'Mississippi appendectomy.'"[23] Black women and other women of color were unnecessarily given hysterectomies to allow doctors in training a chance to practice their skills.

Racist white physicians felt they were doing the larger society a favor by sterilizing black women without telling them. Black women who trusted their obstetricians to deliver their babies were surreptitiously rendered infertile. Black women's bodies became a special target for reproductive injustice.[24] In her book *Killing the Black Body: Race, Reproduction, and the Mean-*

*ing of Liberty*, Rutgers University law professor Dorothy Roberts says that "reproductive freedom is a matter of social justice."[25]

By 1980, sterilization was the most common form of birth control. Black women were given more than their fair share of hysterectomies. In 1983, African Americans made up just 12 percent of the U.S. population but constituted 40 percent of the women sterilized in federally funded family-planning programs.

Black women, men, and children were special targets for risky surgery, drugs, and experiments—abuses and unethical tests disguised as research. Many African Americans wonder what they had done to the government, medical establishment, and even the Army to justify having these institutions declare war on them.

The U.S. Army has conducted hundreds of chemical and biological weapons (BW) "experiments" that deliberately targeted the unsuspecting public, especially African Americans. From 1942 to1977, the U.S. military released disease-causing germs in at least forty-eight open-air tests. In 1900, U.S. Army doctor Walter Reed and his colleagues helped discover that yellow fever is caused by a virus transmitted by mosquitoes. Yet, sixty years after Dr. Reed's death, mosquitoes were used in controversial biological warfare experiments carried out on black citizens in Florida and Georgia. Residents were getting sick, but no one knew why. It was not until much later that residents learned of the biological warfare Army "experiments."[26]

In 1956 and 1958, the U.S. Army and the Central Intelligence Agency (CIA) joined forces to test a possible biological weapon. Scientists bred more than four million mosquitoes in a laboratory and released the insects in hordes in Florida and Georgia, including in poor black housing developments in Carver Village (Miami), Florida, and Carver Village (Savannah), Georgia. According to the 1976 *Final Report of the Senate Select Committee to Study Government Operations with Respect to Intelligence Activities*, the Army tests were used to determine if the mosquitoes could be used as "first-strike" biological weapons to infect enemy troops with yellow fever and dengue fever during wartime.

Fort Detrick, located fifty miles from Washington, D.C., is the nation's principal biological and chemical warfare research center. A Fort Detrick Army Chemical Corps report, *Summary of Major Events and Problems* (now unclassified), details the "practicality of employing *Aedes aegypti* mosquitoes to carry a BW agent." The tests show that "mosquitoes could spread over areas of several square miles by means of devices dropped from planes or set up on the ground."

The Army mosquito tests were kept secret for decades and records destroyed. For years, the CIA denied that it had released biological weapons against its own citizens. The truth was brought to light in the late 1970s when the Scientology religious group broke the story; later mainstream media, including the *New York Times*, the *Christian Science Monitor*, the *Atlanta Journal*, and the *Washington Post*, started their own investigation. The investigatory reporting detailed how the biological warfare tests, undertaken with tax dollars, targeted African Americans. By 1960, residents in the two communities involved were plagued with mysterious illnesses, including symptoms of dengue fever and yellow fewer. Some residents even died from their illnesses. The spikes in local diseases and deaths provided enough proof for the Army-CIA team to deem the project an effective biological weapon against the Soviets, the United States' number one Cold War enemy.[27]

Successful public health responses to epidemics and related health emergencies in the future will depend heavily on overcoming this historical legacy of suspicion and distrust.[28] The anthrax attacks of 2001, the SARS epidemic of 2002, and the West Nile virus and avian flu have raised awareness about the importance of preparedness in combatting bioterrorism and emerging infectious diseases. Yet, the public health agencies in the United States have a history of enacting discriminatory policies during epidemics. Because the nation's public health system is the first line of defense in the detection and surveillance of and the response to bioterrorist threats and infectious disease emergencies, public health effectiveness will require trust and cooperation on the part of all segments of our society, including underserved vulnerable populations that are most at risk.

A severe public health crisis could require controversial control measures (e.g., isolation, quarantine, travel restrictions, targeted distribution of medicines or vaccines) whose success will depend on the extent to which individuals cooperate. The difference in willingness to undergo smallpox vaccinations among different populations, for example, becomes problematic when constructing bioterror attack response plans.[29] Thus, it is important that the needs of all of society's members be met.

African Americans also mistrust annual flu shots and are less likely than whites to get vaccinated. In 2003, 45.4 percent of African Americans age sixty-five and older, the group most susceptible to the flu, received the shot, whereas 68.7 percent of whites in that age group did so.[30] Despite the fact that African Americans are 6 percent more likely than whites to die from seasonal flu, many are reluctant to get vaccinated. In addition to fears about drug safety and misinformation (the notion that you can get the flu from the flu vaccine is still alive), mistrust and suspicion abound among older African Americans. Some of this mistrust is attributed to the lingering legacy of the Tuskegee syphilis experiment. Old ghosts of intentional malpractice are still alive and well in the black community.

Differences in levels of trust of public health officials may reflect the divergent cultural experiences of African Americans and whites, as well as differences in expectations of care.[31] Only 1 percent of the nearly twenty million Americans enrolled in biomedical studies are black. Blacks' reluctance to participate in research, though justified, has meant that African Americans often miss out on the latest treatments and breakthroughs.

Many African Americans simply do not trust the medical establishment and mental health providers.[32] Historically, a large segment of the African American community has bypassed traditional mental health providers and turned to the black church and black clergy, placing them in the role of "first responders."[33] In other cases, traditional mental health "first responders," including the Red Cross and FEMA, have bypassed the black community. Generally, black family members, churches, and community organizations fill this important service gap.

Why do blacks mistrust health professionals and biomedical researchers? Is this mistrust a form of misguided paranoia or a response to a legacy of experimentation and failed ethics? Given the actions of some doctors and medical and health researchers, black people have good reason to mistrust some individuals, institutions, and government-financed studies that treat them and their families as human guinea pigs.

Blacks and whites see the world through different lenses. Whites are far more likely to reject the notion that racial inequality remains a major problem in America and that race plays a part in government response to emergencies. A poll taken by the Pew Research Center for the People and the Press show that six in ten African Americans said that government response was slow after Katrina because most of the victims were poor and black. Nearly nine in ten whites rejected the idea that those factors played a part in the emergency response to Hurricane Katrina.[34]

Comparisons are being made between 9/11 and Hurricane Katrina. The victims who made it out of the terrorist attack on the World Trade Center and the Pentagon were instantly called heroes and survivors. There was no debate about what to call them. However, the nearly half-million New Orleans victims of Katrina who miraculously escaped the hurricane and floodwaters and whose homes and businesses were destroyed were first called refugees, then evacuees, and later survivors.

A National Public Radio (NPR) show was devoted to this topic. "Questions are being raised about what to call people who have escaped New Orleans. Are they refugees? Evacuees? Victims? It all depends on who you ask."[35] It took several days before some political pundits and experts recognized that the mostly black, low-income, sick Americans, both young and old, quartered in the New Orleans Superdome were taking offense at being called "refugees." Although many Katrina evacuees and storm survivors may have been treated like foreign refugees, they were not. They were Americans.

## Destruction of the Public Health Safety Net

Hurricane Katrina and the levee breach in 2005 drowned New Orleans's Charity Hospital, which was founded on May 10, 1736, by a grant from the French sailor and shipbuilder Jean Louis, who had died in New Orleans the year before. Louis's last will and testament included funds to open a hospital for the indigent in the colony of New Orleans from his estate.

Even without hurricanes, floods, and natural disasters, many "safety-net" urban public hospitals that serve the poor and uninsured have fallen on hard times. Most urban public hospitals not only provide care for the indigent but also serve their communities in other ways, including serving as major providers for tertiary services such as trauma care and support for homeland security operations; serving as the foundation for primary-care services; continuing to train a significant number of physicians, nurses, and other medical personnel; and providing laboratories for clinical medical research.[36]

Since 1979, the number of public hospitals and public beds in the United States has declined markedly—faster than the corresponding figures for all hospitals.[37] Federal budget cuts such as those included in the Balanced Budget Act of 1997, recent state budget deficits, competition for Medicaid managed-care patients, and the growth in the number of uninsured Americans have led to a decline in revenues among safety-net urban public hospitals.[38] Some hospitals have actually closed their doors.

The first and only public hospital in the nation's capital, D.C. General Hospital, established in 1806, closed in May 2001 after serving the city's residents for nearly two hundred years. The controversial closing of D.C. General ended its inpatient service; the hospital's health-care system for indigents was transferred mostly to Greater Southeast Community Hospital.

In South Central Los Angeles, the Martin Luther King Harbor Hospital, known as Martin Luther King Jr./Drew Medical Center (King/Drew) closed in August 2007. The hospital, founded in 1972, served more than forty-seven thousand patients in 2006. Now these patients will be forced to travel farther distances in life-threatening situations and overwhelm other already under-staffed hospitals.

Even booming Atlanta's Grady Memorial Hospital, one of the nation's largest safety-net hospitals, is teetering on the edge of disaster. Tens of thousands of Atlantans over the past 115 years, more than one in three babies born here in the last decade, entered the world at Grady. Opened in downtown Atlanta in 1892, it was for many years referred to in the plural—"The Gradys"—because it had separate white and black sections. Now it is one of the largest public health systems in the country, an institution that provides five thousand jobs and treats 900,000 patients a year. At present, more than 90 percent of Grady Hospital's patients are uninsured.[39]

A 2005 report from the State University of New York (SUNY) Downstate Medical Center, *Hospital Care in the 100 Largest Cities and Their Suburbs, 1996–2002: Implications for the Future of the Hospital Safety Net in Metropolitan America*, found that, over the six-year study period, public hospitals in major American cities declined in number by 16 percent, from 83 to 70, while the number of public hospitals in suburban areas declined by 27 percent, from 134 to 98. Similarly, the number of for-profit hospitals declined by 11 percent in cities and suburbs, and the number of not-for-profit hospitals declined by 11 percent in cities and by 2 percent in suburbs, leading to "a major increase" in emergency department visits by low-income residents in suburban areas. Public hospitals typically serve the most vulnerable populations, individuals who face major challenges in accessing private health-care services.

## In the Shadow of the Tuskegee Syphilis Study

The federally funded Public Health Service Tuskegee Syphilis Study, in which investigators observed four hundred black male sharecroppers as they passed through the natural course of syphilis and withheld available treatment, is the most frequently used examples of why mistrust of the biomedical community lingers among blacks.[40]

James H. Jones's 1981 book, *Bad Blood: The Tuskegee Syphilis Experiment*, clearly documents that the Tuskegee Syphilis Study (1932–1972) was the "longest nontherapeutic experiment on humans in the history of medicine, and has come to represent not only the exploitation of blacks in medical history, but the potential for exploitation of any population that may be vulnerable because of race, ethnicity, gender, disability, age or social class."[41] The government deliberately withheld treatment from syphilitic men in an effort to determine the natural course of the disease, regardless of the human cost to the subjects, their wives and children, and their communities.

The black men were never told they had syphilis; there was mention, instead, of "bad blood," which had many other meanings to them. They were never told that effective treatment was being withheld. On the contrary, they were led to believe that they were getting free and appropriate medicines, which were, in fact, aspirin and spring tonics. In one particularly cruel deception, the black men who were called in for a spinal puncture, a painful and (under the circumstances) potentially dangerous procedure with absolutely no therapeutic effect, were sent a letter announcing their "last chance for special free treatment."

In July 1973, the civil rights attorney Fred Gray filed a $1.8 billion class-action civil suit against many of the institutions and individuals involved in the study, demanding $3 million in damages for each living participant and the heirs of the deceased. In December 1974, the case was settled for $10 million without ever going to trial. The living participants each received $37,500 in damages, and the heirs of the deceased received $15,000.[42]

Although the survivors of the horrific experiment and the families of the deceased received compensation, no U.S. Public Health Service officer who had been directly involved in the study acknowledged feeling contrition, no apologies were ever tendered, and none of the health officials ever admitted any wrongdoing at an "American Nuremberg." On the contrary, the PHS officers defended their actions and made it clear that they felt they were acting in good conscience. They felt betrayed by the government's failure to defend the study it had commissioned.

On May 16, 1997, to promote healing and reconciliation, President Bill Clinton offered a formal apology. "Today all we can do is apologize, but you have the power. Only you have the power to forgive. Your presence here shows us that you have shown a better path than your government did so long ago. You have not withheld the power to forgive. I hope today and tomorrow every American will remember your lesson and live by it." President Clinton made it clear that the actions taken by the PHS were wrong. He stated: "The United States government did something that was wrong— deeply, profoundly, morally wrong. It was an outrage to our commitment to integrity and equality for all our citizens . . . clearly racist."

The president also announced the creation of government bioethics fellowships for minority students funded by the Department of Health and Human Services. A bioethics center at Tuskegee University, which was not affiliated with the study but whose reputation was tarnished by it, was also established.

## Childhood Lead Poisoning—When Facts Are Not Enough

Lead poisoning is a classic example of an environmental health threat that disproportionately impacts low-income children and children of color. Childhood lead poisoning is a preventable disease. Why are children still being poisoned? Former Health and Human Secretary Louis Sullivan tagged it the "number one environmental health threat to children."[43] Lead poisoning continues to be a major health threat to children in the United States, especially poor children, children of color, and children living in inner cities. An estimated 1.7 million children ages one to five years have blood lead levels of 10 ug/dl (micrograms per deciliter) or greater. More than 28.4 percent of all low-income African American children are lead poisoned, whereas only 9.8 percent of low-income white children are so afflicted.

Over the past four decades, the Centers for Disease Control and Prevention has lowered the threshold for lead levels considered dangerous in children by 88 percent, from 60 to 10 micrograms per deciliter (mcg/dl), which it defines as the "level of concern." The lead problem has by no means been solved. Rather, the demographics have shifted. Some groups, mainly children of color and poor children living in the inner city, continue to suffer from high rates of lead poisoning.

Before Hurricane Katrina, more than 50 percent (some studies place this figure at around 70 percent) of children living in the inner-city neighborhoods of New Orleans had blood lead levels above the guideline of 10 micrograms per deciliter.[44] The percentage of children with lead poisoning in some New Orleans black neighborhoods was high as 67 percent.[45]

Even 10mcg/dl is not safe. Some medical and health professionals advocate lowering the threshold to 2.5 mcg/dl.[46] The World Health Organization estimates the effect of lead poisoning to be about one to three points of IQ lost for each 10 ug/dl lead level. At higher levels, the effect may be larger. Lead affects almost every organ and system in the body, including the kidneys and the reproductive system.

The environmental justice framework adopts a public health model of prevention (elimination of the threat before harm occurs) as the preferred strategy. Impacted communities should not have to wait until causation or conclusive "proof" is established before preventive action is taken. For example, the framework offers a solution to the lead problem by shifting the primary focus from *treatment* (after children have been poisoned) to *prevention* (elimination of the threat via abating lead in houses).

The Natural Resources Defense Council, the NAACP Legal Defense and Educational Fund, the ACLU, and the Legal Aid Society of Alameda County joined forces in 1991 and won an out-of-court settlement worth between $15 million and $20 million for a blood lead testing program in California. It took a lawsuit, *Matthews v. Coye*, brought by a parent and a community organization to bring about a federal mandate for lead testing in some 557,000 poor children who receive Medicaid.[47]

In 1991, the California Department of Health Services (CDHS) Child Health and Disability Prevention (CHDP) Program issued a directive to physicians to screen all children under the age of six when they underwent health assessments. This historic agreement triggered similar actions in other states that had failed to live up to federally mandated screening.[48]

> Lead screening is an important element in this problem. However, screening is not the solution. Prevention is the solution. Surely, if termite inspections can be mandated to protect individual home investment, a lead-free home can be mandated to protect public health. Ultimately, the lead abatement debate, public health (who is affected) vs. property rights (who pays for cleanup), is a value conflict that will not be resolved by the scientific community.

On January 31, 2003, the U.S. Centers for Disease Control and Prevention released its *Second National Report on Human Exposure to Environmental Chemicals*, a report that includes information on the concentrations of 116 chemicals measured in blood and urine specimens in a sample of the population for the years 1999 and 2000.[49] Progress has been made, but concerns remain. According to the report, between 1999 and 2002, 1.6 percent of children ages one to five years had elevated blood lead levels (levels greater than or equal to 10 micrograms per deciliter). The percentage had decreased from 4.4 percent for the period 1991–1994.

The federal government in 1978 banned lead paint. There have been numerous attempts in recent years to target lead paint in class actions. Since 1990, more than thirty lawsuits filed by individuals, cities, and states against companies that sold lead-based paint have failed or been inconclusive.[50] This pattern is similar to product liability lawsuits that failed for decades against the tobacco industry. It would cost between $50 billion and $100 billion to eradicate lead poisoning in the United States. It also costs the economy to do nothing. Government and taxpayers have incurred significant health, educational, and other social costs because of the presence of lead-based paint in public and private buildings, including housing.

Inspired in part by the tobacco industry settlements, states, counties, municipalities, school districts, and housing authorities have joined in lawsuits against the lead industry for medical and other costs associated with lead poisoning caused by exposure to deteriorated lead paint in homes. The legal assault on big tobacco yielded a $240 billion settlement from cigarette makers after states took on the industry in a series of lawsuits.[51] Similarly, the lead lawsuits seek unspecified money damages from eight manufacturers and a trade association. To date, all such lawsuits against the lead industry have failed. But, then, the same was true for the failed lawsuits filed for decades against the tobacco industry.

### The East Baltimore Childhood Lead Paint Experiment

The Kennedy Krieger Institute, a center affiliated with Johns Hopkins University Medical Center, in Baltimore, Maryland, came under fire in 2006 over its research methods and ethics in a study of different ways to rid lead paint in homes with children.[52] In the study, which ran from 1993 to 1995, landlords were paid to recruit families with healthy children to live in one hundred lead-contaminated homes in the mostly black and poor East Baltimore neighborhood ; in these homes, children were intentionally exposed to high lead levels.[53] The children, who were susceptible to brain damage if they ate lead paint chips, were to be tested periodically to see how effective methods developed to reduce the levels of lead-based paint. The EPA and the U.S. Department of Housing and Urban Development funded the $1 million study.[54]

A half-dozen lawsuits were filed against Kennedy Krieger, including one brought by two East Baltimore mothers that charged the researchers with knowingly endangering young children's health by allowing them to live in homes where the removal of old lead paint was incomplete. The Maryland Court of Appeals condemned the study in a ruling that permitted the suit filed on behalf of the two children, who allegedly suffered brain damage from lead exposure, to go forward.[55] And, after a decade, in September 2011, a class-action lawsuit was filed in Baltimore City Circuit Court against the Kennedy Krieger Institute over the lead paint study. The latest lawsuit claims the institute "selected children and their parents who were predominantly from a lower economic strata and minorities . . . and used these children as known guinea pigs in these contaminated houses to complete this study." The lawsuit also questions the fact that nothing in the research was designed to treat the children for lead poisoning.[56] The case is still pending.

The research protocol of the Kennedy Krieger researchers was detailed in a 2004 *Journal of Medical Ethics* article:

> In order to test their interventions, the presence of small children in houses was required. The Kennedy Krieger researchers encouraged, and in some case required landlords to rent premises to families with young children. Children living in study houses were also encouraged to continue living in the houses. The repair and maintenance costs ranged from $1,650 up to $6,000–$7,000 for the more comprehensive level. Full lead abatement cost $20,000 per house. Some of the landlords who were required to employ only partial treatment to their properties were publicly funded.[57]

In August 2001, Judge Dale R. Cathell of the Maryland Court of Appeals concluded that the Kennedy Krieger lead nontherapeutic study was "inappropriate" and that the Johns Hopkins Institutional Review Board (IRB) had "abdicated [its] responsibility to protect human subjects."[58] The judge likened the Kennedy Krieger study to experiments carried out by Nazi doctors on prisoners at the Buchenwald concentration camp during World War II and to the Tuskegee Syphilis Study carried out by the U.S. Public Health Service, described earlier in this chapter.[59]

Just months before the court ruled in favor of the parents in the *Ericka Grimes v. Kennedy Krieger Institute, Inc.* lawsuit, the principal investigator on the questionable Kennedy Krieger Institute lead experiment turned his attention to the soil in East Baltimore neighborhoods that had severe problems with lead paint. Using a $446,231 grant from the U.S. Department of Housing and Urban Development (HUD) for a two-year study, Kennedy Krieger scientists spread fertilizer made from human and industrial wastes on yards in poor, black neighborhoods to test whether it might protect children from lead poisoning in the soil.[60]

Families were assured that the sewage sludge was safe and were never told about any harmful ingredients. Nine low-income families agreed to let researchers till the sludge into their yards and plant new grass in exchange for food coupons and free lawns.[61] A comparable experiment was conducted by the U.S. Department of Agriculture Department (USDA) and the Environmental Protection Agency in a similarly poor, black neighborhood in East St. Louis, Illinois.

The issue caused such concern that it prompted Senator Barbara Boxer, a California Democrat who chaired the powerful Energy and Public Works Committee Commerce in Congress, to hold hearings on the experiment as part of a wider look into the health impact of using sludge and compost as fertilizers. Johns Hopkins defended its sludge study and criticized the AP story—calling the story "inaccurate and misleading." The disagreement between Johns Hopkins and the AP was not resolved. However, a 2002 report from the National Academy of Sciences concluded that, while nobody had documented harm of sludge to human health, more health studies were needed to address "persisting uncertainty" about the potential risks.[62]

## Pesticide Tests on Children in Florida

On September 22, 2004, the EPA announced the launching of a study intended to learn more about how young children come into contact with household pesticides and other chemicals in their homes. According to the EPA's press release, the study, called the Children's Environmental Exposure Research Study (CHEERS), would have involved following sixty children from birth through three years of age, for two years.[63] The American Chemistry Council, which represents 135 companies, including pesticide manufacturers, agreed to pay $2.1 million of the $9 million research project.[64]

The study was designed to monitor children in their homes. Participants were to keep records of their pesticide and household product use, and the researchers would measure the concentrations of the chemicals in the children's homes in order to determine how the children are exposed to chemicals that are present in consumer products used in the home.[65] Even some rank-and-file EPA scientists questioned the ethics of the two-year experiment, which would have given the families of sixty children in Duval County, Florida, $970 each, as well as a camcorder and children's clothing, in exchange for allowing their children to participate.[66]

Shortly after the announcement by the EPA, a number of environmental and children health groups began to question the American Chemistry Council's involvement on the study and the study's design. The involvement of a trade organization elicited wide criticism from the scientific community. Many questioned the EPA's ability to stay impartial while conducting a study funded by chemical manufacturers. Others questioned the need for the $2.1 million since the agency's budget for research was $572 million.[67]

One issue with the study design that specifically concerned environmental justice advocates was that the researcher were planning to use six

Duval County Health Department clinics and three local hospitals as the sites of participant recruitment. According to the study, the six health clinics "primarily serve individuals with lower incomes," and the three hospitals reported that 51 percent of all births at their facilities were to nonwhite mothers, with 62 percent of all mothers having only received an elementary or secondary education.[68]

Scientists also questioned the ethical standards of the study, even though the EPA claimed that the study had already undergone independent reviews and complied with human-subject safety standards. The study design did not allow for intervening if infants or toddlers showed signs of developmental problems or registered alarmingly high exposure levels in their urine samples. Instead, families would continue in the study so long as researchers were notified when each pesticide application occurred.[69] Also, the scientists argued that the financial incentives could force a poor family to use household chemicals in order to qualify for the study and gain the incentives.

On April 8, 2005, under pressure from Senator Barbara Boxer, a California Democrat, and Senator Bill Nelson, a Florida Democrat, the EPA's acting administrator, Stephen L. Johnson, canceled the Children's Health Environmental Exposure Research Study.[70] The Democratic senators said they would block Senate confirmation of the agency's new head if the pesticide study was not canceled.

### Will Government Response to Bioterrorism Be Fair?

Today, responding to the threat of terrorism has become a top national security issue and the centerpiece of homeland security. The term "terrorism" has gotten a lot of attention in recent years, with the emphasis on foreigners assaulting the United States and its interests. There is no internationally agreed upon legal definition of terrorism. One definition of terrorism is "a threat or the use of violence (including kidnapping, extortion, assault, and murder) by an individual or organization that targets innocent civilians."[71] Terrorism is used to further the perpetrator's ideological, political, and religious goals.

The history of the United States is filled with acts of individual and state-sponsored terrorism against blacks, comprising chattel slavery, lynchings, mutilations, physical intimidation, cross burnings, bombings, and government-sanctioned terrorism, including release of disease-causing agents by the U.S. military.[72] American apartheid facilitated unethical and questionable experimentation on black populations that was sanctioned by the U.S. government and enforced by law, violence, and terror. Unfortunately, an important segment of black life in America is a story of domestic terrorism.

Since the terrorist attacks on the World Trade Center in New York and the Pentagon in Washington, D.C., and the plane crash in Pennsylvania in 2001, the national homeland security agenda has been preoccupied with fighting terrorism. In order for homeland security and emergency preparedness programs to be effective, they must have the cooperation and trust of all Americans.[73]

A homeland security agenda that ignores privacy and civil liberties will undermine public trust, leading people to refuse to fully participate in critical public health activities. We are far more likely to "succeed in preventing and responding to a potential act of bioterrorism if we embrace the principle that advancing public health and preserving individual liberties are symbiotic and inextricable."[74] Boston University health professor George Annas says that protecting basic human and constitutional rights is essential to effective coordination of medicine and public health. He wrote:

> It is unnecessary and counterproductive to sacrifice basic human rights to respond to bioterrorism. Constructive public health legislation, which must be federal, cannot be carefully drafted under panic conditions. When it is, like the "model act," it will predictably rely on broad, arbitrary state authority exercised without public accountability. Public health should resist reverting to its nineteenth-century practices of forced examination and quarantine, which will simply encourage people to avoid physicians, hospitals, and public health practitioners they now trust and actively seek out in emergencies. Upholding human rights is essential to public trust and is ultimately our best defense against the threat of terrorism in the twenty-first century.[75]

On October 15, 2001, a worker in the office of then-Senate Majority Leader Tom Daschle opened a letter containing anthrax spores, *Bacillus anthracis*, the bacterium that causes the disease anthrax, triggering a public health emergency. Anthrax is an acute infectious disease. A similar letter was mailed to U.S. Senator Patrick Leahy. The Leahy letter, which contained a highly purified "weapon-grade" *B. anthracis* preparation, was opened at the U.S. Army Medical Research Institute of Infectious Disease at Fort Detrick, Maryland.[76] These were the first cases of anthrax infection related to an intentional release of anthrax in the United States.[77]

About a month later, twenty-two cases of anthrax had been identified in the United States, and a wide array of people had been exposed in the Washington area. Five people died. No cases of anthrax occurred among the Capitol Hill population. However, four cases of inhalation anthrax originated at the Brentwood U.S. Postal Facility in Washington, D.C., where one contaminated letter was handled four days before it was opened.[78] Brentwood is Washington, D.C.'s main mail-processing facility, operating twenty-four hours daily, seven days a week. Two postal workers at the facility, Joseph Curseen Jr., age forty-seven, of Clinton, Maryland, and Thomas Morris Jr., fifty-five, of Suitland, Maryland, died from anthrax exposure.[79] In December 2002, the Brentwood postal facility was renamed the Curseen-Morris Mail Processing and Distribution Center in their honor.

A $100 million lawsuit was filed by the government watchdog group Judicial Watch in 2002, charging that the Brentwood employees, of whom nearly 95 percent are black, were assured during the anthrax crisis that the building was safe and were reprimanded if they questioned that judgment.[80] The suit was dismissed in 2004 by District Judge Rosemary Collyer of the District of Columbia, who found that Postal Service officials were immune to the charges that they left employees in harm's way during the attacks.

African Americans constitute 10.6 percent of the U.S. labor force. More than 21 percent of postal workers are African Americans; 8 percent are Hispanic; 8 percent are Asian Americans; and 0.06 percent are American Indian or Alaska Native. The Postal Service is one of the leading employers of minorities and women. People of color make up 38 percent of the postal workforce, and women account for nearly 40 percent. Women represent 49 percent and minorities nearly 30 percent of employees at the Executive and Administrative Schedule (EAS) level, which includes midlevel managers and supervisors. People of color constitute 26 percent of the Postal Service's 748 executives, women nearly 29 percent. African Americans make up 58.7 percent of postal workers in Atlanta, 58.1 percent in New Orleans, 48.5 percent in Chicago and Houston, 47.1 percent in Washington, D.C., 42.2 percent in Miami, 39.3 percent in Dallas, 33.4 percent in New York, 30.2 percent in Philadelphia, and 29.3 percent in Los Angeles.

Health officials did not focus their attention on the Brentwood postal center until nine days after the tainted letter was discovered. A 2005 Rand Corporation study, *In Their Own Words: Lessons Learned from Those Exposed to Anthrax*, examined why postal workers and U.S. Senate staffers in Washington lost trust in the public health system after they were exposed to a letter contaminated with anthrax spores.[81] Findings from focus group interviews revealed that, among Brentwood postal workers, lack of trust involved the perception that unfair treatment on the basis of race/ethnicity and socio-economic status had occurred; among U.S. Senate staffers, it derived from perceptions of inconsistent and disorganized messages.[82] The Rand report recommended that future communications on public health emergencies closely involve people from exposed population groups. The report also suggested that well-known people from the groups be enlisted to help authorities spread consistent and forthright information about each health emergency, even about existing uncertainties.

Eventually, public health officials advised 2,743 people from the postal facility and 600 from the Senate Hart office building to take preventive antibiotics for sixty days. The fact that government officials received anthrax treatment before the post office employees did not help officials gain the trust of the African American postal workers. Ron Walters, a professor of political science at the University of Maryland, summed up the incident: "It was botched, and would seem to have a smell of racism because 80 percent of the people who work in [the post office in the Brentwood section of Washington] were African American. There was no thought given to the fact that [postal workers] should be immediately tested because all of the focus went to the Senate and its staff."[83] About five hundred of the Brentwood employees opted to retire early or walked away from their postal duties after the Washington distribution center became a target in the terrorism war.

A 2004 Rand Corporation study in Los Angeles County found that 76.6 percent of white and 73.1 percent of Latino respondents believed that the public health system would respond fairly in a bioterrorist event.[84] Only 63 percent of African Americans and 68 percent of Asian/Pacific Islanders felt that the public health system would do so. The Rand study concluded: "To strengthen bioterrorism preparedness, public health officials must continue to improve perceived fairness among African Americans and Asian/Pacific Islander communities."[85]

In February 2010, more than eight years after the anthrax-laced letters killed five people and terrorized the entire nation, the FBI closed its investigation into the case.[86] Those killed by the spores included two postal workers in Washington, D.C., a New York City hospital worker, a Florida photo editor, and a ninety-four-year-old Connecticut woman who had no known contact with any of the poisoned letters. Seventeen other people were sickened. In a ninety-two-page report, the FBI concluded that Bruce E. Ivins, a microbiologist who had worked with anthrax for decades as part of the vaccine program at the Army's biodefense laboratory at Fort Detrick, Maryland, was a suspect in the anthrax case. Ivins had killed himself on July 29, 2008, after FBI agents had focused on him for two years as the lead suspect in what was called the "Amerithrax" investigation and prosecutors prepared to indict him for the attacks.

In a ninety-six-page prosecutor's summary report and 2,700 pages of documents, FBI investigators concluded that Ivins concocted the anthrax-by-mail attack in hopes of creating a scare that would rescue an anthrax vaccine program that he had helped create but that by 2001 was in danger of failing.[87] Investigators also concluded that the anthrax bacteria used in the attack originated in Ivins's lab and that he was one of a few scientists with both access to the spores and the skills needed to create the deadly powder sent to news media and U.S. Senate offices in September and October 2001.

### Chemical Plants Insecurity Versus Community Safety

Pollution from chemical plants located in populated areas pose a health threat to nearby residents.[88] The plants themselves also pose a threat as possible targets for terrorism. While the Department of Homeland Security has spent billions of dollars shoring up plant security, little attention has been given to reducing elevated health threats to "fenceline" communities, that are disproportionately poor and people of color. These "environmental justice communities" also have a disproportionately large share of sick people. Residents in environmental justice communities are the most vulnerable populations during mass evacuations caused by natural and man-made disasters.

The response by FEMA in New Orleans and along the Gulf Coast after Katrina should alert the nation to the inadequacy of our national emergency preparedness and emergency planning. The Louisiana petrochemical corridor—the stretch from Baton Rouge to New Orleans—is a ticking time bomb. Many of the residents who live near the petrochemical plants and refineries in the Texas, Louisiana, Mississippi, and Alabama Gulf Coast regions are poor, working class, and people of color. Historically, these communities have received unequal protection from government.

The emergency response in the aftermath of Katrina did nothing to build trust among fenceline communities that for decades had been on the frontline of pollution assaults from nearby industry. These same communities would also be on the frontline if there were a terrorist attack on the chemical plants. Since the September 11 attacks, federal officials have warned the chemical industry that terrorist attacks could turn hazardous-materials plants into weapons of mass destruction.[89] Deaths in the wake of a terrorist attack on U.S. chemical facilities could easily exceed the loss of life suffered on September 11.

To date, there has never been a terrorist attack on a U.S. chemical facility. However, there have been more than three thousand accidents involving more than ten thousand pounds of hazardous materials since 1987, with smaller incidents occurring daily. In 2009, according to Dan Cooler, a senior analyst in the office of intelligence and analyst at the Department of Homeland Security (DHS), "the nation's process industry remains vulnerable to terrorist attacks, and that is an unacceptable level of risk. U.S. chemical plants remain targets of interest to foreign and domestic terrorists seeking a dramatic attack that could cause mass casualties and major economic impact."[90] Still, many chemical facilities lack adequate safeguards. In assessing the general terrorist risk to plants, the Justice Department determined that the threat was "both real and credible" and that the outcome of an attack on chemical plants could be more serious than the result of an attack on nuclear power plants, which undergo regular security assessments by the Nuclear Regulatory Commission. The Justice Department concluded that "the ubiquitousness of industrial facilities possessing toxic chemicals and their proximity to population centers also make them attractive targets."[91] In its August 2006 report, *Chemical Facility Security*, the Congressional Research Service concluded:

> Historically, there have been very few terrorist attacks on chemical facilities in the United States. Therefore, the estimated risk of death and injury from such attacks in the immediate future is low relative to the likelihood of other hazardous events, such as industrial accidents or terrorist attacks on other targets using conventional weapons. For any individual chemical plant, the risk of attack is extremely small. However, the overall risks to chemical facilities may be increasing.

Even before the sad events of 9/11, the Agency for Toxic Substances and Disease Registry warned us about the weak site security at "two communities in the United States: a large city in a desert with chemical and entertainment industries, and a county containing several major chemical manufacturing facilities located along a river valley."[92] The two communities were Kanahwa Valley, West Virginia, and Las Vegas, Nevada. The ATSDR study noted:

Terrorists, warring factions, and saboteurs use chemicals commonly found in communities in industrialized nations to create improvised explosives, incendiaries, and chemical agents. Common chemicals may be used because standard military chemical agents may be difficult or dangerous to manufacture, access, or disperse.[93]

After 9/11, Congress enacted the Public Health Security and Bioterrorism Preparedness and Response Act of 2002 (P.L. 107-188) and the Maritime Transportation Security Act (MTSA, P.L. 107-295), requiring the Department of Homeland Security to prepare vulnerability assessments and emergency response plans for "critical infrastructure," including chemical facilities that supply drinking water or are located in ports, as well as security plans for chemical facilities in ports.[94]

Six to seven months after September 11, 2001, the *Pittsburgh Tribune-Review* published its investigation of plant security, which showed (on the basis of reporters' trips to thirty plants in western Pennsylvania that had filed risk management plans under the Clean Air Act, Section 112) that "anyone has unfettered access to more than two dozen potentially dangerous plants in the region." The investigation concluded that "security was so lax at 30 sites that in broad daylight a *Tribune* reporter—wearing a press pass and carrying a camera—could walk or drive right up to tanks, pipes and control rooms considered key targets for terrorists."[95]

A second series of *Tribune-Review* articles described a similar investigation of thirty additional plants in Houston, Baltimore, and Chicago and concluded that security was lax at some of "the potentially deadliest plants" in all three cities; access to some sites owned by corporations with large security budgets was easy, as employees, customers, neighbors, and contractors "not only let a stranger walk through warehouses, factories, tank houses and rail depots, but also gave directions to the most sensitive valves and control rooms," and nineteen sites were accessible thanks to "unguarded rail lines and drainage ditches, dilapidated or nonexistent fences, open doors, poorly angled cameras and unmanned train gates."[96] An April 2010 *Houston Chronicle* article reports that 113 facilities in the Houston area have been identified as potential targets, yet a decade after 9/11, securing them remains problematic.[97]

A 2002 Brookings Institution report ranked chemical facilities third in the number of fatalities that could occur as the result of a terrorist attack.[98] Fenceline communities are especially vulnerable. However, releases of toxic chemicals can kill and injure people located relatively far from the accidents.

As a result, failure to identify and evaluate opportunities to reduce the risks from relatively rare plant accidents, not to mention intentional attacks, could ultimately lead to thousands of fatalities, injuries, and evacuations.

The Surgeon General of the U.S. Army identified chemical plants as second only to bioterrorism in evaluating terrorist threats to the United States. Of the nation's 15,000 chemical facilities, the U.S. General Accounting Office reports that 123 are close enough to population centers to potentially endanger more than one million people if a terrorist attack were to occur.[99] These plants represent "15,000 weapons of mass destruction." Some 700 plants are close enough to put 100,000 people at risk, and about 2,900 are close enough to put at least 10,000 lives at risk. A single breached chlorine tank could cause 17,500 deaths.[100]

In July 2004, the Homeland Security Council issued fifteen national planning scenarios to guide federal, state, and local homeland security preparedness activities. Included in these scenarios are two that refer to industrial chemical releases. The planning figures cited for a hypothetical refinery attack include 350 fatalities and an additional 1,000 casualties. It estimated that a hypothetical chlorine release could cause 17,500 fatalities, 10,000 severe injuries, and 100,000 additional casualties.[101]

Far too few chemical companies have changed the processes and the chemicals they use to make their facilities inherently safer. Instead, most industries and their lobbying organizations have placed emphasis on increasing physical security measures. Moreover, some plans have limited the public's "right-to-know" and restricted access to information on the potential impact of an attack on chemical plants to public health and safety. Also, "limitations have been placed on the information any individual can obtain about a chemical facility and its vulnerability zone."[102]

The zone-of-vulnerability estimates are derived from "worst-case scenario" projections of how far a chemical could travel offsite and still maintain toxic concentrations in various weather conditions and the number of people living within that distance and their vulnerability. Some 15.6 million Americans live inside a vulnerability zone for an oil refinery that uses hydrofluoric acid. Overlapping vulnerability zones pose even greater danger to residents who live, work, and play nearby.[103]

In November 2001, the Children Environmental Health Network and a coalition of medical, nursing, health science, public health, consumer, and faith professionals and organizations issued a "Statement on Protecting Public Health and Hazards Reduction (Chemical Plants, Terrorism, and Right-to-Know)" protesting the government's and the industry's attack on the public right-to-know.

> The terrorist acts of September 11 have in particular heightened awareness of the dangers posed to communities by potential releases of hazardous chemicals in our midst. While valid security concerns have been raised, some current proposals would unduly deny information and forewarning about hazards to those who could be harmed. Moreover, the appropriate release of information would actually help to protect and serve our communities, our citizens, and public health. Limiting access to information should not be a substitute for effective policies and actions that prevent and control environmental hazards. Limiting the unnecessary production and release of hazardous chemicals on a routine basis, coupled with the right-to-know about the presence and release of such chemicals, will make our nation, and the world, a safer place.[104]

In 2004, the public's right to know was again attacked by the Bush administration and a modification proposed by the EPA of the Toxic Release Inventory (TRI) program, which is widely credited with reducing toxic chemical releases by 65 percent. In 2004, nearly thirty-eight million pounds of toxic chemicals known to cause or suspected of causing reproductive disorders were released by U.S. companies into the air and water each year.

In December 2006, the EPA announced final rules that would undermine the TRI program by eliminating detailed reports from more than five thousand facilities that release up to two thousand pounds of chemicals every year and eliminating detailed reports from nearly two thousand facilities that manage up to five hundred pounds of chemicals known to pose some of the worst threats to human health, including lead and mercury.

In April 2007, the Bush administration announced new security requirements for the nation's high-risk chemical plants, marking the first across-the-board attempt to require companies to head off potential catastrophic terrorist attacks involving the theft or explosive release of toxic chemicals stored in densely populated urban areas.[105] In June 2008, the Department of Homeland Security (DHS) announced that more than seven thousand facilities, from chemical plants to colleges, were being designated "high-risk" sites for potential terrorist attacks.[106] The facilities include chemical plants, hospitals, colleges and universities, oil and natural gas production and storage sites, and food and agricultural processing and distribution centers.

The DHS compiled the list from thirty-two thousand facilities nation-wide and narrowed it to seven thousand on the basis of factors such as proximity to population centers, the volatility of chemicals on site, and how the chemicals are stored and handled. The facilities were given ninety days to conduct site-specific assessments of security vulnerabilities. DHS was also to conduct additional assessments, divide the facilities into four tiers, and help the plants develop security plans. Residents on the fence-line and experts have worried that terrorists could attack chemical facil-ities near large cities, turning them into large bombs. "Recent overseas attacks typically have involved an initial blast created by a truck-borne bomb that has penetrated an outer perimeter, followed by an infantry attack by terrorists armed with assault rifles, hand grenades, and other explosives. Terrorists are interested in any potential target that could, if attacked, produce visually dramatic results, broad economic impact and mass casualties."[107]

Some environmental advocates say Homeland Security rules cater to industry and not public safety. A Greenpeace analysis of 2006 lobbying records identified 215 industry lobbyists that spent between $16.4 million and $74.5 million to defeat strong chemical-plant security legislation. On the other hand, the Department of Homeland Security spent just $10 million on actual chemical security for fiscal year 2007 and requested $25 million for chemical security by DHS for fiscal 2008.[108]

*Conclusion*

There is clear evidence that the social environment in which we are born, live, work, and play affects our health. Numerous social determinants of health studies now link racism to ill health and health disparities. These dis-parities exist across the entire health care establishment, from small neigh-borhood clinics to large university-based teaching hospitals. Inequality is making some of us sick.

A health equity movement has emerged in response to these disparities. This movement seeks change through enhancing health services; equaliz-ing care across racial and ethnic populations; improving access to services, insurance, and transportation; increasing the number of African American health professionals; and strengthening health institutions that serve African Americans and other people of color. These actions are desperately needed in the face of declining "safety net" public hospitals in cities where African Americans are concentrated.

African Americans tend to receive a lower quality of health care across a range of diseases and clinical settings, including public and private hospitals and teaching and nonteaching hospitals. Many of these inequities result from unconscious racial bias, while others flow from institutional and structural racism that allow black health to be valued less than white health.

The unfair treatment to which African Americans are subjected and the poor quality of the service they receive lead many to mistrust the health-care system, biomedical research, and government immunization programs. The legacy of human experimentation dressed up as research has left a bitter memory in the minds of young and old African Americans. The lack of trust has limited African American participation in clinical trials and has meant that many blacks miss out on many of the latest treatments and breakthroughs—research that could help address diseases that disproportionately impact black people.

There is little doubt that dangerous, involuntary, unethical, and nontherapeutic experimentation and chemical and biological warfare tests performed on African Americans have left a negative and lasting mark. Historically, African Americans (men, women, and children) have been singled out as special targets for risky experiments—abuses masked as research. It has been difficult for many blacks to erase the historical memory and to overcome the sorry legacy of the Tuskegee syphilis study, the forced sterilization of black women, the lead and pesticide studies that used black children as human guinea pigs, or the Army mosquito biological weapons tests performed on unsuspecting black public-housing residents.

The government response to the 2001 Washington, D.C., anthrax attack left doubts in the minds of many African Americans, including postal workers who were on the frontline of the attack. Again, questions of fairness and trust emerged as major concerns among postal workers. These concerns have not waned with time. Will the government protect postal workers from bioterrorism attacks? Will the government response to bioterrorism be fair? These questions are important as the nation prepares for potential threats from bioterrorism and emerging infectious diseases such as West Nile virus and avian flu.

Success in addressing health emergencies and bioterrorism threats will depend heavily on securing the trust and cooperation of the various publics, including the African American community. In the event of a bioterrorism attack or the release of a biological agent or a deadly virus in a major city, how will African Americans perceive and respond to controversial control measures such as isolation, quarantine, travel restrictions, or targeted distribution of medicines or vaccines? How will the government respond if a chemical plant is attacked by a terrorist? The same questions of fairness and equity are being asked by residents who live on the fenceline with chemical plants and who live next to railways that traverse their communities while carrying dangerous cargo.

Even after billions of dollars have been spent by the Department of Homeland Security, many chemical facilities still lack adequate safeguards. Fenceline residents worry about a possible terrorist attack on chemical plants, although this has never happened in this country. They also worry about the routine toxic emissions from these chemical plants—pollution that residents are forced to endure twenty-four hours a day, seven days a week. Some residents get sick; others die.

Although real health threats to fenceline communities come from chemical plant pollution, not terrorism, government attention has been focused on shoring up plant security, while little attention has been given to reducing pollution threats or transitioning to less toxic and less volatile chemicals, employing "green chemistry," and introducing cleaner production practices. Clean production strategies include using materials that incorporate technical innovations (e.g., biodegradability), environmentally friendly products (such as those designed for reuse and disassembly), and low-polluting facility design (e.g., zero-discharge facilities), as well as following broader policy schemes such as shifting taxes and extending producer responsibility for products.

How can we defuse the potential chemical time bombs that are located in the midst of populated areas? Some experts argue that this will require changing the entire chemical production process to include a "green chemistry" philosophy that encourages the design of products and processes that reduce or eliminate the use and generation of hazardous substances. Green chemistry applies across the life cycle, including the design, manufacture, and use of a chemical product. Vulnerable fenceline communities could benefit from clean production and green chemistry investments. They would also be made safer by increased plant security. Dismantling the separate and unequal emergency preparedness and response apparatuses will make us a safer and more secure nation.

# Critical Conditions

## *Fixing a Broken System*

Some population groups in the United States are more vulnerable to natural and human-induced disasters than others.[1] There are clear links among race, economic power, and vulnerability.[2] Some racial and ethnic communities face an increased risk and vulnerability as a result of where they have settled and the level of protection they are provided.[3] In the real world, all communities are not created equal. Equal protection has eluded many communities that are located in low-lying flood plains, on the fenceline with dangerous polluting industries, and where railways haul their deadly cargo.[4]

People of color experience different consequences of environmental hazards and disasters than whites. A study from the National Academy of Sciences Institute of Medicine concluded that government, public health officials, and the medical and scientific communities need to place a higher value on the problems and concerns of environmental justice communities.[5] The study also confirmed what most impacted communities have known for decades: minority and low-income communities are exposed to higher levels of pollution than the rest of the nation and experience certain diseases in greater numbers than more affluent, white communities.[6]

Emergency planners at the FEMA have known for decades which populations are most vulnerable and what types of people are most likely to be left behind in disasters—individuals who are poor, sick, very elderly or very young, and people of color. Racial disparities exist in disaster preparedness, communication, physical impacts, psychological impacts, emergency response, recovery, and reconstruction.[7] In 2001, FEMA experts ranked a hurricane striking New Orleans, a terrorist attack on New York City, and a strong earthquake in San Francisco as the top three catastrophic disasters most likely to occur in the country.[8]

Even after Hurricane Katrina, significant disparities exist in the amount of culturally tailored information available for vulnerable at-risk populations, and there is a need improve development and dissemination of culturally appropriate emergency risk communication designed to reach low-income minorities.[9] Studies show that blacks are more likely to suffer from delayed posttraumatic stress disorder (PTSD) than whites.[10] Two months after Katrina struck, more than 2,300 children were still separated from their families, down from more than 4,500 reported separated just after the storm.[11] One can only imagine the mental anguish and stress these children and families went through.

## Stranded by Natural and Man-Made Disasters

Transportation is a major component in emergency preparedness and evacuation planning. There is a clear connection between social inequities and the existence of policies, or the lack of policies, for evacuating individuals who do not have transportation to leave the city. Disaster evacuation plans all across the nation assume that people own a car. Nearly eleven million households in the United States lack vehicles.[12] This translates into more than twenty-eight million Americans who would have difficulty evacuating their area in the event of an emergency.

In 1997, to encourage better disaster planning, FEMA, under the Clinton administration, launched Project Impact, a pilot program that provided funding for communities to, among other things, assess their vulnerable populations and make arrangements to get people without transportation to safety. The program reached 250 communities and proved quite effective. However, the Bush administration ended the program in 2001, and funds once earmarked for disaster preparation were shifted elsewhere.[13]

Being left behind has not been headline news for millions of central-city residents who have struggled to get dollars allocated for public transit. Cars not only are an essential part of evacuation plans but also often make the difference between being employed and unemployed. Unequal access to automobile ownership contributes to the racial economic divide and vulnerability to natural and man-made disasters.

There is a clear racial disparity in who can escape natural disasters by car. It should not be a surprise to anyone that people of color are considerably more likely to be left behind in a natural disaster, since fewer people of color than whites own cars. In addition to having lower rates of car ownership, people of color tend to make up a majority of the population in U.S. cities that are at risk of hurricanes: in Miami, 79 percent; in New Orleans, 73 percent; in New York City, 65 percent; and in Houston, 58 percent.[14]

In *Stalling the Dream: Cars, Race and Hurricane Evacuation* report, Lui et al. arrived at some insightful conclusions:

- In all eleven major cities that have had five or more hurricanes in the past one hundred years (Houston, Miami, Fort Lauderdale, Orlando, Jacksonville, St. Petersburg, Tampa, New York City, Providence, Boston, and New Orleans), people without cars are disproportionately people of color.
- If they were to face a mandatory evacuation order during a disaster, 33 percent of Latinos, 27 percent of African Americans, and 23 percent of whites say that lack of transportation would be an obstacle to their evacuating, according to the National Center for Disaster Preparedness.
- Evacuation planning tends to focus on traffic management for those with cars and on institutionalized people, not on noninstitutionalized people without vehicles. New Orleans had only one-quarter the number of buses that would have been needed to evacuate all carless residents.
- In the counties affected by Hurricanes Katrina, Rita, and Wilma in 2005, only 7 percent of white households have no car, whereas 24 percent of blacks, 12 percent of Native Americans and 14 percent of Latino households are carless.[15]

Eleven percent of African American families and 21 percent of Latino families have missed out on medical care because of transportation issues, whereas only 2 percent of white families have done so, according to the National Center for Disaster Preparedness. Generally, public transit in the United States is viewed as the transportation of last resort or as a novelty for tourists, resulting in dramatic differences in convenience, comfort, and safety between motorists and nonmotorists and, therefore, between wealthy and poor, white and black, and able and disabled.[16] Millions of jobs are unreachable for those who lack automobiles, thereby locking many families into permanent poverty, unemployment, and underemployment.

In June 2006, the Department of Homeland Security (DHS) released the *National Plan Review*, a comprehensive, nationwide assessment of the adequacy of emergency plans for each state and for the seventy-five largest urban areas.[17] DHS found these plans particularly insufficient with regard to evacuation planning for the carless and "special needs" populations—individuals who cannot simply jump into their cars and drive away. Evacuation of low-mobility and special-needs groups is an area that, while included in most state emergency operation plans, has been largely unaddressed by state DOTs.

The DHS notes that large swaths of the population have special needs that must be addressed in evacuation plans, including the carless (9 percent of U.S. households), residents with a physical or mental disability (13 percent of residents) or who face a language barrier (8 percent), the elderly (40 percent of whom have a disability), and those living in group quarters such as nursing homes and assisted living facilities (2 percent of residents).

The private automobile is still the most dominant travel mode of every segment of the American population, including the poor and people of color. Car ownership is almost universal in the United States, with more than 90 percent of American households owning at least one motor vehicle.[18] Clearly, private automobiles provide an enormous advantage to their owners in seeking employment. Private automobiles are also the principal mode of urban evacuation; having a car can mean the difference between being trapped and escaping from natural disasters.

Nationally, 87.6 percent of whites, 83.1 percent of Asians and of Hispanics, and 78.9 percent of blacks rely on a private car to get around. Lack of car ownership and inadequate public transit service in many central cities and metropolitan regions with a high proportion of "captive" transit dependents exacerbates social, economic, and racial isolation—especially for low-income people of color who already have limited transportation options.

Only 7 percent of white households do not own a car, whereas 24 percent of African American households, 17 percent of Latino households, and 13 percent of Asian American households are carless.[19] African Americans are nearly three and a half times more likely to lack a car than whites, Latinos about two and a half times more likely. In Georgia, African Americans are more than four times more likely than whites to lack access to a car.

On March 31, 2010, Clayton County, Georgia, a suburban county south of Atlanta, shut down C-Tran, its bus service, stranding more than 8,500 riders who use the service daily, because of a budget shortfall of $1.3 million. More than half of C-Tran riders do not have regular access to a car. Local residents took about two million rides a year on C-Tran. In 2006, Clayton County had an estimated population of 271,240, with a racial makeup that was 20.4 percent white non-Hispanic, 62.9 percent African American, 5 percent Asian, 11.3 percent Hispanic or Latino, 0.4 percent American Indian or Alaska Native, 0.1 percent Pacific Islander, and 1.5 percent multiracial.

Ironically, the shutdown of C-Tran occurred in a county that has the highest unemployment rate in metro Atlanta. Clayton County's unemployment rate for January 2010 was 12.9 percent overall, higher than that in Cobb County (10.1 percent), DeKalb County (10.8 percent), Fulton County (11.1

percent), or Gwinnett County (9.8 percent).This is not a small point, given the fact that metro Atlanta tops the list of cities with decentralized employment. According to a 2009 Brookings study, *Job Sprawl Revisited: The Changing Geography of Metropolitan Employment*, the majority of entry-level jobs in metro Atlanta are not within a quarter-mile of public transportation. In 2006, only 9.3 percent of metro Atlanta's jobs were located within a three-mile radius of the central business district (CBD), 27.5 percent were located within a ten-mile radius, and 63.2 percent were located outside the ten-mile ring.[20]

In urban areas across the United States, African Americans and Latinos make up more than 54 percent of transit users (62 percent of bus riders, 35 percent of subway riders, and 29 percent of commuter rail riders). Nationally, however, only about 5.3 percent of all Americans use public transit to get to work. African Americans are almost six times as likely as whites to use mass transit to get around. Urban transit is especially important to African Americans, more than 88 percent of whom live in metropolitan areas, with 53.1 percent inside central cities. Nearly 60 percent of transit riders are served by the ten largest urban transit systems, and the remaining 40 percent are served by the other five thousand transit systems. Evacuation plans that are centered on the premise that the population will use private transportation are faulty and will universally fail. These policies privilege middle- to upper-class, able-bodied, and nonelderly households that are more likely to own cars, while simultaneously excluding the poor, most people of color, the disabled, and the elderly because many of them lack the physical mobility or transportation to evacuate.

In the case of Hurricane Katrina, emergency transportation planners failed the most vulnerable of our society. Katrina highlighted the mobility problem many of our nation's nondrivers and transit-dependents residents face every day. Addressing transportation equity in the nation's cities, suburbs, and rural areas will have positive health impacts by combining community efforts to build strong institutions and better infrastructure with regional policies to foster equitable public and private investment. If the developers of transportation policies were more democratically accountable, the potential for community change that is racially and economically just and environmentally sustainable might be greater.

Unequal access to transportation alternatives in disasters heightens the vulnerability of the poor, the elderly, the disabled, and people of color. Individuals with private automobiles have a greater chance of "voting with their feet" and escaping threats from hurricanes than do individuals who are dependent on the government to provide emergency transportation. Too often buses (public transit and school buses), vans (para-transit), and trains do not come to the rescue of low-income, elderly, disabled, or sick people or people of color.

Rising fuel prices are stranding millions of Americans on the economic sideline, forcing them to alter their budgets, rethink their driving patterns, and change their mode of travel. Soaring gas prices are pushing more Americans to take public transit and to ditch their cars. This increase in mass transit ridership is noteworthy because it occurred when the economy was declining and fares increasing. Families in rural communities where transit is nonexistent are forced to dig deeper into their wallets—with spending on gasoline often rivaling what people spend on food and housing.

The movement for transportation equity has traveled a long way. Yet, it still has many miles to go before we eliminate inequities within and between regions. Encouraging a balanced regional transportation approach makes economic, social, environmental, and health sense, since the future of cities, suburbs, and rural areas are inextricably interdependent. Public transit is in big trouble. Without additional transit funding from Congress in the form of emergency aid or an infrastructure-focused jobs bill, transit service will continue to deteriorate, leaving millions of Americans stuck and stranded, paying higher fares for less service.

This national crisis was highlighted in *Stranded at the Station*, one of the systematic analyses that documents the devastation caused by transit cuts and fare increases in America's communities.[21] The report found that nearly 90 percent of transit systems were forced to raise fares or cut service in 2008; among the twenty-five largest transit operators, ten agencies raised fares more than 13 percent; 59 percent of public transit systems cut service or raised fares; more than half of all transit systems transferred funds from capital improvements to operations, threatening operators' ability to keep systems in a state of good repair; seven out of ten transit systems projected budget shortfalls in their next fiscal year; and 47 percent of transit systems laid off workers or were considering doing so in the future.

Americans without access to an alternative form of transportation, the majority of whom are older, African American or Hispanic, and senior populations, are being left stranded without access to lifeline services. These trends have important implications for economic opportunity as well as disaster response. Transportation spending has always been about opportunity and equity. Writing in the foreword to *Highway Robbery: Transportation Racism and New Routes to Equity*, Congressman John Lewis of Georgia summed up the challenge that lies ahead: "Our struggle is not over. The physical signs are gone, but the legacy of Jim Crow transportation is still with us."[22]

Transportation spending programs do not benefit all populations equally. If one follows where transportation dollars go, one can tell who is important and who is not. The lion's share of transportation dollars is spent on roads, while urban transit systems are often left in disrepair. Nationally, 80 percent of all surface transportation funds are earmarked for highways, and 20 percent are earmarked for public transportation. On average, states spend just fifty-five cents per person of their federal transportation funds on pedestrian projects, less than 1 percent of their total federal transportation dollars. Average spending on highways came to $72 per person.[23]

Generally, states spend less than 20 percent of federal transportation funding on mass transit.[24] The current federal funding scheme is biased against metropolitan areas. The federal government allocates the bulk of transportation dollars directly to state DOTs. Many of the road-building fiefdoms are no friend to urban transit. Just 6 percent of all federal highway dollars are suballocated directly to the metropolitan regions.[25] Although local governments within metropolitan areas own and maintain the vast majority of the transportation infrastructure, they receive only about 10 percent of every dollar they generate.[26] Many transportation spending projects leave millions of African Americans on the side of the road.[27]

## Widening Disparities and Increased Risks

Disasters often worsen preexisting health disparities between whites and African American children and families, whose needs are only marginally being met before disasters strike. The Association of Black Psychologists (ABPsi) developed *Guidelines for Providing Culturally Appropriate Services for People of African Ancestry Exposed to the Trauma of Hurricane Katrina*; these guidelines urge mental health providers to be "especially aware of the culturally specific issues salient for the African American survivors and their experience."[28] The ABPsi guidelines stated:

> Mental health providers should also be aware that because of the history of racism and White supremacy in this country, many African Americans experience a mistrust of perceived White institutions (e.g., police, education, work, politics, law, mental health agencies). FEMA and the Red Cross are not exempt from this historically conditioned suspicion and mistrust.

There are racial differences in medical care, with African Americans being more likely to receive differential and most often inadequate medical care than Whites which contributes to an ever deepening distrust.[29]

In *Disaster Response to Communities of Color: Cultural Responsive Intervention*, Columbia University professor Robert T. Carter asserts that "training associated with responding to communities of color must be grounded in the worldview and cultural patterns of the community."[30] Some of his key recommendations for cultural responsive interventions include these:

- The predisaster preparedness plan should include training for crisis personnel that has a strong focus on self-exploration of the responder. The self-exploration should be geared to building awareness of one's own culture to facilitate interaction across race/ethnicity.
- As soon as possible in responding to a disaster, deploy racially and culturally diverse response teams, especially in communities of color.
- Training of crisis-response teams should emphasize that, within targeted groups, such as children or the elderly, health-care workers, first responders, and underserved cultural groups, there will be racial and cultural variation.
- Disaster response would be enhanced if there were predisaster interaction between responders and members of the various communities of color. The involvement might be focused on other community needs and concerns. The interaction would be designed to build relationships and mutual knowledge between the sets of culturally different people that will need to trust one another during a crisis.
- The training of health-care providers should include consideration not only of the effects of the first time traumatic effects but also the effects of prior traumatic experiences, including experiences that result from daily living (e.g., sudden death, car accidents, violence, and discrimination).
- Training of crisis response teams would be enhanced if group specific information regarding communities of color were taught. For instance, when specific ethnic and racial groups are discussed, the groups that reside in the area under consideration in the state should be represented.[31]

Past studies have found that blacks are also mistrustful of agencies staffed largely by whites and are less willing to turn to them for aid.[32] Katrina exposed weaknesses within the Red Cross. Many African American leaders questioned the Red Cross's ability to meet the needs of disaster survivors. African Americans also have little faith in the government's to respond to their needs. For example, six in ten Hurricane Katrina evacuees living in shelters in the Houston area said the slow response to the storm made them feel that government didn't care about people like them, according to a poll by the *Washington Post,* the Henry J. Kaiser Family Foundation, and the Harvard School of Public Health.[33]

Disasters push poor people deeper into poverty and exacerbate unemployment and crowding among families with children. African Americans are more likely to experience a decline in standard of living than whites following natural disasters.[34] Many African Americans and other people of color also have greater difficulty recovering from disasters because they have lower incomes and fewer savings, experience greater unemployment, have less insurance, and have limited access to information and communication channels.

Ownership of property, land, and business is still a central part of the American dream of success—a dream that has eluded millions of Americans. A 1999 *USA Today* survey of experts singled out "wealth disparity" as the biggest issue in cities' development for the next fifty years.[35] The growing economic disparity between various racial and ethnic groups has a direct correlation with the existence of institutional barriers in housing, lending, employment, education, health, and transportation. Housing discrimination denies a substantial segment of people of color communities a basic form of wealth accumulation and investment through home ownership.[36]

Wealth is what families own (and is often passed down from generation to generation), combined with income and other financial assets that families have at their disposal to use in the short term and in the long term for securing opportunities and a desired standard of living and pursuing the "good life." Wealth, unlike income, is usually passed along to one's children. Melvin Oliver and Thomas Shapiro, in their book *Black Wealth/White Wealth,* show that the average black family holds only ten cents of wealth for every dollar that whites possess.[37] The typical white family is worth $81,000, whereas the typical black family is worth only $8,000.[38] This wealth gap holds true for otherwise equally achieving blacks and whites. In 1984, the average white family in the sample group held around $20,000 more in assets than the average black family, according to a 2010 study conducted by the Institute on Assets and Social Policy at Brandeis University. By 2007, the "racial wealth gap" had increased by $75,000."[39]

The post-2008 meltdown in the housing market increased the black-white wealth gap. A 2011 Pew study found the median wealth of white households to be twenty times that of black households and eighteen times that of Hispanic households.[40] These wealth ratios are the largest since the government began reporting such data a quarter century ago and are roughly twice the size of the ratios that had prevailed for these three groups for the two decades prior to the Great Recession that ended in 2009.

The purchase of a home is the largest investment most families will make in their lifetimes. Home ownership is a cushion against inflation, the cornerstone of wealth creation, and a long-term asset that can secure advantages and transfer across generations. It is also the "most critical pathway for transformative assets,"[41] defined by Thomas Shapiro as "inherited wealth lifting a family beyond their own achievement."[42] Home ownership is still the cornerstone of the American Dream, but it doesn't seem exactly the path to wealth right now. "The aggressive promotion of risky sub-prime mortgages in neighborhoods largely populated by African Americans is leading to geographic concentrations of foreclosures."[43] Subprime mortgages are very damaging to a community because they are so concentrated geographically.

About 60 percent of America's middle-class families' wealth is derived from their homes.[44] Middle class families are struggling and have been since 2000. Their economic security has erased in a few years, a result of (1) a decline in financial security associated with the cost of medical emergencies, (2) a decrease in the number of households that have an emergency fund of three months  of income to 4 percent in 2007 from 30.5 percent in 2005 and 39.4 percent in 2000; and (3) financial losses imposed by unemployment such that in 2007, 44.1 percent of families had enough wealth to cover unemployment whereas in 2005 that figure was 44.0 percent, and 2000 it was 51.0 percent.[45] Only 48 percent of blacks own their homes, far behind the nationwide home-ownership rate of 68 percent. Sadly, the American Dream is beyond the reach of millions of Americans because of closed home ownership opportunities. In his book *The Hidden Cost of Being African American*, Shapiro says the penalty in net worth for being black amounts to $136,173, and the net financial asset penalty is $94,426.[46] In 2010, Shapiro concludes that "The fourfold increase in the wealth gap reflects a variety of public policies, such as tax cuts on investment income and inheritances, which benefit the wealthiest Americans. Persistent discrimination in housing, credit and labor markets are [sic] also factors that likely played a role in the widening of the gap."[47]

Disasters increase competition for housing in unaffected areas. They therefore place a special burden on black renters and homebuyers seeking replacement housing, exposing them to housing discrimination. The result is a "discrimination tax" that ends up costing black renters and homebuyers more than whites for comparable housing.[48] Generally, blacks spend more time, more effort, and more money than whites in their search for comparable housing.[49] Disasters also expose the survivors to price gouging, home-repair scams, banking and insurance redlining, and predatory lending practices.

Studies show that some banks and lending institutions avoid making loans in heavily black and low-income areas that they serve. In 1977, Congress passed the Community Reinvestment Act (CRA) to encourage depository institutions to help meet the credit needs of the communities in which they operate, including low- and moderate-income neighborhoods. Despite the law, some lenders still discriminate against entire neighborhoods.[50]

Many banks and mortgage companies use predatory lending practices to target black neighborhoods for the sale of high-rate loans. This practice is referred to as "reverse redlining." Predatory lending hits blacks especially hard.[51] Risk factors do not explain racial differences in subprime lending.[52] The 2002 *Risk or Race* explains lending disparities:

The persistent racial disparities in levels of subprime lending found in this analysis do not, in and of themselves, constitute conclusive proof that there is widespread discrimination in the subprime lending markets. These disparities do, however, raise serious questions about the extent to which risk alone could account for such patterns. Discrimination has been a persistent problem in the home finance markets in the United States. The history of mortgage lending discrimination adds weight to the need to explore more fully the role that discrimination plays in the subprime markets through either differential treatment of individual minority borrowers or through the effects of industry practices.[53]

Predatory lending creates separate and unequal housing opportunities.[54] Predatory practices by some subprime lenders have resulted in extremely high foreclosures in once-stable neighborhoods.[55] A 2003 Association of Community Organizations for Reform Now (ACORN) report, *The Great Divide*, found that "lower-income and minority homebuyers, primarily African Americans, have become more and more reliant on subprime loans when buying a home."[56]

African Americans borrowers are more likely than white borrowers to enter into high-cost loans. This racial disparity exists even for African Americans who qualify for traditional loans. African Americans in New Orleans are more than three times as likely as white borrowers to get high-interest loans. The ACORN report found that African American applicants for conventional loans were two and one-third times more likely to be turned down for a mortgage than white applicants.

One of every three African American applicants, 29.83 percent, were denied conventional home purchase loans in 2002, down from 39.73 percent in 2000 and 56.6 percent in 1997.[57] In 2004, African Americans in New Orleans were twice as likely as their white counterparts to have their loan applications rejected—20.41 percent versus 10.5 percent.[58]

The percentage of conventional loans made to African Americans also lags far behind their percentage of the population. For example, African Americans make up almost 13 percent of the country's population but receive just 5.1 percent of the conventional loans. Lenders also fail to adequately serve low- and moderate-income communities, which make up 26 percent of the population but receive just 11 percent of the conventional loans.[59]

In December 2005, the National Fair Housing Alliance (NFHA) released a report, *No Home for the Holidays: Report on Housing Discrimination Against Hurricane Katrina Survivors*, documenting high rates of housing discrimination against African Americans displaced by Hurricane Katrina.[60] NFHA conducted tests over the telephone to determine what both African American and white homeseekers were told about unit availability, rent, discounts, and other terms and conditions of apartment leasing. In 66 percent of these tests—forty-three of sixty-five instances—white callers were favored over African American callers.

NFHA also conducted five matched-pair tests in which persons of different races visited specified apartment complexes. In those five tests, whites were favored over African Americans three times. NFHA conducted an investigation of rental housing practices in five states based on the five matched-pair tests used to determine whether victims of Katrina would be treated unfairly because of their race. From mid-September through mid-December 2005, the NFHA conducted telephone tests of rental housing providers in seventeen cities in five states: Alabama (Birmingham, Mobile, Huntsville, and Montgomery); Florida (Gainesville, Tallahassee, and Pensacola); Georgia (Atlanta, Columbus, Macon, and Savannah); Tennessee (Nashville, Chattanooga, and Memphis); and Texas (Houston, Dallas, and Waco). On the basis of the evidence uncovered by this testing, the NFHA filed five race-based housing discrimination complaints against rental housing complexes located in Dallas, Texas; Birmingham, Alabama; and Gainesville, Florida.

Generally, low-income and African American disaster victims spend more time in temporary shelters and are more vulnerable to permanent displacement than are their middle-income and white counterparts. More than one million Louisiana residents fled Hurricane Katrina, of which an estimated 100,000 to 300,000 could end up permanently displaced. The powerful storm ravaged an eight-parish labor market that supported 617,300 jobs.[61] In September, nearly 100,000 Katrina evacuees were still housed in 1,042 barrack-style shelters scattered across 26 states and the District of Columbia.[62] In 2011, the federal Department of Housing and Urban Development reached a legal settlement in a civil rights lawsuit over Louisiana's Road Home program, which distributed aid to those trying to rebuild homes destroyed by Hurricane Katrina. Under the settlement, $62 million in aid will be distributed to 1,400 mainly minority homeowners whose homes are not habitable.

FEMA contracted for 120,000 mobile homes for Louisiana, Mississippi, and Alabama storm victims until they could find more permanent housing in homes and apartments. However, the pace of getting evacuees out of shelters was slow because few sites were been found with the necessary infrastructure—water, sewer, and electricity—to accommodate the trailers. Six weeks after the storm hit, FEMA had placed 4,662 Louisiana families in trailers, hotel rooms, or cruise ships docked in New Orleans.[63]

Some Louisiana parishes near New Orleans adopted "emergency ordinances" limiting the density of mobile home parks.[64] Some small white rural towns adopted NIMBY-ism (Not in My Back Yard) to keep out "temporary housing."[65] No one, including FEMA (which provided the trailers and mobile homes), homeowners (who were trying to protect their property values) and storm victims (who had to live in tight quarters), would have been served well if temporary or permanent "Katrina ghettos" were created.

Mobile homes are derisively known as "storm magnets" because of the endless reports over the years of trailer parks being demolished during bad weather. More than nine thousand families were living in temporary FEMA housing in Florida when Hurricane Dennis slammed into the Florida Panhandle in July 2004. That number was down from a peak of about fifteen thousand after four hurricanes hit the state in 2004.[66]

African Americans seeking housing in the Deep South are routinely met with discrimination. Disasters worsen this problem and intensify the competition for affordable housing. East Baton Rouge Parish's population surged from 425,000 to 1.2 million as a result of Katrina.[67] Katrina made Baton Rouge one of the "fastest-growing" regions in the country.[68] The influx of these new residents to the region created traffic gridlock and crowded the schools. Many of the mostly white suburban communities and small towns were not known for their hospitality toward blacks. Thus, thousands of black hurricane evacuees faced the added burden of "closed doors" and housing discrimination, while their white counterparts were given preference based on "white privilege."

## The Color of Disaster Relief

FEMA and the Red Cross, and HUD for that matter, have done little to address institutional barriers that block housing and other aid from flowing to African Americans who have historically been underserved by local and state governments.[69] The San Francisco-based writer Jeff Chang and his colleagues observed this problem while traveling the Gulf Coast after Hurricane Katrina:

> In many instances, FEMA and the Red Cross simply left African American populations unserved. In Biloxi, many African Americans remain camped outside of their demolished houses and apartments, and under highway overpasses, awaiting aid from FEMA and the Red Cross. In the poor, rural, still racially segregated Jefferson Davis County, the Red Cross set up at the single registered church, which was white; and African Americans watched as relief trucks drove past their towns and churches. Where FEMA and the Red Cross failed, the community organizations stepped in to provide food, shelter, medical aid and family reunion information.
>
> Across rural Mississippi, black churches such as Crossroads Ministry were the first responders to isolated residents. In Algiers, LA, Malik Rahim's Common Ground Collective has fed, housed and provided medical care to tens of thousands of people. The 21st Century Youth Leadership Project opened its camp outside of Selma, AL., to a surge of 200 families.[70]

Who gets approved for loans is not always based on how much money a person makes or on his or her debt ratio or credit score. Race operates in the mortgage industry before and after disasters. In 2004, the nation's ten largest banks denied African American applicants twice as often as whites.[71] African Americans were four times as likely as whites to pay high interest rates for mortgage loans. African Americans with incomes above $100,000 a year were charged higher interest rates than whites with incomes below $40,000.

Studies over the past three decades clearly document a relationship between racial redlining and disinvestment decisions and neighborhood decline.[72] Redlining exists when a mortgage application with a given set of applicant, property, and loan characteristics is more likely to be denied in a minority than in a white neighborhood.[73] Redlining "hits the poor where they live."[74] It accelerates the flight of full-service banks, food stores, restaurants, and other shopping centers in inner-city neighborhoods.[75]

Small businesses are the lifeblood of the U.S. economy. Hurricane Katrina wiped out up to half of New Orleans's 115,000 small businesses.[76] The number of minority-owned businesses, most of which are small, increased 31 percent to more than four million from 1997 to 2002, according to the Census Bureau, which conducts a survey every five years.[77] Overall, the number of U.S. businesses grew 10 percent in the period, to twenty-three million. Minorities owned 18 percent of those twenty-three million, up from 15 percent in 1997.

Blacks made up a significantly large share of the populations of the three Gulf Coast states hardest hit by Katrina—Louisiana, Mississippi, and Alabama; they made up 32.5 percent of the population in Louisiana, 36.3 percent in Mississippi, and 26 percent in Alabama when the storm hit. Disasters hit small and minority-owned businesses hardest because they are often under-capitalized, vulnerable, and sensitive to even small market shifts.

The U.S. Census Bureau reports that, in 1997, New Orleans had 9,747 black-owned companies, 4,202 Hispanic-owned companies, and 3,210 Asian-owned companies. Among the minority-owned companies in Biloxi-Gulfport, Mississippi, 1,305 were black-owned, 273 were Hispanic-owned, and 1,063 were Asian-owned. Mobile, Alabama, had 2,770 black-owned businesses, 478 Hispanic-owned businesses, and 549 Asian-owned businesses.[78]

Katrina affected more than two thousand black-owned businesses in Mississippi. These companies generated more than $126 million in sales and receipts in 2004.[79] Katrina also adversely affected more than twenty thousand black-owned businesses in Louisiana that had generated sales and receipts of $886 million in 2004. There was a good chance that most of these businesses would not reopen if assistance did not arrive quickly. Nearly one in four black-owned companies in New Orleans and Biloxi had closed by 2008, a rate 52 percent higher than the rate for white-owned businesses, according to the Political and Economic Research Council, a North Carolina think tank.[80]

Katrina negatively impacted more than sixty thousand black-owned businesses in the Gulf Coast region that generated $3.3 billion a year.[81] This is not a small point since most black-owned businesses employ blacks. Black-owned companies met roadblocks and were virtually frozen out of the cleanup and rebuilding of the Gulf Coast region after Katrina and the more recent BP Deepwater Horizon oil spill—where less than 5 percent of the BP cleanup dollars went to companies owned by people of color.[82] The matter was complicated by the U.S. Labor Department's decision to temporarily suspend the affirmative-action rule and no-bid contracts.[83] Billions of dollars were spent cleaning up the mess left by Katrina, but only 1.5 percent of the $1.6 billion awarded by FEMA went to minority businesses, less than a third of the 5 percent normally required by law.[84] The U.S. Army Corps of Engineers awarded about 16 percent of $637 million in Katrina contracts to minority-owned companies.

After Katrina, President Bush suspended the Davis-Bacon Act, passed in 1931 during the Great Depression, which sets a minimum pay scale for workers on federal contracts by requiring that contractors pay the prevailing or average pay in the region.[85] Some leaders saw the suspension of the prevailing wage combined with the relaxation of federal rules requiring employees to hire only people with proper documents as spurring an influx of low-wage illegal immigrant workers.[86] This heightened tension between African Americans and Latino immigrant workers. President Bush, facing mounting pressure from Democrats, moderate Republicans, organized labor, and workers in the Gulf Coast region, later reinstated the prevailing-wage rule.[87] The relaxation-of-documents rules was designed to assist Gulf Coast hurricane victims who lost their IDs and was not intended as a suspension of U.S. immigration laws.

Complaints about being shut out of the Gulf Coast reconstruction were not limited to minority-owned businesses. Many white Gulf Coast workers and businesses also railed about being left out as they saw out-of-state companies receiving the lion's share of the contracts. The annual payroll alone in the metropolitan areas hardest hit by Hurricane Katrina—New Orleans, Biloxi, and Mobile—exceeded $11.7 billion in 2002. About 75 percent of the businesses in the disaster area were nonemployer businesses such as sole proprietorships. Of the remaining small businesses, 80 percent had fewer than twenty employees. Small businesses employed 273,651 workers in the New Orleans area, 54,029 in Biloxi, and 107,586 in Mobile.

FEMA and the U.S. Small Business Administration (SBA) were swamped with requests for disaster assistance. FEMA doesn't offer small-business loans, but it does provide emergency cash grants up to $26,200 per person for housing, medical, and other disaster-related expenses.[88] Some Katrina victims claimed they were unfairly denied emergency aid and accused FEMA of leaving them behind a second time.[89]

The size of the staff at the SBA loan-processing center in Fort Worth, Texas, was tripled in response to Katrina. SBA disaster loans served as the only salvation for companies without insurance or whose insurance didn't cover all the damage. SBA offers two types of loans to small businesses, defined as those with fewer than five hundred employees. One, the physical (property) disaster business loan, provides businesses of any size with funds to repair or replace real estate, equipment, fixtures, machinery, and inventory. The second, the economic injury disaster loan, is available to small businesses that have suffered substantial economic injury as a result of a disaster. Both types of disaster loans fund up to $1.5 million in repair costs.[90]

SBA disaster loans are not just for small businesses; the agency makes the majority of its disaster loans to homeowners and renters. Homeowners and renters were eligible for low-interest disaster loans from the SBA to be used for repairing or rebuilding damage to private property caused by Katrina.[91] Homeowners could borrow up to $200,000 to repair or replace damaged or destroyed real estate, and homeowners and renters could borrow up to $40,000 to repair or replace damaged or destroyed personal property, including vehicles.

SBA's disaster home loans have low interest rates (less than 3 percent) and long terms (up to thirty years), helping to make recovery more financially affordable. Business Physical Disaster Loans are available to businesses to repair or replace disaster-damaged property owned by the business, including real estate, inventories, supplies, machinery, and equipment. Businesses of any size are eligible, as are private, nonprofit organizations such as charities, churches, and private universities. The federal government is expected to provide financial assistance even as private insurance companies are withdrawing disaster coverage from homeowners in hurricane-prone regions. However, most rebuilding funds after disasters come from private insurance, not the government.[92]

Before and after disasters strike, black business entrepreneurs are significantly more likely to be denied bank credit, and, when they do receive credit, they receive smaller loans than do comparable nonminority businesses. A 2005 *New York Times* study discovered that the Small Business Administration had processed only a third of the 276,000 home loan applications it had received.[93] During the same period, the SBA had rejected 82 percent of the applications it received, a higher percentage than in most previous disasters. Well-off neighborhoods like New Orleans's Lakeview received 47 percent of the loan approvals, while poverty-stricken neighborhoods received 7 percent. The loan denial problem is not limited to poor black areas. Middle-class black neighborhoods in New Orleans East also had lower loan approval rates than white districts. This trend, if continued, could hinder the rebuilding of black New Orleans neighborhoods.

Historically, black-owned banks have provided loans and other services to black communities that were redlined by white banks and mortgage companies. Dryades Savings and Loan and Liberty Bank are two well-established black-owned lending institutions in New Orleans. *Black Enterprise Magazine* lists Liberty Bank as the third-largest African American bank in the United States. Liberty Bank and Dryades Bank had assets of $348.2 million and $102.9 million at the time of Katrina.[94] Before Katrina, Liberty Bank operated nine branches in New Orleans, three in Baton Rouge, and one in Jackson, Mississippi. Katrina cost Liberty Bank an estimated $40 million.[95] In 2008, it dropped to fifth place among black-owned banks, with assets of $320 million.

A study from the Milken Institute and the U.S. Department of Commerce emphasized the need for removing barriers to minority business development.[96] African Americans make up about 12 percent of the U.S. population and 4 percent of all U.S. business owners. Minority businesses are vital for community development, since minority businesses are more likely to employ minority workers and thus provide them with an important entry point into the labor market.

Any threat to black businesses can have a destabilizing effect on black communities.[97] Involuntary relocation may also have a negative impact on black companies' ability to stay in business. This is complicated by the fact that black business failure rate is higher than the failure rate of white businesses. Some of the reasons cited for the higher black business failure rate are the lack of access to business or personal loans, poor cash flow, sales problems, and racial discrimination. Black-owned businesses face a different array of challenges. Statistically, minorities lack financial and social capital. On average, they have lower incomes, fewer assets, and less access to government and private contracts than white businesses.[98]

### Insuring Against Disaster

African American households are more likely than white households to lack health insurance. The uninsured rate for African Americans is more than one and a half times the rate for white Americans. Nearly 16 percent of Americans did not have health insurance in 2003, up from 14.2 percent in 2000.[99] The percentage of low-income Hispanics who lack insurance is exceptionally high, with three-quarters (76 percent) of Hispanic adults with incomes below 200 percent of the federal poverty level uninsured at some time during the year. The figure for low-income African Americans is 44 percent and that for low-income whites 46 percent. Disparities persist across income levels; 40 percent of Hispanic adults with incomes over 200 percent of poverty were uninsured during the year, compared to about one-quarter (23 percent) of African American adults and 12 percent of white adults in that income group.[100]

A 2001 Commonwealth Fund survey discovered that Hispanics and African Americans were the most likely ethnic groups in the United States to be uninsured, with 46 percent and 33 percent of working-age Hispanics and African Americans, respectively, lacking insurance for all or part of the twelve months prior to the survey.[101] In comparison, the same study found that one-fifth of both whites and Asian Americans ages eighteen through sixty-four lacked health coverage for all or part of the previous 12 months.[102] In 2009, sixty-three percent of African American adults with incomes under 200 percent above the poverty line reported having one of four chronic diseases (hypertension, heart disease, diabetes, or asthma) or a disability, whereas half of low-income whites and 39 percent of low-income Hispanic adults did so. Forty-five percent of African American adults but only 32 percent of whites and 23 percent of Hispanics in the higher income group with incomes over 200 percent of poverty report health problems.[103]

African American households are also less likely to have homeowners and rental insurance to cover storm losses and temporary living expenses.[104] They are also less likely than whites to have insurance with major companies as a result of decades of insurance redlining.[105] African Americans are more likely than whites to receive insufficient insurance settlement amounts. How insurance claims are settled can impact black households' and black neighborhoods' ability to recover from disaster. Ultimately, this form of discrimination harms the wealth creation of individual households and siphons off investments needed to rebuild black communities.

Many white insurance companies routinely redline black neighborhoods. Although insurance redlining is illegal, it is still practiced. It is not uncommon to find African Americans who live in majority-black zip codes paying twice the insurance premium that whites pay for comparable housing in mostly white suburban zip codes.[106] Race also matters in urban credit and insurance markets.[107] The insurance industry, like its housing industry counterpart, "has long used race as a factor in appraising and underwriting property."[108] In general, black neighborhoods are left with check-cashing stations, pawnshops, storefront grocery stores, liquor stores, and fast-food operations, all well buttoned up with wire mesh and bulletproof glass.[109]

A 1997 Urban Institute insurance study found that people of color face widespread racial barriers. The study used black, Latino, and white testers who presented themselves as homeowners seeking insurance. The black and Latino testers were discriminated against 53 percent of the time in such areas as coverage and premium rates.[110] Four major insurance companies (American Family, Allstate, State Farm, and Nationwide) launched initiatives to end the long-standing tradition of redlining. However, many other companies only change their practices if they are caught.

A 1996 *Atlanta Journal-Constitution* survey discovered stark disparities in property insurance rates between black and white Atlanta neighborhoods.[111] Insurance redlining and subprime abusive lending practices known as "predatory lending" go hand in hand and hit minority homeowners with excessive mortgage fees, interest rates, penalties, and insurance charges that raise the cost of refinancing by thousands of dollars for individual families.[112] The redlining issue prompted newspaper reporter Shelly Emling to title her story "Insurance: Is It Still a White Man's Game?"[113] Emling answered her own question: "Insurance companies create pricing zones that are mostly white or mostly black, and homeowners in the black zones are paying top dollar."[114]

Insurance redlining is not isolated to individual insurance agents. The practice is widespread among both big and small companies. The largest insurance companies in Georgia (i.e., State Farm, Allstate, Cotton States, Cincinnati Insurance, and USAA) routinely charged consumers 40 to 90 percent more to insure homes in Atlanta's predominately black neighborhoods than they charged for similar or identical houses in mostly white suburbs.[115] The premium disparity holds true whether blacks live in the low-income Vine City neighborhood or in the wealthy Cascade neighborhood that houses Atlanta's black elite. As the racial composition of a neighborhood becomes mostly black, the price of homeowner insurance rises dramatically.[116]

Using the state rates for a hypothetical $125,000 brick house (with $250 deductible), the 1996 *Atlanta Journal-Constitution* study concluded, "State Farm and Allstate, Georgia's largest insurers, tend to charge their highest rates in zip codes that also contain the highest proportion of black residents."[117] The premium differentials become apparent when one compares the hypothetical $125,000 brick house in different locations in metropolitan Atlanta. To insure that house in black sections of Atlanta cost about $612 a year; in Buckhead, the rate falls to $459. In Cobb, Gwinnett, and north Fulton, all more than 80 percent white, the price falls to $363 a year.

The premium differentials between black and white neighborhoods cannot be explained solely by loss data related to theft, vandalism, fire, and larceny crimes. In reality, the *Atlanta Journal-Constitution* study found that the highest loss ratios were not in black areas. (A loss ratio is the sum an insurance company pays in claims measured against the amount it collects in premiums. For example, a ratio of 68 percent means that a company paid out sixty-eight cents for each dollar it collected. In general, a company that has a loss ratio of 65 percent or lower turns a healthy profit.)

The loss ratio in mostly black Allstate Zone 2 (Central Atlanta) was 79 percent, yet homeowners there pay a whopping average $705 in annual premiums. On the other hand, the loss ratio in mostly white Atlanta Zone 18 (North Fulton, Northwest DeKalb) was 92 percent, and the homeowners there paid an average of $349—less than half what was paid by residents in Zone 2. There is little doubt that the mostly white suburban communities with the highest loss ratios are not paying their fair share. These premium disparities illustrate the benefits suburban whites derive from discrimination.

After the four hurricanes hit Florida in 2004, insurers began increasing the price for home insurance there by as much as 30 percent, with some homeowners hit with increases more than 50 percent. Five years after Katrina, home insurance in some storm-ravaged Gulf Coast area of Louisiana, Mississippi, and Alabama shot up more than 30 percent, while rates in the rest of the country increased by 7.6 percent for the same period.[118] The problem for disaster victims is compounded by homeowners who are still dealing with the limitations of their pre-Katrina coverage.

Disasters often set the stage for a tug of war between insurers and disaster victims. The total economic losses from Katrina were expected to exceed $125 billion, with insured losses totaling more than $71 billion. How much financial responsibility the insurance companies end up bearing depends on how insurers handled the claims—whether damage was blamed on the wind or on the floods.

FEMA estimated that the majority of households and businesses in the twelve Hurricane Katrina-affected counties in Alabama, Mississippi, and Louisiana did not have flood coverage. FEMA also estimated that 12.7 percent of the households in Alabama, 15 percent of those in Mississippi, and 46 percent of those in Louisiana had flood insurance. Similarly, only eight percent of the businesses in hurricane-affected counties in Alabama, 15 percent in Mississippi, and 30 percent in Louisiana had flood coverage.

Disasters expose the unequal treatment of African Americans and intensify long-running disputes between insurance companies and consumers who live in redlined neighborhoods. Disputes revolve around where standard homeowner's insurance coverage ends and flood insurance begins. For decades, consumers, black and white, have complained that insurance companies have denied their claims on the basis that damage was not wind-related but was caused by flooding. Damage from rising water is covered only by government-backed flood insurance.

Because of the enormity of the damage in the wake of Katrina, insurance companies tried to categorize a lot of legitimate wind claims as flood-related. This problem of white-collar insurance "looting" hit low-income, elderly, and disabled people and people of color hardest, because these groups were likely to have their insurance through small companies. The disaster researchers Walter G. Peacock and Chris Girard made this point in their study of Hurricane Andrew in South Florida:

> Traveling through the neighborhoods in South Dade after Hurricane Andrew was a graphic lesson in racial differences in insurance coverage. Due to the absence of street signs and even house numbers it was very difficult to find specific addresses. To aid insurance adjusters many homeowners spray painted the name of their insurance companies, along with their addresses, on the outside walls of their homes. Driving through predominately White neighborhoods, such as the famous Country Walk development, revealed a virtual *Who's Who* of insurance companies: State Farm, Allstate, and Prudential. In contrast, a drive through predominately Black areas showed names that were far from familiar, such as Utah, Delta, Ocean Casualty, and Florida Fire and Casualty. At minimum, this anecdotal evidence suggests some degree of the market segmentation reflected in the dual economy literature.[119]

Because of Jim Crow segregation, many African American consumers in the Louisiana, Mississippi, and Alabama Gulf Coast region may be concentrated in the secondary insurance market, getting coverage from smaller and less well-known insurance companies. This proved problematic for Katrina victims. Nearly a dozen small insurance companies collapsed after Hurricane Andrew, cost the industry about $23 billion in 2011 dollars. Andrew was the most expensive single hurricane until Katrina.

Many, if not most, Katrina victims lacked the resources to hire lawyers to fight the insurance companies. In an attempt to head off a floodgate of insurance disputes, Mississippi Attorney General Jim Hood filed suit to block insurance companies from denying flood claims when those floods are caused by wind. He claimed that the insurance exclusion of water damage violated Mississippi's Consumer Protection Act and "deprives consumers of any real coverage choices."[120] The lawsuit also accused some insurance companies of forcing storm victims into signing documents that stipulated that their losses are flood-related, not wind-related, before they could receive payment or emergency expenses; the lawsuit would ban such practices.[121] Such a practice is tantamount to economic blackmail.

By September 7, 2005, State Farm, the largest home and automobile insurer in the Gulf Coast region, had begun processing 223,000 Katrina-related claims.[122] (State Farm was eventually dropped from Hood's lawsuit.) The insurance industry had to grapple with the largest-ever loss and with a record number of individual claims—1.6 million from Katrina, another million from hurricanes Rita and Wilma.[123] Companies are not required to disclose their claims practices, including how quickly claims are processed or how many are denied and for what reason. This places consumers at a sizable disadvantage when disputing settlements they perceive to be unfair and inadequate.

## Protecting Public Health

African Americans are more likely than whites to live in neighborhoods where industrial pollution is suspected of posing a significant health danger.[124] Historically, African Americans and communities of other people of color have borne a disproportionate burden of pollution from incinerators, smelters, sewage treatment plants, chemical industries, and a host of other polluting facilities. Clear differences exist between racial groups in terms of disease and death rates. African Americans and low-income populations experience higher-than-average exposures to hazardous-waste facilities.

The federal Superfund program designates hazardous-waste sites for cleanup on the basis of their level of contamination and the threat they pose to human health. The program has failed to provide equal protection to African American communities. Despite the type of contamination discovered at various sites and in residents' wells and the resulting illnesses in communities near the sites, various levels of government have knowingly allowed black families near Superfund sites, abandoned toxic-waste dumps, injection wells, and municipal landfills to be poisoned with lead, arsenic, dioxin, TCE, DDT, PCBs, and a host of other deadly chemicals.

Race maps closely with pollution, vulnerability, and unequal protection. Numerous studies show that African Americans and other people of color are concentrated in or near communities with abandoned hazardous-waste sites. Polluting industries have followed the path of least resistance, as a result of which many black communities have become environmental "sacrifice zones." Not only are people of color differentially impacted by toxic contamination, but also they can expect differential treatment from the government. It takes longer for sites in black communities to get listed and cleaned up than sites in white communities. Polluters also receive stiffer penalties for polluting white communities than for contaminating black communities. Unequal environmental protection places African Americans at special risk and contributes to environmental health disparities.

Historically, emergency response to industrial accidents has been skewed by race. Black workers and black residents are often left behind or are the last to be evacuated or relocated during natural and human-induced disasters, placing their health at elevated risks. Generally, industrial spills, leaks, and explosions that routinely occur in black communities are not reported as "accidents" but are viewed by the industry and the government alike as the price of doing business. This underreporting of industrial accidents disproportionately affects the health, safety, and well-being of African Americans whose homes are concentrated in industrial corridors.

Living on the fenceline with dangerous industries or near the tracks where railway lines haul their deadly cargo can be stressful. A disproportionately large number of black communities are located next to industrial corridors and along transportation routes that expose their residents to potential ticking time bombs—leaks and explosions, accidental or deliberate. Improving the safety and security of communities located on the fenceline with our nation's railways and industrial plants has taken a back seat to funding and actions directed toward securing these facilities against a potential terrorist attack.

When accidents and health emergencies occur, compensation is often biased in favor of whites. Black lives are valued less than white lives. Generally, black victims receive less compensation than white victims for comparable losses. Racial disparities in victim compensation are reinforced and buttressed by industry, insurance companies, banks, public health systems, the courts, and the government. African American disaster victims often must wait longer than whites for relief, recovery, and reconstruction assistance.

Trust in all levels of government differs widely across racial and ethnic groups—and for good reasons. African Americans and whites view the world through very different lenses. Whites are less likely than blacks to see race and racism as influential in the way the government responds to environmental hazards, industrial accidents, natural and human disasters, and bioterrorism threats. The legacy of being left behind and of receiving differential treatment have left many African Americans suspicious and mistrustful of government and the medical establishment, including biomedical research, environmental cleanup, industrial facility permitting, and the "war on terrorism."

After centuries of government deception and medical abuse, millions of African Americans still have unanswered questions. Can we trust the government to protect us? Will the government response be fair? These becomes more than rhetorical questions given the fact that in many instances it was government actions that perpetrated the injustice. Too often, government-sponsored human experimentation—white doctors with black subjects—is "abuse disguised as research."[125] The journalist and ethics scholar Harriett A. Washington aptly tagged the practice "medical apartheid."[126]

Hurricane Katrina exposed the systematic weakness in the nation's emergency preparedness and emergency response systems. The response undermined homeland security. It also reinforced what many African Americans already felt deep down and what Kanye West proclaimed on national television in September 2005 after Hurricane Katrina: "George Bush does not care about black people." A similar charge could easily be leveled at government actions during the Mississippi flood of 1927, the Okeechobee hurricane of 1928, the Tuskegee syphilis experiment of 1932–1972, the U.S. Army and CIA biological warfare experiments at Carver Village in Florida, the TCE well contamination in Dickson in 1988, or the 2001 anthrax attack at the Washington, D.C., Brentwood post office.

Finally, the response to Hurricane Katrina was no fluke. Unfortunately, eight decades of "Katrina responses" to public health emergencies, environmental hazards, industrial accidents, and natural and human-induced disasters have left blacks less safe and less secure than whites in their homes, schools, neighborhoods, and workplaces. There can be no homeland security if people do not have homes to go to and if they lose trust in the government's willingness to respond to an emergency in an effective, fair, and just way.

# Notes

INTRODUCTION

1. Daniels, Kettl, and Kunreuther 2006, 4.
2. Bullard and Wright 2008, 2009.
3. Ramirez, Baker, and Metzler 2008.
4. LaViest 2002.
5. Frazier, Margai, and Tettey-Fio 2003.
6. Dreier, Mollenkopf, and Swanstrom 2001.
7. California Newsreel 2008.
8. Bullard 2005b.
9. Bullard 2007a.
10. Bullard 2000a.
11. Frey 2001.
12. Bullard 1991, 161.
13. Stack 1997; Bullard 2007b.
14. Frey 2001.
15. Bullard 1991, 45–74.
16. Frey 2001, 5.
17. Burch 2002.
18. Frey 2001.
19. Bullard 2007a; Cashin 2004.
20. Bositis, 2007.
21. Bullard 2000a.
22. Lerner 2010.
23. Bullard and Wright 2009.
24. Schueler, 1992, 46–47.
25. Kromm and Ernst 2000.
26. Bullard 2005c; Pastor, Bullard, Boyce, Fothergill, Morella-Frosch, and Wright 2006; Bullard and Wright 2009.
27. Cole and Foster 2000; Bullard 2000b.
28. Greenpeace 1993, 1–2.

CHAPTER 1

1. Bullard 2007a.
2. Dicum 2006.
3. Honey 2007.
4. Bullard 1983.
5. Bullard 1987.
6. Bullard 2005c.
7. Snyder 2002.
8. Schwartz 2002.
9. Mack 2002.
10. Bullard and Wright 1986; 1996.
11. Commission for Racial Justice 1987.
12. Bullard 2005b.

CHAPTER 2

1. Williams 2003.
2. U.S. General Accountability Office 2007.
3. U.S. General Accountability Office 2007.
4. Fields, Huang, Solomon, Rotkin-Ellman, and Simms 2007.
5. Ibid., 838.
6. Banerjee 2011.

CHAPTER 3

1. Gunn 2003, 1.
2. Oxfam International 2008.
3. Smith 2005, Hartman and Squires 2006.
4. Steinberg 2003.
5. Abramovitz 2001.
6. Knowlton, Rotkin-Ellman, Geballe, Max, and Solomon 2011.
7. Simms 2005.
8. Smith 2005.
9. Comerio 1998.
10. Jackson 2005.
11. Wisner, Blaikie, Cannon, and David 1994, 11.
12. Wisner, Blaikie, Cannon, and David 1994, 12.

13. Guinier and Torres 2002.

14. Guinier and Torres 2002, 11.

15. Boyce 2000.

16. Boyce 2000, 254.

17. Cannon, Davis, Blaikie, and Wisner 2004.

18. Cutter, Boruff, and Shirley 2003.

19. Cutter 2002.

20. Cutter 2005.

21. Bullard and Wright 2009.

22. Roberts and Parks 2006; Adger, Paavola, Huq, and Mace 2006.

23. Frumkin, Hess, Luber, Mallay, and McGeehin 2008; Jackson and Shields, 2008.

24. Pastor, Bullard, Boyce, Fothergill, Morella-Frosch, and Wright 2006; Brunsma, Overfelt, and Picou 2007; Mann 2006; Cooper and Block, 2006; Horne 2006; van Heerden and Bryan 2006.

25. Adger, Paavola, Huq, and Mace 2006; Roberts and Parks 2006; Frumkin, Hess, Luber, Mallay, and McGeehin 2008; Jackson and Shields 2008.

26. Pace 2005.

27. Congressional Black Caucus Foundation, 2004, 2.

28. Patz, Kinney, Bell, Goldberg, Hogrefe, Khoury, Knowlton, Rosenthal, Rosenzweig, and Ziska 2004.

29. Bell, Goldberg, Hogrefe, Kinney, Knowlton, Lynn, Rosenthal, Rosenzweig, and Patz 2007.

30. Bullard and Wright 2009; Brinkley 2006; Dyson 2006; Horne 2006; Pastor, Bullard, Boyce, Fothergill, Morella-Frosch, and Wright 2006.

31. Rivkin 2007.

32. Gerberding 2007.

33. Union of Concerned Scientists 2011.

34. Emrich and Cutter 2011.

35. Centers for Disease Control 2000, 2004.

36. *USA Today* 2005.

37. Tanneeru 2005.

38. Ho 2005, A1.

39. Beady and Bolin 1986.

40. Bolin and Bolton 1986.

41. Barry 1998.

42. Howard 1984.

43. Barry 1998.

44. Daniel 1977, Daniel 1972, 153.

45. *Chicago Defender* 1927.

46. Brochu 2003.

47. Kleinberg 2003.

48. Klinkenberg 1992.

49. Barnes 1998.

50. Kleinberg 2004.

51. Kleinberg 2004.

52. Barnes 1998.

53. Klinkenberg 1992.

54. Brochu 2003.

55. Hurston 1998.

56. Klinkenberg 1992.

57. Williams 2003.

58. Colten and Welch 2003.

59. Fletcher 2011.

60. Remnick 2005.

61. Bullard 2005b.

62. Dahl 1983.

63. Bullard 1987.

64. Bullard 1987; Bullard 2000a.

65. Hester 1980, 20.

66. Bullard 1987.

67. National Advisory Commission on Civil Disorders 1968.

68. Bullard 2000b.

69. Bullard 1983.

70. Rosen 1994; Bullard 1996b.

71. McDonald 1979.

72. Bullard 2006b.

73. Baker 1994.

74. Kaniasty and Norris 1995.

75. Cannon, Davis, Blaikie, and Wisner 2004.

76. Pittman 2002.

77. Peacock, Morrow, and Gladwin 1992.

78. Peacock, Morrow, and Gladwin 1992.

79. Peacock, Morrow, and Gladwin 1992.

80. Harrison 1994, 3.

81. Georgia Emergency Management Agency 2004.

82. Board of Regents of University System of Georgia 2004.
83. Harrison 1994.
84. Mittal and Powell 2000.
85. Estes 2001.
86. Associated Press 2008a.
87. Wing, Freedman, and Band 2002.
88. Segrest 2001.
89. Wing, Freedman, and Band 2002.
90. Wing, Freedman, and Band 2002.
91. Solow 2004.
92. Associated Press 1999.
93. Cain 2000
94. Waggoner 2000.
95. Brown 2001.
96. Brown 2001.
97. Tilove 2005.

CHAPTER 4

1. Regional Planning Commission of Orleans 1969; Braubbach and Borah 1981.
2. Pastor, Bullard, Boyce, Fothergill, Morello-Frosch, and Wright 2006.
3. Tibbetts 2006
4. Bullard 2005b.
5. Bullard and Wright 2009.
6. Gabe, Falk, McCarthy and Mason 2005.
7. Bullard 2006b.
8. Eaton and Nixon 2005.
9. Mildenberg 2011.
10. National Fair Housing Alliance 2005.
11. Bullard 2005c.
12. *Business Week* 2005.
13. Luther 2007.
14. Jordan 2006.
15. Shields 2006.
16. U.S. Army Corps of Engineers 2006.
17. U.S. Environmental Protection Agency 2006b.
18. Nossiter 2005.
19. Filosa 2006.
20. Varney and Moller 2005.
21. Dart 2006.
22. Burdeau 2005.

23. O'Driscoll 2005.
24. Martin 2006.
25. Russell 2005.
26. Luther 2007.
27. Luther 2007.
28. Pardo 2006.
29. Eaton 2006.
30. Eaton 2006.
31. Russell 2006.
32. Dunn 2006.
33. Jervis 2008a.
34. Dewan 2007.
35. Kromm and Sturgis 2008.
36. Walsh 2007.
37. Babington 2005, A04.
38. Apartment Rating 2011.
39. National Fair Housing Alliance 2005.
40. Berry 2007.
41. Alfred 2008, 12.
42. Jervis 2008b, 4A.
43. Alfred 2008.
44. Liu and Plyer 2008.
45. Alfred 2008, 16.
46. Kromm and Sturgis 2007.
47. Martell 2006.
48. Deep South Center for Environmental Justice 2006.
49. Simmons 2006.
50. Williams 2006.
51. Solomon and Rotkin-Ellman 2006.
52. U.S. Environmental Protection Agency 2006b.
53. Varney 2006.
54. Brown 2006.
55. U.S. General Accountability Office 2007.
56. U.S. General Accountability Office 2007.
57. Fields, Huang, Solomon, Rotkin-Ellman, and Simms 2007.
58. Spake 2007.
59. Hampton 2006.
60. Schwartz 2007; Spake 2007; Hampton 2006; Johnson 2007.
61. Hampton 2006; Damon 2007; Brunker 2006.

62. Schwartz 2007; Brunker 2006.

63. Committee on Oversight and Government Reform 2007.

64. Committee on Oversight and Government Reform 2007.

65. Damon 2007; Babington 2007.

66. Alberts 2007; Damon 2007; Babington 2007.

67. Johnson 2007.

68. Cruz 2007.

69. Burdeau 2007.

70. Treadway 2007.

71. Maugh and Jervis 2008.

72. Alberts 2007.

73. New Orleans Food Policy Advisory Committee 2008.

74. New Orleans Food Policy Advisory Committee 2007.

75. Burdeau 2008.

76. U.S. Army Corps of Engineers Interagency Performance Evaluations Task Force 2007.

77. Schwartz 2007.

CHAPTER 5

1. Lavelle and Coyle 1992, 2.

2. Bullard 1996a.

3. Bullard 2009b.

4. U.S. Environmental Protection Agency 2010b.

5. Bullard 2000a.

6. Russell 2009.

7. Koons 2009.

8. Hiar 2011.

9. Reynolds 1980.

10. Haggerty 1980.

11. Haggerty 1980.

12. Bullard 2000a.

13. Brown, Mullins, Richitt, Flatman, and Black 1985; Dallas Alliance Environmental Task Force 1983.

14. Dallas Alliance Environmental Task Force 1983, 3.

15. U.S. Environmental Protection Agency 1983.

16. U.S. Environmental Protection Agency 2005.

17. Rawlins 2003.

18. Bullard 2005c.

19. Lyttle 2000.

20. U.S. Department of Justice 2008, 4.

21. Associated Press 2008.

22. Hammer 2008b.

23. Associated Press 2008c.

24. Hammer 2008b.

25. Hammer 2008c.

26. Agency for Toxic Substances and Disease Registry 1989; U.S. Environmental Protection Agency 1992.

27. Agency for Toxic Substances and Disease Registry 1989, 2.

28. Satchel 1997.

29. Hauserman and Olinger 1996.

30. *Pensacola News Journal* 2003.

31. Blumenthal 2006.

32. Welborn 2005a.

33. Welborn 2005b, 2006.

34. Sorg 2006.

35. Sorg 2006.

36. U.S. Environmental Protection Agency 2006a.

37. Welborn 2008.

38. McElheney 2006.

39. Gallentine 2001.

40. Aued 2007.

41. Owens 2008.

42. *Athens Banner-Herald* 2007.

43. Aued 2008.

CHAPTER 6

1. Bullard, Mohai, Saha, and Wright 2007.

2. U.S. Bureau of the Census 2000b.

3. Property Deed 1956.

4. Tetra Tech EM Inc. 2004.

5. Tetra Tech EM Inc. 2004, 15.

6. Haliburton NUS Environmental Corporation 1991, ES-1.

7. Haliburton NUS Environmental Corporation 1991, 9.

8. Haliburton NUS Environmental Corporation 1991, 17.

9. Haliburton NUS Environmental Corporation 1991, 31.

10. Haliburton NUS Environmental Corporation 1991, 17.

11. Tetra Tech EM Inc. 2004, 19.

12. Tetra Tech EM Inc. 2004, 51.

13. U.S. Bureau of Census the 2000.

14. Herbert 2006.

15. Shapiro, Meschede, and Sullivan 2010.

16. Shapiro, Meschede, and Sullivan 2010, 2.

17. Edwards 2003.

18. McWhorter 1988.

19. Agency for Toxic Substances and Disease Registry 2003.

20. U.S. Environmental Protection Agency 2011.

21. Tetra Tech EM Inc. 2004, Appendix B 3-4.

22. Letter from Wayne Aronson, Acting Chief Drinking Water Section, Municipal Facilities Branch, U.S. Environmental Protection Agency, to Mr. Harry Holt, December 3, 1991.

23. Aronson 1991.

24. Moss 1991.

25. Moss 1992a.

26. Sanders 1992.

27. Sanders 1992.

28. Tetra Tech EM Inc. 2004, 28.

29. Appendix B, "Chronology of Event, Dickson County Landfill," 14–15.

30. Gresham Smith and Partners 2000.

31. Tetra Tech EM Inc. 2004, 28.

32. Tennessee Department of Environment and Conservation n.d.

33. Centers for Disease Control and Prevention 2001.

34. Shabecoff and Shabecoff 2008, 7.

35. Cornwell 2004.

36. Cornwell 2003.

37. Kimbro 2006.

38. Bullard 2006b; Duke 2007; Gordy, 2007; Rysavy 2007b.

39. Tetra Tech EM Inc. 2004, 28.

40. Repsher 1994.

41. Bullard et al 2007.

42. Tetra Tech EM Inc. 2004, 27.

43. Letter from Patricia Thompson 1993.

44. Environmental News Service 2008.

45. Gadd 2011.

CHAPTER 7

1. Purvis and Claflin 2003.

2. Kocieniewski 2006.

3. Jordan 1998.

4. Skidmore 1941.

5. Musick 1999.

6. Lucas and Paxton 1999.

7. Cherniack 1986.

8. Lowney 2008; Spangler 2008.

9. Rampton and Stauber 2001, 75.

10. Flournoy 1994, J8.

11. Rampton and Staubner 2001, 78.

12. Cherniack 1986.

13. Gunn 2003, 49.

14. Cherniack 1986.

15. Lucas and Paxton 1999.

16. Tyler 1982, Skidmore 1941, Cherniack 1986.

17. Rosner and Markowitz 1991, 98.

18. Rosner and Markowitz 1991, 98.

19. Lucas and Paxton 1999.

20. Gauley Bridge, West Virginia Forum 2008.

21. National Transportation Safety Board 1998.

22. National Transportation Safety Board 1998, 3–4.

23. Fthenakis 2001.

24. Fthenakis 2001, 246.

25. Justice 1996, A1.

26. CNN News Briefs 1995.

27. Justice 1995.

28. Justice 1995.

29. Shipley 1995.

30. Amar and Cochran 1996.

31. Chappie 2005.

32. Hanemann 2003.

33. Hanemann2008.
34. "Railroad Sued for Water Pollution in South Carolina Wreck" 2008; DeMayo 2008.
35. Daily 2005, Reed 2005, Ethridge 2005, Brundrett 2005.
36. Reed 2005.
37. Noland 2005.
38. Bogdanich and Drew 2005.
39. Brundrett 2005.
40. Brundrett 2005.
41. Brundrett 2005.
42. Hall 2005.
43. Jordan 2005.
44. Richards 2008.
45. U.S. Department of Justice, 2010.
46. Wikipedia 2008.
47. Fountain 2005, Planet Ark World Environmental News 2006.
48. Cappiello 2006b.
49. Fountain 2006, Daily News 2006.
50. Cappiello 2006c.
51. Cappiello 2006b, 2006c.
52. Cappiello 2006c, Daily News 2006.
53. Fountain 2006.
54. Fountain 2006.
55. Fountain 2006.
56. Daily News 2006.
57. Daily News 2006.
58. Dewan 2009.
59. U.S. Environmental Protection Agency 2009b.
60. Morton 2009.
61. Sturgis 2009.
62. Reeves 2009.
63. Bullard 2000a.
64. Tennessee Valley Authority 2009, 14.
65. Donn and Weiss 2010.
66. Associated Press 2010b.
67. Lombard 2010.
68. Bullard 2010.
69. Mock 2010.
70. Schleifstein 2010.
71. British Petroleum 2010.
72. Jackson 2010.
73. Farrell 2010.

74. Scallan 2010.
75. U.S. Environmental Protection Agency 2009b.
76. Gordon 2009.
77. Bullard 2005a.
78. Faulkner 2010.
79. U.S. Environmental Protection Agency 2007b.
80. Environmental Justice Integrity Project and Earthjustice 2009.
81. U.S. Environmental Protection Agency 2010.
82. Bullard 2000b.
83. Raines 2010b.
84. Bullard, Mohai, Saha, and Wright 2007.

CHAPTER 8

1. California Newsreel 2008.
2. Gornick 2000.
3. Steelfisher 2004,
4. Sullivan Commission 2004.
5. California Newsreel 2008.
6. Mays, Cochran, and Barnes 2006.
7. Smedley, Smith, and Nelson 2002.
8. Byrd and Clayton 2001; LaViest 2002.
9. Green, Linda, Gleser, Leonard, Korol, and Winget 2007.
10. Schneider, Zaslavsky, and Epstein 2001.
11. Blendon, Scheck, Donelan, Hill, Smith, Beatrice, and Altman 1995.
12. Petersen 2002.
13. Gamble 1997; Corbie-Smith, Thomas, Williams, and Moody-Ayers 1999; LaViest, Nickerson, and Bowie 2000; Corbie-Smith, Thomas, and St. George 2002; Freimuth, Quinn, Thomas, Cole, Zook, and Duncan 2001; Shavers, Lynch and Burmeister 2001; Washington, 2006.
14. McGary 1999.
15. Blendon, Cassidy, Perez, Hunt, Fleischfresser, Benson, and Herrmann 2007.
16. Hughes-Halbert, Armstrong, Gandy, and Shaker 2006.

17. Braunstein, Sherber, Schulman, Ding, and Powe 2008.

18. Braunstein , Sherber, Schulman, Ding, and Powe 2008, 1.

19. Gamble 1993; Dula 1994; Washington 2006.

20. Washington 2006, 7.

21. Kevles 1985.

22. Davis 1981.

23. Washington 2006, 204.

24. Roberts 1997.

25. Roberts 1997.

26. Washington 2006.

27. Trocheck 1980.

28. Smith 1999.

29. Micco, Gurmankin, and Armstrong 2004.

30. Centers for Disease Control and Prevention 2005.

31. Boulware, Cooper, Ratner, LaVeist, and Powe 2003.

32. Brandon, Isaac, and LaVeist 2005.

33. Neighbors, Musick, and Williams 1998; Taylor, Chatters, and Levin 2004.

34. Page and Puente 2005.

35. Pesca 2005.

36. Anderson, Boumbulian, and Pickens 2004.

37. Bovbjerg, Marsteller, and Ullman 2000.

38. Anderson, Boumbulian, and Pickens 2004.

39. Dewan and Sack 2007.

40. Corbie-Smith 1999.

41. Jones 1993.

42. Reverby 2000.

43. Sullivan 1991.

44. Mielke 1999.

45. Rabito, White, and Shorter 2004.

46. Lamphear 2001.

47. *Matthews and People United for a Better Oakland v. Coye* 1991.

48. Lee 1992.

49. Centers for Disease Control and Prevention 2003.

50. McDiarmid and Shine 2003.

51. Torry 1999.

52. Kaiser 2001.

53. Spriggs 2004, 176–181.

54. Bor 2001.

55. Court of Appeals of Maryland 2000.

56. Williams 2011.

57. Spriggs 2004, 177.

58. Court of Appeals of Maryland, 2000, 85; Glantz 2002, Paulson 2006.

59. Court of Appeals of Maryland 2000, 9–10.

60. Bor and Kohn 2008, Heilprin and Vineys 2008.

61. Heilprin and Vineys 2008.

62. Ritter 2008.

63. U.S. Environmental Protection Agency Research and Development 2004.

64. Eilperin 2004.

65. U.S. Environmental Protection Agency 2004.

66. Eilperin 2004; *Grist Online* 2004.

67. Eilperin 2004.

68. Heilprin 2005.

69. World Combined Sources 2004.

70. Heilprin 2005.

71. Washington 2006, 365.

72. Washington 2006.

73. Working Group on "Governance Dilemmas" in Bioterrorism Response 2004.

74. Goldman 2005.

75. Annas 2002.

76. Levy and Sibel 2003, 107.

77. U.S. General Accounting Office 2001.

78. Centers for Disease Conrol and Prevention 2003.

79. Blanchard, Haywood, Stein, Tanielian, Stoto, and Lurie 2005.

80. Leonnig 2004.

81. Blanchard, Haywood, Stein, Tanielian, Stoto, and Lurie 2005.

82. Hughes 2002.

83. Eisenman, Wold, Setodji, Hickey, Lee, Stein, and Long 2004.

84. Shane 2010.

85. Warrick 2010, A01.

86. Bullard 2005c.
87. Bullard 1996b.
88. Gremaldi and Gugliotta 2002.
89. Hinds 2001.
90. Kamalick 2010.
91. Gremaldi and Gugliotta 2002.
92. Agency for Toxic Substances and Disease Registry 1999a.
93. Agency for Toxic Substances and Disease Registry 1999b, 1.
94. Schierow 2006.
95. Prine 2002a.
96. Prine 2002b.
97. Hatcher 2010.
98. O'Hanlon, Orszag, Daalder, Destler, Gunter, Litan, and Steinberg 2002.
99. U.S. General Accounting Office 2004.
100. *New York Times* 2005.
101. U.S. General Accounting Office 2004.
102. Purvis and Claflin 2003, 8; Shea 2005.
103. Purvis and Claflin 2003, 13.
104. Children's Environment Health Network 2001, 1.
105. Hsu 2007, A10.
106. Ahlers 2008.
107. Kamalick 2009, 1.
108. Hinds, Kay, and Varela 2008.


CHAPTER 9

1. Blaikie, Cannon, and Wisner 1994.
2. Fothergill, Enrique, Maestas, and DeRouen-Darlington 1999.
3. Moore, Barker, and Legator 2004.
4. Bullard 2005b.
5. Institute of Medicine1999.
6. Institute of Medicine 1999.
7. Fothergill, Enrique, Maestas, and DeRouen-Darlington 1999.
8. Berger 2001.
9. James, Hawkins, and Rowel 2007.
10. Green, Linda, Gleser, Leonard, Korol, and Winget 1990.
11. Ong 2005; Emily 2005.
12. Wellner 2005.
13. Elliston 2004.
14. Lui, Dixon, and Leondar-Wright 2006.
15. Lui, Dixon, and Leondar-Wright 2006, 1.
16. Litman 2006.
17. U.S. Department of Homeland Security 2006.
18. Pucher and Renne 2003.
19. Sanchez , Stolz, and Ma 2003.
20 Transportation for America and Transportation Equity Network 2009
21. Kneebone 2009.
22. Bullard, Johnson, and Torres 2004.
23. Surface Transportation Policy Project 2000.
24. Sanchez, Stolz, and Ma 2003.
25. Puentes and Bailey 2003.
26. Ashe 2003.
27. Bullard 2005c.
28. Association of Black Psychologists 2005.
29. Association of Black Psychologists 2005.
30. Carter 2004.
31. Carter 2004.
32. Kaniasty and Norris 2000; Gourash 1978; Padgett, Patrick, Burns, and Schlesinger 1995.
33. Morin and Rein 2005.
34. Bolton and Stanford 1991.
35. El Nasser 1999.
36. Bullard, Grigsby, and Lee 1994; Diamond, Diamond, and Noonan 1996.
37. Oliver and Shapiro 1995.
38. Oliver and Shapiro 1995, 47.
39. Blake 2010.
40. Kochlar et al. 2011.
41. Oliver and Shapiro 1995, 3.
42. Oliver and Shapiro 1995, 10.
43. Planetizen 2007.
44. Oliver and Shapiro 1995, 107.
45.Weller and Logan 2008, 1–2.
46. Oliver and Shapiro 1995, 56.
47. Blake 2010, 1.
48. Yinger 1999; Bullard 2007a.
49. Bullard, Grigsby, and Lee 1994.

50. Bullard, Johnson, and Torres 2000; Feagin 2001.

51. *CNN Money* 2002.

52. Bradford 2002.

53. Bradford 2002.

54. ACORN 2004.

55. Canner 1999; U. S. Department of Housing and Urban Development and U. S. Department of Treasury Joint Task Force 2000; Bullard, Johnson, and Torres 1999.

56. ACORN 2003, 3.

57. ACORN 2003, 5.

58. Federal Financial Institutions Examination Council 2004.

59. Federal Financial Institutions Examination Council 2004, 1–3.

60. National Fair Housing Alliance 2005.

61. Randolph 2005.

62. Frank 2005.

63. Maggi 2005.

64. Maggi 2005.

65. Chang, Soundararajan, and Johnson 2005.

66. Becker 2005.

67. Naughton and Hosenball 2005.

68. Mulligan and Fausset 2005.

69. Gregory 2005.

70. Gregory 2005, 3.

71. Appelbaum and Mellnik 2005.

72. Feins and Bratt 1983; Bullard 2007b.

73. Yinger 1995.

74. Feldstein 1994.

75. Squires 1998.

76. Goddard 2005.

77. U.S. Bureau of the Census 2002b.

78. U.S. Bureau of the Census 2002b.

79. Hughes 2005, 149.

80. Liberto 2009, 1.

81. Hughes 2005, 150.

82. Hing 2010.

83. Associated Press 2005b.

84. Yen 2005.

85. Edsall 2005.

86. Pickel 2005.

87. Witte 2005.

88. Abrams 2005.

89. Sullivan 2005.

90. Rosenberg 2005.

91. Willis 2005.

92. Comerio 1998.

93. Eaton and Nixon 2005.

94. Hughes 2005.

95. U.S. Bureau of the Census 2002a.

96. Yago and Pankratz 2000.

97. National Black Business Council 1996; Sibley-Butler 1991.

98. Enchautegui, Fix, Loprest, von der Lippe, and Wissoker 1997.

99. Grohol 2009, 1.

100. DeNavas-Walt, Proctor, and Mills 2004.

101. Duchon, Schoen, Doty, Davis, Strumpf, and Bruegman 2000.

102. Duchon, Schoen, Doty, Davis, Strumpf, and Bruegman 2000.

103. Grohol 2009, 1.

104. Bolin and Bolton 1986.

105. Peackcock and Girard 1997.

106. Bullard, Johnson, and Torres 2000.

107. Dymski 1995; Squires 1996a.

108. Squires 1996b.

109. Bullard, Grigsby, and Lee 1994.

110. Smith and Clous 1997.

111. Emling 1996, A16.

112. U.S. Department of Housing and Urban Development 2009, 2.

113. Emling 1996, A17.

114. Emling 1996, A16.

115. Emling 1996, A16.

116. Emling 1996, A16.

117. Emling 1996, A16.

118. Treaster 2005.

119. Peackcock and Girard 1997.

120. Lee 2005.

121. Paul 2005.

122. State Farm Insurance 2005.

123. Starkman 2005.

124. Pace 2005; Bullard, Mohai, Saha, and Wright 2007.

125. Grady 2007.

126. Washington 2006.

# References

Abramovitz, J. N. 2001. *Worldwatch Paper #158: Unnatural Disasters*. Washington, DC: Worldwatch Institute. October.

Abrams, R. 2005. "Helping Small Businesses in the Wake of Katrina." *USA Today*. September 1.

ACORN. 2003. *The Great Divide: Home Purchase Mortgage Lending Nationally and in 115 Metropolitan Areas*. Washington, DC: ACORN. October.

ACORN. 2004. *Separate and Unequal: Predatory Lending in America*. Washington, DC: ACORN. February.

Adger, W. N., J. Paavola, S. Huq, and M. J. Mace. 2006. *Fairness in Adaptation to Climate Change*. Cambridge: MIT Press.

African American Registry, Albany State University. Available at http://www.aaregistry. org/historic_events/view/albany-state-university-founded (accessed December 18, 2011).

Agency for Toxic Substances and Disease Registry. 1989. *Health Assessment: Koppers Superfund Site*. Texarkana, TX: U.S. Environmental Protection Agency.

Agency for Toxic Substances and Disease Registry. 1999. *Industrial Chemicals and Terrorism: Human Health Threat Analysis Mitigation and Prevention*. Atlanta, GA: ATSDR. Available at http://www.environmentaldatapages.com/Terror/terror.htm (accessed June 30, 2008).

Agency for Toxic Substances and Disease Registry. 1999. *Public Health Assessment—Agriculture Street Landfill, New Orleans, Orleans Parish, Louisiana*. Atlanta, GA: ATSDR. June.

Agency for Toxic Substances and Disease Registry. 2003. *Managing Hazardous Materials Incidents*. Volume III: *Medical Management Guidelines for Acute Chemical Exposures: Trichloroethylene (TCE)*. Atlanta, GA: U.S. Department of Health and Human Services, Public Health Service.

Ahlers, M. 2008. "Agency Says 7,000 Sites at 'High Risk' of Terrorist Attack." CNN News. June 20. Available at http://www.cnn.com/2008/US/06/20/terror.risk/ (accessed July 1, 2008).

Alabama Department of Archives and History. N.D. "This Week in Alabama History, Compiled by Month." Available at http://www.archives.state.al.us/thisweek/month.html (accessed June 24, 2008).

Alberts, S. 2007. "Katrina Survivors Suffer in 'FEMA Dirty Little Secret' Trailers." August 28. Available at http://www.canada.com/nationalpost/news/story.html?id=d3cob8fa-31d3-4695-a806-5cfd2fef53e5&k=35727 (accessed July 17, 2008).

Alfred, D. 2008. *Progress for Some, Hope and Hardship for Many*. New Orleans: Louisiana Family Recovery Corps. May.

Alliance for Healthy Homes. N.D. "Government Lawsuits Against the Lead Industry." Available at http://www.afhh.org/aa/aa_legal_remedies_lawsuits.htm (accessed June 19, 2008).

Amar, A. R., and J. L. Cochran. 1996. "Do Criminal Defendants Have Too Many Rights?" *American Criminal Law Review* 33 (Summer): 1193.

Anderson, R. J., P. J. Boumbulian, and S. S. Pickens. 2004. "The Role of U.S. Public Hospitals." *Academic Medicine, Journal of the Association of American Medical Colleges* 72 (12): 1162–68.

Andrulis, D. P., and L. M. Duchon. 2005. "Hospital Care in the 100 Largest Cities and Their Suburbs, 1996–2002: Implications for the Future of the Hospital Safety Net in Metropolitan America." Brooklyn, NY: SUNY Downstate Medical Center. August.

Annas, G. J. 2002. "Bioterrorism, Public Health, and Human Rights." *Human Law Journal* 21 (6): 94–97.

Appelbaum, B., and T. Mellnik. 2005. "The Hard Truth in Lending: Blacks 4 Times More Likely Than Whites to Get High Rates." *Charlotte Observer.* August 28.

Ashe, V. H. 2003. Testimony before the U.S. House of Representatives Transportation and Infrastructure Committee. May 7.

Associated Press. 2001. "Maryland Court Scolds Researchers in Lead Paint Study." August 21. Available at http://www.usatoday.com/news/nation/2001/08/21/lead-paint.htm (accessed December 15, 2011).

Associated Press. 2005a. "Flood Insurance Funding to Resume." *Clarion Ledger* (Jackson). November 19. Available at http://www.clarionledger.com/apps/pbcs.dll/article?AID=/20051119/NEWS0110/511190344/0/FEAT07 (accessed June 30, 2008).

Associated Press. 2005b. "Rally: Give Locals Larger Slice of Katrina Reconstruction Work." October 29. Available at http://www.nola.com/newsflash/weather/index.ssf?/base/news-20/1130615644103460.xml&storylist=hurricane (accessed June 1, 2008).

Associated Press. 2007. "Texas Toxic Town Lures Industry While Residents Wheeze." *International Herald Tribune.* October 27.

Associated Press. 2008a. "Black Farmers File New Suit Against USDA." *USA Today.* June 4.

Associated Press. 2008b. "Feds Settle with City Over Agricultural Street Landfill Site." *Times-Picayune.* May 29.

Associated Press. 2008c. "Scientists Scrutinize Toxic FEMA Trailers." *USA Today.* February 16.

Associated Press. 2010a. "BP Puts Gulf Oil Spill Cost at Nearly $4 Billion." *Atlanta Journal-Constitution.* July 19.

Associated Press. 2010b. "Is Oil Spill Waste Being Mishandled? Mound of Oily Sand Sits Uncovered at Gulf State Park." June 23.

Association of Black Psychologists. 2005. "Guidelines for Providing Culturally Appropriate Services for People of African Ancestry Exposed to the Trauma of Hurricane Katrina." September 29. Available at http://www.abpsi.org/special/hurricane-info1.htm (accessed June 30, 2008).

*Athens Banner-Herald.* 2007. "Landfill Agreement Reveals a Dirty Little Secret." December 17.

Aued, B. 2007. "Deal Not to Dump Trash: Clarke, Oglethorpe Likely to Expand Landfill Despite '92 Pact with Residents." *Athens Banner-Herald.* December 15.

Aued, B. 2008. "Environmental Group Pressing for Landfill Talks: Expansion Concerns." *Athens Banner-Herald.* January 4.

Babcock, R. 1982. "Houston Unzoned, Unfettered, and Mostly Unrepentent." *Planning* 48: 21–23.

Babington, C. 2005. "Some GOP Legislators Hit Jarring Notes in Addressing Katrina." *Washington Post.* September 5.

Babington, C. 2007. "FEMA Slow to Test Toxicity of Trailers." *USA Today.* Available at http://www.usatoday.com/news/topstories/2007-07-19-2231201740_x.htm (accessed July 1, 2008).

Baker, E. J. 1994. *Hurricane Hugo, Puerto Rico, the Virgin Islands, and Charleston, South Carolina, September 17-22, 1989.* Available at http://www.nap.edu/books/0309044758/html/166.html (accessed June 22, 2008).

Banerjee, Neela. 2011. "Gulf Oil Spill: BP Gets Most Blame in Government Report." *Los Angeles Times.* September 14.

Barnes, J. 1998. *Florida's Hurricane History.* Chapel Hill: University of North Carolina Press.

Barry, J. M. 1998. *Rising Tide: The Great Mississippi Flood of 1927 and How It Changed America.* New York: Simon and Schuster.

Beady, Jr., C. H., and R. C. Bolin. 1986. "The Role of the Black Media in Disaster Reporting to the Black Community." Working Paper No. 56. Institute for Behavioral Science, University of Colorado.

*Bean v. Southwestern Waste Management Corp.* 1979. In *Great American Court Cases*, ed. Mark F. Mikula and L. Mpho Mabunda (Gale Cengage, 1999). Available athttp://www.enotes.com/american-court-cases/bean-v-southwestern-waste-management-corp (accessed June 30, 2008).

Becker, A. 2005. "Storm-Resistant Homes a Long Time Coming: Left Homeless Last Year Still Holed Up in Temporary Housing." *Dallas Morning News.* August 28, 6A.

Beegley, S., M. Hager, and S. Agrest. 1985. "Maybe It Could Happen Here." *Newsweek.* February 4.

Bell, M. L., R. Goldberg, C. Hogrefe, P. L. Kinney, K. Knowlton, B. Lynn, J. Rosenthal, C. Rosenzweig, and J. A. Patz. 2007. "Climate Change, Ambient Ozone, and Health in 50 U.S. Cities (2007). *Climate Change* 82: 61–76.

Berger, E. 2001. "Keeping Its Head Above Water." *Houston Chronicle.* December 1.

Berry, D. B. 2007. "Testers Play Crucial Role in Exposing Discrimination." *USA Today.* September 28.

Blaikie, P. T., T. Cannon, and B. Wisner. 1994.*At Risk: Natural Disasters, People's Vulnerability, and Disasters.* New York: Routledge.

Blake, R. 2010. "Skin Color Wealth Gap: White Average $95K Richer Than Blacks." *ABC News.* May 18. Available at http://abcnews.go.com/Business/study-finds-wealth-gap-blacks-whites-quadrupled/story?id=10670261 (accessed December 17, 2011).

Blanchard, J. C., Y. Haywood, B. D. Stein, T. L. Tanielian, M. Stoto, and N. Lurie. 2005. "In Their Own Words: Lessons Learned from Those Exposed to Anthrax." *American Journal of Public Health* 95, no. 3 (March): 489–95.

Blendon, R. J., A. C. Scheck, K. Donelan, C. A. Hill, M. Smith, D. Beatrice, and D. Altman. 1995. "How White and African Americans View Their Health and Social Problems. Different Experiences, Different Expectations," *Journal of the American Medical Association* 273 (4): 341–46.

Blendon, R. J., T. Buhr, E. F. Cassidy, D. J. Perez, K. A. Hunt, C. Fleischfresser, J. M. Benson, and M. J. Herrmann. 2007. "Disparities in Health: Perspectives of a Multi-Ethnic, Multi-Racial America." *Health Affairs* 26, no. 5 (2007): 1437–47.

Blumenthal, R. 2006. "Texas Lawsuit Includes a Mix of Race and Water." *New York Times.* July 9.

Board of Regents of University System of Georgia. 2004. "Albany State President Portia Shields to Step Down at Year's End." December 11. Available at http://www.usg.edu/news/2004/121104.phtml (accessed June 22, 2008).

Bogdanich, W., and C. Drew. 2005. "Deadly Leak Underscores Concerns About Rail Safety." *New York Times.* January 9.

Bolin, R., and P. A. Bolton. 1986. *Race, Religion, and Ethnicity in Disaster Recovery.* Boulder: Institute of Behavioral Science, University of Colorado.

Bolton, R., and L. Stanford. 1991. "Shelter, Housing and Recovery: A Comparison of U.S. Disasters." *Disaster* 12 (1): 24–34.

Bor, J. 2001. "Kennedy Krieger Doctor Defends Lead Paint Study: Researcher Disputes High Court's Findings." *Baltimore Sun.* August 18.

Bor, J., and D. Kohn. 2008. "Researcher Faces Outcry." *Baltimore Sun.* May 1.

Borenstein, S., and T. Bren. 2010. "BP Oil Spill, Gushing More Than 2 Months, Hits Some Record as Gulf of Mexico's Biggest Ever." *Chicago Tribune.* July 1.

Bositis, D. "Black Political Power in the New Century." In *The Black Metropolis in the Twenty-First Century: Race, Power, and the Politics of Place*, ed. R. D. Bullard. New York: Rowman and Littlefield.

Boulard, G. 2009. "Rebuilding the Gulf Coast: The High Rates of Property Insurance in the Post-Katrina Era has made Rebuilding Difficulty." *State Legislatures.* May 1. Available at http://www.thefreelibrary.com/Rebuilding+the+Gulf+Coast%3a+the+high+rates+of+property+insurance+in...-a0163198706.

Boulware, L. E., L. A. Cooper, L. E. Ratner, T. A. LaVeist, and N. R. Powe. 2003. "Race and Trust in the Health Care System." *Public Health Reports* 118 (4): 358–65.

Bourne, J. K. 2004. "Gone with the Water." *National Geographic.* October. Available at http://altreligion.about.com/gi/dynamic/offsite.htm?site=http://www3.nationalgeographic.com/ngm/0410/feature5/ (accessed June 30, 2008).

Bovbjerg, R. R., J. A. Marsteller, and F. C. Ullman. 2000. *Health Care for the Poor and Uninsured After Public Hospital's Closure or Conversion.* Washington, DC: Urban Institute.

Boyce, J. J. 2000. "Let Them Eat Risk? Wealth, Rights, and Disaster Vulnerability." *Disasters* 24 (3): 254–61.

Bradford, C. 2002. *Risk or Race? Racial Disparities and the Subprime Refinance Market.* Washington, DC: Neighborhood Revitalization Project. May.

Brandon, D. T., L. A. Isaac, and T. LaVeist. 2005. "The Legacy of Tuskegee and Trust in Medical Care: Is Tuskegee Responsible for Race Differences in Mistrust of Medical Care?" *Journal of the National Medical Association* 97 (7): 951–56.

Broadwater, L. 2011. "Kennedy Krieger Sued Over Lead Paint." *Baltimore Sun.* September 15. Available at http://articles.baltimoresun.com/2011-09-15/news/bs-md-murphy-suit-20110915_1_mark-farfel-blood-lead-levels-paint-study (accessed December 15, 2011).

Braubbach, R., and E. Borah. 1981. *The Second Battle of New Orleans: A History of the Vieux Carré Riverfront-Expressway Controversy.* Tuscaloosa: University of Alabama Press.

Braunstein, J. B., N. S. Sherber, S. P. Schulman, E. L. Ding, N. R. Powe. 2008. "Race, Medical Researcher Distrust, Perceived Harm, and Willingness to Participate in Cardiovascular Prevention Trials." *Medicine* 87 (1): 1–9.

Brinkley, D. 2006. *The Great Deluge: Hurricane Katrina, New Orleans, and the Mississippi Gulf Coast.* New York: William Morrow.

British Petroleum (BP). 2010. "Recovered Oil/Waste Management Plan Houma Incident Command." Deepwater Horizon Incident, April 22.

Brochu, N. S. 2003. "Florida's Forgotten Storm: The Hurricane of 1928." *Sun-Sentinel.* September 14.

Brooks, J. 2008. "Hearing Marks Milestone in Spill Case: Union Tank Car's $3 millon Deemed Fair for Members." *Daily News.* April 30. Available at http://www.gobogalusa.com/articles/2008/04/30/news/news02.txt (accessed December 15, 2011).

Brown, F. D. 2001. "The Destruction of Princeville, the Nation's Oldest Black-Governed Community." EarthAfrica News Service. April 9.

Brown, K. W., J. W. Mullins, E. P. Richitt, G. T. Flatman, and S. C. Black. 1985. "Assessing Soil Lead Contamination in Dallas, Texas." *Environmental Monitoring and Assessment* 5: 137–54.

Brown, M. 1987. The Toxic Cloud: The Poisoning of America's Air. New York: Harper and Row.

Brown, M. 2006. "Final EPA Report Deems N.O. Safe." *Times-Picayune.* August 19.

Brundrett, R. 2005. "Blacks Say They Were Left Until Last: Sheriff Denies That White Graniteville Neighborhoods Were Evacuated First." *TheState.com.* January 18. Available at http://www.thestate.com/mld/thestate/news/special_packages/10669304.htm (accessed June 27).

Brunker, M. 2006. "FEMA Trailers 'Toxic Tin Cans?'" July 23. Available at http://risingfromruin.msnbc.com/2006/07/are_fema_traile.html (accessed August 1, 2006).

Brunsma, D., L. D. Overfelt, and J. S. Picou. 2007. *The Sociology of Katrina: Perspectives in a Modern Catastrophe.* New York: Rowman and Littlefield.

Bullard, R. D. 1983. "Solid Waste Sites and the Black Houston Community." *Sociological Inquiry* 53 (2): 273–88.

Bullard, R. D. 1984. "Endangered Environs: The Price of Unplanned Growth in Boomtown Houston." *California Sociologist* 7: 84–102.

Bullard, R. D. 1987.*Invisible Houston: The Black Experience in Boom and Bust.* College Station: Texas A&M University Press.

Bullard, R. D. 1991. *In Search of the New South: The Black Urban Experience in the 1970s and 1980s.* Tuscaloosa:University of Alabama Press.

Bullard, R. D. 1996a. "Environmental Justice: It's More Than Waste Facility Siting." *Social Science Quarterly* 77: 493–99.

Bullard, R. D. 1996b. *Unequal Protection: Environmental Justice and Communities of Color.* San Francisco: Sierra Club Books.

Bullard, R. D. 2000a. *Dumping in Dixie: Race, Class, and Environmental Quality.* Boulder, CO: Westview Press.

Bullard, R. D. 2000b. "Environmental Racism in the Alabama Blackbelt." Environmental Justice Resource Center. October 9. Available at http://www.ejrc.cau.edu/envracismalablackbelt.htm (accessed May 14, 2010).

Bullard, R. D. 2005a. "Blacks Left Behind in Deadly Chlorine Gas Leak." Graniteville, SC, Environmental Justice Resource Center Report Series. February. Available at http://www.ejrc.cau.edu/pamhallinterview.html (accessed June 27, 2008).

Bullard, R. D. 2005b. "Katrina and the Second Disaster: A Twenty-Point Plan to Destroy Black New Orleans." December 23. Available at http://www.ejrc.cau.edu/Bullard-20PointPlan.html (accessed July 17, 2008).

Bullard, R. D. 2005c. *The Quest for Environmental Justice: Human Rights and the Politics of Pollution*. San Francisco: Sierra Club Books.

Bullard, R. D. 2006a. "A Twenty-Point Plan to Destroy Black New Orleans." *News Media America*. February 1. Available at http://news.newamericamedia.org/news/view_article.html?article_id=ad54cb41686743ebb33ed2eb16647b16 (accessed May 24, 2009).

Bullard, R. D. 2006b. "Poisoned Water, Government Response, and Race." *Dissident Voice*. August 31. Available at http://www.dissidentvoice.org/Aug06/Bullard31.htm (accessed June 28, 2008).

Bullard, R. D. 2007a. *The Black Metropolis in the Twenty-First Century. Race, Power, and the Politics of Place*. New York: Rowman and Littlefield.

Bullard, R. D. 2007b. "Equity, Unnatural Disasters, and Race: Why Environmental Justice Matters." Research in Social Problems and Public Policy. Special Issue on Equity and the Environment 15 (1): 51–85.

Bullard, R. D. 2009a. "Poisoned Communities Put Spotlight on EPA Region 4." *OpEd News*. October 24, 2009. Available at http://www.opednews.com/articles/Poisoned-Communities-Put-S-by-Robert-Bullard-091021-905.html (accessed May 12, 2010).

Bullard, R. D. 2009b. "Sept. 5 Labor Day 'Call to End Toxic Racism' Rally in Dickson, Tennessee." OpEdNews. August 26. Available at  http://www.opednews.com/articles/Sept-5-Labor-Day—Call-by-Robert-Bullard-090825-326.html (accessed December 15, 2011).

Bullard, R. D. 2010. "BP's Waste Management Plan Raises Environmental Justice Concerns." *Dissident Voice*. July 29.

Bullard, R. D, and B. Wright. 2008. "Disastrous Response to Natural and Man-Made Disasters: An Environmental Justice Analysis Twenty-Five Years After Warren County." *UCLA Journal of Law and Environmental Policy* 26, no. 2: 217–253. Available at http://www2.law.ucla.edu/jelp/Articles/26-2%20Article%20PDFs/UCLA%20JELP%20 26-2%20Bullard-Wright.pdf .

Bullard, R. D., and B. Wright. 2009. *Race, Place and Environmental Justice After Hurricane Katrina: Struggles to Reclaim, Rebuild and Revitalize New Orleans and the Gulf Coast*. Boulder, CO: Westview Press.

Bullard, R. D., and B. H. Wright. 1986. "The Politics of Pollution: Implications for the Black Community." *Phylon* 47 (1): 71–78.

Bullard, R. D., J. E. Grigsby III, and C. Lee, eds. 1994. *Residential Apartheid: The American Legacy*. Los Angeles: UCLA Center for African American Studies.

Bullard, R. D., G. S. Johnson, and A. O. Torres. 1999. "Race, Equity, and Smart Growth: Why People of Color Must Speak for Themselves." Atlanta: Environmental Justice Resource Center, Clark Atlanta University. December. Available at http://www.sactaqc.org/Resources/Literature/Access_Equity/Race_Equity_Smartgrowth.htm (accessed June 30, 2008).

Bullard, R. D., G. S. Johnson, and A. O. Torres. 2004. *Highway Robbery: Transportation Racism and New Routes to Equity*. Boston:  South End Press.

Bullard, R. D., G. S. Johnson, and A.O. Torres, eds. 2000. *Sprawl City: Race, Politics and Planning in Atlanta*. Washington, DC: Island Press.

Bullard, R. D., P. Mohai, R. Saha, and B. Wright. 2008. "Toxic Wastes and Race at Twenty: Why Race Still Matters After All These Years." *Environmental Law* 38 (2): 371–411.

Bullard, R. D., Paul Mohai, Robin Saha, and Beverly Wright. 2007. *Toxic Wastes and Race at Twenty, 1987–2007.* Cleveland: United Church of Christ.

Burch, Audra D. S. 2002. "Blacks Go South in Reverse Migration." *Miami Herald.* December 15.

Burdeau, C. 2005. "New Orleans Area Becoming a Dumping Ground." Associated Press. October 31.

Burdeau, C. 2007. "Amid Toxic Worries, FEMA Wants Hurricane Victims Out of Trailers." Available at http://www.examiner.com/a-875419~Amid_toxin_worries__FEMA_wants_hurricane_victims_out_of_trailers.html (accessed August 1, 2007).

Burdeau, C. 2008. "Leaky New Orleans Levee Alarms Experts." *Times-Picayune.* May 21.

Bureau of Labor Statistics. 2005. "Employment Situation Summary: October 2005." November 4. Available at http://www.bls.gov/news.release/empsit.nro.htm (accessed June 30, 2006).

Burke, G. 2010. "AP News Break: Coast Guard, EPA Clamp Down on How BP Handles Oily Beach Trash from Gulf Spill." *Star Tribune.* July 1.

*Business Week.* 2005. "The Mother of All Toxic Cleanups." September 26. Available at http://www.businessweek.com/magazine/content/05_39/b3952055.htm (accessed December 21, 2005).

Byrd, M., and L. Clayton. 2001. *An American Health Dilemma: Race, Medicine, and Health Care in the United States, 1900–2000.* New York: Routledge.

Cain, J. D. 2000. "After the Flood: Princeville, North Carolina, Recovers from Flooding Caused by Hurricane Floyd in 1999." *Essence.* September.

California Newsreel. 2008. "Unnatural Causes . . . Is Inequality Making Us Sick?" Backgrounder from the Unnatural Causes Health Equity Database. Available at http://www.unnaturalcauses.org/assets/uploads/file/primers.pdf (accessed November 28, 2009).

Callahan, D., and B. Jennings. 2002. "Ethnics and Public Health: Forging a Strong Relationship." *American Journal of Public Health* 92: 169–76.

Canner, G. 1999. "The Role of Specialized Lenders in Extending Mortgages to Low-Income and Minority Homebuyers." *Federal Reserve Bulletin* 85 (11): 709–23.

Cannon, T., I. Davis, P. Blaikie, and B. Wisner. 2004. *At Risk: Natural Hazards, People's Vulnerability, and Disasters.* New York: Routledge.

Cappiello, D. 2006a. Refinery Release. "Residents Wake Up to Oil-Laden Fog: ExxonMobil Site in Baytown Coats Nearby Homes and Cars With Lubricant." *Houston Chronicle.* January 25.

Cappiello, D. 2006b. "Delay in Oil-Spill Notification Probed: Government Officials Question Why Exxonmobil Took So Long to Alert Them." *Houston Chronicle.* January 26.

Cappiello, D. 2006c. "Flawed Response to Spill Exposed: When an Exxon Neighbor Reported Leak, No Help Came." *Houston Chronicle.* March 26.

Carter, R. T. 2004. *Disaster Response to Communities of Color: Cultural Responsive Intervention.* Report prepared for the Connecticut Department of Mental Health and Addiction, Connecticut Department of Children and Families, University of Connecticut Health Center, Center for Trauma Response, Recovery and Preparedness, and Yale University School of Medicine (February 18).

Cashin, Sheryll D. 2004. *The Failures of Integration: How Race and Class Are Undermining the American Dream.* New York: Public Affairs.

Centers for Disease Control. 2000. "Death Rates from 72 Selected Causes by Year, Age Groups, Race, and Sex: United States 1979–98." Hyattsville, MD: National Center for Health Statistics.

Centers for Disease Control and Prevention. 2001. "Epi-Aid Trip Report: Possible Cluster of Orofacial Clefts." EPI-2001-08. Atlanta: CDC.

Centers for Disease Control and Prevention. 2003. "Second National Report on Human Exposure to Environmental Chemicals." Atlanta: CDC. January 31. Available at http://www.cdc.gov/exposurereport/ (accessed June 19, 2008).

Centers for Disease Control and Prevention.2003. "Follow-up of Deaths Among U.S. Postal Service Workers Potentially Exposed to Bacillus Anthracis—-District of Columbia, 2001–2002." MMWR, October 3, 52 (39): 937–938.

Centers for Disease Control and Prevention. 2004. "Asthma Prevalence, Health Care Use and Mortality 2000–2001." Available at http://www.cdc.gov/nchs/products/pubs/pubd/hestats/asthma/asthma.htm (accessed June 1, 2008).

Centers for Disease Control and Prevention. 2005. "Influenza Vaccination Levels Among Persons Aged >65 Years and Among Persons Aged 18–64 Years with High-Risk Conditions—United States, 2003." *Morbidity and Mortality Weekly Reports* 54 (41): 1045–49.

Centers for Disease Control and Prevention. No date. "Blood Lead Level Laboratory Reference System." Available at http://www.cdc.gov/lead/guidelines.htm (accessed June 19, 2008).

Chang, J., T. Soundararajan, and A. Johnson. 2005. "Getting Home Before It's Gone." *Alternet.org.* September 26. Available at http://www.alternet.org/katrina/25930 (accessed June 1, 2008).

Chappie, C. 2005. "Paying for Their Pain." *Times-Picayune.* May 29.

Cherniack, M. 1986. *The Hawk's Nest Incident: America's Worst Industrial Disaster.* New Haven: Yale University Press.

*Chicago Defender.* 1927. "Refugees Cry for Help in Hunger Zone." April 30.

*Chicago Tribune.* 2005. "Feds Under Fire for Moving Evacuees to Hotels." October 13.

Children's Environmental Health Network. 2001. "Statement on Protecting Public Health and Hazards Reduction (Chemical Plants, Terrorism, and Right-to-Know)." Mapcruzin.com. November. Available at http://www.mapcruzin.com/news/rtk111001a.htm (accessed June 30, 2008).

*CNN Money.* 2002. "Subprime Lenders Target Minorities: Study Finds African-Americans, Hispanics Pay Higher Loan Rates Than Whites with Similar Incomes." May 1.

CNN News Briefs. 1995. "New Evacuations Ordered Due to Chemical Spill." October 25. Available at http://www.cnn.com/US/Newsbriefs/9510/10-24/ (accessed June 28, 2008).

Cole, L., and S. Foster. 2000. *From the Ground Up: Environmental Racism and the Rise of the Environmental Justice Movement.* New York: New York University Press.

Colten, C. E., and J. Welch. 2003. "Hurricane Betsy and Its Effects on the Architecture Integrity of the Bywater Neighborhood: Summary." May.

Comerio, M. C. 1998. *Disaster Hits Home: New Policy for Urban Housing Recovery.* Berkeley: University of California Press.

Commission for Racial Justice. 1987. *Toxic Wastes and Race in the United States.* New York: United Church of Christ.

Committee on Homeland Security. 2011. "Homeland Security Committee Passes Bill to Secure U.S. Chemical Facilities from Terrorist Attack." June 22. Available at http://homeland.house.gov/press-release/homeland-security-committee-passes-bill-secure-us-chemical-facilities-terrorist-attack (accessed December 16, 2011).

Committee on Oversight and Government Reform. 2007. "Committee Probes FEMA's Response to Reports of Toxic Trailers." July 19. Available at http://oversight.house.gov/story.asp?ID=1413 (accessed July 17, 2008).

Consumeraffairs.com. 2005. "Class Action Suit Filed Against AIG over Katrina Claims." October 13. Available at http://www.consumeraffairs.com/news04/2005/katrina_aig.html (accessed June 1, 2008).

Cooper, C., and R. Block. 2006. *Disaster: Hurricane Katrina and the Failure of Homeland Security*. New York: Time Books.

Congressional Black Caucus Foundation. 2004. *African Americans and Climate Change: An Unequal Burden*. Washington, DC: CBCF, Inc. July 21.

Corbie-Smith, G. 1999. "The Continuing Legacy of the Tuskegee Syphilis Study: Considerations for Clinical Investigation." *American Journal of Medical Science* 317 (1): 5–8.

Corbie-Smith, G., S. B. Thomas, M. V. Williams, and S. Moody-Ayers. 1999. "Attitudes and Beliefs of African Americans Toward Participation in Medical Research." *Journal of General Internal Medicine* 14: 537–46.

Corbie-Smith, G., S. B. Thomas, and D. Marie M. St. George. 2002. "Distrust, Race, and Research." *Archives of Internal Medicine* 162: 2458–63.

Cornwell, K. 2003. "Contamination Problems Date Back Almost 40 Years." *Dickson Herald* (Tennessee). October 2.

Cornwell, K. 2004. "County Commission Tables Decision to Pay Families' Water Bills." *Dickson Herald* (Tennessee). June 9.

Corrosion Doctors. 2008. "Explosion Due to Corrosion by Process Chemicals." Available at http://www.corrosion-doctors.org/ProcessIndustry/Bogalusa-explosion.htm (accessed June 27, 2008).

Court of Appeals of Maryland. 2000. *Ericka Grimes v. Kennedy Krieger Institute, Inc. and Myron Higgins, a Minor, etc. et al. v. Kennedy Krieger Institute, Inc.* Available at http://www.law.uh.edu/healthlaw/law/statematerials/Marylandcases/grimesvkennedykreiger.pdf (accessed June 30, 2008).

Cruz, G. 2007. "Grilling FEMA over Its Toxic Trailers." *Time*. Available at http://www.time.com/time/nation/article/0,8599,1645312,00.html (accessed July 17, 2008).

Cuevas, F. 2005. "Fla. Eyes on Strengthening Wilma." *Atlanta Journal-Constitution*. October 18, A6.

Cutter, S. L. 2002. American Landscapes: The Regionalization of Hazards and Disasters. Washington, DC: Joseph Henry Press.

Cutter, S. L. 2005. "The Geography of Social Vulnerability: Race, Class, and Catastrophe." In Social Science Research Council, *Understanding Katrina: Perspectives from the Social Sciences*. New York: Social Science Research Council.

Cutter, S. L., B. J. Boruff, and W. L. Shirley. 2003. "Social Vulnerability to Environmental Hazards," *Social Science Quarterly* 84 (no. 1): 242–61.

Dahl, J. 1983. "It's Just Disgusting: Bordersville Residents Are Bitter over Burning of Hurricane Debris." *Houston Chronicle*. October 9.

Daily, K. 2005. "Deadly Derailment." *Aiken Standard* (South Carolina). January 7.

Daily News. 2006. ExxonMobil. *National Petroleum News.* August 27. Available at http://www.npnweb.com/daily/news.asp?a=565349 (accessed June 28, 2008).

Dallas Alliance Environmental Task Force. 1983. *Final Report.* Dallas, TX: Dallas Alliance. June 29.

Damon, A. 2007. "FEMA Covered Up Toxic Danger in Trailers Given to Katrina Victims." July 21. Available at http://www.wsws.org/articles/2007/jul2007/fema-j21.shtml (accessed July 17, 2008).

Daniel, P. 1972. *The Shadow of Slavery: Peonage in the South, 1901–1969.* Urbana: University of Illinois Press.

Daniel, P. 1977. *Deep'n as It Come: The 1927 Mississippi River Flood.* New York: Oxford.

Daniels, R. L., D. F. Kettl, and H. Kunreuther. 2006. *On Risk and Disaster: Lesson from Katrina.* Philadelphia: University of Pennsylvania Press.

Dart, D. 2006. "Junk Cars, Boats Slow Recovery in Big Easy." *Atlanta Journal-Constitution.* July 5.

Davis, Angela. 1981. *Women, Race, and Class.* New York: Vintage Books.

Deep South Center for Environmental Justice at Dillard University. 2006. "Project: A Safe Way Back Home." Available at http://www.dscej.org/asafewayhome.htm (accessed July 2, 2006).

DeNavas-Walt, C., B. D. Proctor, and R. J. Mills. 2004. *Income, Poverty, and Health Insurance Coverage in the United States: 2003.*Washington, DC: U.S. Census Bureau.

de Vries, D. 2002. "An Integrated Council Level Spatial Impact Assessment of Hurricane Floyd Combining Data on Damages and Social Vulnerability." Working Paper, Carolina Population Center Spatial Analysis Unit, University of North Carolina at Chapel Hill (December), 2–3.

Dewan, S. 2007. "Road to New Life After Katrina Closed to Many." *New York Times.* July 12.

Dewan, Shaila. 2009. "Clash in Alabama over Tennessee Coal Ash." *New York Times.* August 30.

Dewan, S., and S. Stack. 2008. "A Safety-Net Hospital Falls into Financial Crisis." *New York Times.* January 8.

Diamond, H., L. Diamond, and P. F. Noonan. 1996. *Land Use in America.* Washington, DC: Island Press.

Dickson, S. 2007. "County Seeks New Transfer Site." *Carrboro Citizen.* November 21.

Dickson, S. 2008. "County Board Reviews Transfer Site Complaint." *Carrboro Citizen.* January 24.

Dicum, G. 2006. "Justice in Time: Meet Robert Bullard, the Father of Environmental Justice." *Grist Magazine.* March 14. Available at http://www.grist.org/news/maindish/2006/03/14/dicum/ (accessed June 24, 2008).

Donn, J., and M. Weiss. 2010. "27,000 Abandoned Oil and Gas Well in the Gulf of Mexico." *Gulf Oil Catastrophe News.* July 9.

Draffan, G. "Corporate Profiles: Union Carbide." 2008. April 3. Available at http://www.endgame.org/carbide.html (accessed June 28, 2008).

Dreier, P., J. Mollenkopf, and T. Swanstrom. 2001. *Place Matters: Metropolitics for the Twenty-First Century.* Lawrence: University Press of Kansas.

Duchon, L., C. Schoen, M. M. Doty, K. Davis, E. Strumpf, and S. Bruegman. 2000. "Security Matters: How Instability in Health Insurance Puts U.S. Workers at Risk." Findings from the *Commonwealth Fund 2001 Health Insurance Survey*. New York: Commonwealth Fund. Available at http://www.cmwf.org (accessed June 1, 2008).

Duke, L. 2007. "A Well of Pain." *Washington Post*. March 20.

Dula, A. 1994. "African American Suspicion of the Healthcare System Is Justified: What Do We Do About It." *Cambridge Quarterly of Healthcare Ethics* 3: 347–57.

Dunn, M. 2006. "Debris Removal Need Trumps Protest." *The Advocate*. May 8.

Dymski, G. A. 1995. "The Theory of Bank Redlining and Discrimination: An Exploration." *Review of Black Political Economy* 23 (Winter): 37–74.

Dyson, M. E. 2006. *Come Hell or High Water: Hurricane Katrina and the Color of Disaster*. New York: Basic Books.

Eaton, L. 2006. "A New Landfill in New Orleans Sets Off a Battle." *New York Times*. May 8. Available at http://www.nytimes.com/2006/05/08/us/08landfill.html?ex=1151035200&en=99305c0b4651e848&ei=5055&partner=RRCOLUMBUS (accessed July 15, 2006).

Eaton, L., and R. Nixon. 2005. "Loans to Homeowners Along Gulf Coast Lag." *New York Times*. December 15. Available at http://www.nytimes.com/2005/12/15/national/nationalspecial/15loans.html?ref=smallbusinessadministration (accessed December 17, 2011).

Ebner, D. 2010. "Up to 60,000 Barrels Flowing in Gulf: U.S." *Globe and Mail*. June 15.

Eckholm, E. 2007. "Foreclosures Force Suburbs to Fight Blight." *The New York Times*, March 23. Available at http://www.nytimes.com/2007/03/23/us/23vacant.html?_r=1&th=&oref=...(accessed December 16, 2011).

Edsall, T. B. 2005. "Bush Suspends Pay Act in Areas Hit by Storm." *Washington Post*. September 9, D3.

Edwards, H. 2003. "Family Blames Health Woes on Dickson's Landfill." *Dickson Herald*. September 2.

Eilperin, J. 2004. "Chemical Industry Funds Aid EPA Study: Effect of Substances on Children Probed." *Washington Post*. October 26, A23.

Eisenman, D. P., C. Wold, C. Setodji, S. Hickey, B. Lee, B. D. Stein, and A. Long. 2004. "Will Public Health's Response to Terrorism Be Fair? Racial/Ethnic Variations in Perceived Fairness During a Bioterrorist Event." *Biosecurity and Bioterrorism: Biodefense Strategy, Practice, and Science* 2 (3): 146–56.

El Nasser, H. 1999. "Urban Experts Pick Top Factors Influencing Future." *USA Today*. September 27, A4.

Ellick, A. B. 2008. "Tons of PCBs May Come Calling at a Down-at-the-Heels Texas City." *New York Times*. June 19.

Elliston, J. 2004. "Disaster in the Making." *Orlando Weekly*. October 21, 2004.

Emily, J. 2005. "Katrina Leaves Children Separated from Their Anguished Parents." *Dallas Morning News*. September 14.

Emling, S. 1996. "Black Areas in City Pay Steep Rates." *Atlanta Journal-Constitution*. June 30.

Emrich, Christopher T., and Susan L. Cutter. "Social Vulnerability to Climate-Sensitive Hazards in the Southern United States." *Weather, Climate and Society AMS Journal* 3 (July 2011): 193–208.

Enchautegui, M. E., M. Fix, P. Loprest, S. C. von der Lippe, and D. Wissoker. 1997. *Do Minority-Owned Businesses Get a Fair Share of Government Contracts?* Washington, DC: Urban Institute.

Environmental Integrity Project and Earthjustice. 2009. *Coming Clean: What the EPA Knows About the Dangers of Coal Ash.* Washington, DC: EIP. May.

Environmental News Service. 2005. "Thousands of Chlorine Evacuees Return Home." January 18. Available at http://www.ens-newswire.com/ens/jan2005/2005-01-18-03.asp (accessed June 28, 2008).

Environmental News Service. 2008. "Water Contamination Suit Filed Against Dickson County, Tennessee." March 10. Available at http://www.ens-newswire.com/ens/mar2008/2008-03-10-097.asp (accessed June 28, 2008).

Environmental Policy Institute. 2005. "Katrina Evacuees Face Extreme Levels of Joblessness." November 9. Available at http://www.epinet.org/content.cfm/webfeatures_snapshots_20051109 (accessed June 1, 2008).

*Environmental Science News.* 2007. "FEMA's Toxic Trailers Exposed." July 25. Available at http://www.ens-newswire.com/ens/jul2007/2007-07-25-02.asp (accessed July 17, 2008).

Estes, C. 2001. "Second Chance for Black Farmers." *Yes!* Summer.

Ethridge, K. 2005. "Town Picks Up Pieces after Train Wreck." *Augusta Chronicle.* January 21.

Fadden, R. R., S. E. Lederer, and J. D. Moreno. 1996. "U.S. Medical Researchers, the Nuremberg Doctors Trials, and the Nuremberg Code: A Review of Findings of the Advisory Committee on Human Radiation Experiments." *Journal of the American Medical Association* 276: 1667–71.

"Fairer Treatment for Katrina's Victims." 2011. *New York Times.* July 11. Available at http://www.nytimes.com/2011/07/12/opinion/12tue3.html (accessed December 17, 2011).

Farrell, D. A. 2010. "Oil-Spill Debris Might Be Coming to County Landfill." *Picayune Item,* July 3.

Faulkner, L. 2010. "Perry County Landfill Bankruptcy Raises Questions." *Selma Times-Journal.* January 27.

Feagin, J. R. 1985. "The Global Context of Metropolitan Growth: Houston and the Oil Industry." *American Journal of Sociology* 90: 1204–30.

Feagin, J. R. 2001. *Racist America: Roots, Current Realities and Future Reparations.* New York: Routledge.

Federal Emergency Management Agency. 1999. "Hazard Mitigation at Work: Two Alabama Communities." Atlanta: FEMA Region IV. April 15.

Federal Emergency Management Agency. 2004. *Hurricane Pam Exercise Concludes.* Press release. July 23. Available at http://www.fema.gov/news/newsrelease.fema?id=13051 (accessed June 1, 2008).

Federal Financial Institutions Examination Council. 2004. *Home Mortgage Disclosure Act, Aggregate Report Search by State.* Washington, DC. Available at http://www.ffiec.gov/hmdaadwebreport/aggwelcome.aspx (accessed June 1, 2008).

Feins, J. D. and R. G. Bratt. 1983. "Barred in Boston: Racial Discrimination in Housing." *Journal of the American Planning Association* 49: 344–55.

Feldstein, M. 1994. "Hitting the Poor Where They Live." *Nation* 58. April 4.

Fields, L., A. Huang, G. Solomon, M. Rotkin-Ellman, and P. Simms. 2007. *Katrina's Wake: Arsenic-Lased Schools and Playgrounds Put New Orleans Children at Risk.* New York: Natural Resource Defense Council.

Filosa, G. 2006. "House Razing Costs to Rise for N.O." *Times-Picayune.* May 22.

Finch, S. 2006. "Ag Street Landfill Case Gets Ruling: City Ordered to Pay Residents of Toxic Site." *Times-Picayune.* January 27.

Fischbein, N. 2005a. "Waiting for Updates in Tallevast." *Bradenton Herald*. March 15.

Fischbein, N. 2005b. "Tallevast Plume Bigger Than Thought: Residents Concerned." *Bradenton Herald*. April 16.

Fischbein, N. 2005c. "Tallevast Residents File Lawsuit." *Bradenton Herald*. September 3.

Fischbein, N. 2006. "Lockheed Done Looking for Tallevast Plume Boundaries." *Bradenton Herald*. October 6.

Flournoy, C. 1994. "In the War for Justice, There's No Shortage of Environmental Fights." *Dallas Morning News*. July 3.

Flournoy, C., and R. L. Loftis. 2000. "Toxic Neighbors: Residents of Projects Find Common Problem, Pollution." *Dallas Morning News*. October 1.

Fothergill, A., E. Enrique, G. M. Maestas, and J. DeRouen-Darlington. 1999. "Race, Ethnicity and Disaster in the United States: A Review of the Literature." *Disaster* 23 (2): 156–73.

Fountain, K. 2005. "Exxon Scrubs 'Greasy' Spill from Cars, Homes." *Baytown Sun*. January 25.

Fountain, K. 2006. "County Suing Exxon over Archia Court Spill." *Baytown Sun*. August 12.

Frank, T. 2005. "Blanco Pushes FEMA for Hotel Rooms." *USA Today*. September 21.

Frazier, John W., Florence M. Margai, and Eugene Tettey-Fio. 2003. *Race and Place*. Boulder, CO: Westview Press.

Freimuth, V. S., S. C. Quinn, S. B.Thomas, G. Cole, E. Zook, and T. Duncan. 2001. "African Americans' View on Research and the Tuskegee Syphilis Study." *Social Science and Medicine* 52 (2): 797–808.

Frey, William H. 2001. "Census 2000 Shows Large Black Return to the South, Reinforcing the Region's 'White-Black' Demographic Profile." PSC Research Report No. 01-473. Ann Arbor: University of Michigan. May.

Frumkin, H., J. Hess, G. Luber, J. Mallay, and M. McGeehin. 2008. "Climate Change: The Public Health Response." *American Journal of Public Health* 98 (3): 1–11.

Fthenakis, V. M. 2001. "A Release of Nitrogen Oxides in Bogalusa, Louisiana and Similarities of Causation to the Bhopal MIC Release." *Journal of Loss Prevention in the Process Industries* 14: 245–50.

Gabe, T., G. Falk, M. McCarthy, and V. W. Mason. 2005. *Hurricane Katrina: Social-demographic Characteristics of Impacted Areas*. Washington, DC: Congressional Research Service Report RL33141. November.

Gallentine, S. 2001. "The Old Home Place." *Banner-Herald*. April 7.

Gamble, V. N. 1997. "Under the Shadow of Tuskegee: African Americans and Health Care." *American Journal of Public Health* 87 (11): 1773–78.

Georgia Emergency Management Agency. 2004. *GEMA Marks 10th Anniversary of State's Worst Flood*. July 5.

Glantz, L. H. 2002. "Nontherapeutic Research with Children." *American Journal of Public Health* 92: 1070–73.

Gerberding, J. L. 2007. Climate Change and Public Health Statement of M.D., M.P.H. Director, Centers for Disease Control and Prevention Administrator, Agency for Toxic Substances and Disease Registry, U.S. Department of Health and Human Services, Testimony Before the Committee on Environment and Public Works, United States Senate, Delivery Expected at 10:00 a.m. Tuesday, October 23.

Goddard, J. 2005. "No People, No Power, No Money: A City Struggling to Live Again." *Times.* November 12.

Goldman, J. 2005. "Balancing in a Crisis? Bioterrorism, Public Health, and Privacy." *Journal of Health Law* 38 (3): 481–527.

Gordon, T. 2009. "Dumping Ash, and Cash on Perry County." *Birmingham News.* November 15.

Gordy, C. 2007. "Troubled Waters." *Essence.* July.

Gornick. M. 2000. *Vulnerable Populations and Medicare Services: Why Do Disparities Exist?* New York: Century Foundation Press.

Gourash, N. 1978. "Help-Seeking: A Review of Literature." *American Journal of Community Psychology* 6: 413–23.

Grady, D. 2007. "White Doctors, Black Subjects: Abuse Disguised As Research." *New York Times.* January 23.

Green, A. R., R. Dana, Carney, D. J. Pallin, L. H. Ngo, K. L. Raymond, L. I. Iezzoni, and M. B. Banaji. 2007. "Implicit Bias Among Physicians and Its Prediction of Thrombolysis Decisions for Black and White Patients." *Journal of General Internal Medicine* 22 (9): 1231–38.

Green, J. D., M. C. Linda, G. C. Gleser, A. C. Leonard, M. Korol, and C. Winget. 1990. "Buffalo Creek Survivors in the Second Decade: Stability of Stress Symptoms." *American Journal of Orthopsychiatry* 60 (1): 43–54.

Green, R. 2008. "Small-Town Residents Living on Deadly Ground." *Miami Herald.* May 3.

Greenpeace. 1993. The Case for a Ban on All Hazardous Waste Shipment from the United States and Other OECD Member States to Non-OECD States. June.

Gregory, G. 2005. "Trying to Get It Right This Time." *Time.* September 19.

Gremaldi, J. V., and G. Gugliotta. 2002. "Chemical Plants Feared as Targets." *Washington Post.* December 16, A01.

Gresham Smith and Partners. 2000. USGS Dye Tracer Study: Summary and Results of Dye-Tracer Tests Conducted at the Dickson County Landfill, Tennessee, 1997 and 1998, Appendix B. April, 2.

*Grist Online.* 2004. "EPA Denies Poor Families Camcorders: Controversial EPA Pesticide Study Put on Hold." November 10. Available at http://www.grist.org/news/daily/2004/11/10/ (accessed June 19, 2008).

Grodin, M. A. 1996. "Legacies of Nuremberg: Medical Ethics and Human Rights." *Journal of the American Medical Association* 276: 1682–83.

Grohol, J. M. 2009. "Psych Central—Hispanic and African American Adults Are Uninsured at Rates One and Half to Three times Higher Than Whites." August 1. Available at http://psychcentral.com/news/archives/2006-08/cf-haao72606.html (accessed December 17, 2011).

Guinier, L., and G. Torres. *The Miner's Canary: Enlisting Race, Resisting Power, Transforming Democracy.* Cambridge, MA: Harvard University Press.

Gunn, Angus A. 2003. *Unnatural Disasters: Case Studies of Human-Induced Environmental Catastrophes.* Westport, CT: Greenwood Press.

Haar, C. M., and J. S. Kayden. 1999. *Zoning and the American Dream: Promises Still to Keep.* Chicago: American Planning Association.

Haggerty M. 1980. "Crisis at Indian Creek." *Atlanta Journal and Constitution Magazine* (January 20): 14–25.

Haliburton NUS Environmental Corporation. 1991. "Final Report: Site Inspection Dickson County Landfill, Dickson, Dickson County, Tennessee." Report prepared for the U.S. Environmental Protection Agency. October 10.

Hall, P. 2005. "Blacks Left Behind in Deadly Chlorine Gas Leak, Graniteville, S.C." Interview conducted by Robert D. Bullard, Graniteville, SC. March 4. Available at http://www.ejrc.cau.edu/pamhallinterview.html (accessed June 28, 2008).

Hammer, D. 2008a. "Court Upholds Dump Housing Payout." *Times-Picayune*. June 30.

Hammer, D. 2008b. "Contaminated Homes Denied Funds." *Times-Picayune*. March 27.

Hammer, D. 2008c. "Court Upholds Dump Housing Payout." *Times-Picayune*. July 1.

Hampton, M. 2006. "Formaldehyde in FEMA Travel Trailers Making People Sick." August 8. Available at http://www.homelandstupidity.us/2006/08/08/formaldehyde-in-fema-travel-trailers-making-people-sick/ (accessed July 17, 2008).

Hanemann, M. 2003. "Slow Pay." *Daily News* (Bogalusa, Louisiana). December 19.

Harrison, E. 1994. "Legacy of Racism Dams up Post-Flood Effort in Georgia." *Los Angeles Times*. August 26.

Hartman, C., and G. Squires. 2006. *There Is No Such Thing as a Natural Disaster: Race, Class and Hurricane Katrina*. New York: Routledge.

Hasnain-Wynia, W., R. D. W. Baker, D. Nerenz, J. F., A. C. Beal, M. B. Landrum, R. Behal, and J. S. Weissman. 2007. "Disparities in Health Care are Driven By Where Minority Patients Seek Care." *Archives of Internal Medicine* 167 (12):1233–39. Available at http://www.commonwealthfund.org/usr_doc/1038_Hasnain-Wynia_disparities_hlt_care_ArchIntMed.pdf?section=4039.

Hatcher, Monica. 2010. "Only a Handful of Houston Plants Checked for Safety Standards." *Houston Chronicle*. April 5.

Hauserman, J., and D. Olinger. 1996. "EPA to Evacuate Mount Dioxin." *St. Petersburg Times*. October 4, 1A.

Heilprin, J. 2004. "EPA Suspends Study on Kids and Pesticides." *Washington Post*. November 10.

Heilprin, J. 2005. "EPA Cancels Controversial Pesticide Study: EPA Cancels Study That Would Have Paid Families While Studying Children Exposed to Pesticides." *Associated Press*. April 8.

Heilprin, J. 2008. "Sludge Tested as Lead Poisoning Fix in Poor Black Neighborhoods." *Democracy Now*, April 23. Available at http://www.democracynow.org/2008/4/23/sludge_tested_as_lead_poisoning_fix (accessed December 15, 2011).

Heilprin, J., and K. S. Vineys. 2008. "Sludge Spread Around City Homes." *Batimore Sun*. April 14.

Herbert, B. 2006. "Poisoned on Eno Road." *New York Times*. October 2.

Hester, G. A. 1980. "Bordersville: Catching up to the 20th Century." *Playsure*. January.

Hinds, R. 2001. "Is the U.S. Chemical Industry Our Weakest Link Against Terrorist Attacks." Testimony of Rick Hinds, Legislative Director, Greenpeace Toxics Campaign, Before the Subcommittee on Superfund, Toxics, Risk, and Waste Management of the Senate Environment and Public Works Committee, November 14. Available http://epw.senate.gov/107th/greenpeace_1114.htm (accessed June 19, 2008).

Hinds, R., T. Kay, and K. Varela. 2008. "238 Lobbyists Led the Chemical Industry Campaign Against Strong Laws and Regulations in 2007." Washington, DC: Greenpeace. May. Available at http://www.greenpeace.org/raw/content/usa/press-center/reports4/238-lobbyists-led-the-chemical.pdf (accessed July 1, 2008).

Hing, Julianne. 2010. "Blacks Locked Out of Oil Spill Cleanup Jobs, says NAACP." *Color-Lines.* July 20.

Ho, D. 2005. "The Worst Hurricane Season Ever." *Atlanta Journal-Constitution.* November 30.

Honey, M. K. 2007. *Going Down Jericho Road: The Memphis Strike, Martin Luther King's Last Campaign.* New York: W. W. Norton.

Horne, J. 2006. *Breach of Faith: Hurricane Katrina and the Near Death of a Great American City.* New York: Random House.

*Houston Chronicle.*1979. "Judge Denies Request to Halt Dump Opening." December 22.

*Houston Chronicle.* 1985. "OSHA Cites Union Carbide with Neglecting Safety Policy." October 1, 7. Available at http://bhopal.net/oldsite/presscoverage/houstonchronicle/archive/19851001-wilfulneglect.html (accessed June 28, 2008).

Howard, W. 1984. "Richard Wright's Flood Stories and the Great Mississippi River Flood of 1927: Social and Historical Backgrounds." *Southern Literary Journal* 16 (2) (Spring): 44–62.

Hsu, S. S. 2007. "U.S. Announces New Chemical Plant Security Rules." *Washington Post.* April 3.

Hughes, A. 2002. "Cures for the Privileged? Government Officials Receive Anthrax Treatment Prior to Post Office Employees." *Black Enterprise.* January.

Hughes, A. 2005."Blown Away by Katrina." *Black Enterprise.* November.

Hughes-Halbert, C., K. Armstrong, O. Gandy, and L. Shaker. 2006. "Racial Differences in Trust in Health Care Providers." *Archives of Internal Medicine* 166: 896–901.

Hunter, M. 2005. "Schools Take in Displaced Students." *CNN.com.* September 12. Available at http://www.cnn.com/2005/EDUCATION/09/07/katrina.schools/ (accessed June 1, 2008).

Hurston, Z. N. 1998. *Their Eyes Were Watching God.* New York: Harper Perennial Classics.

Institute of Medicine. 1999.*Toward Environmental Justice: Research, Education, and Health Policy Needs.* Washington, DC: National Academy Press.

Intergovernmental Panel on Climate Change. 2007. *Climate Change 2007: Impacts, Adaptation and Vulnerability.* Cambridge: Cambridge University Press.

Intergovernmental Panel on Climate Change. 2007. *Climate Change: Impacts, Adaptation and Vulnerability.* New York: Working Group II Contribution to the Fourth Assessment and Cambridge University Press.

International Federation of the Red Cross and Red Crescent Societies. 2004. *World Disaster Report 2004.*Geneva, Switzerland: IFRC. Available at http://www.ifrc.org/publicat/wdr2004/ (accessed June 1, 2008).

Jackson, L. P. 2010. "Seven Priorities of EPA's Future." Memorandum to All Employees. January 12. Available at http://blog.epa.gov/administrator/2010/01/12/seven-priorities-for-epas-future/ (accessed July 22, 2010).

Jackson, R., and K. N. Shields. 2008. "Preparing the U.S. Health Community for Climate Change." *Annual Review of Public Health* 29 (25): 1–17.

Jackson, S. 2005. "Un/natural Disasters, Here and There." In Social Science Research Council, *Understanding Katrina: Perspectives from the Social Sciences.* New York: Social Science Research Council. Available at http://understandingkatrina.ssrc.org/Jackson/.

James, X., A. Hawkins, and R. Rowel. 2007. "An Assessment of the Cultural Appropriateness of Emergency Preparedness Communication for Low- Income Minorities." *Journal of Homeland Security and Emergency Management* 4 (3): article 13.

Jervis, R. 2008a. "New Orleans' Homeless Rate Swells to 1 in 25." *USA Today.* March 17.

Jervis, R.. 2008b. "New Orleans to Begin Citing Trailer Residents." *USA Today.* July 14.

Johnson, A. 2007. "FEMA Suspends Use of 'Toxic' Trailers." Available at http://www.msnbc.msn.com/id/20165754/ (accessed July 17, 2008).

Jones, J. H. 1993. *Bad Blood: The Tuskegee Syphilis Experiment.* 2nd ed. New York: Free Press.

Jones, N. B. 2008. "Waste Issue Needs Fair Solution." *Chapel Hill News.* January 20.

Jordan, J. 1998. "Hawk's Nest." *West Virginia Historical Society Quarterly* 12 (2): 1–3.

Jordan, J. 2005. "Lawyers for Railroad, S.C. Town Seek Deal." *Washington Post.* May 25.

Jordan, L. J. 2006. "Washington Extends Full Pickup Costs of Hurricane Debris Removal." WWLTV.com. June 29. Available at http://www.wwltv.com/cgi-bin/bi/gold_print.cgi (accessed July 1, 2006).

Justice, G. 1995. Group: "Gas Leak Response Racist." *Times-Picayune.* October 29, B1.

Justice, G. 1996. "Police in the Dark After Tanker Blast 911 Records Show Confusion." *Times-Picayune.* April 23.

Kaiser, J. 2001. "Court Rebukes Hopkins for Lead Paint Study." *Science* 293: 1567–69.

Kamalick, J. 2009. "Trusted Market Intelligence for the Global Chemical and Energy Industries." ICIS News, June 29. Available at http://www.icis.com/Articles/2009/06/29/9228412/us-chemical-plants-still-targets-of-interest-for-terrorists.html (accessed December 16, 2011).

Kaniasty, K., and F. H. Norris. 1995. "In Search of Altruistic Community: Patterns of Social Support Mobilization Following Hurricane Hugo." *American Journal of Community Psychology* 4 (23) (August ): 447–77.

Kaniasty, K., and F. H. Norris. 2000. "Help-Seeking Comfort and Receiving Social Support: The Role Of Ethnicity and Context of Need." *American Journal of Community Psychology* 28 (4): 545–81.

Kevles, D. 1985. *In the Name of Eugenics: Genetics and the Uses of Human Heredity.* New York: Knopf.

Kimbro, P. L. 2006. "County, City Settle Landfill Lawsuits with Families." *Dickson Herald.* November 7.

Kimbro, P. L. 2008."Lawsuit Wants Dickson to Clean Waste." *Tennessean.* March 6.

King, R. 2001. "Shifting Landscape." *Times-Picayune.* March 26.

Kleinberg, E. 2003. *Black Cloud: The Deadly Hurricane of 1928.* New York: Carroll and Graf.

Kleinberg, E. 2005. "The Florida Flood That Accounted for the Most Deaths of Black People in a Single Day (Until Katrina)." George Mason University History News Network, September 6. Available at http://hnn.us/articles/15373.html.

Klinkenberg, J. 1992. "A Storm of Memories." *St. Petersburg Times.* July 12.

Kneebone, E. 2009. *Job Sprawl Revisited: The Changing Geography of Metropolitan Employment.* Washington, DC: Brookings. April.

Knowlton, Kim, M. Rotkin-Ellman, L. Geballe, W. Max, and G. Solomon, 2011. "Health costs of six climate change-related events in the United States, 2002–2009." *Health Affairs* 30 (11): 2167–76.

Kocieniewski, D. 2006. "Despite 9/11 Effect, Railyards Are Still Vulnerable." *New York Times*. March 27.

Kochlar, Rakesh, Richard Fry, and Paul Taylor. 2011. *Wealth Gaps Rise to Record Highs between Whites, Blacks, Hispanics*. Washington DC: Pew Research Center. June 26.

Krauss, C., and J. M. Broder. 2010. "BP Resumes Work to Plug Oil Leak After Facing Setback." *New York Times*. May 27.

Kromm, C., and K. Ernst. 2000. *Gold and Green Report*. Durham, NC: Institute for Southern Studies.

Kromm, C., and S. Sturgis. 2007. *Blueprint for Gulf Renewal: The Katrina Crisis and a Community Agenda for Action*. Durham, NC: Institute for Southern Studies. August/September.

Kromm, C., and S. Sturgis. 2008. *Hurricane Katrina and the Guiding Principles of Internal Displacement: A Global Human Rights Perspective on a National Disaster*. Durham: Institute for Southern Studies. January.

Kunzelman, M. 2007. "Mississippi Sues State Farm Over Katrina Deal." June 11. Available at http://www.msnbc.msn.com/id/19176625/ns/business-us_business/t/mississippi-sues-state-farm-over-katrina-deal/# (accessed December 17, 2011).

Labouisse, M. 1974. "Architecture: The Ironical History of Louis Armstrong Park." *New Orleans*. July.

Lakshimo, R. 2008. "Indians Pressure Dow on Bhopal Cleanup." *Washington Post*. March 29, A1.

Lamphear, B. P. 2001. "Environmental Lead Exposure and Children's Intelligence at Blood Lead Concentration Below 10 mg/dl." APA Presidential Plenary Session, Pediatric Academy Society meeting, April 30.

LaVeist, T. A. 2002. *Race, Ethnicity, and Health: A Public Health Reader*. New York: Jossey-Bass.

LaVeist, T. A., K. J. Nickerson, and J. V. Bowie. 2000. "Attitudes About Racism, Medical Mistrust, and Satisfaction with Care Among African Americans and White Cardiac Patients." *Medical Care Research Review* 57 (1): 146–61.

Lavelle, M., and M. Coyle. 1992. "Unequal Protection." *National Law Journal*. September, S1–S2.

Lee, A. 2005. "Wind or Water: The Debate Rages, but Who Will Pay?" *Sun Herald (South Mississippi)*. December 21.

Lee, B. L. 1992. "Environmental Litigation on Behalf of Poor, Minority Children, *Matthews v. Coye*: A Case Study." Paper presented at the Annual Meeting of the American Association for the Advancement of Science, Chicago. February 9.

Leonnig, C. D. 2004. "Brentwood Postal Workers Push Lawsuit over Anthrax." *Washington Post*. April 30. Available at http://www.washingtonpost.com/ac2/wp-dyn/A54534-2004Apr29?language=printer (accessed December 19, 2011).

Lerner, S. 2007. *Diamond: A Struggle for Environmental Justice in Louisiana's Chemical Corridor*. Cambridge, MA: MIT Press.

Lerner, S. 2008. "Tallevast, Florida: Rural Residents Live Atop Groundwater Contaminated by High-Tech Weapons Company." *The Collaborative on Health and the Environment*. Available at http://www.healthandenvironment.org/articles/homepage/3829 (accessed June 25, 2008).

Lerner, S. 2010. *Sacrifice Zones: The Front Lines of Toxic Chemical Exposure in the United States*. Cambridge, MA: MIT Press.

Letter from Patricia Thompson to Claudia Brand, ICF Kaiser, August 31, 1993, pp. 1-2.

Levy, Barry S., and Victor W. Sibel. 2003. *Terrorism and Public Health: A Balanced Approach to Strengthening Systems and Protecting People.* New York: Oxford University Press.

Liberto, J. 2009. "Black Businesses Hit Hard in New Orleans: African American Owners Exited the Business Community in Higher Numbers Than White Owners—and Those that Returned Face More Challenges." *CNN Money.* August 20. Available at http://money.cnn.com/2009/08/19/news/economy/New_Orleans_black_businesses/ (accessed December 16, 2011).

Litman, T. 2006. *Evaluating Transportation Equity: Guidance for Incorporating Distributional Impacts in Transportation Planning.* Victoria, BC: Victoria Transport Policy Institute. March 8.

Liu, A., and A. Plyer. 2008. *The New Orleans Index: Tracking Recovery of the New Orleans Metro Area.* The Brookings Institution and Greater New Orleans Community Data Center. August.

Lombard, C. 2010. "Where Does Oil Spill Clean-up Waste Go." *Fox 10-TV News.com,* Mobile, Alabama. July 8.

Lowney, J. 2008. "Overviews of the Book of the Dead." Available at http://www.english.uiuc.edu/maps/poets/m_r/rukeyser/hawksnest.htm (accessed June 28, 2008).

Lucas, A., and A. Paxton. 1999. Cherniack, *Hawks Nest Incident* (Spring). Available at http://www.english.uiuc.edu/maps/poets/m_r/rukeyser/hawksnest.htm (accessed June 28, 2008).

Lui, M., E. Dixon, and B. Leondar-Wright. 2006. *Stalling the Dream: Cars, Race and Hurricane Evacuation.* Boston: United for a Fair Economy. January 10.

Luther, L. 2007. *Disaster Debris Removal After Hurricane Katrina: Status and Associated Issues.* Washington, DC: Congressional Research Service Report to Congress. June 16.

Lyttle, A. 2000. *Agricultural Street Landfill Environmental Justice Case Study.* Michigan: University of Michigan School of Natural Resource and Environment. Available at http://www.umich.edu/~snre492/Jones/agstreet.htm (accessed June 22, 2008).

Lyttle, A. 2003. *Agriculture Street Landfill Environmental Justice Case Study.* University of Michigan School of Natural Resources, Ann Arbor, Michigan. January.

Mack, K. 2002. "Acres Homes as Impoverished Today as It Was 10 Years Ago." *Houston Chronicle.* November 19.

Maggi, L. 2005. "Shelter Shutting: Next Steps." *Times-Picayune.* October 14.

Majority Staff of the Subcommittee on Investigations and Oversight of the Committee on Science and Technology. 2009. "The Agency for Toxic Substances and Disease Registry (ATSDR):Problems in the Past, Potential for the Future?" Report to U.S. House of Representatives of Subcommittee Chairman Brad Miller. March 10. Available at http://democrats.science.house.gov/Media/file/Investigations/ATSDR%20Staff%20Report%2003%2010%2009.pdf (accessed May 13, 2010).

Mann, E. 2006. *Katrina's Legacy: White Racism and Black Reconstruction in New Orleans and the Gulf Coast.* Los Angeles: Frontline Press.

Martell, B. 2006. "Horse Racing Returns to New Orleans." *Associated Press.* November 23.

Martin, A. 2006. "Katrina's Garbage Rates a Category 5." *Chicago Tribune.* January 4.

*Matthews and People United for a Better Oakland v. Coye.* 1991. U.S. District Court, N. D. California. No. C 90 3620 EFL.

Maugh, T. H., and J. Jervis. 2008. "FEMA Trailers Toxic, Tests Show." *Los Angeles Times*. February 15.

Mays, Vivkie M., Susan D. Cochran, and Namdi W. Barnes. 2007. "Race, Raced-Based Discrimination, and Health Outcomes Among African Americans." *Annual Review of Psychology* 58: 201–25.

McDiarmid, H., and D. Shine. 2003. "State Slow to Act on Lead Paint Threat." *Detroit Free Press*. January 24.

McElheney, J. 2006. "Payne vs. Payout of Burying Garbage." *Rachel's Democracy & Health News* no. 864. December 7.

McGary, H. 1999. "Distrust, Social Justice, and Health Care." *Mount Sinai Journal of Medicine* 66 (4): 236–40.

McLaughlin, M. No date. "Center Says Eastern North Carolina Lags the State on Infrastructure, Human Needs." North Carolina Center for Public Policy News Release. Available at http://www.nccppr.org/easternnc2.html (accessed June 22, 2008).

McWhorter, M. 1988. Letter to Harry Holt and Lavenia Holt. Division of Solid Waste, Tennessee Department of Health and Environment. December 8.

Members Scholars of the Center for Progressive Reform. 2005. *An Unnatural Disaster: The Aftermath of Hurricane Katrina*. New York: Center for Progressive Reform, September.

Micco, E., A. D. Gurmankin, and K. Armstrong. 2004. "Differential Willingness to Undergo Smallpox Vaccination Aamong African-American and White Individuals." *Journal of General Internal Medicine* 19 (5): 451–55.

Mielke, H. 1999. "Lead in the Inner Cities: Policies to Reduce Children's Exposure to Lead May Be Overlooking a Major Source of Lead in the Environment." *American Scientist* 87 (1) (January-February).

Mittal, A., and J. Powell. 2000. "The Last Plantation." *Food First*. Available at http://www.foodfirst.org/pubs/backgrdrs/2000/w00v6n1.html (accessed June 25, 2008).

Mock, Brentin. 2010. "Minorities See Little Green in BP Oil Spill Jobs." *TheRoot.com*. July 13.

Moore, S., M. Daniel, L. Linnan, M. Campbell, S. Benedict, and A. Meier. 2004. "After Hurricane Floyd Passed: Investigating the Social Determinants of Disaster Preparedness and Recovery." *Family and Community Health* 27 (3): 204–17.

Morin, R., and L. Rein. 2005. "Many New Orleans Evacuees Won't Return." *Washington Post*. September 15.

Morris, D. L., P. J. Barker, and M. S. Legator. 2004. "Symptoms of Adverse Health Effects Among Residents from Surrounding Chemical-Industrial Complexes in Southeast Texas." *Archives of Environmental Health* 59 (3): 160–65.

Morton, J. 2009. "An Estimated 3.9 Million Tons of Coal Ash Destined for Perry County." *Tuscaloosa News*. June 29.

Moss, T. A. 1991. Letter to Nathan Sykes. Drinking Water Section, Municipal Facilities Branch, U.S. Environmental Protection Agency, Region IV. December 17.

Moss, T. A. 1992a. Letter to Dickson County File. Ground Water Management Section, Tennessee Department of Health and Environment. January 6.

Moss, T. A. 1992b. Letter to Dickson County File. Ground Water Management Section, Tennessee Department of Health and Environment. March 13.

Mulligan, T. S., and R. Fausset. 2005. "Baton Rouge a Booming Haven for the Displaced." *Los Angeles Times*. September 7.

Musick, M. 1999. "Union Carbide: A Case of Environmental Disregard and Disrespect." Available at http://www.bhopal.net/oldsite/oldwebsite/musick.html (accessed June 28, 2008).

NAACP Legal Defense and Education Fund. 2010. *Holt v. Scovill*. News Update. Available at http://naacpldf.org/case/holt-v-scovill (accessed June 5, 2011).

National Advisory Commission on Civil Disorders. 1968. *Report of the National Advisory Commission on Civil Disorders*. New York: E. P. Dutton.

National Black Business Council. 1996. "National Black Business Council Fact Sheet 1996."

National Fair Housing Alliance. 2005. "No Home for the Holidays: Report on Housing Discrimination Against Hurricane Katrina Survivors—Executive Summary." Washington, DC: NFHA, December 20. Available at http://www.nationalfairhousing.org/html/Press%20Releases/Katrina/Hurricane%20Katrina%20Survivors%20-%20Report.pdf (accessed June 1, 2008).

National Institute of Environmental Health Sciences. No date. *Environmental Diseases from A to Z*. NIH Publication No. 96-4145. Available at http://www.niehs.nih.gov/health/topics/agents/lead/index.cfm (accessed June 19, 2008).

National Oceanic and Atmospheric Administration. 2010. "NOAA Expands Fishing Closed Area in Gulf of Mexico." *NOAANews*. July 4, 2010. Available at http://www.noaanews.noaa.gov/stories2010/20100704_closure.html (accessed Jul7 22, 2010).

National Transportation Safety Board. 1998. Hazardous Materials Accident Brief, Accident NTSB Abstract HZB-98/01. Available at http://www.ntsb.gov/publictn/1998/HZB9801.htm (accessed June

National Weather Service. 2002. Elba Alabama Levee Dedication. Southern Regional Headquarters. May 13. Available at http://www.srh.noaa.gov/tlh/hydro/Elba_Levee_Dedication/Elba_Levee_Dedication.htm (accessed June 24, 2008).

Natural Resources Defense Council. 2011. "Press Release." December 8. Available at http://www.nrdc.org/media/2011/111208.asp (accessed December 15, 2011).

Naughton, K., and M. Hosenball. 2005. "Cash and 'Cat 5' Chaos." *Newsweek*. September 26, 36.

Neighbors, H. W., M. A. Musick, and D. R. Williams. 1998. "The African American Minister: Bridge or Barrier to Mental Health Care?" *Health Education Psychology* 25: 759–77.

Nelson, R. 2005. "Not in My Backyard Cry Holding Up FEMA Trailers." *Times-Picayune*. December 26.

New Orleans Food Policy Advisory Committee. 2008. *Building Healthy Communities: Expanding Access to Fresh Food Retail*. New Orleans, LA: New Orleans Food Policy Advisory Committee.

*New York Times*. 2005. "Time for Chemical Plant Safety." December 27.

Noland, D. 2005. "What Went Wrong; Toxic Train Wreck." April. Available at http://www.popularmechanics.com/technology/transportation/1513937.html (accessed June 28, 2008).

Nossiter, A. 2005. "Thousands of Demolitions Are Likely in New Orleans." *New York Times*. October 2.

O'Donnell, C. 2008. "State Admits Tallevast Pollution Study Way Off Mark." *Herald-Tribune*. March 31.

O'Driscoll, Patrick. 2005. "Cleanup Crews Tackle Katrina's Nasty Leftovers." *USA Today*. December 11.

O'Hanlon, M. E., P. R. Orszag, I. H. Daalder, I. M. Destler, D. Gunter, R. E. Litan, and J. Steinberg. 2002. *Protecting the American Homeland*. Washington, DC: Brookings Institution Press. March.

Oliver, M. O., and T. M. Shapiro. 1995. *Black Wealth/White Wealth: A New Perspective on Racial Inequality*. New York: Routledge.

Ong, B. 2005. "Fractured Families." *Newsweek*. October 6.

Organic Consumers Association. No date. "EPA and Chemical Industry to Study Effects of Known Toxic Chemicals on Children." Available at http://www.organicconsumers.org/epa-alert.htm (accessed June 19, 2008).

Owens, C. 2008. "County Set to Seize Site for Landfill: Will Use Eminent Domain." *Athens Banner-Herald*. May 12.

Oxfam International. 2008. Rethinking Disasters: Why Death and Destruction Is Not Nature's Fault but Human Failure. New Delhi: Oxfam International.

Pace, D. 2005. "Minorities Suffer Most from Industrial Pollution." MSNBC. December 13. Available at http://www.msnbc.msn.com/id/10452037/ (accessed June 30, 2008).

Padgett, D., C. Patrick, B. Burns, and H. Schlesinger. 1995. "Use of Mental Health Services by Black and White Elderly." In *Handbook on Ethnicity, Aging, and Mental Health*, ed. D. Padgett. Westport, CT: Greenwood Press.

Page, A. 1986. "The Union Carbide Institute Plant: The Perception of Risk." Paper presented at the annual meeting of the Society for the Study of Social Problems. New York (August ), 27–30.

Page, S., and M. Puente. 2005. "Poll Shows Racial Divide on Storm Response." *USA Today*. September 13.

Pardo, A. 2006. "The Battle of Chef Menteur: The Movement to Close a New Orleans Landfill Presses On." *Reconstruction Watch*. July 6. Available at http://www.reconstructionwatch.org/index.php?s=20&n=56 (accessed July 15, 2006).

Pastor, M., R. D. Bullard, J. K. Boyce, A. Fothergill, R. Morella-Frosch, and B.Wright. 2006. *In the Wake of the Storm: Environment, Disaster and Race after Katrina*. New York: Russell Sage Foundation.

Patz, J. A., P. L. Kinney, M. L. Bell, R. Goldberg, C. Hogrefe, S. Khoury, K. Knowlton, J. Rosenthal, C. Rosenzweig, and L. Ziska. 2004. *Heat Advisory: How Global Warming Causes More Bad Air Days*. New York: Natural Resource Defense Council.

Paul, P. C. 2005. "You've Got to Make Them Feel Good About Something." *Atlanta Journal-Constitution*. September 18.

Paulson, Jerome A. 2006. "An Exploration of Ethical Issues in Research in Children's Health." *Environmental Health Perspective* 114 (10): 1603–8.

Peacock, W. G., and C. Girard. 1997. "Ethnic and Racial Inequalities in Hurricane Damage and Insurance Settlements." In *Hurricane Andrew: Ethnicity, Gender, and the Sociology of Disasters*, ed. W. G. Peacock, B. H. Morrow, and H. Gladwin. New York: Routledge.

Peacock, W. G., B. H. Morrow, and H. Gladwin. 1992. *Hurricane Andrew: Ethnicity, Gender, and the Sociology of Disasters*. Miami: Florida International University, Laboratory for Social and Behavioral Research. New York: Routledge.

*Pensacola News Journal*. 2003. "Superfund Homes Set for Demolition." November 30, A1.

Pesca, M. 2005. "Are Katrina's Victims 'Refugees' or 'Evacuees'?" NPR.org. September 5. Available at http://www.npr.org/templates/story/story.php?storyId=4833613 (accessed June 19, 2008).

Petersen, L. A. 2002. "Racial Differences in Trust: Reaping What We Have Sown?" *Medical Care* 40 (2): 81–84.

Pickel, M. L. 2005. "Immigrant Workers Rile New Orleans." *Atlanta Journal-Constitution.* October 19.

Pittman, C. 2002. "Storm's Howl Fills the Ears of Survivors." *St. Petersburg Times.* August 18.

*Planet Ark World Environmental News.* 2006. "Texas Probes Oily Residue Near Exxon Refinery."

Planetizen. 2007. "Africa Americans Among First Victims of Subprime Meltdown." March 23. Available at http://www.planetizen.com/node/23382 (accessed December 16, 2011.)

Presser, S. B. 2006. "The Bogalusa Explosion, Single Business Enterprise, Alter Ego, and Other Errors: Academics, Economics, Democracy, and Shareholder Limited Liability: Back Towards a Unitary Abuse Theory of Piercing the Corporate Veil." *Northwestern University Law Review* 100, no. 1: 405–35. Available at http://www.law.northwestern.edu/lawreview/v100/n1/405/LR100n1Presser.pdf.

Prine, C. 2002a. "Lax Security Exposes Lethal Chemical Supplies." *Pittsburgh Tribune-Review.* April 7.

Prine, C. 2002b."Chemicals Pose Risks Nationwide." *Pittsburgh Tribune-Review.* May 5.

Property Deed. 1956. Dickson County, State of Tennessee. September 22.

Pucher J., and J. L. Renne. 2003. "Socioeconomics of Urban Travel: Evidence from the 2001 NHTS." *Transportation Quarterly* 57, no. 3: 49–77.

Puentes, Robert, and Linda Bailey. 2003. *Improving Metropolitan Decision Making in Transportation: Greater Funding and Devolution for Greater Accountability.* Washington, DC: Brookings Institution.

Purvis, Meghan, and Warrant Claflin. 2003. *Needless Risk: Oil Refineries and Hazards Reduction.* University of Pennsylvania Environment Research and Policy Center. Philadelphia: University of Pennsylvania Environment Research and Policy Center.

Quinn, Sandra Crouse, Tammy Thomas, and Carol McAllister. 2005. "Biosecurity and Bioterrorism: Biodefense Strategy, Practice." *Science* 3 (3): 207–15.

Rabito, F. A., L. E. White, and C. Shorter. 2004. "From Research to Policy: Targeting the Primary Prevention of Childhood Lead Poisoning." *Public Health Reports* 119 (May/June).

Raines, B. 2010a. "Alabama Becoming Popular Place to Ship Nation's Garbage." *Alabama Press-Register.* January 17.

Raines, B. 2010b. "BP Buys Gulf Scientists for Legal Defense, Roiling Academic Community." *Alabama Press-Register.* July 16.

Ramirez, L. K. B., E. A. Baker, and M. Metzler. 2008. *Promoting Health Equity: A Resource to Help Communities Address Social Determinants of Health.* Atlanta: U.S. Department of Health and Human Services, Centers for Disease Control and Prevention.

Rampton, S., and J. Stauber. 2001. *Trust Us, We're Experts: How Industry Manipulates Science and Gambles with Your Future.* New York: Jeremy P. Tarcher/Putman.

Randolph, N. 2005. "State Will Suffer Sans N.O." *Advocate.* September 11.

Rawlins, W. 2003. "Dump's Days Fade." *News and Observer.* November 11. Available at http://www.ncwarn.org/media/Related%20News%20Articles/art-11-11-03DumpsDaysFade.htm (accessed December 1, 2004).

Reed, Z. 2005. Graniteville Train Derailment. Available at http://www.zimmreed.com/graniteville-derailment.htm (accessed June 28, 2008).

Reeves, J. 2009. "EPA Allows TVA to Dump Spilled Coal Ash in Alabama: Critics Say Plan Unfair to Some of State's Poorest." *Associated Press.* July 2.

Regional Planning Commission of Orleans. 1969. "History of Regional Growth of Jefferson, Orleans, and St. Bernard Parishes." November, 13.

Remnick, D. 2005. "High Water: How Presidents and Citizens React to Disaster." *The New Yorker.* October 3.

Repsher, C. J. 1994. Letter to Mrs. Ann Sullivan. Tennessee Department of Environment and Conservation. September 8.

Reverby, Susan M. 2000. *Rethinking the Tuskegee Syphilis Study.* Chapel Hill: University of North Carolina Press.

Reynolds, B. 1980. "Triana, Alabama: The Unhealthiest Town in America." *National Wildlife* 18 (August): 33.

Richards, G. 2008. "Norfolk Southern, S.C. Textile Firm Settle in Train Wreck." *Virginia Pilot.* April 8.

Ricketts, T. C., and D. L. Pope. 2002. "Demography and Health Care in Eastern North Carolina." *North Carolina Medical Journal* 62: 20–25.

Ritter, Malcolm. 2008. "John Hopkins Raps AP Story on Lead Experiment." *USA Today.* June 13.

Rivkin, A. C. 2007. "Climate Change Testimony Was Edited by White House." *New York Times.* October 25.

Roberts, D. 1997. *Killing the Black Body: Race, Reproduction and the Meaning of Liberty.* New York: Vintage Books.

Roberts, J. T., and B. Parks. 2006. A Climate of Injustice: Global Inequality, North-South Politics, and Climate Policy. Cambridge, MA: MIT Press.

Robison, C., and S. Levine. 2005. "Perry, White Thrash FEMA." *Houston Chronicle.* November 1.

Roderick, Bill A. 2009. Letter from Bill A. Roderick, Acting EPA Inspector General, to Robert D. Bullard, Director of the Environmental Justice Resource Center at Clark Atlanta University. November 10.

Rose, M. 2008. "Protests Spark New Search for Waste-Transfer Site." *Daily Tar Heel.* January 1.

Rosen, R. 1994. "Who Gets Polluted: The Movement for Environmental Justice." *Dissent* (Spring): 223–30.

Rosenberg, J. M. 2005. "Small Business Loans Help with Rebuilding." *Houston Chronicle.* September 4.

Rosner, D., and G. Markowitz. 1991. *Deadly Dust: Sillicosis and the Politics of Occupational Disease in Twentieth Century America.* Princeton: Princeton University Press.

Russell, G. 2005. "Landfill Reopening Is Raising New Stink." *Times-Picayune.* November 21. Available at http://www.nola.com/news/t-p/frontpage/index.ssf?/base/news-4/1132559045240640.xml (accessed July 2, 2006).

Russell, G. 2006. "Chef Menteur Landfill Testing Called a Farce: Critics Say Debris Proposal 'Would Be a Useless Waste of Time.'" *Times-Picayune.* May 29.

Russell, K. 2009. "Clean Water Laws Are Neglected, at a Cost in Suffering." *New York Times.* September 12.

Rysavy, T. F. 2007. "Environmental Justice for All." *Co-Op America Quarterly.* 73 (Fall):13–19. Available at http://community-wealth-org./pdfs.articles-publications/green/article-rysavy.pdf.

Sanchez, T. A., R. Stolz, and J. Ma. 2003. *Moving to Equity: Addressing Inequitable Effect of Transportation Policies on Minorities.* Cambridge, MA: Civil Rights Project, Harvard University.

Sanders, D. 1992. Memorandum. Tennessee Department of Health and Environment. February 12.

Sapien, J. 2010. "Senior Public Health Official Reassigned in Wake of Congressional Inquiries." *ProPublica.* January 22. Available at http://www.propublica.org/feature/senior-cdc-official-reassigned-howard-frumkin (accessed May 13, 2010).

Satchel, M. 1997. "A Black and Green Issue Moves People." *U.S. News and World Report.* April 21.

Scallan, M. "Gulfport Supervisor Rejects BP's Plan to Use Landfill for Oil Spill Waste." *Biloxi Sun Herald.* June 8.

Schierow, L. 2006. *Chemical Facility Safety.* Congressional Research Service Report to Congress. Washington, DC: Congressional Research Service. August 2.

Schleicher, A. 2005. "School Bells Ring for Children Displaced by Hurricane Katrina." *NewsHour with Jim Lehrer.* September 7. Available at http://www.pbs.org/newshour/extra/features/july-dec05/katrina_9-07.html (accessed June 1, 2008).

Schleifstein, Mark. 2010. "Environmental Justice Concerns Arising from Gulf of Mexico Oil Spill Aired." *Times-Picayune.* June 15.

Schneider, E. C, Alan M. Zaslavsky, and A. M. Epstein. 2002. "Racial Disparities in the Quality of Care for Enrollees in Medicare Managed Care, Mental Illness." *Journal of the American Medical Association* 287 (10): 1288–94.

Schueler, Donald. 1992. "Southern Exposure." *Sierra* 77 (November/December): 45–47.

Schwartz, M. 2002. "Though City Touts Neighborhood Initiatives, Many Have Yet to Bring Substantial Change." *Houston Chronicle.* September 19.

Schwartz, J. 2007. "Army Corps Details Flood Risks Facing New Orleans." *New York Times.* June 20.

Schwartz, S. M. 2007. "Deja Vue, Indeed: The Evolving Story of FEMA's Toxic Trailers." July 16. Available at http://www.toxictrailerscase.com/ (accessed July 17, 2008).

Segrest, M. 2001. *Looking for Higher Ground: Disaster and Response in North Carolina After Hurricane Floyd.* Durham, NC: Urban-Rural Mission.

Shabecoff, P., and A. Shabecoff. 2008. *Poisoned Profits: The Toxic Assault on Our Children.* New York: Random House.

Shane, S. 2010. "F.B.I. Laying Out Evidence, Closes Anthrax Case." *New York Times.* February 19.

Shapiro, T. M., T. Meschede, and L. Sullivan. 2010. *The Racial Wealth Gap Increases Fourfold.* Research and Policy Brief, Brandeis University. May.

Shavers, V. L., C. F. Lynch, and L. F. Burmeister. 2001. "Factors That Influence African Americans' Willingness to Participate in Medical Research Studies." *Cancer* 91 (S1): 233–36.

Shea, D. A. 2005. "Legislative Approaches to Chemical Facility Security." Report to Congress. Washington, DC: Congressional Research Service. July 12.

Shields, G. 2006. "Five Parishes to Receive Help with Debris Cleanup." *Advocate* (Baton Rouge). June 30.

Shipley, S. 1995. "Cochran Fires Up Crowd for Bogalusa Class Action." *Times-Picayune.* November 10, A1.

Shrivastava, P. 1987. *Bhopal: Anatomy of a Crisis.* Cambridge, MA: Ballinger.

Sibley-Butler, J. 1991. *Entrepreneurship and Self-Help Among Black Americans: A Reconsideration of Race and Economics.* Albany: State University of New York Press.

Simmons, A. S. 2006. "New Orleans Activists Starting from the Ground Up." *Los Angeles Times.* March 24.

Simms, A. 2005. "Unnatural Disasters." *The Guardian.* October 15. Available at http://www.guardian.co.uk/climatechange/story/0,12374,1063181,00.html (Accessed June 30, 2008).

Simms, A. 2005. "Unnatural Disasters." *The Guardian.* October 15. Available at http://www.guardian.co.uk/climatechange/story/0,12374,1063181,00.html (Accessed June 30, 2008).

Sisk, T. 2007a. "Patterns Emerge on Race and Environment." *Carrboro Citizen.* November 15.

Sisk, T. 2007b. "The Grassroots of Environmental Justice." *Carrboro Citizen.* November 8.

Skidmore, H. 1941. *Hawk's Nest.* New York: Doubleday.

Smedley, B. D., A. Y. Smith, and A. R. Nelson. 2002. *Unequal Treatment: Confronting Racial and Ethnic Disparities in Healthcare.* Washington, DC: National Academy of Sciences.

Smith, C. 1999. "African Americans and the Medical Establishment." *Mount Sinai Journal of Medicine* 66 (4): 280–81.

Smith, N. 2005. "There Is No Such Thing as a Natural Disaster." *Understanding Katrina: Perspectives from the Social Sciences.* New York: Social Science Research Council.

Smith, S. L., and C. Clous. 1997. "Documenting Discrimination by Homeowners Insurance Companies Through Testing." In *Insurance Redlining: Disinvestment, Reinvestment, and the Evolving Role of Financial Institutions,* ed. Gregory D. Squires. Washington, DC: Urban Institute.

Snyder, M.. 2002. "Neglected Neighborhoods: Hasty Annexations Left a Legacy of Blighted Neighborhoods." *Houston Chronicle.* November 19.

Sole, M. W. 2004. Letter to Winston Smith, Director, Waste Management Division, U.S. Environmental Protection Agency. June 29. Available at http://www.dep.state.fl.us./secretary/news/2004/tal/epa_letter.pdf (accessed June 25, 2008).

Solomon, G. M., and M. Rotkin-Ellman. 2006. "Contaminants in New Orleans Sediments: An Analysis of EPA Data." New York: Natural Resource Defense Council. February. Available at http://www.nrdc.org/health/effects/katrinadata/sedimentepa.pdf (accessed July 1, 2006).

Solow, B. 2004. "Cracks in the System," *Independent Weekly.* September 8. Available at http://indyweek.com/durham/2004-09-08/cover.html (accessed June 22, 2008).

Sorg, Lisa. 2006. "Not a Drop to Drink." *San Antonio Current.* May 3.

South Carolina State Emergency Operations Center. 2005. *Aiken County/Graniteville Train Derailment. Situation Report #1.* January 6. Available at http://www.scemd.org/news/sitreps/graniteville-05/Graniteville_train_wreck1-010605.pdf (accessed June 28, 2008).

Spake, A. 2007. "Dying for a Home: Toxic Trailers Are Making Katrina Refugees Ill." *Nation.* February 15. Available at http://www.alternet.org/katrina/48004/ (accessed July 17, 2008).

Spangler, P. 2008. *The Hawks Nest Tunnel.* Proctorville, OH: Wythe-North.

Spies, S. 2007. "Nelson Rethinks Waste Site Decision." *News Observer.* October 27.

Spriggs, M. 2004. "Canaries in the Mines: Children, Risk, Non-Therapeutic Research, and Justice." *Journal of Medical Ethics* 30 (2): 176–81.

Squires, G. 1996a. "Policies of Prejudice: Risky Encounters with the Property Insurance Business." *Challenge* 39. July.

Squires, G. 1996b. "Race and Risk: The Reality of Redlining." *National Underwriter (Property and Casualty/Risk and Benefits Management)* 100 (September 16): 63, 70.

Squires, G. 1998. "Forgoing a Tradition of Redlining for a Future of Reinvestment." *Business Journal Serving Greater Milwaukee* 15. July 24.

Stack, Carol B. 1997. Call to Home: African Americans Reclaim the Rural South. New York: Basic Books.

Starkman, D. 2005. "Same Insurance Claims, Different Results in La. Town." *Washington Post.* November 26.

Starr, M., M. Hager, W. J. Cook, and C. Friday. 1985."America's Toxic Tremors." *Newsweek.* August 26, 18–19.

State Farm Insurance. 2005. "State Farm: Hurricane Katrina Claims Top 200,000." September 8. Available at http://www.statefarm.com/media/release/hurr_katrina2.asp (accessed June 1, 2008).

Steelfisher, Gillian K. 2004. "Addressing Unequal Treatment." *Issue Brief* (November). Prepared for the Commonwealth Fund and the John F. Kennedy School of Government Bipartisan Congressional Health Policy Conference, January 15–17. Available at http://www.commonwealthfund.org/usr_doc/SteelFisher_unequaltreatment_cong2004_709.pdf?section=4039 (accessed June 19, 2008).

Steinberg, T. 2003. *Acts of God: The Unnatural History of Natural Disasters in America.*New York: Oxford University Press.

Sturgis, S. 2009. "Dumping in Dixie: TVA Sends Toxic Coal Ash to Poor Black Communities in Georgia and Alabama." *Facing South.* May 12. Available at http://southernstudies.org/2009/05/tva-sends-spilled-coal-ash-to-impoverished-black-communities-in-georgia-and-alabama.html (accessed May 14, 2010).

Sullivan, B. 2005. "FEMA Grants Leave Some Behind." MSNBC. October 19. Available at http://www.msnbc.msn.com/id/9655113 (accessed June 1, 2008).

Sullivan Commission on Diversity in the Healthcare Workforce. 2004. U.S. Health Care Professions Separate and Unequal: Sullivan Commission—Lack of Diversity May Be Greatest Cause of Health Disparities. Durham, NC: Sullivan Commission, Duke University School of Medicine (September).

Sullivan, L. 1991. Remarks at the first annual conference on childhood lead poisoning. In *Preventing Child Lead Poisoning:Final Report.*Washington, DC: Alliance to End Childhood Lead Poisoning (October).

Surface Transportation Policy Project. 2000. "Mean Streets 2000: Pedestrian Safety, Health and Federal Transportation Spending." Progress, June/July, 2. Available at http://www.transact.org/report.asp?id=181

Tanneeru, M. 2005. "It's Official: 2005 Hurricanes Blew Records Away." *CNN.com.* December 30. Available at http://www.cnn.com/2005/WEATHER/12/19/hurricane.season.ender/ (accessed June 22, 2008).

Taylor, R. J., L. M. Chatters, and J. Levin. 2004. *Religion in the Lives of African Americans: Social, Psychological, and Health Perspectives.* Thousand Oaks, CA: Sage.

Tennessee Department of Environment and Conservation. No date. "Community Meeting Questions and Answers." December 3. Available at http://www.state.tn.us/environment/swm/ppo/response.pdf (accessed December 3, 2006).

Tennessee Valley Authority. 2009. Off-Site Ash Disposal Options Analysis Work Plan. June 30.

Tennessean. 2011. "NRDC: $5M to Benefit County." Available at http://www.tennessean.com/article/20111209/DICKSON01/312080103/Settlement-final-Holt-Orsted-says-restores-right-clean-water. (accessed December 15, 2011).

Tetra Tech EM. 2004. Dickson County Landfill Reassessment Report. A Report Prepared for the U.S. EPA, Region IV. Atlanta. March 4.

Thomas, C. B. 2005."Hurricane Katrina: The Cleanup." *Time*. November 28.

Thompson, P. 1993. Letter to Claudia Brand. ICF Kaiser. August 31, 1–2.

Tibbetts, J. 2006. "Louisiana's Wetlands: A Lesson in Nature Appreciation." *Environmental Health Perspective* 114 (January): A40–A43.

Tilove, J. 2005. "Saved by Its Own History, Oldest Black Town Celebrates Birthday." *Newhouse News Service*. February 17. Available athttp://www.newhousenews.com/archive/tilove021705.html (accessed June 22, 2008).

Torry, S. 1999. "Lead Paint: The Next Big Legal Target." *Washington Post*. June 10, A1.

Transportation for America and Transportation Equity Network. 2009. *Stranded at the Station: The Impact of the Financial Crisis in Public Transportation*. Washington, DC: Transportation Equity Network. August.

Treadway, T. 2007. "Formaldehyde Testing on Travel Trailers to Start in September, FEMA Tells Hastings, Mahoney." August 23. Available at http://www.tcpalm.com/news/2007/aug/23/congressmen-question-fema-availability-travel-trai/ (accessed July 17, 2008).

Treaster, J. B. 2005. "Gulf Coast Insurance Expected to Soar." *New York Times*. September 24.

Trocheck, K. 1980. "Savannah Residents Angered by Army's '56 Mosquito Test." *Atlanta Journal*. November 10.

Tyler, A. 1982. *Dust to Dust, the Hawk's Nest Tunnel Tragedy*. New York: Gallery.

Uchitelle, L. 2005. "Jobs Surged Last Month in Rebound from Storm." *New York Times*. December 3.

Union Carbide. 1998. *Responsible Care Progress Report*. Danbury, CT: Union Carbide Corporation.

Union of Concerned Scientists. 2011. "Climate Change and Your Health: Rising Temperatures, Worsening Ozone Pollution." June. Washington, DC: UCS.

United Church of Christ Commission for Racial Justice. 1987. *Toxic Wastes and Race in the United States*. New York: UCC Commission for Racial Justice.

United Nations Counter-Terrorism Implementation Task Force. 2011. Interagency Coordination in the Event of a Terrorist Attack Using Chemical or Biological Weapons or Materials. Report of the Working Group on Preventing and Responding to Weapons of Mass Destruction Attacks. New York: United Nations. Available at http://www.un.org/en/terrorism/ctitf/pdfs/ctitf_wmd_working_group_report_interagency_2011.pdf.

U.S. Army Corps of Engineers. 2006. "Questions and Answers: Hurricane Recovery and Levee Issues." January 18. Available at http://www.mvn.usace.army.mil/tgf/Q&A01.htm (accessed July 1,

U.S. Army Corps of Engineers Interagency Performance Evaluations Task Force. 2007. Risk and Reliability Report. June 20. Available at http://nolarisk.usace.army.mil/ (accessed July 1, 2008).

U.S. Bureau of the Census. 2000. "State and County Quick Facts." Available at http://quickfacts.census.gov/qfd/states/47/47043.html (accessed December 1, 2006).

U.S. Bureau of the Census. 2002a. "Numbers of Americans with and without Health Insurance Rise, Census Bureau Reports." September 30.

U.S. Bureau of the Census. 2002b. "Survey of Minority-Owned Business Enterprises." Washington, DC: U.S. Bureau of the Census.

U.S. Department of Homeland Security. 2006. "National Plan Review Phase 2 Report." Washington, DC: DHS. June 16.

U.S. Department of Housing and Urban Development. 2009. "Subprime Lending Report. Unequal Burden: Subprime Lending in Atlanta Income and Racial Disparities in Subprime Lending." Available at http://archives.hud.gov/reports/subprime/subpratl.cfm (accessed December 17, 2011).

U.S. Department of Housing and Urban Development and U. S. Department of Treasury Joint Task Force. 2000. "Curbing Predatory Home Mortgage Lending." Washington, DC: U.S. Department of Housing and Urban Development and U.S. Department of Treasury.

U.S. Department of Justice. 2008. Proposed Consent Decree: *United States of America v. City of New Orleans et al.* June 16. Available at http://www.usdoj.gov/enrd/Consent_Decrees/City_New_Orleans/r_City_Of_New_Orleans_Consent_DecreeFinal.pdf (accessed June 19, 2008).

U.S. Environmental Protection Agency. 1983. "Report of the Dallas Area Lead Assessment Study." Dallas, TX: U.S. Environmental Protection Agency Region IV, 8.

U.S. Environmental Protection Agency. 1992. "Koppers Site Update: EPA Announces Amended Record of Decision for Site." March 5.

U.S. Environmental Protection Agency. 2000. "Assessment of the Incentive by Public Disclosure of Off-Site Consequences Analysis Information for Reduction in the Risk of Accidental Releases." Washington, DC: U.S. Environmental Protection Agency. April 18.

U.S. Environmental Protection Agency. 2005. "RSR Corp. (Murph Metals) Texas." U.S. Environmental Protection Agency Region VI (April 13), 8. Available at http://www.epa.gov/docs/region06/6sf/pdffiles/0602297.pdf#search='west%20dallas%20superfund%20site%20cleanup%20epa%202005 (accessed June 19, 2008).

U.S. Environmental Protection Agency. 2006a. "Preliminary Observations and Recommendations, Panola County, TX Ground Water Contamination OIG Complaint #2004-059." July 6.

U.S. Environmental Protection Agency. 2006b. "Release of Multi-Agency Report Shows Elevated Lead Levels in New Orleans Soil, Consistent with Historic Levels of Urban Lead," *EPA Newsroom.* March 4. Available at http://yosemite.epa.gov/opa/admpress.nsf/o/BA5F2460D6C777F58525714600693B5B (accessed July 17, 2008).

U.S. Environmental Protection Agency. 2007a. "Complete Assessment Needed to Ensure Rural Texas Community Has Safe Drinking Water." Dallas, TX: Office of Inspector General, Report No. 2007-P-00034. September 11.

U.S. Environmental Protection Agency. 2007b. "Human and Ecological Risk Assessment of Coal Combustion Wastes (Draft)." Research Triangle Park, NC: Research Triangle Institute, August 6. Available at http://wvrhrc.hsc.wvu.edu/docs/2009-05-12_human_and_ecological_risk_assessment_of_coal_combustion_wastes.pdf.

U.S. Environmental Protection Agency. 2009a. "Environmental Justice Analysis: Perry County, Alabama." Atlanta, GA: U.S. Environmental Protection Agency Region IV. September 23.

U.S. Environmental Protection Agency. 2009b. "EPA Approves Plan for Disposal of Coal Ash from TVA Kingston Site at the Arrowhead Landfill in Perry County, Alabama." EPA Region IV, Press release. July 1. Available at http://yosemite.epa.gov/opa/admpress. nsf/2ac652c59703a4738525735900400c2c/02ec745d4bba7547852575e700476a8f!OpenDo cument (accessed May 14, 2010).

U.S. Environmental Protection Agency. 2010. "EPA Announces Plans to Regulate Coal Ash." EPA News Release. May 4. Available at http://yosemite.epa.gov/opa/admpress. nsf/docf6618525a9efb85257359003fb69d/4eca022f6f5c501185257719005dfb1b!OpenDocu ment (accessed May 17, 2010).

U.S. . Environmental Protection Agency Research and Development. 2004. "EPA Conducts Study on Young Children's Exposures to Household Chemicals in Duval County, Florida." News release. September 22. Available at http://www.fluoride-alert.org/pesticides/cheers/cheers.epa.news.sept.22.04.htm (accessed June 19, 2008).

U.S. Environmental Protection Agency and Louisiana Department of Environmental Quality. 2005. "Top State and Federal Environmental Officials Discuss Progress and Tasks Ahead After Katrina." News Release. September 30. Available at http://www. deq.state.la.us/news/pdf/administratorjohnson.pdf#search='katrina%20debris%20 350%2C000%20automobiles (accessed July 2, 2006).

U.S. General Accounting Office. 2001. "Bioterrorism: Public Health Response to Anthrax Incidents of 2001." Report to the Honorable Bill Frist, Majority Leader, U.S. Senate. Washington, DC: U.S. General Accounting Office. October.

U.S. General Accounting Office. 2007. "Hurricane Katrina: EPA's Current and Future Environmental Protection Efforts Could Be Enhanced by Addressing Issues and Challenges Faced on the Gulf Coast." Report to Congressional Committees. Washington, DC: U.S. General Accounting Office. June.

U.S. General Accounting Office. 2004. "Homeland Security: Federal Action Needed to Address Security Challenges at Chemical Facilities." Publication GAO-04-482T. Washington, DC: U.S. General Accounting Office. February 23.

U.S. House of Representatives Committee on Science and Technology. "Toxic Trailers— Toxic Lethargy: How the Centers for Disease Control and Prevention Has Failed to Protect the Public Health." Staff Report. September 22, 2008. Available at http:// democrats.science.house.gov/Media/File/Commdocs/ATSDR_Staff_Report_9.22.08. pdf (accessed May 13, 2010).

U.S. Small Buisness Administration.(n.d.) "Fact Sheet About U.S. Small Business Administration (SBA) Disaster Loans." Available at http://www.sbaonline.sba.gov/ide/groups/ public/documents/sba_homepage/serv_dadisastr_loan_factsht.pdf.

USA Today. "October Likely to Be Another Busy Month for Hurricanes." October 4.

Van Heerden, Ivor, and Mike Bryan. 2006. The Storm: What Went Wrong and Why: Hurricane Katrina, The Inside Story from One Louisiana Scientist. New York: Viking.

Varney, J. 2006. "Senators Grill Corps, FEMA: Hearing Details Waste in Relief Spending." Times-Picayune. April 11.

Varney, J., and J. Moller. 2005. "Huge Task of Cleaning Up Louisiana Will Take at Least a Year." *Newhouse News Service*. October 2. Available at http://www.newhousenews.com/archive/varney100305.html (accessed July 2, 2006).

Velliquette, B. 2008. "Sites for Transfer Station Ranked." *Herald-Sun*. June 19.

Waggoner, M. 2000. "Hurricane Floyd Hit Poor Hardest." *Detroit News*. February 16.

Walsh, B. 2007. "Feds Oppose Full Replacement of N.O. Public Housing Units." *Times-Picayune*. September 26.

Warrick, J. 2010. "FBI Investigation of 2001 Anthrax Attacks Concluded, U.S. Releases Details." *Washington Post*. February 20.

Washington, H. A. 2006. *Medical Apartheid: The Dark History of Medical Experimentation on Black Americans from Colonial Times to the Present*. New York: Doubleday.

Weisel, E. 2005. "Without Conscience." *New England Journal of Medicine* 325: 1511–13.

Weisenmiller, M. 2007. "Environment-US: Toxins Threaten to Uproot Entire Town." *IPS-Inter Press Service*. November 1. Available at http://ipsnews.net/news.asp?idnews=39889 (accessed June 25, 2008).

Welborn, V. 2005a. "East Texas Families Fight Contamination of Wells." *Shreveport Times*. August 23.

Welborn, V. 2005b. "Government Agencies Respond to East Texas Residents' Water Woes." *Shreveport Times*. September 12.

Welborn, V. 2006. "Request Leads to Records on Contamination." *Shreveport Times*. March 21.

Welborn, V. 2008. "Bethany Finally Getting Fresh Water." *Shreveport Times*. June 17.

Wellner, A. S. 2005. "No Exit." *Mother Jones*. September 13.

Wellner, C.E., and A. Logan. 2008. *America's Middle Class Still Losing Ground*. July. Washington, DC: Center for American Progress. Available at http://www.americanprogress.org/issues/2008/07/pdf/middleclasssqueeze.pdf (accessed December 17, 2011).

Williams, J. 2003. "Answers: Hurricane Betsy Hits Florida, Smashed New Orleans in 1965." *USA Today*. October 21.

Williams, L. 2006. "Groups Warn About Arsenic in Soil." *Times-Picayune*.

Williams, Timothy. 2011. "Racial Bias Seen in Study of Lead Dust and Children." *New York Times*. September 15.

Willis, G. 2005. "Disaster Relief: 5 Tips: How to Call on the Disaster Relief Resources You Need." *CNN/Money*. September 16. Available at http://money.cnn.com/2005/09/16/pf/saving/willis_tips/ (accessed June 30, 2008).

Wing, S., S. Freedman, and L. Band. 2002. "The Potential of Flooding on Confined Animal Feeding Operations in Eastern North Carolina." *Environmental Health Perspectives* 110, no. 4: 387–91.

Wisner, B., P. Blaikie, T. Cannon, and I. David. 1994. *At Risk: Natural Hazards, People's Vulnerabilities and Disasters*. New York: Routledge.

Witte, G. 2005. "Prevailing Wages to Be Paid Again on Gulf Coast." *Washington Post*. October 27.

Woodall, J. 2008. "Board Lays Out Site Criteria." *Daily Tar Heel*. February 12.

Working Group on Governance Dilemmas in Bioterrorism Response. 2004. "Leading During Bioattacks and Epidemics with the Public's Trust and Help." *Biosecurity Bioterrorism* 2, no. 1: 25–40.

World Combined Sources. 2004. "EPA Pays Families to Expose Kids to Pesticides." *People's Weekly World Newspaper*. November 4. Available at http://www.pww.org/article/articleprint/6060/ (accessed June 19, 2008).

Worldwatch Institute. 2003. "Fact Sheet: The Impacts of Weather and Climate Change." September 23. Available at http://www.worldwatch.org/press/news/2003/09/15/ (accessed June 22, 2008).

Worldwatch Institute. 2005. "Unnatural Disaster: The Lessons of Katrina." September 2. Available at http://www.worldwatch.org/press/news/2005/09/02 (Accessed June 30, 2008).

Yago, G., and A. Pankratz. 2000. *The Minority Business Challenge: Democratizing Capital for Emerging Domestic Markets*. Los Angeles: Milken Institute, U.S. Department of Commerce, Minority Business Development Agency. September 25.

Yen, H. 2005. "Minority Firms Getting Few Katrina Pacts." *Business Week*. October 4.

Yinger, J. 1995. *Closed Doors, Opportunity Lost: The Continuing Cost of Housing Discrimination*. New York: Russell Sage Foundation.

Yinger, J. 1999. "Sustaining the Fair Housing Act." *Cityscape: A Journal of Policy Development and Research* 4: 93–105.

# Index

9/11 attacks, 198

21st Century Youth Leadership Project, 222

*Acts of God* (Steinberg), 47

Adams, George, 120

affordable housing, 221–222

African Americans: Agency for Toxic Substances and Disease Registry (ATSDR), suspicions of, 102; air quality, 3; asthma, deaths from, 54; biological weapons testing on, 186–187, 233; "Black Belt," percent of population in, 5; black/white wealth gap, 217–218; BP Deepwater Horizon oil spill cleanup jobs, 173, 224; car ownership, 210; climate change, 51–52; compensation for losses, 232; confined animal feeding operations (CAFOs), 69; Congress, seats held in, 6; elected officials, number of, 6; environmental problems facing, 177; farmers, 67–69, 130–131; Federal Emergency Management Agency (FEMA), 188, 222; in fenceline communities (*see* fenceline communities); "food deserts," 92; hazardous waste sites, 23; health care, 181–183, 206–207; health insurance, 226–227; high-cost loans, 219–220; home ownership, 12–13, 218; Housing and Urban Development (HUD), 222; Hurricane Betsy (1965), 60; industrial pollution, 231; insurance, 75, 230; land ownership, 67–68; living standards following disasters, 217; marginalization of, 25; mental health, 215–216; middle-income, 19–20; mistrust of agencies staffed largely by whites, 216; mistrust of Agency for Toxic Substances and Disease Registry (ATSDR), 102; mistrust of biomedical research, xvii, 184, 233; mistrust of Centers for Disease Control and Prevention (CDC), 59; mistrust of environmental cleanup, 233; mistrust of Environmental Protection Agency (EPA), 59; mistrust of Federal Emergency Management Agency (FEMA), 59; mistrust of flu shots, 187–188; mistrust of government, xvii, 28, 41, 59–60, 125, 184, 216–217, 233; mistrust of health care system, 184–185; mistrust of Housing and Urban Development (HUD), 59; mistrust of industrial facility permitting, 233; mistrust of medical establishment, xvii, 188, 233; mistrust of Red Cross, 215, 216–217; mistrust of "war on terrorism," 233; in New Orleans, 31; ozone standards, 54; poisoning of in the South, 7–8; postal workers, 199; posttraumatic stress disorder (PTSD), 210; public transit use, 213; Red Cross, 188, 222; relocation from Archia Court (Baytown, Texas), 167; relocation under Superfund program, 119; reproductive injustice, 185–186; residential segregation, 65; the South, 4–6, 19; sterilization of black women, 185–186, 207; Superfund program, 231; toxic contamination, 102; transportation, 211, 212; unequal protection afforded, 1–2; U.S. Supreme Court, xvi; vulnerability, 65; "wrong complexion for protection," belief in, xvi, 28

Agency for Toxic Substances and Disease Registry (ATSDR): African Americans' mistrust of, 102; to environmental justice leaders, 101; post-Katrina health care and testing, 97; post-Katrina response in New Orleans, 101–102; response to Hurricane Katrina (2005), 98, 188; security at chemical plants, 202–203

confined animal feeding operations (CAFOs), 69

Congress. *See* U.S. Congress

Congressional Black Caucus Foundation (CBCF), 51–52

Congressional Research Service, 79, 202

construction and demolition (C&D) land-fills: Dickson County, Tennessee, 127, 130; post-Katrina New Orleans, 80–81

Cooler, Dan, 202

COP15 (15th annual UN Climate Change Conference, Copenhagen, 2009), xviii

COP16 (16th annual UN Climate Change Conference, Cancun, 2010), xviii

Corexit dispersant, 172

Corps of Engineers (COE): Carver Terrace contamination (Texarkana), 116–117; Escambia relocation, 119; Executive Order 12898, 96; Fort Worth District, 116; Lake Okeechobee dike, 58–59; minority businesses, 224; New Orleans East landfill, 80; post-Katrina dem-onstration cleanup project, 35–36, 37; Princeville Dike, North Carolina, 70, 71; retrofitting and rebuilding levees, 50, 71, 93–94; toxic contamination in Triana, Alabama, 105

Cotton States insurance company, 228

crisis response teams, 216

Crossroads Ministry, 222

CSX White Bluff derailment cleanup, 129, 152

Curseen, Joseph, Jr., 199

Cutter, Susan L., 50

Dallas, Texas: East Oak Cliff, 107, 108; George Loving Place public hous-ing project, 108; lead contamination, 106–109; Maro Booth Day Care Center, 108; NFHA race-based discrimination complaint against, 220; West Dallas, 106–109; West Dallas Boys Club, 108

Dallas Health Department, 107, 109

*Dallas Morning News* (newspaper), 99, 108

Daschle, Tom, 198

Davis-Bacon Act, 224

DeBerry, Texas, 120–123

deed restrictions, 14, 63

Deep South Center for Environmental Justice (DSCEJ): founding, 32; Hurricane Katrina (2005), xvi; Minority Worker Training Program, 33; National Institute of Environmental Health Sciences (NIEHS), 33; Natural Resources Defense Council (NRDC), 32; programs, 32–33; Safe Way Back Home project, 33, 35, 85–86

deepwater drilling moratorium, 45

DeKalb County, Georgia, 5, 212

Delta By-Products, Inc., 114

Delta insurance company, 230

*dichloro-diphenyl-tricloroethane* (DDT), 105–106

dichloroethylene (DCE), 143

Dickson, Tennessee, 130–142, 145–147; dif-ferential treatment of blacks and whites, 146–147; environmental racism, 130–131, 145–146; Holt family lawsuit against, 138–139, 147; Jim Crow, 127; settlement agreement, 147; treatment of black fami-lies, 131–139; treatment of white families, 139–142. *See also* Holt family

Dickson County, Tennessee: apology to Holt family, 147; "cleft lip/palate cluster" in, 138–139; NIMBY (Not in My Back Yard), 142; PIBBY (Place in Blacks' Back Yard ), 130; policy recommendations, 148–149; taxes, 127

Dickson County Circuit Court, 138

Dickson County Commissioners, 148, 154

Dickson County landfill, 126–155; balefills, 128, 129; cadmium, 129; *Chronology of Events–Dickson County Landfill* (EPA), 134, 152–155; contaminated water, 132–133; CSX White Bluff derailment cleanup, 129; *Dickson County Landfill Reassessment Report* (EPA), 129; Ebbtide Corporation (Winner Boats), 129; Envi-ronmental Protection Agency (EPA), 129, 135–136, 137, 148; environmental rac-ism, 127; government response to, 233; Holt family nearness to, 137; industrial waste solvents, 129; leachate, 129–130;

founders, 9; goals, 7; impact, 21; influence, 25; King, Martin Luther, Jr., 11; leaders' view of Agency for Toxic Substances and Disease Registry (ATSDR), 101; leaders' view of Environmental Protection Agency, 101; National People of Color Environmental Leadership Summit, First (1991), 21; National People of Color Environmental Leadership Summit, Second (2002), 22; National Wildlife Federation (NWF), 18; Obama administration, 178; organizations supporting, 20; the South, 4–7; trigger, 110; Warren County, North Carolina, 17, 110, 130

Environmental Justice Resource Center (EJRC), xvi, 22–23, 101

environmental justice statutes: District of Columbia, 22; New Hampshire, 22; state passing, number of, 22

environmental policies, Southern, 6

environmental protection: dominant paradigm, 3–4; environmental justice framework, 3–4, 24, 192–193; risk, 3–4

Environmental Protection Agency (EPA): African Americans' mistrust of, 59; Agriculture Street landfill site inspection, 113; asbestos emissions standards, 96; Children's Environmental Exposure Research Study (CHEERS), 196–197; *Chronology of Events–Dickson County Landfill*, 134, 152–155; collusion with state environmental agencies, 103, 104–105; creation, 103; cumulative risk assessment in facility permitting, 180; Dickson County landfill, 135–136, 137, 148; *Dickson County Landfill Reassessment Report*, 129, 136, 140; East Baltimore childhood lead paint experiment, 194; environmental justice (EJ), 174; environmental justice leaders, 178; to environmental justice leaders, 101; Escambia Wood Treating Superfund site, 119; Executive Order 12898, 96, 176; fertilizer made from sewage sludge, 195; Hall Gaffney Learning Center inspection, 164; Holt-Orsted, Sheila, 150–151; Koppers Superfund site, 116; lead contamina-

tion in West Dallas, Texas, 106–107, 109; "Mount Dioxin" (Pensacola), 118–119; National Ambient Air Quality Standard, 107; National Environmental Justice Advisory Council (NEJAC), 21, 119, 173; Natural Resources Defense Council (NRDC), 32; Nixon, Richard, 103; under Obama administration, 104; Office of Inspector General (OIG) investigation of, 103; Office of Solid Waste and Emergency Response (OSWER), 169, 173, 177; Office on Environmental Equity, 21; ozone standards, 54; "Perry County Environmental Justice Analysis," 169; post-Katrina clean bill of health, 114; post-Katrina demonstration cleanup project, 33, 34–36, 37–39, 79–80, 85–87; post-Katrina soil contamination, 87, 88–89; record of decision (ROD) (1988), 116; Region IV, 101, 102–103, 129, 168–169; Region VI Emergency Response, 120; relocation of African Americans under Superfund program, 119; response to environmental and civil rights complaints, 104–105; response to Hurricane Katrina (2005), 98; safe drinking water, 122–123; saltwater injection wells in DeBerry, Texas, 122; Sumter County hazardous waste landfill, 103–104; Superfund laws, enforcement of, 100–105; Tennessee Valley Authority (TVA) coal ash spill (2008-2009), 169–170; Title VI complaints, 104–105; Toxics Inventory Release (TRI), 205; trichloroethylene (TCE), 133

"environmental racism" (the term), 130

environmental racism: *Bean v. Southwestern Waste Management Corp.*, 15–16; book publishing industry, 18; Dickson, Tennessee, 130–131, 145–146; Dickson County landfill, 127; EPA Region IV, 168–169; Gaylord Chemical Company tank car accident (1995), 162; Hawk's Nest Tunnel construction deaths from silicosis, 159; Hurricane Alicia (1983), 60–64; solid-waste facilities, siting of, 14; Warren County (Afton) PCB landfill, 111–112

environmental refugees, number of, 48
environmental rights and civil rights, 17
epidemics, discriminatory policies during, 187
*Erika Grimes v. Kennedy Krieger Institute, Inc.,* 195
Escambia County Commission, 119
Escambia Treating Company (ETC), 118
Escambia Wood Treating site ("Mount Dioxin"), 119
ethnicity, 65, 209
evacuation planning: carrels and "special needs" populations, 211–212; differential treatment in, 161–162, 163–164, 210; private transportation, 213
Executive and Administrative Schedule (EAS), 199
Executive Order 12898: Clinton, Bill, 21, 176; Corps of Engineers (COE), 96; environmental justice leaders, 178; environmental justice movement, 21; Environmental Protection Agency (EPA), 96; Federal Emergency Management Agency (FEMA), 96; National Environmental Policy Act (NEPA), 21–22; New Orleans, post-Katrina, 96; Tennessee Valley Authority (TVA) coal ash spill (2008-2009), 169
expanded site inspection (ESI) of Agriculture Street landfill, 113
extended producer responsibility (EPR), 179
Exxon Valdez oil spill (1989), 45, 171
ExxonMobil Baytown refinery gas spill (2006), 156, 165–167

FBI, 200–201
Federal Emergency Management Agency (FEMA): African Americans, 188, 222; African Americans' mistrust of, 59; emergency cash grants, 224–225; Executive Order 12898, 96; FEMA trailers, 89–91, 101–102, 115, 221; flood coverage estimates, 229; Hazardous Mitigation Fund, 95; help from, 28; housing and aid for African Americans, 222; minor-

ity businesses, 224; mistrust of, 215; post-Katrina cleanup, 79; post-Katrina demonstration cleanup project, 34, 35–36; post-Katrina grants, 74; post-Katrina infrastructure allocation, 84–85; President's Council on the Future of Princeville, North Carolina, 71; Princeville Recovery Plan, 71; Project Impact, 210; top catastrophic disasters, 209
federal farm loan and assistance program, racism in, 69
Federal Procurement Data System (FPDS), 173
Federation of Southern Cooperatives, 68
fenceline communities: African Americans, 7; chemical facilities/plants, 201, 203, 208; clean production, 208; green chemistry, 208; industrial accidents, 156, 176; the South, 7
fenceline community performance bonds, 180
fertilizer made from sewage sludge, 195
flood coverage, 229
floods: deliberate flooding, 60; economic mobility, 11/; Elba, Alabama, 11; human activity, 71; Hurricane Betsy (1965), 41, 59; Hurricane Floyd (1999), 70; post-Katrina New Orleans, 94; poverty, 11; Princeville, North Carolina, 70–72; tropical storm Alberto (1994), 66–67; wetlands and marshes, 43
Florida: African Americans' reverse migration to, 5; biological weapons testing on black citizens, 186; Carver Village (Miami), 186, 233; differential treatment of remains of black and white storm victims, 58; Duval County, 196–197; Fort Lauderdale, 211; Gainesville, 220; home insurance, 229; Hoover dike, 59; Hurricane Andrew (1992), 65, 230; Hurricane Dennis (2005), 221; Lake Okeechobee, 57, 58–59; Miami, 211; Okeechobee Hurricane (1928), 57–59; Palm Beach County, 57; Pensacola, 118–119; pesticide tests on children, 196–197; Springhill Regional Landfill, 175

Housing Authority of New Orleans (HANO), 81, 113, 114

Houston, 13–17; Acres Homes neighborhood, 16; black neighborhoods, 16–17; Bordersville, 60–62; carless population, 211; Community Development Block Grant (CDBG) program, 61; deed restrictions, 14, 63; Fifth Ward, 60; Fourth Ward, 15, 63; garbage incinerators, siting of, 15, 62–63; Hispanics, 62–63; landfills, siting of, 15, 62, 63; "Mount Trashmore," 12; mountains in, 13; no zoning policy, 13–14, 62; nonresidential facilities, siting of, 14, 63–64; North Forest Independent School district, 12; Northeast Community Action Group (NECAG), 12; Northwood Manor subdivision, 12–13, 16, 20; "pibby" (Place in Blacks' Back Yard ), 14; residential services, 16; Second Ward ("Segundo Barrio"), 15, 63; security at chemical plants, 203; solid-waste facilities, siting of, 14–15, 17, 62; South Main, 60; South Park, 60; Sunnyside, 60, 62; "super neighborhoods," 16; Third Ward, 60; Trinity Gardens neighborhood, 14; waste disposal facilities, siting of, 64; Whispering Pines landfill, 12, 13, 16

*Houston Chronicle* (newspaper), 16, 203

Houston-Galveston area, Hurricane Alicia (1983), 60–64

Houston Super Neighborhood Program, 16

Hudson, David, 121, 122

Humane Society of Dickson County, 137

hurricanes: 2005 season, 55; deaths from, 55; differential treatment of remains of black and white storm victims, 58; emergency responses to, 55

Hurricane Alex (2010), 45

Hurricane Alicia (1983), 60–64

Hurricane Andrew (1992), 65, 230

Hurricane Betsy (1965): African Americans, 60; Agriculture Street landfill, 37, 113; deliberate flooding, 60; floods, 41, 59; government response to, 42; government response to disasters, 59; Hurri-

cane Katrina (2005) compared to, 41–42; legal challenge, 59; New Orleans, 27–28, 37, 40–42, 59–60; Schiro, Victor, 60

Hurricane Camille (1969), 42

Hurricane Dennis (2005), 54, 221

Hurricane Floyd (1999), 69–72

Hurricane Hugo (1989), 64

Hurricane Ivan (2004), 42

Hurricane Katrina (2005): carless population, 211; damages, extent in square miles, xv; damages, lasting, xviii; death toll, 55; debris from, 79; Deep South Center for Environmental Justice (DSCEJ), xvi; displacement, 54; economic losses, 229; emergency transportation, 213; evacuees, 221; evacuees in Atlanta, xvi; government response to, xvi, 33–35, 36, 37–39, 43–44, 98–99, 188, 201–202; Gulf Coast, 8; homes destroyed by, 31; Hurricane Betsy (1965) compared to, 41–42; impact's scale, 48; insurance companies, collapse of small, 230; insured losses, 229; jobless rate for returnees, 77; "Katrina Cottages," 90–91; loan denials, 225–226; Louisiana, 221; New Orleans, xv–xvi, 8, 24–25, 28–32, 41–42, 73–74, 189, 223 (*see also* New Orleans, post-Katrina); payroll of affected areas, 224; personal experience of, author's, 28–32; poverty, 52; public transit use, 213; social vulnerability, 8

*Hurricane Katrina* (GAO), 88

*Hurricane Katrina* report (GAO), 36

"hurricane party," 42

Hurricane Rita (2005), 54, 84, 85, 211, 231

Hurricane Wilma (2005), 211, 231

Hurston, Zora Neale, 58

*In the Wake of the Storm* (Russell Sage Foundation), 73–74

*In Their Own Words* (Rand Corporation), 199–200

Indiana, 7

industrial accidents, 156–180; ammonium nitrate explosion (Texas City, 1947), 159; Arrowhead landfill, 168–170;

industrial accidents (*continued*)
BP Deepwater Horizon oil spill (2010)
(*see* BP Deepwater Horizon oil spill);
chlorine gas, 163; clean production,
178, 179; cumulative risk assessment
in facility permitting, 180; extended
producer responsibility (EPR), 179;
ExxonMobil Baytown refinery gas spill
(2006), 156, 165–167; fenceline communities, 156, 176; fenceline community performance bonds, 180; Gauley
Bridge, West Virginia, mine disaster
(1930), 156, 157–160; Gaylord Chemical
Company tank car accident (1995), 156,
160–163; Good Neighbor Agreements,
179; Hawk's Nest Tunnel construction deaths from silicosis, 157–160;
nitrogen tetroxide, 160–161; Norfolk
Southern Railway train wreck (2005),
156, 163–165; persistent, bioaccumulative, and toxic pollutants (PBTs), phase
out of, 178; policy recommendations,
178–180; process gas oil (PGO), 165;
right-to-know, community and worker,
179; safety data for all chemicals,
179–180; safety permits, 180; silicosis,
158–159; Tennessee Valley Authority
(TVA) coal ash spill (2008-2009), 156,
167–171; waste reduction legislation, 179
industrial chemical releases, 204
industrial pollution, 101, 231
Institute, West Virginia, 160
Institute for Southern Studies, 6
Institute of Medicine (IOM), 182–183, 209
Institute on Assets and Social Policy, 217
insurance, 226–231; African Americans, 75,
226–227, 230; Asians/Pacific Islanders,
227; claims, 227; collapse of small companies after Katrina, 230; flood coverage,
229; health insurance, 226–227; Hispanics, 227; homeowners and rental insurance, 227, 229; premiums, 227, 228–229;
property insurance, 228; redlining,
227; secondary insurance markets, 230;
settlement amounts, 227; white-collar
insurance "looting," 230

"Insurance: Is It Still a White Man's
Game?" (Emling), 228
Intergovernmental Panel on Climate
Change (IPCC), 52
*Invisible Houston* (Bullard), 60
IPC, Inc., 114
Ivins, Bruce E., 200

Jackson, Lisa P., 102, 169, 173, 177
Jefferson Davis Parish Landfill, 175
Jefferson Parish Sanitary Landfill, 175
Jim Crow: Dickson, Tennessee, 127; Elba,
Alabama, 10–11; Holt family, 149; legacy
and residuals, 25, 184; Mississippi River
Flood (1927), 56; place, 3; residential
segregation, 65; secondary insurance
markets, 230; Texarkana, Texas, 115;
transportation, 215
*Job Sprawl Revisited* (Brookings Institu-
tion), 213
Johns Hopkins Institutional Review Board
(IRB), 195
Johns Hopkins University, 184, 196
Johnson, Andrew, 67
Johnson, Lyndon, 41
Johnson, Stephen L., 197
Jones, A. W., 60
Jones, James H., 190–191
*Journal of Medical Research*, 195
Judicial Watch, 199

Kanahwa Valley, West Virginia, 202
Kansas City Southern and Illinois Central
railroad, 162
"Katrina Cottages," 90–91
"Katrina ghettos," 221
Kennedy Krieger Institute, 194–195
Kentucky, 7
*Killing the Black Body* (Roberts), 185–186
King, Martin Luther, Jr., 11
Kingston, Tennessee, 170
Kingston Fossil Plant, 167
Kitchens, Ron, 121
Kleinberg, Eliot, 57
Koppers Company, 115
Koppers Superfund site, 116, 117

Maritime Transportation Security Act (MTSA), 203
Martin Luther King Jr./Drew Medical Center (Los Angeles), 189–190
Maryland: African Americans' reverse migration to, 5; Fort Detrick, 186, 198, 200–201; Prince George's County, 5
Maryland Court of Appeals, 194–195
Massachusetts General Hospital, 183
maximum contaminant level (MCL): Dickson County landfill, 129; trichloroethylene (TCE), 133–134, 135, 136, 153–154
McDonald, Gabrielle, 64
McGinn County, Tennessee, 168
*Medical Apartheid* (Washington), 185
Meiburg, A. Stanley, 101
Mellon Institute, 158
Memphis sanitation workers strike, 11
mental health, 215–216
metyl tertiary butyl ether (MTBE), 120
Miami, Florida, 211
Milken Institute, 226
*Miner's Canary, The* (Gunier and Torres), 49
minority businesses, 223–224
Minority Worker Training Program, 33
Mississippi: Biloxi-Gulfport, 223; black population, 223; Central Landfill, 175, 176; Consumer Protection Act, 231; economic performance indicators, 7; FEMA trailers, 89; fenceline communities, 201; flood coverage, 229; Greenville, 56; Mounds Landing, 56; Pecan Grove Landfill, 175, 176; secondary insurance markets, 230
Mississippi River Flood (1927), 55–56, 233
Mississippi River Gulf Outlet Canal (MRGO), 41
Mixon, Judy, 166
Mobile, Alabama, 223
Mock, Brentin, 173
Model Eugenical Sterilization Law (1914), 185
*Money Magazine,* 83–84
mortgage industry, 222
Mounds Landing, Mississippi, 56

"Mount Dioxin" (Escambia Wood Treating site), 119
"Mount Trashmore," 12
Murray, Richard O., 116

NAACP Legal Defense and Education Fund (LDF): blood lead testing program settlement, 193; Carver Terrace contamination (Texarkana), 117; environmental justice movement, 20; Holt family lawsuit, 147, 151; Hurricane Betsy (1965) legal challenge, 59
National Academy of Sciences, 196, 209
National Ambient Air Quality Standard, 107
National Black Environmental Justice Network (NBEJN), xv
National Center for Environmental Health (NCEH), 101–102
National Center fro Disaster Preparedness, 211
National Environmental Justice Advisory Council (NEJAC), 21, 119, 173
National Environmental Policy Act (NEPA), 21–22
National Fair Housing Alliance (NFHA), 59, 77, 220
National Flood Protection Program, 95
National Hurricane Center, 57
National Institute of Environmental Health Sciences (NIEHS), 33
*National Law Journal,* 100–101
National Lawyers Guild Sugar Law Center, 20
National Oceanic and Atmospheric Administration (NOAA), 172
National People of Color Environmental Leadership Summit, 21, 22
*National Plan Review* (DHS), 211–212
National Priorities List (NPL), 113
National Public Radio (NPR), 188
National Resources Cluster Transition Team, 21
National Transportation Safety Board (NTSB), 160–161
*National Wildlife* (magazine), 105

National Wildlife Federation (NWF), 18
Nationwide insurance company, 228
Native Americans, 19, 182, 199, 211
"natural" disasters: black farmers, 68;
deaths and health problems from, 48,
54; economic losses worldwide, 47–48;
future losses, 48; human activity, 47–48,
71; legacy of unfairness, 50–54; location-
specific benefits, 49; media coverage,
55; people affected worldwide, 47; social
injustice, 47; vulnerability, 48–49. *See
also* floods; hurricanes; weather-related
disasters
Natural Resources Defense Council
(NRDC): blood lead testing program
settlement, 193; Deep South Center for
Environmental Justice (DSCEJ), 32; Environmental Protection Agency (EPA), 32;
Holt family lawsuit, 147, 151, 155; "natural"
disasters, estimated deaths and health
problems, 48, 54; post-Katrina demonstration cleanup project, 37; post-Katrina
soil contamination, 87, 89
Nelson, Bill, 197
New Deal, 158
New Hampshire, 22
New Hope, South Carolina, 163–164
New Orleans, 26–42; African Ameri-
cans, 31; Agriculture Street landfill, 37,
112–115; carless population, 211; Central
City, 92–93; Charity Hospital, 189;
Chef Menteur Highway landfill, 80–81;
coastal wetland loss, 73; Convention
Center, 94; cultural traditions, 26–27;
Fair Grounds, 85; French Quarter, 28,
41; Gentilly, 41, 93, 94; Gordon Plaza
subdivision, 112–113; government,
African Americans' mistrust of, 28, 41;
grocery stores, 91–92; homeless rate, 82;
Hurricane Alex (2010), 45; Hurricane
Betsy (1965), 27–28, 37, 40–42, 59–60;
Hurricane Camille (1969), 42; Hurricane Ivan (2004), 42; Hurricane Katrina
(2005), xv–xvi, 8, 24–25, 28–32, 41–42,
73–74, 189, 223 (*see also* New Orleans,
post-Katrina); "hurricane," meaning of,

27; "hurricane party" in, 42; Lake Vista,
60; Lakeview, 94; Lower Ninth Ward, 27,
31, 41, 59, 60, 75, 79, 93, 94; Mardi Gras,
26–27; McDonogh #35 high school,
39–40; Michoud, 93; minority-owned
companies, 223; Moton Elementary
School, 113; New Orleans East, 27, 31, 41,
75, 85, 92, 93, 94; Old Gentilly landfill,
80; population, pre-Katrina, 84; postal
workers in, 199; Press Park subdivision,
112–113; St. Thomas redevelopment,
81–82; shopping centers, 91–92; site of,
73; social vulnerability, 8; Superdome,
94; supermarkets, residents per, 92;
Upper Ninth Ward, 41, 93, 94; Uptown,
28, 41, 95; West Lake Forest, 93
New Orleans, post-Katrina, 73–99;
20-point plan to destroy black New
Orleans, 74–78; Agency for Toxic Substances and Disease Registry (ATSDR),
101–102; balancing green building and
social justice, 97–98; black cultural
heritage downplayed, 77; black land
grab via eminent domain, 76; black-
owned businesses, 223–224; cars lost,
79; construction and demolition (C&D)
landfills, 80–81; demonstration cleanup
project, 33–34, 78–81, 84–87; depopulation and displace of black communities,
95; disaster vouchers, 83; discriminatory
environmental cleanup standards, 75;
elections held without Voting Rights Act
safeguards, 78; environment and health
standards, enforcement of, 96; environmental assessment, 96; environmental
health, 36; environmental justice (EJ),
96; Environmental Protection Agency
(EPA) clean bill of health, 114; environmental training and "green jobs"
initiative, 98; Executive Order 12898, 96;
"expulsive" zoning, 76; federal aid to residents, 84–85; FEMA grants, 74; FEMA
infrastructure allocation, 84–85; FEMA
trailers, 89–91; financial assistance for
returning evacuees, 76; financial difficulties, 114; food desert, 91–93;

New Orleans, post-Katrina (*continued*)
formaldehyde exposure, 89; future
flooding, 94; government response to,
88, 188; "greenbuilding" restrictions
on redevelopment, 75; home rebuilding, 85; homes needing to be demolished, 79; house prices, 83; housing
discrimination against evacuees, 77, 83;
independent environmental testing and
monitoring, 96–97; insurance claims
using "wind or water" trap, 75; insurance redlining, 75; job discrimination
against returning evacuees, 77; "Katrina
Cottages" affordable housing initiative,
90–91; loan denials, 225–226; "low-
lying" neighborhoods sacrificed to save
wetlands, 75–76; monitoring of air and
water quality, 97; names for people who
escaped/survived, 188–189; oversight
board created to manage funds, 78;
policy recommendations, 95–98; "policy surge," 95; preference for mixed-
income "integrated" housing, 77–78;
promotion of a smaller, more upscale
New Orleans, 76; public housing, abandonment of commitment to, 77; public
housing, demolition of, 81–84; racial
disparities in adaptation and recovery,
83; rebuilding of levees and floodwalls,
93–95; rebuilding plan, 31, 36, 76;
removal of contaminated sediments,
97; rents, 83, 84; returnees, number of,
84; SBA loans, 74–75; school rebuilding, construction delayed, 78; schools
for returning children, 97; as "second
disaster," 74; small businesses, 223; soil
contamination, 32–34, 37–38, 85, 87,
88–89; soil-eating publicity stunt, 35,
87; treatment of exposure to toxins,
97; Vietnamese American families, 81;
waste management guidance, 96
New Orleans Public School Board (NOPS),
113, 114
"New South," 4–5
*New York Times* (newspaper): biological
weapons testing on black citizens, 187;

Brown, Chuck Carr, 81; clean water
laws, violations of, 104; Dickson County
landfill, 130; post-Katrina SBA loans,
74; racial disparities in government
response to toxic contamination, 120;
SBA home loan application, 225
Nicholas County, West Virginia, 159
NIMBY (Not in My Back Yard), 124, 142,
221
Ninth U.S. Circuit Court of Appeals, 104
nitrogen tetroxide, 160–161
Nixon, Richard, 103
*No Home for the Holidays* (NFHA), 220
nonresidential facilities in Houston, 14,
63–64
Norfolk Southern Railway train wreck
(2005), 156, 163–165
North Carolina: African Americans'
reverse migration to, 5; Department of
Environment and Natural Resources
(DENR), 109; Freedom Hill, 70; Hur-
ricane Floyd (1999), 69–72; Princeville,
70–72; Princeville Dike, 70; Rocky
Mount, 71; Warren County, 17, 109–112,
130, 169; Warren County (Afton) PCB
landfill, 109–110
North Forest Independent School district,
12
Northeast Community Action Group
(NECAG), 12
notices of violations (NOVs), 129
Nuclear Regulatory Commission, 202

Obama, Barack, 170
Obama administration: BP's waste management, 176; deepwater drilling moratorium, 45; environmental justice (EJ),
169; environmental justice leaders, 178;
EPA under, 104; leaders of contaminated
communities, 102
Occupational Safety and Health Administration (OSHA), 161
Ocean Casualty, 230
Odom, Lula, xv
Office of Inspector General (OIG), 103,
122–123

Staubner), 158–159
Tuskegee syphilis study, 184, 188, 190–192, 207, 233
Tuskegee University, 170, 191–192

*Unequal Treatment* (Institute of Medicine), 182–183
Uniform Relocation Act, 117
Union Carbide and Carbon Corporation, 157, 159, 160
Union of Concerned Scientists, 54
Uniontown, Alabama, 168, 169, 170–171
United Church of Christ (UCC): Environmental Justice Resource Center (EJRC), 23; *Toxic Wastes and Race at Twenty* report, 17, 144, 177; *Toxic Wastes and Race* report, 17, 126
United Church of Christ (UCC) Commission on Racial Justice, 17, 21
U.S. Army, 186–187, 204
U.S. Army Corps of Engineers. *See* Corps of Engineers (COE)
U.S. Coast Guard, 46, 174, 176
U.S. Congress: EPA's handling of Dickson County landfill, 148; Hurricane Katrina, response to, 36, 43–44; seats held by African Americans, 6
U.S. Department of Agriculture (USDA): disaster relief (1997) for black farmers, 67–69; fertilizer made from sewage sludge, 195
U.S. Department of Commerce, 226
U.S. Department of Health and Human Services (DOH), 191
U.S. Department of Homeland Security (DHS): *National Plan Review*, 211–212; terrorist risks to chemical plants, 202, 205–206, 208
U.S. Department of Justice (DOJ): Agriculture Street landfill, 114; Carver Terrace contamination (Texarkana), 116; Holt family, 148; Norfolk Southern Railway train wreck settlement (2005), 165; terrorists risks to chemical plants, 202
U.S. Department of Labor (DOL), 71, 224
U.S. House of Representatives Committee on Science, Space, and Technology Subcommittee on Investigations and Oversight, 102
U.S. Housing and Urban Development (HUD): African Americans, 222; Agriculture Street landfill, 115; East Baltimore childhood lead paint experiment, 194; fertilizer made from sewage sludge, 195; housing and aid for African Americans, 222; post-Katrina disaster vouchers, 83; post-Katrina public housing, 77, 82; President's Council on the Future of Princeville, North Carolina, 71; Press Park, New Orleans, 113; Road Home program settlement, 221
U.S. Senate: Committee on Environment and Public Works Subcommittee on Environmental Health, 36; Committee on Environment and Public Works Subcommittee on Superfund and Waste Management, 36–37; *Final Report of the Senate Select Committee to Study Government Operations with Respect to Intelligence Activities* (1976), 186
U.S. Supreme Court, xvi
United Steel Workers (USW), 33, 34, 85–86
University of California, Los Angeles (UCLA), 22
University of Pennsylvania, 184
*Unnatural Causes* (PBS documentary), 181
Urban Institute, 228
*USA Today* (newspaper), 217
USAA, 228
Utah insurance company, 230

Vicksburg Chemical Company, 160–161, 162–163
volatile organic compounds (VOCs), 141–142
Voting Rights Act (1965), 78
vulnerability: African Americans, 65; class, 50, 72; climate change, 51, 53, 54; ethnicity, 209; "natural" disasters, 48–49; race, 72, 209; residential segregation, 65; risk, 49–50; social creation, 50; social vulnerability, 8, 50; weather-related disasters, 53, 72

vulnerability zones, 204

*Wall Street Journal* (newspaper), 83
Walters, Ron, 200
"war on terrorism," 233
Warren County, North Carolina, 17,
  109–112, 130, 169
Warren County (Afton) PCB landfill,
  109–110
Washington, Harriett A., 185, 233
Washington Parish, Louisiana, 79
*Washington Post* (newspaper), 187, 217
waste disposal facilities: Alabama, 171;
  "Black Belt," 170; BP Deepwater Horizon
  oil spill (2010), 171–176; Houston, 64;
  siting of, 64; in the South, 172–173
Waste Management, Inc., 80, 103, 174,
  176
waste reduction legislation, 179
weather-related disasters: disaster displacement, 48; frequency and intensity, 48;

the South, 4; vulnerability, 53, 72. *See
  also* "natural" disasters
West, Kanye, 233
West Dallas, Texas, 106–109
West Nile virus, 187
West Virginia: economic performance
  indicators, 7; Gauley Bridge mine disas-
  ter (1930), 156, 157–160; Hawk's Nest
  Tunnel construction deaths from sili-
  cosis, 157–160; Institute, 160; Kanahwa
  Valley, 202; Nicholas County, 159
Westchester Insurance Company, 162
Whispering Pines landfill, 12, 13, 16
Williams, Margaret, 119
World Health Organization (WHO), 182,
  192
Wright, Beverly, 17–18, 20

Xavier University, xvi, 173

zone-of-vulnerability estimates, 204

# About the Authors

ROBERT D. BULLARD is Dean of the Barbara Jordan-Mickey Leland School of Public Affairs at Texas Southern University in Houston. He is author of many books, including *The Black Metropolis in Twenty-First Century: Race, Power, and the Politics of Place*; *Race, Place and Environmental Justice After Hurricane Katrina: Struggles to Reclaim, Rebuild, and Revitalize New Orleans and the Gulf Coast*; and *Environmental Health and Racial Equity in the United States: Building Environmentally Just, Sustainable and Livable Communities.*

BEVERLY WRIGHT is the founding director of the Deep South Center for Environmental Justice (DSCEJ) at Dillard University New Orleans and co-chair of the National Black Environmental Justice Network and the Environmental Justice Climate Change (EJCC) Initiative. She is the author of many books, including *In the Wake of the Storm: Environment, Disaster, and Race After Katrina*; *Toxic Wastes and Race at Twenty: 1987–2007*; and *Race, Place and Environmental Justice After Hurricane Katrina: Struggles to Reclaim, Rebuild, and Revitalize New Orleans* and the Gulf Coast. She is a native of New Orleans and a survivor of Hurricane Katrina.

CPSIA information can be obtained
at www.ICGtesting.com
Printed in the USA
LVHW112025191218
601087LV00001B/2/P